Imperialism and Underdevelopment

Imperialism and Underdevelopment:
a reader

edited by Robert I. Rhodes

New York and London

Contents

Introduction   xi

PART I

IMPERIALISM IN HISTORICAL AND CONTEMPORARY PERSPECTIVE

Introduction   1

1. The Development of Underdevelopment
   by Andre Gunder Frank   4

2. The American Empire and the U.S. Economy
   by Harry Magdoff   18

3. The Alliance for Progress
   by David Horowitz   45

4. Pakistan: The Burden of U.S. Aid
   by Hamza Alavi and Amir Khusro   62

5. Aluminum Profits and Caribbean People
   by Philip Reno   79

6. On the Mechanisms of Imperialism: The Case of Brazil
   by Andre Gunder Frank   89

7. The Meaning of Economic Imperialism
   by James O'Connor   101

PART II

THE UNDERDEVELOPED ECONOMY AND ECONOMIC POLICY

Introduction   153

1. On Economic Planning in Tropical Africa
   by Terence K. Hopkins   156

2. The Stages of Economic Growth of a Primary Producer in the
   Middle of the Twentieth Century
   by Dudley Seers   163

3. Mineral Development and Economic Growth
   by Charles E. Rollins   181

4. Agricultural and Economic Development
   by Thomas Balogh   205

5. International Corporations, Labor Aristocracies, and Economic
   Development in Tropical Africa
   by Giovanni Arrighi   220

6. Foreign Capital and Social Conflict in Indonesia, 1950–1958
   by Hans O. Schmitt   268

PART III

POLITICS, CLASS CONFLICT, AND UNDERDEVELOPMENT

Introduction   283

1. On the Political Economy of Backwardness
   by Paul A. Baran   285

2. The Pitfalls of National Consciousness—Africa
   by Frantz Fanon   302

3. The Middle-Class Military Coup
   by José Nun   323

4. The Politics of Pseudo-Planning in a Primary-Producing Nation
   by Philip Ehrensaft   358

5. Problems of Socialism in Southeast Asia
   by Malcolm Caldwell   376

Bibliography   405

Notes on the Contributors

HAMZA ALAVI and AMIR KHUSRO are Pakistani economists. Dr. Alavi has published a number of articles on Indian and Pakistani development. He is presently studying agrarian questions in rural India.

GIOVANNI ARRIGHI is an Italian economist. He has taught at University College in Dar es Salaam, Tanzania, and is now teaching in Milan, Italy. His collection of essays, *Economic Development and Superstructure in Africa*, has just been published in Italy and will soon be published in English by Monthly Review Press.

THOMAS BALOGH is one of England's most distinguished development economists. He is presently a fellow at Balliol College, Oxford University. A collection of his articles has been published as *The Economics of Poverty* (1966).

PAUL A. BARAN was Professor of Economics at Stanford University before his death in 1964. His published works include *The Political Economy of Growth* (1957), and, with Paul M. Sweezy, *Monopoly Capital*. A collection of his articles has just been published as *The Longer View : Essays Toward a Critique of Political Economy* (1970).

MALCOLM CALDWELL is a Lecturer in the Economic History of Southeast Asia at the School of Oriental and African Studies, London, and author (with James C. Henderson) of *The Chainless Mind : A Study of Resistance and Liberation* (1968).

PHILIP EHRENSAFT is an Assistant Professor of Sociology at the University of California at Santa Cruz. He has done extensive field work in the British West Indies and Africa. He recently edited, with Amitai Etzioni, *Anatomies of America : Sociological Perspectives* (1969).

vii

FRANTZ FANON was a black psychiatrist and Algerian revolutionary. He is author of *The Wretched of the Earth* (1961), *Black Skin, White Masks* (1952), *Toward the African Revolution* (1964), and *Studies in a Dying Colonialism* (1959).

ANDRE GUNDER FRANK has taught economics and social science at the universities of Iowa, Michigan State, and Wayne State, and was visiting professor of economics at Sir George Williams University in Montreal. In Latin America, he has taught at the universities of Brasilia, Chile, and the National University of Mexico. His work has been widely published in journals and he has written two books, *Capitalism and Underdevelopment in Latin America* (1967) and *Latin America: Underdevelopment or Revolution* (1969).

TERENCE K. HOPKINS, formerly an Associate Professor of Sociology at Columbia University, is now teaching at the State University of New York at Binghamton. He has done field work in Uganda and taught at the University of the West Indies (Trinidad). Professor Hopkins and Immanuel Wallerstein are presently preparing a book on the comparative study of national societies.

DAVID HOROWITZ is an editor of *Ramparts*. He is the author of *Student*; *Shakespeare: An Existential View*; and *The Free World Colossus*. He has recently edited two books: *Marx and Modern Economics* (1969) and *Corporations and the Cold War* (1970).

HARRY MAGDOFF is the author of *The Age of Imperialism: The Economics of U.S. Foreign Policy* (1969). He worked for many years in government, and is at present co-editor, with Paul Sweezy, of *Monthly Review*.

JOSE NUN is an Argentinian sociologist. He was a visiting professor of political science at the University of California, Berkeley, from 1964 to 1966. He is currently employed by the United Nations Commission for Latin America on a study of comparative urban politics in Latin America.

JAMES O'CONNOR is on the faculty of the economics department at San Jose State College. He has published many articles on Cuban development and on development economics. His most recent book is *Origins of Socialism in Cuba* (1970).

PHILIP RENO worked as an economist for the Social Security Board during the New Deal and the War Labor Board during the Second World

War. Since then he has worked as an organizational and educational director for various unions, and as a newspaper editor. He has traveled extensively in Latin America and the Caribbean, and is the author of *The Ordeal of British Guiana* (1964).

CHARLES E. ROLLINS received his Ph.D. in economics from Stanford University in 1955. His field of study is raw materials development and economic growth.

HANS O. SCHMITT is an Associate Professor Economics at the University of Wisconsin. He has done field work in Indonesia, Europe, and Latin America and published articles on Asian development and the international monetary system.

DUDLEY SEERS is director of the Institute of Development Studies at the University of Sussex. He has been a consultant to the governments of Malta, Jamaica, Trinidad, and Ghana, and is a past director of the Economic Development Division of the Economic Commission for Africa. A collection of his articles will be published shortly.

Introduction

The study of development is usually confined to an evolutionary perspective. That is to say, development is defined as a set of interdependent processes through which a "traditional" social structure is transformed into a "modern" social structure. Within this evolutionary frame, each of the social sciences (often in splendid isolation) has constructed elaborate theories. Thus, for example, in economics we have "stages of growth" theories; psychologists contrast the authoritarian or traditional man with creative, achievement-oriented, or modern man; political scientists construct elaborate classification schemes which purport to distinguish between traditional and modern forms of government; and sociologists discuss the increasing division of labor in society.

These efforts have, with few exceptions, been remarkably ahistorical. The history of the underdeveloped world, a history of colonialism, is ignored. The result has been a pervasive tendency to label as "traditional" any characteristic of the underdeveloped world which has been an obstacle to development.

In contrast to this perspective, the central theme of this volume is the assertion that the colonial experience is of crucial significance in the analysis of underdevelopment. Colonialism is not viewed merely as an experience which has had an impact on the minds of men in the underdeveloped world. Rather, it is studied as the historical process which created underdevelopment. The underdeveloped country is seen as a colonial society whose structure has been determined by hundreds of years of European and, more recently, United States domination. Moreover, the structures that continue to link the developed and underdeveloped worlds are treated as crucial data which must be analyzed. No attempt is made to confine discussion within the boundaries of particular academic disciplines. Instead, articles have been chosen that emphasize the interrelatedness of phenomena which are often treated as if they were independent.

The articles in the first section ("Imperialism in Historical and Contemporary Perspective") deal primarily with the economic interests which the developed nations have in the underdeveloped world, and the power they exercise in the defense of these interests. Since the United States is the major imperial power today, the major focus is upon its activities, but this does not imply that the United States is the only imperial power.

The second section ("The Underdeveloped Economy and Economic Policy") deals with the problem of planning within the context of a set of constraints involving, on the one hand, the limits imposed by economic ties with the developed world and, on the other hand, the political realities which have developed out of the colonial experience.

The third section ("Politics, Class Conflict, and Underdevelopment") analyzes these political realities and relates them both to the phenomenon of imperialism and to the economic difficulties which have been created by the colonial and neo-colonial experiences.

Each section is preceded by a short introduction.

Part I

Imperialism in Historical and Contemporary Perspective

Introduction

Adherents of the evolutionary perspective picture a transition in terms of the stages through which all societies (with perhaps minor variations) evolve. Consequently, it is taken as axiomatic that contact between "traditional" and modern societies will lead to the development of the former. In his essay entitled "The Development of Underdevelopment," Andre Gunder Frank challenges this view on a number of basic grounds. He argues that the underdeveloped world can hardly be regarded as traditional since the capitalist system has "effectively and entirely penetrated even the apparently most isolated sectors of the underdeveloped world." This penetration, he suggests, has made the economies of the underdeveloped countries dependent upon those of the developed nations. The consequence has been "a satellite development which [is] neither self-generating nor self-perpetuating." He supports his thesis with an historical survey which indicates that "satellites experience their greatest economic development and especially their most classically capitalist industrial development if and when their ties to their metropolis are weakest."

Frank's article supports the view that the relationship between the developed capitalist world and the underdeveloped world is inherently exploitative. That is to say, it leads to the continued enrichment of some nations and the perpetual stagnation and poverty of other nations. Need this be the case? This question is examined in Harry Magdoff's book *The Age of Imperialism*.[1] In the concluding chapter of this work, "The American Empire and the U.S. Economy," Magdoff examines the extent

---

1. Harry Magdoff, *The Age of Imperialism* (New York and London: Monthly Review Press, 1969).

1

to which our economic system is dependent upon foreign trade and foreign investment. His analysis supports the view that our dependency is very great and is, furthermore, increasing at a rapid rate. However, he does not attempt to explain our foreign policy in purely economic terms. On the contrary, he suggests that our political, military, and economic interests are complementary. "Just as the fight against Communism helps the search for profits," he concludes, "so the search for profits helps the fight against Communism. What more perfect harmony of interests could be imagined?"

The articles which follow Magdoff's deal with specific aspects of U.S. foreign activities and their relationship to underdevelopment.

In his analysis of the Alliance for Progress, David Horowitz argues that despite its rhetoric of reform the Alliance "had built into it resistance to land and tax reforms." Further, he argues that its emphasis on the protection of foreign and private investments and monetary stability prevents the kinds of structural change which are necessary if Latin America is to develop.

The article by Hamza Alavi and Amir Khusro is an unusually detailed examination of the impact of United States aid on Pakistani development. The authors show how, through contributing a small proportion of the total cost of each of many development projects, the United States gains a decisive role in their execution. Consequently, the United States is able to demand that unnecessary experts be hired, unnecessary services bought, and U.S. products be purchased. In this way much of our aid expenses are recovered immediately and Pakistani firms are placed at a competitive disadvantage. Moreover, Alavi and Khusro argue that the sale of U.S. surplus commodities depresses local agricultural markets and enables the United States to accumulate large quantities of rupees which aid our attempts to control the Pakistani economy and discourage active industrialization.

Philip Reno's article, "Aluminum Profits and Caribbean People," illustrates the problem faced by many countries in the underdeveloped world. Where a number of countries are dependent upon the export of a single commodity—whose market is dominated by an international cartel—the primary producer receives little of the wealth taken out of the ground.

In "On the Mechanisms of Imperialism: The Case of Brazil," Andre Gunder Frank describes the mechanisms through which capital is transferred from an underdeveloped country to the United States, and examines the economic effects which these mechanisms have upon the underdeveloped country. Frank's description of the mechanisms that enable U.S. firms to control and exploit the Brazilian economy through the use of Brazilian capital, financial institutions, and special legal privileges is of particular interest.

"The Meaning of Economic Imperialism" by James O'Connor is a concise summary of theories of economic imperialism. O'Connor traces the changing historical meaning of economic imperialism and relates modern imperialism to both the foreign policy and the economic character of the modern capitalist state.

I

Andre Gunder Frank

The Development of
Underdevelopment

We cannot hope to formulate adequate development theory and policy for the majority of the world's population who suffer from underdevelopment without first learning how their past economic and social history gave rise to their present underdevelopment. Yet most historians study only the developed metropolitan countries and pay scant attention to the colonial and underdeveloped lands. For this reason most of our theoretical categories and guides to development policy have been distilled exclusively from the historical experience of the European and North American advanced capitalist nations.

Since the historical experience of the colonial and underdeveloped countries has demonstrably been quite different, available theory therefore fails to reflect the past of the underdeveloped part of the world entirely, and reflects the past of the world as a whole only in part. More important, our ignorance of the underdeveloped countries' history leads us to assume that their past and indeed their present resembles earlier stages of the history of the now-developed countries. This ignorance and this assumption lead us into serious misconceptions about contemporary underdevelopment and development. Further, most studies of development and underdevelopment fail to take account of the economic and other relations between the metropolis and its economic colonies throughout the history of the worldwide expansion and development of the mercantilist and capitalist system. Consequently, most of our theory fails to explain the structure and development of the capitalist system as

---

This essay originally appeared in the September 1966 issue of *Monthly Review* and is included in *Latin America : Underdevelopment or Revolution* (New York and London: Monthly Review Press, 1969).

a whole and to account for its simultaneous generation of underdevelopment in some of its parts and of economic development in others.

It is generally held that economic development occurs in a succession of capitalist stages and that today's underdeveloped countries are still in a stage, sometimes depicted as an original stage of history, through which the now-developed countries passed long ago. Yet even a modest acquaintance with history shows that underdevelopment is not original or traditional and that neither the past nor the present of the underdeveloped countries resemble in any important respect the past of the now-developed countries. The now-developed countries were never *under*developed, though they may have been *un*developed. It is also widely believed that the contemporary underdevelopment of a country can be understood as the product or reflection solely of its own economic, political, social, and cultural characteristics or structure. Yet historical research demonstrates that contemporary underdevelopment is in large part the historical product of past and continuing economic and other relations between the satellite underdeveloped and the now-developed metropolitan countries. Furthermore, these relations are an essential part of the structure and development of the capitalist system on a world scale as a whole. A related and also largely erroneous view is that the development of these underdeveloped countries and, within them of their most underdeveloped domestic areas, must and will be generated or stimulated by diffusing capital, institutions, values, etc., to them from the international and national capitalist metropoles. Historical perspective based on the underdeveloped countries' past experience suggests that, on the contrary, in the underdeveloped countries economic development can now occur only independently of most of these relations of diffusion.

Evident inequalities of income and differences in culture have led many observers to see "dual" societies and economies in the underdeveloped countries. Each of the two parts is supposed to have a history of its own, a structure, and a contemporary dynamic largely independent of the other. Supposedly, only one part of the economy and society has been importantly affected by intimate economic relations with the "outside" capitalist world; and that part, it is held, became modern, capitalist, and relatively developed precisely because of this contact. The other part is widely regarded as variously isolated, subsistence-based, feudal, or pre-capitalist, and therefore more underdeveloped.

I believe, on the contrary, that the entire "dual society" thesis is false and that the policy recommendations to which it leads will, if acted upon, serve only to intensify and perpetuate the very conditions of underdevelopment they are supposedly designed to remedy.

A mounting body of evidence suggests, and I am confident that future historical research will confirm, that the expansion of the capitalist system over the past centuries effectively and entirely penetrated even the apparently most isolated sectors of the underdeveloped world. Therefore, the economic, political, social, and cultural institutions and relations we now observe there are the products of the historical development of the capitalist system no less than are the seemingly more modern or capitalist features of the national metropoles of these underdeveloped countries. Analogously to the relations between development and underdevelopment on the international level, the contemporary underdeveloped institutions of the so-called backward or feudal domestic areas of an underdeveloped country are no less the product of the single historical process of capitalist development than are the so-called capitalist institutions of the supposedly more progressive areas. In this paper I should like to sketch the kinds of evidence which support this thesis and at the same time indicate lines along which further study and research could fruitfully proceed.

The Secretary General of the Latin American Center for Research in the Social Sciences writes in that Center's journal: "The privileged position of the city has its origin in the colonial period. It was founded by the Conqueror to serve the same ends that it still serves today: to incorporate the indigenous population into the economy brought and developed by that Conqueror and his descendants. The regional city was an instrument of conquest and is still today an instrument of domination."[1] The Instituto Nacional Indigenista (National Indian Institute) of Mexico confirms this observation when it notes that "the mestizo population, in fact, always lives in a city, a center of an intercultural region, which acts as the metropolis of a zone of indigenous population and which maintains with the underdeveloped communities an intimate relation which links the center with the satellite communities."[2] The Institute goes on to point out that "between the mestizos who live in the nuclear city of the region and the Indians who live in the peasant hinterland there is in reality a closer economic and social interdependence than might at first glance appear" and that the provincial metropoles "by being centers of intercourse are also centers of exploitation."[3]

Thus these metropolis-satellite relations are not limited to the imperial or international level but penetrate and structure the very economic, political, and social life of the Latin American colonies and countries. Just as the colonial and national capital and its export sector become the satellite of the Iberian (and later of other) metropoles of the world economic system, this satellite immediately becomes a colonial and then a national metropolis with respect to the productive sectors and population of the interior. Furthermore, the provincial capitals, which thus are themselves satellites of the national metropolis—and through the latter of the world metropolis—are in turn provincial centers around which their own local satellites orbit. Thus, a whole chain of constellations of metropoles and satellites relates all parts of the whole system from its metropolitan center in Europe or the United States to the farthest outpost in the Latin American countryside.

When we examine this metropolis-satellite structure, we find that each of the satellites, including now-underdeveloped Spain and Portugal, serves as an instrument to suck capital or economic surplus out of its own satellites and to channel part of this surplus to the world metropolis of which all are satellites. Moreover, each national and local metropolis serves to impose and maintain the monopolistic structure and exploitative relationship of this system (as the Instituto Nacional Indigenista of Mexico calls it) as long as it serves the interests of the metropoles which take advantage of this global, national, and local structure to promote their own development and the enrichment of their ruling classes.

These are the principal and still surviving structural characteristics which were implanted in Latin America by the Conquest. Beyond examining the establishment of this colonial structure in its historical context, the proposed approach calls for study of the development—and underdevelopment—of these metropoles and satellites of Latin America throughout the following and still continuing historical process. In this way we can understand why there were and still are tendencies in the Latin American and world capitalist structure which seem to lead to the development of the metropolis and the underdevelopment of the satellite and why, particularly, the satellized national, regional, and local metropoles in Latin America find that their economic development is at best a limited or underdeveloped development.

That present underdevelopment of Latin America is the result of its centuries-long participation in the process of world capitalist development, I believe I have shown in my case studies of the economic and social histories of Chile and Brazil.[4] My study of Chilean history suggests that the Conquest not only incorporated this country fully into the expansion and development of the world mercantile and later industrial capitalist system but that it also introduced the monopolistic metropolis-satellite structure and development of capitalism into the Chilean domestic economy and society itself. This structure then penetrated and permeated all of Chile very quickly. Since that time and in the course of world and Chilean history during the epochs of colonialism, free trade, imperialism, and the present, Chile has become increasingly marked by the economic, social, and political structure of satellite underdevelopment. This development of underdevelopment continues today, both in Chile's still increasing satellization by the world metropolis and through the ever more acute polarization of Chile's domestic economy.

The history of Brazil is perhaps the clearest case of both national and regional development of underdevelopment. The expansion of the world economy since the beginning of the sixteenth century successively converted the Northeast, the Minas Gerais interior, the North, and the Center-South (Rio de Janeiro, São Paulo, and Paraná) into export economies and incorporated them into the structure and development of the world capitalist system. Each of these regions experienced what may have appeared as economic development during the period of its respective golden age. But it was a satellite development which was neither self-generating nor self-perpetuating. As the market or the productivity of the first three regions declined, foreign and domestic economic interest in them waned; and they were left to develop the underdevelopment they live today. In the fourth region, the coffee economy experienced a similar though not yet quite as serious fate (though the development of a synthetic coffee substitute promises to deal it a mortal blow in the not too distant future). All of this historical evidence contradicts the generally accepted theses that Latin America suffers from a dual society or from the survival of feudal institutions and that these are important obstacles to its economic development.

During the First World War, however, and even more during the Great Depression and the Second World War, São Paulo began to build up an industrial establishment which is the largest in Latin America today. The question arises whether this industrial development did or can break Brazil out of the cycle of satellite development and underdevelopment which has characterized its other regions and national history within the capitalist system so far. I believe that the answer is no. Domestically the evidence so far is fairly clear. The development of industry in São Paulo has not brought greater riches to the other regions of Brazil. Instead, it converted them into internal colonial satellites, decapitalized them further, and consolidated or even deepened their underdevelopment. There is little evidence to suggest that this process is likely to be reversed in the foreseeable future except insofar as the provincial poor migrate and become the poor of the metropolitan cities. Externally, the evidence is that although the initial development of São Paulo's industry was relatively autonomous it is being increasingly satellized by the world capitalist metropolis and its future development possibilities are increasingly restricted.[5] This development, my studies lead me to believe, also appears destined to limited or underdeveloped development as long as it takes place in the present economic, political, and social framework.

We must conclude, in short, that underdevelopment is not due to the survival of archaic institutions and the existence of capital shortage in regions that have remained isolated from the stream of world history. On the contrary, underdevelopment was and still is generated by the very same historical process which also generated economic development: the development of capitalism itself. This view, I am glad to say, is gaining adherents among students of Latin America and is proving its worth in shedding new light on the problems of the area and in affording a better perspective for the formulation of theory and policy.[6]

The same historical and structural approach can also lead to better development theory and policy by generating a series of hypotheses about development and underdevelopment such as those I am testing in my current research. The hypotheses are derived from the empirical observation and theoretical assumption that within this world-embracing metropolis-satellite structure the metropoles tend to develop and the satellites to underdevelop. The first hypothesis has already been mentioned above: that in contrast to the development of the world metropolis which is no one's satellite, the development of the national and other subordinate metropoles is limited by their satellite status. It is perhaps more difficult to test this hypothesis than the following ones because part of its confirmation depends on the test of the other hypotheses. Nonetheless, this hypothesis appears to be generally confirmed by the non-autonomous and unsatisfactory economic and especially industrial development of Latin America's national metropoles, as documented in the studies already cited. The most important and at the same time most confirmatory examples are the metropolitan regions of Buenos Aires and São Paulo whose growth only began in the nineteenth century, was therefore largely untrammeled by any colonial heritage, but was and remains a satellite development largely dependent on the outside metropolis, first of Britain and then of the United States.

A second hypothesis is that the satellites experience their greatest economic development and especially their most classically capitalist industrial development if and when their ties to their metropolis are weakest. This hypothesis is almost diametrically opposed to the generally accepted thesis that development in the underdeveloped countries follows from the greatest degree of contact with and diffusion from the metropolitan developed countries. This hypothesis seems to be confirmed by two kinds of relative isolation that Latin America has experienced in the course of its history. One is the temporary isolation caused by the crises of war or depression in the world metropolis. Apart from minor ones, five periods of such major crises stand out and are seen to confirm the hypothesis. These are: the European (and especially Spanish) depression of the seventeenth century, the Napoleonic Wars, the First World War, the Depression of the 1930's, and the Second World War. It is clearly established and generally recognized that the most important recent industrial development—especially of Argentina, Brazil, and Mexico, but also of other countries such as Chile—has taken place precisely during the periods of the two world wars and the intervening Depression. Thanks to the consequent loosening of trade and investment ties during these periods, the satellites initiated marked autonomous industrialization and growth. Historical research demonstrates that the same thing happened in Latin America during Europe's seventeenth-century depression. Manufacturing grew in the Latin American countries, and several of them such as Chile became exporters of manufactured goods. The Napoleonic

Wars gave rise to independence movements in Latin America, and these should perhaps also be interpreted as confirming the development hypothesis in part.

The other kind of isolation which tends to confirm the second hypothesis is the geographic and economic isolation of regions which at one time were relatively weakly tied to and poorly integrated into the mercantilist and capitalist system. My preliminary research suggests that in Latin America it was these regions which initiated and experienced the most promising self-generating economic development of the classical industrial capitalist type. The most important regional cases probably are Tucumán and Asunción, as well as other cities such as Mendoza and Rosario in the interior of Argentina and Paraguay, during the end of the eighteenth and the beginning of the nineteenth centuries. Seventeenth- and eighteenth-century São Paulo, long before coffee was grown there, is another example. Perhaps Antioquia in Colombia and Puebla and Querétaro in Mexico are other examples. In its own way, Chile was also an example since, before the sea route around the Horn was opened, this country was relatively isolated at the end of the long voyage from Europe via Panama. All of these regions became manufacturing centers and even exporters, usually of textiles, during the periods preceding their effective incorporation as satellites into the colonial, national, and world capitalist system.

Internationally, of course, the classic case of industrialization through nonparticipation as a satellite in the capitalist world system is obviously that of Japan after the Meiji Restoration. Why, one may ask, was resource-poor but unsatellized Japan able to industrialize so quickly at the end of the century while resource-rich Latin American countries and Russia were not able to do so and the latter was easily beaten by Japan in the War of 1904 after the same forty years of development efforts? The second hypothesis suggests that the fundamental reason is that Japan was not satellized either during the Tokugawa or the Meiji period and therefore did not have its development structurally limited as did the countries which were so satellized.

A corollary of the second hypothesis is that when the metropolis recovers from its crisis and re-establishes the trade and investment ties which fully reincorporate the satellites into the system, or when the metropolis expands to incorporate previously isolated regions into the worldwide system, the previous development and industrialization of these regions is choked off or channeled into directions which are not self-perpetuating and promising. This happened after each of the five crises cited above. The renewed expansion of trade and the spread of economic liberalism in the eighteenth and nineteenth centuries choked off and reversed the manufacturing development which Latin America had experienced during the seventeenth century, and in some places at the beginning of the nineteenth. After the First World War, the new national industry of Brazil suffered serious consequences from American economic invasion. The increase in the growth rate of Gross National Product and particularly of industrialization throughout Latin America was again reversed and industry became increasingly satellized after the Second World War and especially after the post-Korean War recovery and expansion of the metropolis. Far from having become more developed since then, industrial sectors of Brazil and most conspicuously of Argentina have become structurally more and more underdeveloped and less and less able to generate continued industrialization and/or sustain development of the economy. This process, from which India also suffers, is reflected in a whole gamut of balance-of-payments, inflationary, and other economic and political difficulties, and promises to yield to no solution short of far-reaching structural change.

Our hypothesis suggests that fundamentally the same process occurred even more dramatically with the incorporation into the system of previously unsatellized regions. The expansion of Buenos Aires as a satellite of Great Britain and the introduction of free trade in the interest of the ruling groups of both metropoles destroyed the manufacturing and much of the remainder of the economic base of the previously relatively prosperous interior almost entirely. Manufacturing was destroyed by foreign competition, lands were taken and concentrated into latifundia by the rapaciously growing export economy, intraregional distribution of income became much more unequal, and the previously developing regions became simple satellites of Buenos Aires and through it of London. The provincial centers did not yield to satellization without a struggle. This metropolis–satellite conflict was much of the cause of the long political and armed struggle between the Unitarists in Buenos Aires and the Federalists in the provinces, and it may be said to have been the sole important cause of the War of the Triple Alliance in which Buenos Aires, Montevideo, and Rio de Janeiro, encouraged and helped by London, destroyed not only the autonomously developing economy of Paraguay but killed off nearly all of its population which was unwilling to give in. Though this is no doubt the most spectacular example which tends to confirm the hypothesis, I believe that historical research on the satellization of previously relatively independent yeoman-farming and incipient manufacturing regions such as the Caribbean islands will confirm it further.[7] These regions did not have a chance against the forces of expanding and developing capitalism, and their own development had to be sacrificed to that of others. The economy and industry of Argentina, Brazil, and other countries which have experienced the effects of metropolitan recovery since the Second World War are today suffering much the same fate, if fortunately still in lesser degree.

A third major hypothesis derived from the metropolis-satellite structure is that the regions which are the most underdeveloped and feudal-seeming today are the ones which had the closest ties to the metropolis in the past. They are the regions which were the greatest exporters of primary products to, and the biggest sources of capital for, the world metropolis and which were abandoned by the metropolis when for one reason or another business fell off. This hypothesis also contradicts the generally held thesis that the source of a region's underdevelopment is its isolation and its pre-capitalist institutions.

This hypothesis seems to be amply confirmed by the former super-satellite development and present ultra-underdevelopment of the once sugar-exporting West Indies, Northeastern Brazil, the ex-mining districts of Minas Gerais in Brazil, highland Peru, and Bolivia, and the central Mexican states of Guanajuato, Zacatecas, and others whose names were made world-famous centuries ago by their silver. There surely are no major regions in Latin America which are today more cursed by under-development and poverty; yet all of these regions, like Bengal in India, once provided the life blood of mercantile and industrial capitalist development—in the metropolis. These regions' participation in the development of the world capitalist system gave them, already in their golden age, the typical structure of underdevelopment of a capitalist export economy. When the market for their sugar or the wealth of their mines disappeared and the metropolis abandoned them to their own devices, the already existing economic, political, and social structure of these regions prohibited autonomous generation of economic development and left them no alternative but to turn in upon themselves and to degenerate into the ultra-underdevelopment we find there today.

These considerations suggest two further and related hypotheses. One is that the latifundium, irrespective of whether it appears as a plantation or a hacienda today, was typically born as a commercial enterprise which created for itself the institutions which permitted it to respond to increased demand in the world or national market by expanding the amount of its land, capital, and labor and to increase the supply of its products. The fifth hypothesis is that the latifundia which appear isolated, subsistence-based, and semifeudal today saw the demand for their products or their productive capacity decline and that they are to be found principally in the above-named former agricultural and mining export regions whose economic activity declined in general. These two hypotheses run counter to the notions of most people, and even to the opinions of some historians and other students of the subject, according to whom the historical roots and socioeconomic causes of Latin American latifundia and agrarian institutions are to be found in the transfer of feudal institutions from Europe and/or in economic depression.

The evidence to test these hypotheses is not open to easy general inspection and requires detailed analyses of many cases. Nonetheless, some important confirmatory evidence is available. The growth of the latifundium in nineteenth-century Argentina and Cuba is a clear case in support of the fourth hypothesis and can in ño way be attributed to the transfer of feudal institutions during colonial times. The same is evidently the case of the post-revolutionary and contemporary resurgence of latifundia particularly in the north of Mexico, which produce for the American market, and of similar ones on the coast of Peru and the new coffee regions of Brazil. The conversion of previously yeoman-farming Caribbean islands, such as Barbados, into sugar-exporting economies at various times between the seventeenth and twentieth centuries and the resulting rise of the latifundia in these islands would seem to confirm the fourth hypothesis as well. In Chile, the rise of the latifundium and the creation of the institutions of servitude which later came to be called feudal occurred in the eighteenth century and have been conclusively shown to be the result of and response to the opening of a market for Chilean wheat in Lima.[8] Even the growth and consolidation of the latifundium in seventeenth-century Mexico—which most expert students have attributed to a depression of the economy caused by the decline of mining and a shortage of Indian labor and to a consequent turning in upon itself and ruralization of the economy—occurred at a time when urban population and demand were growing, food shortages became acute, food prices skyrocketed, and the profitability of other economic activities such as mining and foreign trade declined.[9] All of these and other factors rendered hacienda agriculture more profitable. Thus, even this case would seem to confirm the hypothesis that the growth of the latifundium and its feudal-seeming conditions of servitude in Latin America has always been and still is the commercial response to increased demand and that it does not represent the transfer or survival of alien institutions that have remained beyond the reach of capitalist development. The emergence of latifundia, which today really are more or less (though not entirely) isolated, might then be attributed to the causes advanced in the fifth hypothesis—i.e., the decline of previously profitable agricultural enterprises whose capital was, and whose currently produced economic surplus still is, transferred elsewhere by owners and merchants who frequently are the same persons or families. Testing this hypothesis requires still more detailed analysis, some of which I have undertaken in a study on Brazilian agriculture.[10]

All of these hypotheses and studies suggest that the global extension and unity of the capitalist system, its monopoly structure and uneven development throughout its history, and the resulting persistence of commercial rather than industrial capitalism in the underdeveloped world (including its most industrially advanced countries) deserve much more attention in the study of economic development and cultural change than they have hitherto received. Though science and truth know no national boundaries, it is probably new generations of scientists from the underdeveloped countries themselves who most need to, and best can, devote the necessary attention to these problems and clarify the process of underdevelopment and development. It is their people who in the last analysis face the task of changing this no longer acceptable process and eliminating this miserable reality.

They will not be able to accomplish these goals by importing sterile stereotypes from the metropolis which do not correspond to their satellite economic reality and do not respond to their liberating political needs. To change their reality they must understand it. For this reason, I hope that better confirmation of these hypotheses and further pursuit of the proposed historical, holistic, and structural approach may help the peoples of the underdeveloped countries to understand the causes and eliminate the reality of their development of underdevelopment and their underdevelopment of development.

Notes

1. *América Latina*, año 6, no. 4 (October–December 1963), p. 8.
2. Instituto Nacional Indigenista, *Los centros coordinadores indigenistas* (Mexico, 1962), p. 34.
3. *Ibid.*, pp. 33–34, 88.
4. "Capitalist Development of Underdevelopment in Chile" and "Capitalist Development of Underdevelopment in Brazil" in *Capitalism and Underdevelopment in Latin America* (New York and London: Monthly Review Press, 1967 and 1969).
5. Also see "The Growth and Decline of Import Substitution," *Economic Bulletin for Latin America*, vol. 9, no. 1 (March 1964); and Celso Furtado, *Dialectica do Desenvolvimiento* (Rio de Janeiro: Fundo de Cultura, 1964).
6. Others who use a similar approach, though their ideologies do not permit them to derive the logically following conclusions, are Anibal Pinto, *Chile: Un caso de desarrollo frustrado* (Santiago: Editorial Universitaria, 1957); Celso Furtado, *A formação economica do Brasil* (Rio de Janeiro: Fundo de Cultura, 1959) which was recently translated into English and published as *The Economic Growth of Brazil* by the University of California Press; and Caio Prado Junior, *Historia Económica do Brasil*, 7th ed. (São Paulo: Editora Brasiliense, 1962).
7. See for instance Ramiro Guerra y Sanchez, *Azúcar y Problación en las Antillas*, 2nd ed. (Havana, 1942), also published as *Sugar and Society in the Caribbean* (New Haven: Yale University Press, 1964).
8. Mario Góngora, *Origen de los "inquilinos" de Chile central* (Santiago: Editorial Universitaria, 1960); Jean Borde and Mario Góngora, *Evolución de la propiedad rural en el Valle del Puango* (Santiago: Instituto de Sociología de la Universidad de Chile); Sergio Sepúlveda, *El trigo chileno en el mercado mundial* (Santiago: Editorial Universitaria, 1959).
9. Woodrow Borah makes depression the centerpiece of his explanation in "New Spain's Century of Depression," *Ibero-Americana* (Berkeley), no. 35, 1951. François Chevalier speaks of turning in upon itself in the most authoritative study of the subject, "La formación de los grandes latifundios en México," *Problemas Agrícolas e Industriales de México*, vol. 8, no. 1, 1956

(translated from the original French and recently published by the University of California Press). The data which provide the basis for my contrary interpretation are supplied by these authors themselves. This problem is discussed in my "¿Con qué modo de producción convierte la gallina maíz en heuvos de oro?" which originally appeared in *El Día* (Mexico), October 31 and November 28, 1965, and is reprinted in *Latin America: Underdevelopment or Revolution* (New York and London: Monthly Review Press, 1969); and it is further analyzed in a study of Mexican agriculture under preparation.

10. "Capitalism and the Myth of Feudalism in Brazilian Agriculture," in *Capitalism and Underdevelopment in Latin America.*

Harry Magdoff

The American Empire
and the U.S. Economy

Three interrelated views on economic imperialism and United States foreign policy prevail today:

(1) Economic imperialism *is not* at the root of United States foreign policy. Instead, political aims and national security are the prime motivators of foreign policy.

(2) Economic imperialism *cannot* be the main element in foreign policy determination, since United States foreign trade and foreign investment make such relatively small contributions to the nation's overall economic performance.

(3) Since foreign economic involvement is relatively unimportant to the United States economy, it follows that economic imperialism *need not* be a motivating force in foreign policy. Hence some liberal and left critics argue that present foreign policy, to the extent that it is influenced by imperialism, is misguided and in conflict with the best economic interests of this country. If we sincerely encouraged social and economic development abroad, the argument goes, even to the extent of financing the nationalization of United States foreign investment, the rising demand for capital imports by underdeveloped countries would create a more substantial and lasting stimulus to prosperity than the current volume of foreign trade and foreign investment.

Obscuring economic and commercial interests by covering them up or intermingling them with idealistic and religious motivations is hardly a new phenomenon. Wars have been fought to impose Christianity on heathen empires—wars which incidentally also opened up new trade

This essay was originally published in the November 1966 issue of *Monthly Review* and appears as Chapter 5 of *The Age of Imperialism* (New York and London: Monthly Review Press, 1969). Copyright © 1966 by Monthly Review, Inc.

routes or established new centers of commercial monopoly. Even such a crass commercial aggression as the Opium War in China was explained to the United States public by the American Board of Commissioners for Foreign Missions as "not so much an opium or an English affair, as the result of a great design of Providence to make the wickedness of men subserve his purposes of mercy toward China, in breaking through her wall of exclusion, and bringing the empire into more immediate contact with Western and Christian nations."[1]

John Quincy Adams, in a public lecture on the Opium War, explained that China's trade policy was contrary to the law of nature and Christian principles:

> The moral obligation of commercial intercourse between nations is founded entirely, exclusively, upon the Christian precept to love your neighbor as yourself. . . . But China, not being a Christian nation, its inhabitants do not consider themselves bound by the Christian precept, to love their neighbor as themselves. . . . This is a churlish and unsocial system. . . . The fundamental principle of the Chinese Empire is anti-commercial . . . It admits no obligation to hold commercial intercourse with others . . . It is time that this enormous outrage upon the rights of human nature, and upon the first principles of the rights of nations, should cease.[2]

Perhaps the Christian principle of "love thy neighbor" and the more modern ethic that the anti-commercial is also immoral have become so habitual in accepted ways of thought that we have lost the facility to separate the various strands that make up foreign policy. Perhaps the source of the difficulty can be traced to a lack of understanding of what Bernard Baruch called "the essential one-ness of [United States] economic, political and strategic interests."[3]

There will probably be little dispute about the "one-ness" of United States political and national security aims. The only rationale of national security today is "defense" against the Soviet Union and China. To be absolutely safe, it is said, we need also to cope with the "concealed wars" which may appear as internal revolutions or civil war.[4] It is merely coincidental, to be sure, that socialist revolutions destroy the institutions of private ownership of the means of production and thereby violate the Christian precept to love thy neighbor by eliminating freedom of trade and freedom of enterprise in large and important sectors of the earth.

The "one-ness" of the political and national security aims becomes more evident on examination of the political aims, since in this realm of thought our policy-makers and policy-defenders are strict economic determinists. Political freedom is equated with Western-style democracy The economic basis of this democracy is free enterprise. Hence the political aim of defense of the free world must also involve the defense of free trade and free enterprise. The primary departure from this rigid economic determinism appears when dealing with politically unstable nations where, obviously, the art of self-government is not fully developed. In such cases, for the sake of political stability, we permit and encourage military dictatorships, in full confidence that the people of these countries will eventually learn the art of self-government and adopt a free society just so long as the proper underpinning of free enterprise remains.

While our policy-makers and policy-defenders will identify in the most general terms the "one-ness" of the nation's foreign political and national security goals, they usually become quite shy when it comes to the question of the unity of these goals and economic interests. We have come a long way from the very straightforward bulletin prepared in 1922 by the Office of Naval Intelligence on "The U.S. Navy as an Industrial Asset."[5] This report frankly details the services rendered by the navy in protecting American business interests and in seeking out commercial and investment opportunities which the Navy Department brings to the attention of American businessmen.

But today our national aims are presumably concerned only with political and philosophic ideals. Insofar as economic interests are concerned, the tables have been turned: today it is business that is expected to serve the needs of national policy. The problem is how to stimulate private investment abroad. Private foreign investment is considered such a necessary tool of national policy that various forms of investment-guaranty programs have been designed to protect foreign investors against losses due to confiscation, wars, and the uncertainties of currency convertibility.

The interrelation between economic interests and foreign policy is seen more clearly by business-minded observers. Thus the former president and chairman of the World Bank, Eugene R. Black, informs us that "our foreign aid programs constitute a distinct benefit to American business. The three major benefits are: (1) Foreign aid provides a substantial and immediate market for U.S. goods and services. (2) Foreign aid stimulates the development of new overseas markets for U.S. companies. (3) Foreign aid orients national economies toward a free enterprise system in which U.S. firms can prosper."[6]

More specifically, an Assistant Secretary of Commerce for Economic Affairs explains to businessmen that "if these [military and economic] aid programs were discontinued, private investments might be a waste because it would not be safe enough for you to make them."[7]

On a much more elevated plane, we are told by a specialist on international business practice, a teacher at MIT and Harvard: "It would seem that there is a horrible urgency in making Western economic concepts internationally viable if man's dignity is to be preserved—and incidentally, a profitable private business."[8]

And as an indication of how in fact some influential members of the business community see the "one-ness" of economic, political, and security interests, listen to the view expressed in 1965 by the vice-president of Chase Manhattan Bank who supervises Far Eastern operations:

> In the past, foreign investors have been somewhat wary of the over-all political prospect for the [Southeast Asia] region. I must say, though, that the U.S. actions in Vietnam this year—which have demonstrated that the U.S. will continue to give effective protection to the free nations of the region—have considerably reassured both Asian and Western investors. In fact, I see some reason for hope that the same sort of economic growth may take place in the free economies of Asia that took place in Europe after the Truman Doctrine and after NATO provided a protective shield. The same thing also took place in Japan after the U.S. intervention in Korea removed investor doubts.[9]

THE SIZE OF FOREIGN ECONOMIC INVOLVEMENT

But even if we grant the interrelatedness of economic, political, and security interests, how much priority should we assign to economic interests? Specifically, how can one claim that economic imperialism plays a *major* role in United States policy if total exports are less than 5 percent of the Gross National Product, and foreign investment much less than 10 percent of domestic capital investment?

Let us note first that the size of ratios is not by itself an adequate indicator of what motivates foreign policy. Many wars and military operations were aimed at control over China's markets at a time when those markets represented only 1 percent of total world trade. Overall percentages need analytical examination: the strategic and policy-influential areas of business activity need to be sorted out.

Above all, it is important to appreciate that the stake of United States business abroad is many times larger than the volume of merchandise exports. The reason for this is that the volume of accumulated capital abroad controlled by United States business has been increasing at a faster rate than exports. The unique advantage of capital is that it reproduces itself. That is, the output obtained by capital investment produces enough revenue to cover not only costs of labor and raw materials but also the capital and natural resources consumed, plus profits. The annual flow of capital invested abroad is therefore additive: increments to capital enlarge the productive base. Even more important, United States firms abroad are able to mobilize foreign capital for their operations. The net result of the flow of capital abroad and the foreign capital mobilized by American firms is that while production abroad arising out of United States investment was $4\frac{1}{2}$ times larger than exports in 1950, by 1964 this had risen to $5\frac{1}{2}$ times exports. These observations are based on estimates made in a recent study conducted by the National Industrial Conference Board[10] (see table).

| | *Sales (in billions)* | |
	1950	*1964*
Output abroad resulting from U.S. investment		
From direct investment[a]	$24	$ 88
From other investment[b]	20	55
Total	44	143
Sales abroad via exports	10	25
Total output abroad plus exports	$54	$168

[a]As defined by the Department of Commerce, direct investments are branch establishments or corporations in which United States firms own 25 percent or more of the voting stock.
[b]"Other investment" represents mainly stocks and bonds of foreign firms owned by United States firms and individuals.

When the Department of Commerce measures the economic significance of exports, it compares them with the figure for total domestic production of moveable goods—that is, the sales of agricultural products, mining products, manufactures, and freight receipts. The estimated total of moveable goods produced in the United States in 1964 was $280 billion.[11] There are technical reasons which make it improper to compare the $168 billion of sales abroad with $280 billion of domestic output of moveable goods. For example, a portion of our exports is shipped to United States-owned companies as components or semi-finished products. Thus, if we add such exports to output of United States-owned foreign business we are double counting. Adjusting for this and other sources of noncomparability, we arrive at a conservative estimate that the size of the foreign market (for domestic and United States-owned foreign firms) is equal to approximately two-fifths the domestic output of farms, factories, and mines.[12]

If this seems surprising to those who are accustomed to think in terms of Gross National Product, remember that the latter includes government expenditures, personal and professional services, trade, and activities of banks, real estate firms, and stock brokers. But as far as the business of farms, factories, and mines is concerned, foreign business amounts to quite a noteworthy volume relative to the internal market. Nor is this the whole story. These data do not include the considerable amount of sales abroad of foreign firms operating under copyright and patent agreements arranged by United States firms. As an example, one firm in the Philippines manufactures the following brand-name products under restricted licenses of United States firms: "Crayola" crayons, "Wessco" paints, "Old Town" carbon paper and typewriter ribbons, "Mongol" lead pencils, "Universal" paints, and "Parker Quink."

THE GROWING IMPORTANCE OF FOREIGN ECONOMIC ACTIVITY

The increasing relative importance of foreign economic activity is well illustrated by the experience of the manufacturing industries, as shown in Chart I and Table I. Here we compare total sales of domestic manufactures with exports of manufactures and sales of United States direct investments in foreign manufacturing activity. The data are plotted on a semi-logarithmic scale in the chart. Therefore, the narrowing of the distance between the two lines depicts the more rapid rise of the foreign market as compared with the growth of domestic markets.

Equally significant is the comparison of expenditures for plant and equipment in foreign-based and in domestic manufacturing firms (Chart II and Table II). As in the preceding chart, the narrowing of the distance between the two lines is a clear portrayal of the increasing relative importance of business activity abroad. Expenditures for plant and equipment for United States subsidiaries abroad were a little over 8 percent of

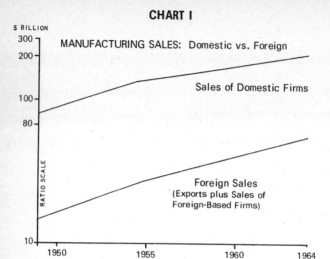

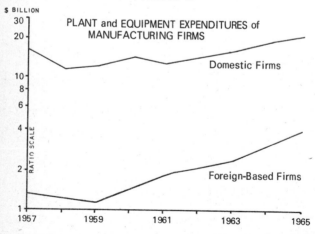

Table I
Manufactures
Foreign and Domestic Sales
(*in billions*)

(1) Year	(2) Exports	(3) Sales by foreign-based U.S. firms	(4) Total foreign sales (2)+(3)		(5) Sales of domestic manufactures	
			Absolute	1950 = 100	Absolute	1950 = 100
1950	$ 7.4	$ 8.4	$15.8	100	$ 89.8	100
1955	12.6	13.9	26.5	168	135.0	150
1960	16.1	23.6	39.7	251	164.0	183
1964	20.6	37.3	57.9	367	203.0	226

Source: Exports: U.S. Bureau of the Census, *Statistical Abstract of the United States: 1965*, pp. 877, 773. 1964 sales of domestic firms: U.S. Bureau of the Census, *Annual Survey of Manufactures, 1964*. Sales of foreign-based U.S. firms: The data for 1950 and 1955 are estimates based on the average relation between sales and investment abroad. (This is the procedure used by the National Industrial Conference Board.) Data for 1960 and 1964: *Survey of Current Business* (September 1962), p. 23; (November 1965), p. 18.

Note: The data in columns (4) and (5) are not strictly comparable (see footnote 12). However, the noncomparability does not destroy the validity of comparing the differences in the rates of growth of the two series.

Table II
Plant and Equipment Expenditures by U.S.
Domestic and Foreign-Based Manufacturing Firms

Year	Domestic firms		Foreign-based firms		Foreign as % of domestic
	Billion $	1957=100	Billion $	1957=100	
1957	$16.0	100	$1.3	100	8.1
1958	11.4	71	1.2	92	10.5
1959	12.1	76	1.1	85	9.1
1960	14.5	91	1.4	108	9.7
1961	13.7	86	1.8	139	13.1
1962	14.7	82	2.0	154	13.6
1963	15.7	98	2.3	177	14.7
1964	18.6	116	3.0	231	16.1
1965	22.5	141	3.9	300	17.3

Source: Foreign-based firms: *Survey of Current Business* (September 1965), p. 28; (September 1966), p. 30. Domestic firms: *Economic Report of the President* (Washington, D.C., 1966), p. 251.

such expenditures of domestic firms in 1957. Last year this had risen to 17 percent.

It is not surprising to find, as shown in Chart III and Table III, that profits from operations abroad are also becoming an ever more important component of business profits. In 1950, earnings on foreign investment represented about 10 percent of all after-tax profits of domestic non-financial corporations. By 1964, foreign sources of earnings accounted for about 22 percent of domestic nonfinancial corporate profits. In evaluating the significance of this we should also take into account (a) the under-statement of foreign earnings because the latter do not include all the service payments transferred by foreign subsidiaries to home corporations, and (b) the financial advantages achieved in allocating costs between the home firms and foreign subsidiaries so as to minimize taxes. Moreover, we are comparing foreign earnings with earnings of all nonfinancial corporations—those that are purely domestic and those that operate abroad as well as in the United States. If we compared foreign earnings with total earnings of only those industries that operate abroad, the share of foreign earnings would of course be much larger than one-fourth.

CHART III

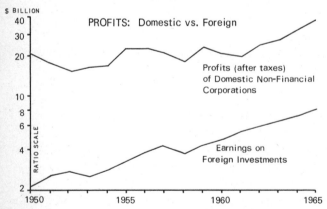

The significance of the last three tables is their representation of the rapid growth of the foreign sector. During the period when the economy as a whole was experiencing a slowing down in the rate of growth, foreign markets were an important source of expansion. For example, in manu-facturing industries during the past ten years domestic sales increased by

Table III
Earnings on Foreign Investments and
Domestic Corporate Profits
(*billions of $*)

	Earnings on foreign investment	Profits (after taxes) of domestic nonfinancial corporations
1950	2.1	21.7
1951	2.6	18.1
1952	2.7	16.0
1953	2.6	16.4
1954	2.8	16.3
1955	3.3	22.2
1956	3.8	22.1
1957	4.2	20.9
1958	3.7	17.5
1959	4.1	22.5
1960	4.7	20.6
1961	5.4	20.5
1962	5.9	23.9
1963	6.3	26.2
1964	7.1	31.3
1965	7.8	36.1

Source: Earnings on foreign investments: U.S. Department of Commerce, *Balance of Payments Statistical Supplement Revised Edition* (Washington, D.C., 1963); *Survey of Current Business* (August 1962, August 1963, August 1964, September 1965, June 1966, September 1966). Profits of nonfinancial domestic corporations: *Survey of Current Business* (September 1965, July 1966).

Note: Earnings include (a) earnings on direct investments abroad, (b) fees and royalties on direct investment transferred to parent companies in the U.S., and (c) income from "other" investments (other than direct) transferred to U.S. owners of these assets.

50 percent, while foreign sales by United States-owned factories increased over 110 percent.

Thus, as far as the commodity-producing industries are concerned, foreign markets have become a major sphere of economic interest and have proven to be increasingly important to United States business as an offset to the stagnating tendencies of the inner markets.

This is quite obvious to American businessmen. The treasurer of General Electric Company put it this way in discussing "the need that American business has to keep expanding its foreign operations":

In this respect, I think business has reached a point in the road from which there is no turning back. American industry's marvelous technology and abundant capital resources have enabled us to produce the most remarkable run of peacetime prosperity in the nation's history. To keep this going, we have for several years sought additional outlets for these sources in foreign markets. For many companies, including General Electric, these offshore markets offer the most promising opportunities for expansion that we can see.[13]

It is also quite obvious that if foreign markets are so important to the commodity-producing industries, they are also of prime importance to the other interest groups, those whose profits and prosperity are dependent upon the welfare of the commodity-producers as well as those who benefit from servicing trade and investment in foreign markets: investment and commercial bankers, stock market speculators, transportation, insurance, etc.

MILITARY SPENDING AND EXPORTS

For a full measure of economic involvement in foreign markets, the impact of military spending—the "defense" program—must also be reckoned with. The growth of our inner and outer markets has, since the founding of the Republic, been associated with the use (actual or threatened) of military force in peace as well as war. Professor William T. R. Fox states the case quite mildly: "The United States Army in peacetime was through most of the nineteenth century, extensively used to aid in the winning of the West, and especially in the suppression of Indian opposition to the opening up of new lands for settlement. Our Navy and Marine Corps, beginning with their exploits against the Barbary pirates were also engaged in making it safe for Americans to live and invest in remote places."[14]

While military activity is today presumably subordinated to national security needs, the "one-ness" of the national security and business interests persists: the size of the "free" world and the degree of its "security" define the geographic boundaries where capital is relatively free to invest and trade. The widespread military bases, the far-flung military activities, and the accompanying complex of expenditures at home and abroad serve many purposes of special interest to the business community: (1) protecting present and potential sources of raw materials; (2) safeguarding foreign markets and foreign investments; (3) conserving commercial sea and air routes; (4) preserving spheres of influence where United States business gets a competitive edge for investment and trade; (5) creating new foreign customers and investment opportunities via foreign military and economic aid; and, more generally, (6) maintaining the structure of world capitalist markets not only directly for the United States but also for its junior partners among the industrialized nations, countries in which United States business is becoming ever more closely enmeshed. But even all of this does not exhaust the "one-ness" of business interest and military activity, for we need to take into account the stake business has in the size and nature of military expenditures as a well-spring of new orders and profits.

As with exports, the significance of military spending for business and the economy as a whole is usually greatly underestimated. One often hears that defense expenditures amount to less than 10 percent of the Gross National Product and that with a proper political environment comparable government spending for peaceful uses could accomplish as much for the economy. A crucial weakness of this approach is its un-critical acceptance of Gross National Product as a thing-in-itself. Because GNP is a useful statistical tool and one which has become entrenched in our ways of thought, we tend to ignore the underlying strategic relationships that determine the direction and degree of movement of the economic aggregates. Instead of examining the requirements of the industrial structure and the dynamic elements of economic behavior, we tend to view the economy as blocks of billions of dollars that may be shifted at will from one column to another of the several categories used by statisticians to construct the measurement of GNP.

To appreciate fully the critical influence of foreign markets and military expenditures on the domestic economy, recognition must be given to their exceptionally large impact on the capital goods industries. But first a comment on the capital goods industries and the business cycle. There are diverse explanations of business cycles, but there can be no disputing the fact that the mechanics of the business cycle—the trans-mission mechanism, if you wish—is to be found in the ups and downs of the investment goods industries. There are cycles which are primarily related to the ebb and flow of inventories, but these are usually short-lived as long as the demand for investment goods does not collapse.

During a cyclical decline, the demand for consumer goods can be sustained for a period by several expedients such as unemployment relief, other welfare payments, and depletion of consumer savings. However, except for the most essential replacement needs, expenditures on investment goods theoretically can go down to zero. Businessmen naturally will not invest unless they expect to make a profit. The result of the diverse behavior of producer goods and consumer goods was classically demonstrated in the depression of the 1930's. During this probably worst depression in our history, purchases of consumer goods declined only 19 percent (between 1929 and 1933). Compare this with the

Table IV
Percent of Total Output Attributable to
Exports and Federal Purchases, 1958

Industry	Percent of output		
	Going into exports	Purchased by federal government	Total of exports and federal purchases
Iron and ferroalloy ores mining	13.5%	12.8%	26.3%
Nonferrous metal ores mining	9.1	35.6	44.7
Coal mining	19.1	6.3	25.4
Ordnance and accessories	1.7	86.7	88.4
Primary iron and steel manufacturing	10.1	12.5	22.6
Primary nonferrous metal manufacturing	10.1	22.3	32.4
Stamping, screw machine products	7.1	18.2	25.3
Other fabricated metal products	8.6	11.9	20.5
Engines and turbines	14.8	19.7	34.5
Farm machinery and equipment	10.0	2.9	12.9
Construction, mining and oil field machinery	26.9	6.1	33.0
Materials handling machinery and equipment	9.4	17.2	26.6
Metalworking machinery and equipment	14.0	20.6	34.6
Special industry machinery and equipment	17.5	4.3	21.8
General industrial machinery and equipment	13.4	15.3	28.7
Machine shop products	7.0	39.0	46.0
Electric industrial equipment and apparatus	9.8	17.0	26.8
Electric lighting and wiring equipment	5.5	14.5	20.0
Radio, TV and communication equipment	4.8	40.7	45.5
Electronic components and accessories	7.6	38.9	46.5
Misc. electrical machinery, equipment and supplies	8.9	15.1	24.0
Aircraft and parts	6.1	86.7	92.8
Other transportation equipment (not autos)	10.1	20.9	31.0
Scientific and controlling instruments	7.3	30.2	37.5

Source: "The Interindustry Structure of the United States," *Survey of Current Business* (November 1964), p. 14.

behavior of the two major types of investment goods during the same period: expenditures for residential construction fell by 80 percent and nonresidential fixed investment dropped 71 percent.

With this as background, let us now focus on the post-Second World War relationship between (a) exports and military demand, and (b) a major category of investment, nonresidential fixed investment goods. Table IV lists the industries producing nonresidential investment goods. It should be noted that a number of these industries also contribute to consumer goods (e.g., steel and machinery for autos) and to residential construction. This table presents the percentages of total demand (direct and indirect) created by exports and purchases of the federal government, which are almost entirely for military needs. These data are for the year 1958, the latest year for which there exists a complete input-output analysis for the United States economy.

As will be noted from Table IV, in only one industry—farm machinery and equipment—did the combined export and military demand come to less than 20 percent of total demand. At the opposite extreme are the military industries par excellence—ordnance and aircraft. For all the other industries, the range of support given in 1958 by exports and military demand is from 20 to 50 percent.

While the available statistical data refer to only one year, the postwar patterns of exports and military expenditures suggest that this tabulation is a fair representation of the situation since the Korean War, and surely a gross underestimate during the Vietnam War. More information and study are required for a more thorough analysis. Meanwhile, the available data warrant, in my opinion, these observations:

(1) Exports and military spending exert a distinctive influence on the economy because they fortify a strategic center of the existing industrial structure. This is especially noteworthy because business investment is not, as is too often conceived, a freely flowing stream. There is a definite interdependence between (a) the existing schedule of wage rates, prices, and profits, (b) the evolved structure of industry (the types of interrelated industries, each built to be profitable at the scale of obtainable domestic and foreign markets), and (c) the direction of profitable new investments. To put it in simpler terms, there are sound business reasons why investments flow in the direction they do and not in such ways as to meet the potential needs of this country—for example, to eliminate poverty, to provide the industry which would create equal opportunity to Negroes,

to develop the underdeveloped regions of the United States, or to create adequate housing. More important, business cannot invest to accomplish these ends and at the same time meet its necessary standards of profit, growth, and security for invested capital. Exports of capital goods and military demand flowing to the capital-goods producers, on the other hand, are uniquely advantageous in that they strengthen and make more profitable the established investment structure; they also contribute to an expansion of the industries that are most harmonious with and most profitable for the existing composition of capital.

(2) The support given by foreign economic involvement—both military and civilian commodities—makes a singular contribution by acting as a bulwark against the slippage of minor recessions into major depressions. It has accomplished this by shoring up one of the strategic balance wheels of the economy, the production of investment-type equipment—by supplying, as we have seen, from 20 to 50 percent of the market for these goods.

(3) We need also to take into account that it is *monopolistic* industry which dominates the volume and flow of investment and that such monopolistic businesses characteristically gear their investment policies to the "sure thing," where good profits and safety of investment are reliably assured. Here the tie-in of government action and foreign policy is of paramount interest. The military-goods market usually has the decided advantage of supplying long-term contracts, often accompanied by enough guarantees to reduce and even eliminate any risk in building additional plant equipment, plant and equipment which may also be used for civilian purposes. In addition, military contracts pay for related research and development expenses, again removing risky aspects of normal investment programs. As for the foreign countries, the United States military presence, its foreign policy, and its national security commitments provide a valuable protective apparatus for the investments made in foreign markets. These foreign investments, together with the demand created by governmental foreign aid, contribute importantly to the demand for the exports of the capital-goods and other manufacturing industries. The confidence in the consistency of government foreign policy and its complementary military policy can, and surely must, act as a valuable frame of reference for the domestic as well as foreign investment practices of monopolistic business.

(4) The extra 20 to 50 percent of business provided by exports plus

military demand (as shown for the key industries in Table IV) provides a much greater percentage of the total profits of these firms. The typical economics of a manufacturing business requires that a firm reach a certain level of productive activity before it can make a profit. Gross overhead costs—depreciation of machinery, use of plant, costs of administration—remain fairly constant at a given level of capacity. Until production reaches a point where at the market price of the final product enough income is produced to meet the overhead and direct costs, a business operates at a loss. Once this "break-even" point is reached, the profitability of the business surges forward until it hits against the limits of productive capacity. Of course the curve of profitability differs from industry to industry and from firm to firm. But the existence of a break-even point, and the upward swing of profits after the break-even point has been passed, is a common characteristic of manufacturing industries. What this means is that for many of the firms in the capital-goods industries, the overlay of 20 to 50 percent of demand from military purchases and exports probably accounts for the major share of the profits, and in not a few firms perhaps as much as 80 to 100 percent of their profits.

MONOPOLY AND FOREIGN INVESTMENTS

One of the reasons frequently given for believing that economic imperialism is an unimportant influence in foreign and military policy is that only a small segment of American business is vitally concerned with foreign or military economic activities. This might be a meaningful observation if economic resources were widely distributed and the majority of domestic-minded business firms could conceivably be mobilized against policies fostered by the small minority of foreign-oriented businesses. But the realities of economic concentration suggest quite the opposite. In manufacturing industries, five corporations own over 15 percent of total net capital assets (as of 1962). The 100 largest corporations own 55 percent of total net capital assets.[15] This means that a small number of firms—with their own strength and that of their allies in finance and mass communication media—can wield an overwhelming amount of economic and political power, especially if there is a community of interest within this relatively small group.

And it is precisely among the giant corporations that we find the main centers of foreign and military economic operations. Just a cursory examination of the 50 largest industrial concerns shows the following types of firms heavily involved in international economic operations and the supply of military goods: 12 in oil, 5 in aviation, 3 in chemicals, 3 in steel, 3 in autos, 8 in electrical equipment and electronics, and 3 in rubber. These 37 companies account for over 90 percent of the assets of the top 50 industrial firms.

The community of interest among the industrial giants in foreign and military operations stems from relations that are not always obvious in terms of the customary statistical categories. First, there is the inter-relationship among the firms via the financial centers of power. Second, there are the direct economic ties of business. While only 5 firms get one-fourth of the volume of military contracts and 25 firms account for more than half of such contracts, a large part of this business is distributed to other businesses that supply these chief contractors.[16] Thus, as we saw in Table IV, the primary nonferrous metal manufacturers who receive very few direct military contracts nevertheless get over 22 percent of their business from military demand. And, third, because of the rich growth potential and other advantages of the military- and foreign-oriented businesses, the postwar merger movement among industrial giants has intermingled the typically domestic with the typically outer-market directed business organizations. The most unlikely seeming business organizations are today planted with both feet in foreign and military business. We see, for example, traditional producers of grain mill pro-ducts and of plumbing and heating equipment acquiring plants that make scientific instruments; meat packing firms buying up companies in the

Table V
U.S. Direct Foreign Investment by Size of Investment (1957)

Value of direct investment by size classes	Number of firms	Percent of total U.S. investment
$ 100 million and over	45	57
$ 50-100 million	51	14
$ 25-50 million	67	9
$ 10-25 million	126	8
$ 5-10 million	166	5
Total	455	93

Source: United States Business Investments in Foreign Countries, U.S. Dept. of Commerce (1960), p. 144.

general industrial machinery field; and many other cross-industry mergers.

The concentration of economic power, so much part of the domestic scene, shows up in even stronger fashion in the field of foreign investment. The basic available data on this are taken from the 1957 census of foreign investments (see Table V). These data refer only to direct investments and do not include portfolio investments or such economic ties as are created by the licensing of patents, processes, and trademarks. We note from this table that only 45 firms account for almost three-fifths of all direct foreign investment. Eighty percent of all such investment is held by 163 firms. The evidence is still more striking when we examine the concentration of investment by industry:

Industry	No. of firms	Percent of total assets held
Mining	20	95
Oil	24	93
Manufacturing	143	81
Public Utilities	12	89
Trade	18	83
Finance and Insurance	23	76
Agriculture	6	83

These data are shown from the viewpoint of total United States foreign investment. If we examined the situation from the angle of the recipient countries, we would find an even higher degree of concentration of United States business activities. But from either perspective, the concentration of foreign investment is but an extension of domestic monopolistic trends. The latter provide the opportunity to accumulate the wealth needed for extensive foreign investment as well as the impetus for such investment.

The question of control is central to an understanding of the strategic factors that determine the pattern of foreign investment. In its starkest form, this control is most obvious in the economic relations with the underdeveloped countries—in the role of these countries as suppliers of raw materials for mass-production industries and as a source of what can properly be termed financial tribute.

Let us look first at the distribution of foreign investment as shown in Table VI. We see here two distinct patterns. In Latin America, Asia, and Africa, the majority of the investment is in the extractive industries.

Although Canada is an important source of minerals and oil, only 35 percent of United States investment is in these extractive industries, with 45 percent going into manufactures. The investment in extractive industries in Europe is minimal: the data on petroleum represent refineries and distribution, not oil wells.

Table VI
Percent Distribution of Direct Foreign Investment by
Area and Industry, 1964

Industry	All areas %	Canada %	Europe %	Latin America %	Africa %	Asia %	Oceania %
Mining	8.0	12.1	0.4	12.6	21.9	1.1	6.3
Petroleum	32.4	23.4	25.6	35.9	51.0	65.8	28.1
Manufacturing	38.0	44.8	54.3	24.3	13.8	17.5	54.1
Public utilities	4.6	3.3	0.4	5.8	0.1	1.8	0.1
Trade	8.4	5.8	12.2	10.7	5.7	7.8	5.5
Other	8.6	10.6	7.1	10.7	7.5	6.0	5.9
Totals	100.0	100.0	100.0	100.0	100.0	100.0	100.0

Source: Calculated from data in *Survey of Current Business* (September 1965), p. 24.

The economic control, and hence the political control when dealing with foreign sources of raw material supplies, is of paramount importance to the monopoly-organized mass production industries in the home country. In industries such as steel, aluminum, and oil, the ability to control the source of raw material is essential to the control over the markets and prices of the final products, and serves as an effective safety factor in protecting the large investment in the manufacture and distribution of the final product. The resulting frustration of competition takes on two forms. First, when price and distribution of the raw material are controlled, the competitor's freedom of action is restricted; he cannot live very long without a dependable source of raw materials at a practical cost. Second, by gobbling up as much of the world's resources of this material as is feasible, a power group can forestall a weaker competitor from becoming more independent as well as discourage possible new competition. How convenient that a limited number of United States oil companies control two-thirds of the "free world's" oil![17]

At this level of monopoly, the involvement of business interests with United States foreign policy becomes ever more close. The assurance of control over raw materials in most areas involves not just another business matter but is high on the agenda of maintaining industrial and financial power. And the wielders of this power, if they are to remain in the saddle, must use every effort to make sure that these sources of supply are always available on the most favorable terms: these foreign supplies are not merely an avenue to great profits but are the insurance policy on the monopolistic position at home.

The pressure to obtain external sources of raw materials has taken on a new dimension during the past two decades, and promises to become increasingly severe. Even though United States business has always had to rely on foreign sources for a number of important metals (e.g., bauxite, chrome, nickel, manganese, tungsten, tin), it has nevertheless been self-reliant and an exporter of a wide range of raw materials until quite recently. This generalization has been a mainstay of those who argued that U.S. capitalism had no need to be imperialistic. But even this argument, weak as it may have been in the past, can no longer be relied on. The developing pressure on natural resources, especially evident since the 1940's, stirred President Truman to establish a Materials Policy Commission to define the magnitude of the problem. The ensuing commission report, *Resources for Freedom* (Washington, D.C., 1952), graphically summarized the dramatic change in the following comparison for all raw materials other than food and gold: at the turn of the century, the U.S. produced on the whole some 15 percent more of these raw materials than was domestically consumed; this surplus had by 1950 turned into a deficit, with U.S. industry consuming 10 percent more than domestic production; extending the trends to 1975 showed that by then the overall deficit of raw materials for industry will be about 20 percent.

Perhaps the awareness of this development was a contributing factor to President Eisenhower's alerting the nation to the unity of political and economic interests in his first inaugural address (January 20, 1953): "We know . . . that we are linked to all free peoples not merely by a noble idea but by a simple need. No free people can for long cling to any privilege or enjoy any safety in economic solitude. For all our own material might, even we need markets in the world for the surpluses of our farms and our factories. Equally, we need for these same farms and factories vital materials and products of distant lands. This basic law of interdependence, so manifest in the commerce of peace, applies with thousand-fold intensity in the event of war."

As is so often the case, economic interests harmonize comfortably with political and security goals, since so many of the basic raw materials are considered essential to effective war preparedness. Quite understandably, the government makes its contribution to the security of the nation as well as to the security of business via diplomatic maneuvers, maintenance of convenient military bases in various parts of the world, military aid to help maintain stable governments, and, last but not least, a foreign aid program which is a fine blend of declared humanitarian aims about industrialization and a realistic appreciation that such progress should not interfere with the ability of supplying countries to maintain a proper flow of raw materials. To do a real job of assuring an adequate supply of raw materials in the light of possible exhaustion of already exploited deposits, and in view of possible needs for missiles and space programs, the government can make its greatest contribution by keeping as much of the world as possible "free" and safe for mineral development. Clarence B. Randall, president of Inland Steel Co. and adviser on foreign aid in Washington, comments on the fortunate availability of uranium deposits in the Belgian Congo as the atom bomb was developed: "What a break it was for us that the mother country was on our side! And who can possibly foresee today which of the vast unexplored areas of the world may likewise possess some unique deposit of a rare raw material which in the fullness of time our industry or our defense program may most urgently need?"[18]

The integration of less developed capitalisms into the world market as reliable and continuous suppliers of their natural resources results, with rare exceptions, in a continuous dependency on the centers of monopoly control that is sanctified and cemented by the market structure which evolves from this very dependency. Integration into world capitalist markets has almost uniform effects on the supplying countries: (1) they depart from, or never enter, the paths of development that require independence and self-reliance; (2) they lose their economic self-sufficiency and become dependent on exports for their economic viability; (3) their industrial structure becomes adapted to the needs of supplying specialized exports at prices acceptable to the buyers, reducing thereby such flexibility of productive resources as is needed for a diversified and growing economic productivity. The familiar symptom of this process is still seen in Latin America where, despite industrialization efforts and the stimulus of two world wars, well over 90 percent of most countries' total exports consists of the export of agricultural and mineral products.[19] The extreme dependence on exports, and on a severely restricted number of export products at that, keeps such economies off balance in their international economic relations and creates frequent need for borrowing. Debt engenders increasing debt, for the servicing of the debt adds additional balance of payments difficulties. And in all such relations of borrowing and lending, the channels of international finance are in the hands of the foreign investors, their business associates, and their government agencies.

The chains of dependence may be manipulated by the political, financial, and military arms of the centers of empire, with the help of the Marines, military bases, bribery, CIA operations, financial maneuvers, and the like. But the material basis of this dependence is an industrial and financial structure which through the so-called normal operations of the marketplace reproduces the conditions of economic dependence.

A critical element of the market patterns which helps perpetuate the underdeveloped countries as dependable suppliers of raw materials is the financial tribute to the foreign owners who extract not only natural resources but handsome profits as well. The following comparison for the years 1950-1965 is a clear illustration of the process and refers to only one kind of financial drain, the income from direct investments which is transferred to the United States:[20]

	Europe	*Canada*	*Latin America*	*All other areas*
			(billions of dollars)	
Flow of direct investments from U.S.	$8.1	$6.8	$3.8	$5.2
Income on this capital transferred to U.S.	5.5	5.9	11.3	14.3
Net	+ $2.6	+ $ .9	− $7.5	− $9.1

In the underdeveloped regions almost three times as much money was taken out as was put in. And note well that besides drawing out almost three times as much as they put in, investors were able to increase the value of the assets owned in these regions manifold: in Latin America, direct investments owned by United States business during this period increased from \$4.5 to \$10.3 billion; in Asia and Africa, from \$1.3 to \$4.7 billion.

The contrasting pattern in the flow of funds to and from Europe indicates a post-Second World War trend. The rapid growth of investment in Europe was in the manufacturing and oil refining fields. The developments in foreign investment in manufacturing are closely related to the normal business drive to (a) control markets and (b) minimize costs of production. The methods used will vary according to the industry and the conditions in each country. The main factors involved in relying on capital investment instead of relying on export trade are:

(1) If the profit rate obtainable by manufacturing abroad is greater than by increasing domestic production.

(2) If it facilitates getting a larger and more secure share of a given foreign market.

(3) If it enables taking advantage of the channels of export trade of the country in which investment is made. Thus, United States business firms in England account for 10 percent of Britain's exports.[21]

(4) If it is possible to pre-empt a field of industry based on new technological developments, usually protected by exercise of patent rights. But the most dramatic development of our times is the spread of United States industry into the computer, atomic energy, and space technology activities of industrialized countries. The rapid spread of these fields is motivated, to be sure, by immediate profit opportunities. But it most likely also has the aim of helping to maintain, and get full advantage of, the technical edge United States business now has as a result of the vast investment made by the United States government in research and development. The dominant position in this technology may be decisive in achieving wider control of the rest of the economy, when and if the new technology becomes the key to the productive forces of a society.

Such investment as is made by United States capital in manufacturing in underdeveloped countries occurs primarily in Latin America, where the percentage of total United States investment in the field of manufacturing is 24 percent. This investment is mainly in light manufacturing industry, including the processing of native food materials. Manufacturing operations in the durable goods field, such as autos, takes the form of assembly plants. This guarantees the export market of components and parts. It also contributes to stabilizing the market for these United States products. It is much easier for a country faced with severe balance of payments difficulties to prohibit imports of a luxury product than to eliminate the import of raw materials and assembly parts which will create unemployment and shut down local industry.

The postwar foreign economic expansion of United States manufacturing firms has resulted in the transformation of many of the giants of United States business into a new form of multinational organization. The typical international business firm is no longer limited to the giant oil company. It is as likely to be a General Motors or a General Electric— with 15 to 20 percent of its operations involved in foreign business, and exercising all efforts to increase this share. It is the professed goal of these international firms to obtain the lowest unit production costs on a worldwide basis. It is also their aim, though not necessarily openly stated, to come out on top in the merger movement in the European Common Market and to control as large a share of the world market as they do of the United States market. To the directors of such organizations the "one-ness" of economic and national interests is quite apparent. The president of General Electric put it succinctly: "I suggest we will perceive: that overriding both the common purposes and cross-purposes of business and government, there is a broader pattern—a 'consensus' if you will, where public and private interest come together, cooperate, interact and become the national interest."[22]

Needless to stress, the term "private interest" refers to private enterprise. Another officer of this corporation grapples with the identity of the private and national interest: "Thus, our search for profits places us squarely in line with the national policy of stepping up international trade as a means of strengthening the free world in the Cold War confrontation with Communism."[23]

Just as the fight against Communism helps the search for profits, so the search for profits helps the fight against Communism. What more perfect harmony of interest could be imagined?

Notes

1. American Board of Commissioners for Foreign Missions, *32nd Annual Report* (1841), as quoted in Richard W. Van Alstyne, *The Rising American Empire* (Chicago: Quadrangle Books, 1965), p. 171. The latter, originally published in 1960 by Oxford University Press, is highly recommended for a better understanding of the continuity of United States foreign policy. See

also Charles A. Beard, *The Idea of National Interest*, reissued in 1966 by Quadrangle Paperbacks with new material; and Lloyd C. Gardner, *Economic Aspects of New Deal Diplomacy* (Madison: University of Wisconsin Press, 1964).

2. *Niles' National Register*, January 22, 1842, pp. 327–328.

3. Foreword to Samuel Lubell, *The Revolution in World Trade and American Economic Policy* (New York: Harper and Brothers, 1955), p. xl.

4. *International Security—The Military Aspect*, Report of Panel II of the Special Studies Project of Rockefeller Brothers Fund (Garden City, N.Y.: Doubleday & Co., 1958), p. 24.

5. The full title reads, *The United States Navy as an Industrial Asset—What the Navy Has Done for Industry and Commerce*. It was written by the Office of Naval Intelligence, U.S. Navy, in October 1922 and published in 1923 by the U.S. Government Printing Office, Washington, D.C. The following excerpt is typical: "In the Asiatic area a force of gunboats is kept on constant patrol in the Yangtse River. These boats are able to patrol from the mouth of the river up nearly 2,000 miles into the very heart of China. American businessmen have freely stated that should the United States withdraw this patrol they would have to leave at the same time. Our Navy not only protects our own citizens and their property, but is constantly protecting humanity in general and frequently actually engages the bands of bandits who infest this region" (p. 4).

6. Eugene R. Black, *The Domestic Dividends of Foreign Aid* in *Columbia Journal of World Business*, vol. 1 (Fall 1965), p. 23.

7. Address by Assistant Commerce Secretary Andrew F. Brimmer at a meeting of the Tax Foundation, Inc., as reported in the *New York Times*, December 5, 1965.

8. Richard D. Robinson, *International Business Policy* (New York: Holt, Rinehart and Winston, 1966), p. 220.

9. *Economic Considerations in Foreign Relations—An Interview with Alfred Wentworth* in *Political*, vol. 1, no. 1 (July 1965), pp. 45–46.

10. *The Conference Board Record*, vol. 3, no. 5 (May 1966), p. 28. See also Judd Polk, Irene W. Meister, and Lawrence A. Veit, *U.S. Production Abroad and the Balance of Payments: A Survey of Corporate Investment Experience* (New York: National Industrial Conference Board, 1966).

11. This total consists of (a) cash receipts from farm marketing plus consumption of farm products in the farm household, (b) value added in manufacturing industries, (c) value of minerals production, and (d) freight receipts.

12. The Department of Commerce estimates that $6.3 billion of exports was shipped to foreign affiliates of United States companies in 1964. Other

sources of noncomparability arise from (a) the estimated $168 billion includes sales of trade organizations, public utilities, and other noncommodity producers, and (b) the data on sales of domestic manufactures are on a value-added basis while the sales of foreign affiliates are on a value-of-shipments basis. Conservative estimates of adjustments to obtain comparability reduce the $168 billion to $110 billion.

13. John D. Lockton, "Walking the International Tightrope." Address to the National Industrial Conference Board, May 21, 1965; published by General Electric Co., Schenectady, N.Y., 1965, pp. 4–5.

14. William T. R. Fox, "Military Representation Abroad," in *The Representation of the United States Abroad*, a report of The American Assembly, Graduate School of Business, Columbia University, New York, 1956, pp. 124–125.

15. *Hearings, Subcommittee on Antitrust and Monopoly of the Committee on the Judiciary*, U.S. Senate, 88th Congress, 2nd Session, Part I, Washington, D.C., 1964, p. 115.

16. *Background Material on Economic Aspects of Military Procurement and Supply: 1964*, Joint Economic Committee of Congress (Washington, D.C., 1964), p. 11.

17. A. George Gols, "Postwar U.S. Foreign Petroleum Investment," in Raymond F. Mikesell, ed., *U.S. Private and Government Investment Abroad* (Eugene, Oregon: University of Oregon Books, 1962), p. 417.

18. Clarence B. Randall, *The Communist Challenge to American Business* (Boston: Little Brown & Co., 1959), p. 36.

19. Joseph Grunwald, "Resource Aspects of Latin American Development," in Marion Clawson, ed., *National Resources and International Development* (Baltimore: Johns Hopkins Press, 1964), p. 315.

20. These are summations of data presented for 1950 to 1960 in U.S. Department of Commerce, *Balance of Payments Statistical Supplement Revised Edition* (Washington, D.C., 1963). The data for 1961 to 1965 appear in the review articles on foreign investment in various issues of the *Survey of Current Business* from 1962 to 1966. The first line in the text table represents net capital outflows of direct investment from the United States. The second line is the sum of dividends, interest, and branch profits, after foreign taxes, produced by direct investments abroad. It does not include the earnings of corporate subsidiaries (as distinguished from branches), which are retained abroad.

21. John H. Dunning, *American Investment in British Manufacturing Industry* (London, 1958).

22. Speech by Fred J. Borch, president of General Electric Company, "Our Common Cause in World Competition," before The Economic Club of

New York, November 9, 1964; printed by General Electric Co., Schenectady, N.Y.

23. Speech by John D. Lockton, treasurer of General Electric Company, "The Creative Power of Profits," at Macalester College, St. Paul, Minn., April 22, 1964; printed by General Electric Co., Schenectady, N.Y.

3

David Horowitz

The Alliance for Progress

The Alliance, whose formal Charter was signed at Punta del Este on August 17, 1961, proposed to utilize $20 billion in foreign capital (including $10 billion in U.S. government funds and $300 million annually in U.S. private capital investment) and $80 billion in capital provided by the Latin Americans themselves, over a ten-year period, to finance an economic growth rate of 2.5 percent.[1] An essential element in the success of this plan, formally recognized as such by the Alliance Charter, was the carrying out of those social and economic reforms necessary to free the productive forces of the continent.

Before proceeding to a consideration of the key points of this program of reform, it might be well to look at the recommendations as a whole. In the main they called for the alleviation of the most glaring inadequacies in diet, housing, and health, the improvement of agriculture through diversification of agriculture, broadening of land ownership, expansion of cultivable acreage and increasing of modern farming techniques, the expansion of industries, the elimination of illiteracy and education of technicians, the enlargement of existing systems of transportation and communications, assurance of fair wages and satisfactory working conditions, reform of tax laws, stabilization of the prices of basic exports, and acceleration of the economic integration of Latin America.

With few exceptions, this same program was prescribed for Cuba by the Foreign Policy Association in 1935, by the World Bank in 1950, and by the United States Department of Commerce in 1956. One can understand, therefore, the comment of Arnold Toynbee (who restricted his observation to a single, but in his view critical, item on the agenda): "Perhaps," he said, "it does need a revolutionary explosion of fifty-megaton power to blow up the . . . road-block that has hitherto ob-

---

This essay originally appeared in *The Socialist Register 1964* (New York: Monthly Review Press, 1964). Copyright © 1964 by The Merlin Press Ltd.

structed both economic and social progress in Latin America so griev-
ously."[2]

Which brings us to specifics. In his speech, President Kennedy
stressed the absolute necessity of social reforms, particularly land and
tax reforms, if the goals of the Alliance were to be achieved: "For unless
necessary social reforms, including land and tax reform, are freely made—
unless we broaden the opportunity for all our people—unless the great
mass of Americans share in increasing prosperity—then our alliance,
our revolution and our dream will have failed."

With regard to land reform, observers like Toynbee were even more
specifically categorical: "In Latin America, agrarian reform is the
necessary starting-point for political, economic, and social change alike"
(emphasis added). Writing in 1962, Toynbee also noted that "the
resistance to the redistribution of the *latifundia* has, so far, been aston-
ishingly and distressingly successful." The reason for this success has
not been probed deeply by spokesmen for the Alliance, who generally
have spoken in terms of inertia, the failure of the "idea" of the Alliance
to take hold; in a highly revealing passage, the Committee of Nine[3]
complained, for example, that the revolutionary nature of the Alliance
had not caught on "because the leaders [i.e., rulers—D.H.] of Latin
America have never presented it as such to their people."[4]

Two Marxist critics (Huberman and Sweezy) have offered a structural
explanation for this pass, which if correct must go a long way in damp-
ening hopes for any future reversal, or for any real reform in Latin
America short of a fifty-megaton revolution. For they suggest that it is
vain to look toward an urban bourgeoisie in Latin America to push
through land reforms in the name of economic efficiency. According to
their analysis, there is no bourgeoisie independent of the latifundists;
through cross-investments and intermarriages, they have become one
and the same group. Further,

> it is very doubtful whether any Latin American bourgeoisie has the will or
> discipline to impose drastic reforms on itself. This explains, for example,
> the otherwise baffling fact that Brazil, where industrial development has gone
> farther and faster in recent years than anywhere else and where an expansion
> of agricultural production has become a matter of extreme urgency, neverthe-
> less does nothing but talk about agrarian reform.[5]

Whether, in fact, this analysis and its conclusions hold rigorously
for every one of the nineteen republics is beyond the scope of the present

essay. One important illustration of its validity, however, which may also serve as an introduction to what the U.S. means by land reform (there are several varieties) is the agrarian program instituted by Guatemala in 1952-1953.

The men who attempted to carry through this reform were middle-class social democrats; the target of the reform was 200,000 acres (eventually 400,000) of uncultivated land owned by the United Fruit Co. (hardly a feudal remnant). The Guatemalan government agreed to pay $600,000 compensation in 3 percent, twenty-five-year bonds, an amount equivalent to the assessed value of the land recorded in 1952 for tax purposes. This payment was termed unacceptable by the company, which was backed by the U.S. government. The U.S. contended that the compensation offered did not conform to the minimum standards of just compensation prescribed by international law, and proceeded to file a claim of $16 million against Guatemala for the expropriated properties.[6] The dispute was settled after the U.S. engineered a coup d'état that toppled the reform-minded regime; the junta which succeeded it immediately returned the lands to United Fruit.

A similar set of events occurred in Cuba. On May 17, 1959, the Agrarian Reform Law was promulgated prohibiting anyone from owning more than 995 acres of farm land or 3,316 acres of ranch land; compensation was based on assessed values (provided by the owners and firms themselves for tax purposes) payable in twenty-year bonds at about 4 percent interest.

> Hardest hit U.S. companies [commented *Time*] are Atlantica del Golfo (with 500,000 acres), the Rionda group (330,000), United Fruit Company (270,000). . . . The companies were officially silent, privately frantic. "This isn't expropriation," cried one sugar executive. "It's confiscation."

On June 11, a U.S. note was delivered to the Cuban government which, while acknowledging Cuba's right to expropriate foreign-owned property, reminded Cuba that "this right is coupled with the corresponding obligation for prompt, adequate and effective compensation." But, as William Appleman Williams has observed:

> no poor or developing country has the funds for "prompt, adequate and effective compensation." . . .
> Hence the American demand is relevant only as a vehicle for the implied threat that the United States will resort to other means if its formal injunction is not honored. This meaning was only slightly veiled in the note to Cuba.

The United States made it clear that it would "seek solutions through other appropriate international procedures" if Cuba did not meet the American conditions.[7]

This same Cuban land reform, according to Toynbee, is "one of those acts of the present Cuban revolution that have set a standard—and a pace—for reform in the rest of Latin America." This is especially so, because "so far the Cuban revolution has not followed suit to the Mexican and Bolivian revolution or the abortive Guatemalan revolution in its agrarian policy."[8] For, in Toynbee's view, these revolutions failed to carry through their agrarian reforms for reasons very closely related to the analysis of Huberman and Sweezy.

In the past, notes Toynbee, the benefits of civilization were monopolized by a small oligarchy of big landlords. These benefits could not be extended to the huge depressed majority without a political and economic revolution. The revolutions which broke the power of the oligarchs were carried out by the "middle class." But this class did not move to share the benefits of civilization with the rest of the depressed majority. Instead, the middle class itself

> has appropriated almost the whole of the increased production which the first phase of the Industrial Revolution has generated; and, in consequence, the great majority of mankind has experienced no appreciable change for the better as a result of the middle-class revolution. . . . From the majority's point of view, what has happened has been merely the replacement of landlord oligarchy by a middle-class oligarchy. The hopes that the masses cherished have been frustrated by the middle class itself as soon as it has ousted the landlords from the saddle and has taken their place.[9]

In Mexico, for example, the redistribution of the land was the first item on the agenda of the revolution for the first thirty years of its course. During the last six years of these thirty, President Cárdenas carried out redistribution wholeheartedly. But after Cárdenas' term, the Partido Revolucionario Institucional, which had been the sole party in power since 1930, "without any breach of solidarity" openly proclaimed "the Mexican Revolution's *volte-face*." "In 1950, the P.R.I. officially discarded the concept of the class struggle and 'democracy of the workers and agrarians' in favour of the 'ideal of the middle classes.'"[10] In this year (1950) 42.2 percent of Mexican workers on the land were still landless, as against only 29.2 percent who were *ejidarios* (in cooperatives) and 26.5 percent who were owner-operators. Less than 1 percent of all farms in private hands occupied 76 percent of the total farm land in private hands.[11] Among the wealthy landowners was the son of the revolutionary General Obregón, now a governor of one of the northern states (his land irrigated at government expense).

Toynbee is more optimistic than Huberman and Sweezy, as he feels that there is a good deal of hope that the middle classes will move "voluntarily to help the industrial and agricultural labouring class to attain the middle class standard of living." If the middle class refuses this opportunity, however, the outlook is bleak: "In the light of past experience, it is, I think, safe to say that, whenever and wherever the middle class tries to sit on the social safety-valve, it is going to bring on itself, sooner or later, the nemesis of being blown sky high."[12]

These observations pinpoint a critical role that the Alliance for Progress was conceived to play. As President Kennedy warned on the first anniversary of the Alliance,

> those who possess wealth and power in poor nations must accept their own responsibilities. They must lead the fight for those basic reforms which alone *can preserve the fabric of their own societies.* Those who make peaceful revolution impossible will make violent revolution inevitable. (Emphasis added—Speech, March 13, 1962, Anniversary of Alliance.)

What then can be said of the kind of "peaceful revolution" that Kennedy and the Alliance sponsors envisaged? Before answering this question we must ask what kind of revolution have they been able to induce?

In terms of land reform, the answer is very little "revolution" at all. After two years, land reforms, according to the *New York Times* (August 18, 1963) "were on the books in ten countries" but "no substantial progress [as of July 1963] had been made in practice." Of these ten countries, moreover, five had had land reform programs prior to the Alliance for Progress. (Mexico since 1917, Bolivia and Guatemala since 1953, Venezuela since 1954, and Colombia since 1961.) The experiences of these countries—and two in particular, Guatemala and Venezuela—suggested an even more negative outlook than the figures indicated.

In Guatemala, as we have seen, the U.S. government frustrated the beginnings of really effective land reform. Toynbee, it should be noted, sees a great deal of promise in the fact that since 1954

> the United Fruit Company has . . . handed over a large part of its land reserves . . . to the present counter-revolutionary regime for continuing . . . the colonization work that the previous revolutionary regime had initiated. This

is a prudent recognition of the persisting force, in Guatemala, of the demand for social justice.[13]

But according to a student of agrarian reform in Latin America (Andre Gunder Frank), "at the rate at which land was distributed in Guatemala in the post-Arbenz years [1955–1961], it would take 148 years for all peasant families to receive some land—if there were no population growth in the meantime."

The Venezuelan program, which was much heralded in some quarters, showed similar results. In March 1963, *Time* magazine reported that 50,000 families received 3.5 million acres of land under the Betancourt program. However,

> in a report recently published jointly by the Venezuelan National Agrarian Institute, the Ministry of Agriculture, the Agrarian Bank and the National Planning Office, it appears that in the last twenty-five years, all put together, no more than 1.4 million acres have been distributed to 35,622 families. . . . On the other hand, it is true that 3.5 million acres were expropriated and paid for, often at exorbitant prices and in cash amounts in excess of the maximum prescribed by law.[14]

One characteristic of the Betancourt program of land reform and of land reforms in general promoted by the U.S. (e.g., abortively in South Vietnam) is that they are mainly *resettlement* programs. They do not involve the breakup of large estates, but the buying of virgin lands, their reclamation, and the transfer of peasant populations to these previously uninhabited areas. Aside from the callousness of transferring indigenous peasant populations from the soil to which they have been attached for centuries, such "reforms" have serious economic and political drawbacks. In particular, they do not break the political power of the oligarchs. Hence, the oligarchs are able to resist adequate land-taxation and land-utilization.

> For these reasons [writes Toynbee] a frontal attack on the *latifundia* would surely have to be made for the sake of economic efficiency and fiscal equity, even if all the landless agricultural workers and all the owners of economically non-viable *minifundia* could be provided for by the opening up of potentially rich virgin lands.[15]

Tax reform presents a similar story. To be sure, as of June 30, 1963, eleven Latin American countries had passed new tax laws to increase revenues. It would be somewhat utopian, however, to expect the same ruling groups that opposed land reform (even with compensation) to impose *significant* new taxes on themselves:

> [In Guatemala] the new income tax law stands in lieu of an old business profits tax that went as high as forty-four per cent. But where the old tax was simple and had relatively few loopholes, the new is riddled with holes. American experts and local lawyers agree unanimously that business has reaped a bonanza with this "tax reform" because it will be paying less this year than the years before under business-profits tax.[16]

Even where reforms were not as fraudulent as this, taxes could not be raised too high (the most radical reform, in Ecuador, called for a 15 percent tax on corporate profits) without conflicting with a major objective of the Alliance, namely "to stimulate private enterprise." For one of the chief lures for private foreign capital is the extremely low tax rate throughout the area.

If the Alliance failed to stimulate the enactment of significant reforms, it is not surprising that the minimal goals of economic growth were not approached either. Indeed, in the second year of the Alliance, Latin American growth taken as a whole actually declined to between 0.6 and 1 percent, which was less than the 1961 levels and not even half the modest Alliance goal of 2.5 percent. Moreover, eleven nations were in the grip of inflation after two years, private foreign investment had declined (despite "guarantees" to investors against revolution and expropriation),[17] and the foreign debt had attained "grave proportions" in some of the countries. Such was the picture drawn by the president of the Inter-American Development Bank.

A failure to reach any accord on stabilizing commodity prices of exports (more than 50 percent of which are sold to the U.S.) further exacerbated the situation. At the third annual meeting of the governors of the Inter-American Development Bank, Finance Minister Jorge Mejía Palacio of Colombia said his country had lost two to three times as much foreign income from falling coffee prices as it had received in Alliance for Progress credits. Until there is a long-term world coffee pact, Señor Mejía asserted, "the help that is given to us, however generous it may be, will not be blood to vitalize our economies, but simply tranquillizers to avoid total collapse." (*New York Times*, April 23, 1962.)

In his speech on the first anniversary of the Alliance, President Kennedy took note of the already present signals of distress and departed from his prepared text to say that those who were discouraged should remember the condition of Europe at the outset of the Marshall Plan. In November 1963, after the São Paulo conference to evaluate the first two years of the Alliance, he drew the same parallel. The comparison, however, cuts both ways.

At a symposium held in June 1962, Felipe Herrera, president of the Inter-American Development Bank (one of the key agencies of the Alliance), also referred to the reconstruction of war-torn Europe, but with the contrary intention of warning his listeners against making facile analogies. First, he noted that the Marshall Plan was aimed at the reconstruction of developed economies, whose productive capacity had been partially destroyed by war. Second, the Marshall Plan represented only a part of total U.S. aid to postwar Europe, some $10.3 billion of $24 billion given between 1945 and 1951.

"During a six-year period, therefore, the flow of U.S. public-resources to Europe averaged some $4 billion per year. In the case of the Alliance for Progress, the flow of U.S. public funds during the decade of the 1960's, is expected to total some $10 billion or an average of $1 billion each year." Furthermore, Herrera noted, "approximately 90 percent of the total funds invested in the Marshall Plan was in the form of outright grants, the 10 percent remaining consisting of loans." In the Alliance for Progress, only 30 percent of the funds invested were to be in the form of outright grants, while 70 percent were to consist of loans.[18]

A difference omitted by Herrera, but significant none the less, was the attitude of the aid recipients toward the success of the project. The feeling among members of Latin America's economic elite was summed up for a Congressional committee in May 1962 by a U.S. businessman:

> The absence of confidence by Latin America's business elite and ruling groups is vividly demonstrated by their own export of capital which, over the past decade, has been in excess of $10 billion. In passing, may I say that this $10 billion represents the amount of flight capital in numbered bank accounts in Switzerland alone. My New York banker friends tell me that the amount of flight capital on deposit in New York, or invested in American securities or bonds, is probably equal to another ten or twelve billion dollars.[19]

This absence of confidence by Latin America's business elite was in effect a confession of their inability to impose the reforms on themselves which were necessary to make the Alliance work. And indeed, as the U.S. trade-unionist Sidney Lens reported in November 1963, the dependence of the Alliance on such men was in large measure responsible for its failures:

> We have been pushing for a "revolution" from the "top-down" rather than from the "bottom-up." We have been asking the oligarchs to sign their own death-warrants by agreeing to land reform, tax reform, and other innovations that will depress their own status. They have replied to our proddings by ruse and fraud.

But this raises a critical question. Why, in fact, did the U.S. insist from the very beginning of the Alliance on "pushing for a revolution from the 'top-down'"? The orthodox answer (the Alliance is seeking to buy a revolution without having to pay the price of violence) could hardly stand in the face of such massive indifference to reform as was evidenced from the beginning by the Latin American oligarchies. For in Latin America the status quo itself is violence, the overall infant mortality rate being four times that of the U.S., the deaths due to curable diseases numbered in hundreds of thousands per year, and the deaths from hunger (not to mention premature old age or the executions carried out by political police in such Alliance countries as Nicaragua and Haiti) add equally shocking figures to the somber toll.

The reason for the United States' unwavering insistence on a "revolution" from the top-down, rather than waiting for, or encouraging, the already present tides of revolutionary populism[20] to sweep the oligarchs away, becomes evident when we view two little-noted aspects of the Alliance program, for these two aspects preclude by their very nature any radical land and tax reform or rapid economic growth. And because they preclude what have been proclaimed as the two key goals of the Alliance, they suggest that these may not in fact be the real, that is to say, the primary purposes, for which the program was constructed.

The first aspect of the Alliance program which demands our attention is a section of the U.S. Foreign Assistance Act which is designed to forestall any radical land or tax reform aimed at U.S. corporations abroad. Since U.S. corporations have large investments in every important area of Latin America, any such injunction is of fundamental significance. According to Section 620 (e) of the Foreign Assistance Act of 1962, the President is instructed to cut off all foreign aid to any country which either nationalizes or places excessive tax burdens upon corporations operating on its territory over 50 percent of whose stock is owned by Americans; the President may continue aid to such countries only if "equitable and speedy" compensation is given, or the rescinding of the taxes takes place within six months.

Under the terms of this Act the $3 million aid program to Ceylon was terminated in the spring of 1963, six months after that country had nationalized several oil companies owned by U.S. citizens. The Ceylon government had offered to pay compensation for the companies in bonds, but both the amount and form of the payment were termed unacceptable by the companies, and hence aid was ended.

The importance of the Act for the Alliance for Progress was made crystal clear even before the Ceylonese case, when the government of Honduras passed an agrarian reform law on September 30, 1962, that would have affected land owned by the United Fruit Company, which dominated the economy of the republic. The United Fruit Company was disturbed by the fact that payment would be in interest bonds and not cash. Of course, no underdeveloped country can possibly pay "promptly" or in cash; indeed, the whole aim of land reform within the context of a national development program is to earn the capital for which, in the present, there is such a crying need. Thus it is highly significant that when the Honduran question was raised in the Senate on October 2, the senators who spoke unanimously supported the viewpoint of the United Fruit Company; the liberal Senator Wayne Morse, chairman of the all-important subcommittee on Latin American Affairs, expressed their consensus when he said: "The Senator from Iowa [Hickenlooper] pointed out that it is contemplated that some script or bond or paper may be offered in payment for this property. Mr. President, there is only one compensation that means anything, and that is hard, cold American dollars."[21]

In view of the fact that it is an announced aim of the Alliance to revolutionize the continent, and to do this by promoting land reform, diversification of agriculture, and rural development through coopera-tives, it does not seem far-fetched to expect that the Alliance itself would make funds available to the government of Honduras in order to com-pensate the United Fruit Company. It is of further significance therefore, that Morse's remarks made painfully evident that such a conception of the Alliance would be unthinkable, even to liberal congressmen.

We must make clear to American investors that if there is a seizure of their property they will get fair compensation. If they do not get fair compensation, we do not propose to take American tax dollars and pour them into any country by way of foreign aid, so that they will in effect get a double take—the property of American investors and the taxpayer's money.

Far from retreating from this position, in the following year Congress added a new amendment making any country which terminated contracts with U.S. companies ineligible for foreign aid. The amendment was aimed at the nationalist governments of Peru and especially Argentina where oil concessions granted illegally by the Frondizi government in 1958 were canceled by the newly elected Illia government in 1963.[22]

If the Alliance had built into it resistance to land and tax reforms (not to mention national development of national resources, since a large proportion of Latin America's resources are exploited by foreign private firms), there was an equally forbidding structural block to economic growth. This block was the emphasis (shared by the U.S. and the banks of the Alliance) on monetary stability, meaning balanced budgets. But this kind of stabilization ruled out "the use of the tool of deficit financing for handling industrialization and agrarian reform." The result of such stabilization on economic growth was noted in a *New York Times* report (Int. Ed., March 25, 1963) on Colombia, which in the early days of the Alliance had been singled out as a prospective "showcase" country:

> [I]f the U.S. has shown strong interest in helping Colombia a main reason has been her relatively stable currency. Aid from abroad is deemed essential to the country's development.
>
> What is now being realized, however, is the difficulty and even the contradictions involved in an austerity policy in an underdeveloped country that is trying to grow.
>
> One diplomat observed recently that the U.S. and the International Bank for Reconstruction and Development had pressed the Government to balance its budget as a condition for helping it with development funds.
>
> But to cut spending by the one billion pesos of the annual government deficit would be to cut back the national product—because of the multiplying effect Government spending has—by ten to fifteen per cent.

(One irony of this is that in a country like Brazil, where inflation was really rampant—the cost of living rose 100 percent in 1963—not even the severest pressures of the Alliance banks could stem the tide. To be sure, aid was cut and resumed only in exchange for pledges that austerity would be imposed, but the Goulart government found it impossible to impose measures against either labor or capital, because of the balance of military and political forces within the country. Moreover, in the absence of the tax, land, and administrative reforms necessary to provide the government with revenues, the state resorted to printing money, thereby increasing the inflation.[23] Meanwhile, the Alliance sponsors found the prospect of Brazil's total collapse frightening enough to warrant a continuation of the resumed aid even in the absence of the necessary countervailing measures. In this way $700 million in foreign credits to Brazil—half Alliance monies—resulted in a dramatically lower growth rate—about 1 percent as compared with 6 percent—than in the years prior to the Alliance. As Brazil contains one-third of the population and more than half the land area of Latin America, what happens there, naturally, is of primary significance.)

This evident concern for preventing any inflationary pressures (even economically "healthy" ones) is motivated, of course, by a primary concern for creating the proper climate for foreign investment, as indeed the *Times* article indicated.

This preoccupation with the climate for foreign private capital even to the point where it conflicted with the claims of national integrity and economic growth can only be understood in the context of the Alliance's own priorities. It is here that we are finally able to understand the negative stance the U.S. has taken toward radical reforms and deficit-financed economic growth, as well as its insistence on making a "revolution" from the top down no matter now reactionary the top may show itself to be.

In an address before the fourth Annual Institute on Private Investments Abroad and Foreign Trade (May 31, 1962) the U.S. coordinator of the Alliance, Teodoro Moscoso, made clear the priorities of the program:

> I would say as emphatically as I can that private enterprise—local and foreign —must respond if the Alliance is to succeed . . . must respond by building the factories, the marketing and the service companies which are the manifestations of mature, developed economies. If the private sector fails, then our own public aid programs will have little effect. We may build some impressive monuments in the decade of Alliance development—dams and highways and schools, but unless the great impetus of the Alliance carries over into the private sector . . . unless the private and corporate savings of Latin America find their way into productive reinvestment rather than into Swiss banks and high living—then I fear that the great hopes born of the Charter of Punta del Este will be deeply disappointed.

In other words, the government-to-government aspect of the program, or public aid, is designed to build the infrastructure for a developed economy while the role of private capital is to develop it.

This is borne out by a breakdown of the aid given, for example, to Mexico in the first two years of the Alliance. Of $700 million committed, $345 million was in the form of stand-by credits to bolster the peso, which could be drawn upon only in a grave monetary crisis. Another $80 million in credit was specifically for U.S. exporters engaged in trade and $14 million went to private borrowers through the Export-Import Bank. Finally, $266 million was promised for development projects (health, housing, schools, water systems, roads, etc.).[24] It should be noted, perhaps, that of $1,500 million disbursed in the first two years of the Alliance, $600 million was in the form of loans from the Export-Import Bank, i.e., loans for the purpose of buying U.S. products, and $150 million was furnished in the form of surplus food, under the "Food for Peace" scheme, "a program which frequently operates on the basis of dumping, causing incalculable harm to local producers."[25]

In yet another speech, this time before the Detroit Economic Club on April 1, 1963, Mr. Moscoso reiterated the basic philosophy of the program from a slightly different point of view. Dealing with what he called the myth that "all that Latin America needs is a friendly climate for private enterprise . . . and the job that the Alliance for Progress is trying to do will be done," Moscoso said: "This view disregards the need for building roads, ports, power plants, and communications systems which must be built at least in great part with public funds and which in many areas are a prerequisite for the effective and profitable investment of private capital."

Latin America had, of course, a very bitter experience with regard to private capital and the dearth of an infrastructure, which Mr. Moscoso did not mention. To cite a typical example, in Guatemala in 1954, 90 percent of the electrification was in the capital city. Four-fifths of the electric power of the country was generated by a U.S.-owned electric company which refused to take the risks involved in bringing electricity to the rest of the country. In Brazil, the U.S.-owned telephone company was so inefficient that in 1962 there were 700,000 people on waiting lists for telephones.[26] When Governor Leonel Brizola of the state of Rio Grande do Sul expropriated a telephone company belonging to International Telephone & Telegraph, resolutions in the House and Senate were offered calling for a halt in aid. The issue was finally settled between the central Brazilian government and the U.S. when "adequate" compensation was agreed upon.

It should be clear from the foregoing that the Alliance for Progress was conceived with a double rather than a straightforward single commitment. Its double commitment was to develop Latin America *through* the influx of private capital and to utilize public funds only in areas which were not directly profitable or where the risks for private enterprise were too great. Moreover, where there was conflict between the means (private capital) and the ends (economic development) it was inevitable from the very structure of the program that the latter, that is, the "goal" itself, would be sacrificed. And indeed, at the São Paulo conference to review the first two years of the program, one Brazilian delegate noted the new U.S. legislation against nationalization of U.S. foreign-based oil companies and said, "It proves one fact, social reforms and private investments don't mix." In recognition of this fact, it was decided that Alliance loans would be channeled through one inter-American agency which would direct them toward strictly economic development projects; social reforms would not be a prerequisite. As one Brazilian commentator concluded, "The *Alianza* was born in Punta del Este and died in São Paulo."[27]

Here we have the answer to our questions. For it must now be clear that the Alliance for Progress was, in fact, formulated with the purpose of heading off the social revolution in Latin America. It was formulated, moreover, not with the intention of replacing the revolution, but of preserving the basic property structure (albeit with the minimal but necessary modifications needed to survive) and, in particular, the stake of U.S. private capital on the continent. This stake, as *New York Times* editor Herbert L. Matthews pointed out in 1959, is by no means small, nor limited to the well-being of individual firms:

> About one-quarter of all our exports go to Latin America and one-third of all our imports come from the area. U.S. private investments in Latin America now reach the amazing total of $9.5 billion. . . . At every point it has to be said "If we did not have Latin America on our side our situation would be desperate." To be denied the products and the markets of Latin America would reduce the U.S. to being a second-rate power.

To ignore these facts and instead to talk of a desire to buy a revolution in order to avoid paying the price of revolutionary violence is the sheerest hypocrisy when placed against the abortive U.S. attempt to launch a civil war in Cuba in April 1961. It is absurd, moreover, when set against the background of U.S. arms aid to Latin America which amounted to $700 million between 1945 and 1963. In 1955, the Colombia Liberal Party leader Eduardo Santos asked: "Against whom are we Latin Americans arming ourselves? . . . what we are doing is building up armies which weigh nothing in the international scale but which are juggernauts for the internal life of each country. Each country is being occupied by its own army." But this is just the point. The traditionally right-wing army is the guarantor of stability in Latin America in the eyes of the oligarchs and their U.S. partners. Only this desire for stability, for preservation of the *essential status quo*, can explain why the Kennedy Administration gave diplomatic recognition to all seven of the military coups against constitutional regimes which took place during its existence, or why Alliance funds were forthcoming to the military dictators in Paraguay, Nicaragua, and Haiti, to the military juntas in Argentina, Peru, Ecuador, El Salvador, and Guatemala, despite Kennedy's much-vaunted declaration that the Alliance was "an alliance of free governments" designed to work "to eliminate tyranny from a hemisphere in which it has no rightful place."

In sum, from the very beginning of the Alliance, its U.S. sponsors have faced a considerable and ever growing task in holding back the nationalism of Latin American bourgeoisies, while at the same time coaxing them to accept "safety-valve" reforms, in restraining the more reactionary of the powerful army leaders, while at the same time depending on them for "stability," and in maintaining this triple alliance against the revolutionary populism of the Latin American masses.

The primary policy of the U.S., not only in Latin America but in the underdeveloped world generally since World War II, has been "containment" in an anti-revolutionary sense. As Toynbee wrote in 1961, "America is today the leader of a world-wide anti-revolutionary movement in defence of vested interests." This is no less accurate a characterization of the post-1961 state of affairs. The primary goal of the Alliance, from the very first, was not progress, but preservation—or more accurately, and with emphasis on the tactical changes introduced by Kennedy—progress only insofar as it was necessary for preservation.

Notes

1. I.e., a growth rate of 5.3 percent, less 2.8 percent population growth.
2. Arnold J. Toynbee, *The Economy of the Western Hemisphere* (London: Oxford University Press, 1962), p. 34.

3. The Committee of Nine is composed of experts who establish norms for the Alliance's development programs and evaluate them.

4. Alonso Aguilar, "Latin America and the Alliance for Progress," Monthly Review pamphlet (New York: Monthly Review Press, 1963).

5. *Monthly Review*, March 1963.

6. *Foreign Capital in Latin America*, Report of the United Nations Department of Economics and Social Affairs (New York, 1955).

7. William A. Williams, *The United States, Cuba, and Castro* (New York and London: Monthly Review Press, 1962), p. 128.

8. Toynbee, *The Economy of the Western Hemisphere*, p. 33.

9. *Ibid.*, pp. 20–21.

10. *Ibid.*, pp. 32–33.

11. *Ibid*. Cf. Andre Gunder Frank, "The Varieties of Land Reform," *Monthly Review*, April 1963.

12. Toynbee, *The Economy of the Western Hemisphere*, p. 23.

13. *Ibid.*, p. 13.

14. Frank, "The Varieties of Land Reform."

15. Toynbee, *The Economy of the Western Hemisphere*, p. 34.

16. Sidney Lens, "Building on Quicksand," *The Commonweal*, November 1, 1963.

17. *New York Times*, Int. Ed., November 12, 1963.

18. William Manger, ed., *The Alliance for Progress: A Critical Appraisal* (Washington, D.C.: Public Affairs Press, 1963), pp. 45–47.

19. *Congressional Record*, 87th Congress, 2nd session, May 10 and 11, 1962; cited in *Monthly Review*, October 1962.

20. The Communist parties, it should be emphasized, are reform-minded, weak, and generally isolated from the mainstream in Latin America.

21. *Congressional Record*, 87th Congress, 2nd session, pp. 20457–20460; cited in N. Gordon Levin, Jr., "Our Men in Honduras," *Dissent*, Autumn 1963.

22. *New York Times*, Int. Ed., November 21, 1963.

23. *Ibid.*

24. *Hispanic-American Report*, April 1963. This is an excellent source of information on the current situation in Latin America, published in Stanford, California. The Alliance built 140,000 new homes in the first two years, but according to an OAS report (1953), 80 percent of the rural population of Latin America lived in housing that met none of the minimum hygiene requirements. (See Manger, *The Alliance for Progress*, p. 33.) The Housing deficit, in the words of the *New York Times* (August 18, 1963), is "unmeasurable" and "increases by an estimated million units annually, or twelve times faster than what the Alliance has been able to provide."

25. Aguilar, "Latin America and the Alliance for Progress."
26. *New York Times*, March 31, 1962.
27. *Newsweek*, November 25, 1963.

4

Hamza Alavi and Amir Khusro

Pakistan: The Burden of U.S. Aid

The role of foreign aid in economic development cannot be judged purely quantitatively. Given a model subsistence economy it may be argued that economic development is impossible without outside aid. But even here the inverse statement would not necessarily be true, viz., that foreign aid, regardless of its nature and manner of administration, would automatically generate a process of growth. In Pakistan, the economy is, of course, an agricultural one from which a substantial surplus is extracted. The economy supports a largely feudal society as well as the over-expanded armed forces, whose upkeep swallows up a large part of our resources. These are channels which drain off resources which could, if properly utilized, provide a domestic basis for capital accumulation. One must also consider the possibility that with a suitable reorganization of our agrarian society, incentives can be created for a considerable expansion of current output. Today sharecropping destroys those incentives because the cultivator is deprived of a large part of the increase in output resulting from any additional investments or extra effort. It would be too much of a digression to attempt to discuss these issues at all fully. But fundamentally the pace of economic development depends upon the kind of social reorganization we can bring about and not merely on the arithmetic measure of material resources that are currently made available. We must therefore take account of the influence of foreign aid on the pattern of our social development.

Nearly four-fifths of all foreign assistance received by Pakistan in the period from 1951 to 1960 came from the United States: America contributed $1,238.4 million out of a total of $1,590 million. Over 75 percent

---

This essay has been excerpted from an article which appeared in *New University Thought*, vol. 2, no. 4 (Autumn 1962).

of all the aid from the U.S., however, came in the form of surplus agricultural commodities.

Definitions can be quite arbitrary, but they should not be so completely misleading as they sometimes are in the jargon of foreign aid. The term which is grossly misleading in the literature on foreign aid is the word "grant." Ordinarily, "grant" is understood to mean a transfer which involves no quid pro quo. Not so for foreign aid, however; according to the UN, classification of aid "transfers described as loans for which no specific schedule of repayment has been arranged should be included as grants." But loans are loans, whether a specific schedule of repayment has been laid down or not. We find that foreign aid such as commodity assistance is classified as "loans," e.g., the "wheat loan," whereas these transactions actually amount to a purchase of the commodities for Pakistani rupees. Of course, the rupees remain in Pakistan, but the character of the transaction is determined by what can be done with them. Some of this money may indeed be disbursed as "grants," but much of it constitutes loans or other kinds of transactions. These are discussed more fully below. Here we wish only to caution our readers against taking literally the term "grants" when reading literature on foreign aid.

CLASSIFICATION OF FOREIGN AID

The amount of military assistance to Pakistan is not shown separately in official statistics although this figure is available for most countries which receive U.S. military aid. It is, however, possible to infer from the available statistics the approximate proportion constituted by military aid. Official statistics show the amount of military aid to all countries except Saudi Arabia and Pakistan. The figures for these two countries are included in the category of "regional" military aid. The total "regional" military aid for the Near East and South Asia from 1946 to 1960 was $574 million. This compares with military aid to Iran amounting to $457.5 million in the same period and $1,924 million to Turkey. But countries like Lebanon received much less—$8.7 million to Lebanon; $17.6 million to Jordan. It is safe to assume that the lion's share of "regional" aid went to Pakistan; Saudi Arabia's portion is likely to be commensurate with aid given to other Arab countries, although, as the custodian of Aramco Oil, it would be expected to receive a little more than the other Arab countries. Part of the total has probably gone for projects having a regional character so that each country participating in the regional "defense" establishment may be considered to have received a share. It is probably safe to conclude that the amount of military aid received by Pakistan during this period amounted to about a quarter of all aid received from the U.S.

Technical assistance : This covers both the services of foreign experts in Pakistan and the training of Pakistani nationals abroad. Technical assistance covers many fields, but as the Colombo Plan for 1960 states: "More than half of the U.S. Technical Cooperation Project funds were devoted to the improvement and expansion of local educational institutions, mainly through contracts with United States universities."

An extraordinary number of experts in a variety of fields has come to Pakistan in the last few years under foreign aid programs. We must differentiate between experts concerned with overall planning and policy-making, and those whose activities are at the operational level of designing and implementing particular projects. Problems arising out of planning and policy-making will be discussed separately later; here we deal only with some general issues.

The International Cooperation Administration (ICA) has a decisive say in the choice of experts, particularly in connection with projects in which there is some aid component. Many of these experts are on loan from U.S. commercial concerns with interests in the projects being undertaken in Pakistan. Most of these experts come on fairly short contracts generally not exceeding two years. It is easy to understand how they experience a conflict of loyalties. It is frequently complained that specifications laid down by such experts are so specific that only the parent firms can supply the material and equipment required. In many cases vital decisions rest with these experts. The government of Pakistan was apprehensive of this and issued a circular in 1958 in an effort to indicate clearly that these experts have an advisory capacity only, and need not perform an executive role. But a mere circular cannot alter such widespread practices, especially when the reports given by the U.S. experts so greatly influence the careers of their Pakistani colleagues. The result very often is that in the implementation of a project the interests of the experts' parent firms override the interests of Pakistan.

A fairly common difficulty is experienced with foreign experts who come to Pakistan on short contracts. Many of them have very little experience in local problems and special requirements. By the time that they have acquired enough experience to be of help to Pakistan it is time for them to return. In cases where these experts are employees of manufacturing concerns in the U.S., a great deal of benefit no doubt accrues to the parent firm. Because of the valuable local experience gained by their men they are placed in a better position for competing in the local market. Very often they are better off in this respect than even Pakistani concerns, which get less government cooperation. There is also another kind of difficulty, viz: that these inexperienced foreign experts are often placed as advisers to qualified Pakistanis who feel that their services are not always given the recognition that they deserve. Moreover, many of the foreign experts are given fabulous salaries by Pakistani standards. In 1958 it was estimated that a foreign expert cost us about Rs. 12,000 a month to keep. This is almost as much as Pakistanis with similar qualifications would expect to get in a year. Very often foreign experts are simply not required, but we are forced to have them. Dr. Sen, the economic and statistical adviser to the Indian Ministry of Food, said in 1952: "There have been cases where we had trained experts of our own and all the technical assistance that we needed was some equipment for them to work with. But we were told that we could set up the equipment only if we were prepared to take the experts with it." When these experts come they do not always keep to their job of giving advice. The Pakistan *Times* (August 25, 1958) reported that "the government's attention has been drawn to the fact that American technicians have often shown too much interest in internal administrative matters and neglected their own duties." The paper reported that Mr. Ataur Rahman, Chief Minister of East Pakistan, had deplored the increase in American interference in internal matters and that he had been able to observe this, during his tenure as chief minister, in relation to certain development projects.

Project assistance: This is aid allocated for particular development projects such as irrigation schemes, power stations, reconstruction of ports, etc. It is a special feature of U.S. project aid that, instead of the U.S. financing the whole of a few selected projects, the aid is distributed over a large number of projects which are being undertaken by the government of Pakistan. Thus, most of our projects come to have an "aid component" which under the terms of the aid agreements automatically brings them under the control of the U.S. Aid Mission. The proportion of the U.S. contribution to the cost of the projects is indicated by the fact that 18.6 percent of the total development expenditure was financed by aid funds, according to the latest annual report of the Colombo Plan. By providing less than a fifth of the expenditure the U.S. Aid Mission acquires control over Pakistan government funds being expended on the projects.

Aid is given for specific projects after they have been approved by the ICA mission at Karachi. The project aid may be grants or loans repayable in rupees. In the case of grants, the government of Pakistan must deposit in a special account an amount of rupees sufficient to cover the total rupee expenditure on the project, which, in any case, must be at least equal to the dollar aid provided for the project. Withdrawals from this account are made at each stage, as the project progresses, only with the approval of the director of the ICA mission in Karachi. The ICA thus secures not only the right of "supervision" over the projects, as provided in the agreements, but has complete control over the expenditure. In this way virtually the entire operation of the government of Pakistan in the field of development comes to be securely within the detailed control of the U.S. Aid Mission.

A large proportion of these funds is in fact recouped by the U.S. in the form of charges for "planning and survey," etc. A statement from a "special correspondent" in the government-controlled Pakistan *Times* (June 11, 1961), stated that by this means the U.S. "take[s] back 50 percent to 60 percent of the total allocation in the name of consultants' and contractors' fees." It is stated that "both in the Warsak and Karnaphuli the estimate of such charges has been as high as over 50 percent." Furthermore, U.S. control over the entire project insures that the Pakistan government is put into a helpless position vis-à-vis U.S. suppliers who quote exorbitant prices for the materials and "services" they provide. Much can be learned about such deals from the business community of Karachi; but in the nature of the case specific evidence can be made available only through a detailed departmental inquiry. There is only one case within our knowledge (and that is in India) where the magnitude of such extortion has been made public. This was in connection with the purchase of locomotives by India with U.S. aid. Although a Japanese quotation for a locomotive was $81,500 as against an American quotation of $178,000, the U.S. Foreign Operations Administration compelled the Indians to place half the contracts with the U.S. supplier. This increased the cost to the Indians by over $4.8 million. India received a loan of $20 million for this purpose, but in effect she received only $15.2 million. She must pay interest on, and ultimately repay the whole of, the $20 million. This manner of inflating the principal of a loan is not unknown in the feudal society of the Indian countryside where ignorant peasants are overcharged by greedy moneylenders. On an international scale this is "aid." (For reports of this transaction see the *New York Times* [September 4 and October 9, 1954].)

The way in which the government of Pakistan is forced into the hands of U.S. suppliers and U.S. contractors is reflected also in a recent report which appeared in the Pakistan *Times*. The report, obviously officially inspired when the government had been let down after promises of generous aid, says:

> It has become difficult for a public servant to convince Pakistani engineers, contractors, or firms of consultants that they were not being discriminated against and discouraged by such agencies [i.e., aid agencies] . . . Agencies like the World Bank are working contrary to this end [of utilizing available local talent and experience] . . . The conditions imposed for participation in the bidding [for tenders for construction projects] are such as would automatically eliminate Pakistani firms . . . It is pointed out that the Jinnah Barrage, Ghulam Mohammed Barrage, Taunsa Barrage, and the Gudu Barrage have all been designed, planned, and executed by Pakistani engineers and contractors. However . . . the World Bank seems to be taking no notice of these facts as neither is the designing likely to be assigned to any local firm of consultants nor is the execution likely to be entrusted to competent local contractors.

Commodity aid: As we have noted, the bulk of U.S. aid to Pakistan is in the form of surplus agricultural commodities. It is not only the principal form in which aid is provided, but it is also a form of aid which gives rise to a set of financial relationships with an influence far beyond what is suggested by the phrase "commodity aid." This aid is provided under two separate legislations, the Mutual Security Act and the Agricultural Trade Development and Assistance Act (P.L. 480).

Under this form of aid, various surplus commodities are shipped to Pakistan *against which payment is made in rupees by the government of Pakistan.* Indeed, the first stage of the transaction can be regarded as nothing more than a purchase of the commodities by Pakistan. The character of the "aid" and its economic significance is then determined by the status of the rupee funds that arise from the transaction, the control of these funds, and the use to which the funds are put. These funds are designated "counterpart funds," for they represent the counterpart of the "community aid" which has been supplied.

The funds arising from the transactions in commodities fall into two categories according to the terms of the legislation under which the commodities are provided:

(1) *Government of Pakistan funds.* Rupee funds so described arise out of commodity aid supplied under the Mutual Security Act. These amounts represent the value of the commodities supplied plus the customs duty, and are intended to finance development projects. But they cannot be spent by the government of Pakistan except with the prior approval of the U.S. Aid Mission. Similarly, funds arising out of commodities supplied under P.L. 480, Title II, for relief purposes, also fall into this category.

(2) *Government of the U.S. funds.* The rupee equivalent of the commodities supplied under P.L. 480, Title I, is credited to a special account which is classified under this category. As for the use of these funds, we give below the "planned uses of rupee funds under Title I, P.L. 480, cumulative total up to the end of 1958" (in millions of U.S. dollars).

Development "grants"	Loans to Pak. govt.	Payment of U.S. obliga- tions	Military procurement	Loans to business	Other uses	Total
12.3	89.1	50.0	79.4	28.7	8.8	268.5

The amount budgeted as "grants" appeared only in the half-year June–December 1958, i.e., after the military regime in Pakistan had taken over. The amounts classified as "payment of U.S. obligations" represent funds disbursed to meet American obligations for which it would otherwise have had to remit dollars to Pakistan. The U.S. is clearly at a great advantage in being able to discharge these obligations by paying in surplus commodities sold to Pakistan at an above-world-average price (see below), instead of paying in dollars which Pakistan may have made better use of. Loans to business firms are restricted under the U.S. legislation either to American concerns or concerns engaged in the marketing of American goods. The figure of $8.8 million shown under "other uses" represents the cost of various "cultural" activities which the U.S. pursues so assiduously in Pakistan. These amounts are classified under: "Information and Education" (by the USIS), "Translation and Publication," and "International Education Exchange." The amount of $89.1 million budgeted as loans to the government of Pakistan represents a financial transaction rather than aid as such. A high rate of interest is paid on these loans about which Pakistan has protested to the U.S. often but without success. And, ultimately, we must repay.

Up to December 1958, Pakistan was given $263.3 million worth of commodities under P.L. 480, Title I (as shown in the statement above), which were paid for in rupees. However, this figure gives an exaggerated picture of the aid provided. This is so because the amount is calculated on the prices charged by the Commodity Credit Corporation of America, *which charges higher prices than those prevailing on the world market*, and because these commodities must be shipped in American bottoms. The *New York Times* reported on June 13, 1953, that shipping wheat aid to Pakistan in American ships would cost $26 per ton as against $12 to $14 per ton in a foreign ship.

P.L. 480 was designed to reduce the accumulation of surplus commodities in the U.S. which the U.S. government has to buy under price-support legislation, and which costs more than a billion dollars a year for storage alone. The pressure to get rid of these commodities has led the Americans to keep countries dependent upon its aid as outlets for these surpluses. There are many instances in which the dependent countries have actually been prevented from undertaking development programs which might interfere with the disposal of these surpluses, regardless of the importance of these programs to the countries concerned. In Formosa, Senator Green tells us, "the point has already been reached where the U.S. Mission has *de-emphasized* rice production despite the fact that an increase in rice export is one of the ways in which Formosa can become self-supporting . . . Our policy in this regard is vitiated by efforts to dispose of our rice surpluses." This has also resulted in a distortion of the agricultural development pattern. C. A. Munkman, an ex-UNRRA official who was attached to the American Aid Mission in Greece, tells of plans for sugar beet production which were put forth several times, but which "have, however, been checked by the American Mission. This has been a major irritant to the Greeks who rightly consider the introduction of sugar beet imperative to their agricultural pattern. The Mission policy is considered to be dominated by the desire to maintain the Greek sugar market for U.S. surpluses."

Pakistan has been made to take commodities under this program which we ourselves have surpluses to dispose of! This is best illustrated by the case of cotton. Pakistan itself is a surplus producer of the long-staple "American-type" cotton, some of which it must export. Yet Pakistan received 174,400 bales of American cotton, most of it (126,000 bales) *during July 1954 and December 1955, when there was already too much cotton on the market.* The effect of this dumping was only to lower further the price of domestic cotton, much to the delight of the local cotton mill owners. This caused distress to cotton growers and also reduced Pakistan's foreign exchange earnings by forcing down the price of cotton. D. C. Swerling pointed out, in his article in the *American Economic Review* for May 1959, that Pakistan, "welcoming P.L. 480 wheat, suffering from our cotton policy," shared the position of many countries. Similar results have been brought about by P.L. 480 aid of tobacco and dairy products. Tobacco imports have served only to force down prices of domestic tobacco and have greatly profited the manufacturers—one foreign manufacturer has a virtual monopoly in this field.

Payment of prices for wheat higher than the prevailing world prices was admitted by Mr. Amjad Ali, the Finance Minister, in September 1958 in the last session of the Pakistan parliament. He justified paying higher prices on the grounds that after all it was all out of aid. But a glance at the uses of the rupee funds generated by P.L. 480 will show that of the equivalent of $268.3 million, no more than $12.3 million was a grant. The rest was U.S. government funds and was disbursed in lieu of dollar remittances. Thus by paying higher prices the government of Pakistan has subsidized the funds of the U.S. government rather than the other way around. Moreover, if we also consider that these rupee funds are made available to the U.S. in return for commodities which we not only do not want but which in some cases actually do us economic harm, we can see for whose benefit this part of the "foreign aid" program is operated.

We can thus see that except perhaps for food grains received during a period of food shortage, commodity aid does not provide us with the kind of resources which might assist us in economic development. It must be remembered that these loans and grants from the U.S.-controlled "counterpart funds," which are held in Pakistan rupees, do not give us control over any resources other than the commodities received. Their only use lies in providing one possible alternative to cover the deficit in government expenditure which arises in the absence of a wide enough tax base. The other alternative would be to resort to domestic borrowing and/or "deficit financing," both of which measures were advocated by the panel of economists set up by the government of Pakistan to study the draft of the Second Five-Year Plan. The present regime has, however, turned away from the use of domestic financial resources and has come to depend more and more on the "counterpart funds," on the plea that the use of domestic resources necessitates deficit financing which is inflationary. But only a small part of domestic financing need involve borrowing from the State Bank. Moreover, withdrawals from accumulated "counterpart funds" are no less inflationary than borrowing from the State Bank. For military expenditure particularly, the government has relied upon withdrawals from the counterpart funds. In 1957-1958, rupees equivalent to $74.3 million were spent from this source for military purposes. Since this expenditure does not appear in the budget, defense expenditure is made to appear less than it really is.

An excessive reliance on the counterpart funds as a source of government spending can be dangerous. The Greek example is instructive. "The U.S. Mission," Munkman says,

> through the counterpart account was by far the largest depositor with the Bank of Greece and consequently was able to influence the credit situation by manipulating this account . . . In late 1951 the Mission imposed a cutback on all major investment projects in progress by imposing a restriction on the release of counterpart funds . . . In 1952 the U.S. withdrew from supporting the budget and investment program and pressed on the Greek government a policy of budgetary stability, cutback in development plans and progressive withdrawal of aid . . . The net result (in the next fiscal year) was a wholesale cancellation of programs or at best a slowing down. Greece was literally spattered with works at all stages of completion liberally plastered with such signs as "Marshall Aid," "Gift of the American People," etc., until the Mission decided that diplomacy required that they should be removed.

In Pakistan, the governments before the military regime were chary of budget support from the counterpart funds. In 1956-1957, during Suharawardy's premiership, Pakistan *paid back* Rs. 7.2 million. The Noon government which followed drew Rs. 177.2 million from this source to finance part of its deficit of Rs. 1,281 million in 1957-1958—the rest being covered by internal borrowing. The present regime has exactly reversed this by depending on foreign support of Rs. 1,010.9 million to finance its budget deficit of Rs. 1,202.1 million for the year 1959-1960.

This adds an important element to U.S. influence over Pakistan's development.

A sufficiently large deposit account in a country allows the U.S. to influence more than the credit situation and the amount of money that is to be spent on various government projects. Any large dependence upon this source of finance by the government enables the U.S. also to have a great deal of say in the overall pattern of development policy. In Pakistan the U.S. government is already able to influence the course of both economic and political development.

In the economic sphere the U.S. government has the right to receive information about all projects on which even a small proportion of aid money is being spent. The agreement providing for commodity assistance grants that the American government has an interest in the monetary stability of Pakistan, thus enabling it formally to have its say in our financial policy. This control is possible through a series of measures— formal and informal—which have developed since the beginning of the aid programs. The aid agreements between the United States and Pakistan enjoin the Pakistan government to foster and maintain the stability of its currency and to promote development on a "sound basis." To insure that these conditions of aid are complied with, the United States has the right to send observers, as described above. Thus U.S. experts are associated at all levels of policy-making. This means in effect that the U.S. interpretation of what is "sound policy" prevails.

Economic aid, though it is all channeled through the ICA, comes under numerous agreements and is given on a yearly basis. This arrangement has long been criticized for leading to waste and delays since no long-term planning, so essential for any large projects, can be done. But it has the advantage of preventing the U.S. from being forced into a position where it has either to withhold aid completely or to tolerate the receiving country's taking a course contrary to American wishes. By the threat of cutting down future aid for particular projects, the ICA can force the receiving country to submit to its plans. Two cases are given here as examples of this mode of pressure. In 1959, the U.S. withdrew an offer of aid for the construction of power lines from Multan to Lyallpur. The project was to have cost $3.5 million and was agreed on between the ICA and the Pakistan Industrial Development Corporation. The first installment was to have arrived in February of that year. Washington vetoed the plan, it is believed, as a reprisal for the agreement with

Czechoslovakia for the extension of the Maple Leaf Cement Factory. In this case PIDC was able to complete the project on its own, but in view of the expense involved in larger projects at different stages of completion, one can imagine the desire to avoid a cut in aid when so much has already been committed to a project. When such a cut can affect a very large number of projects, the cut itself need not actually be used—the mere threat of such a step would make any government so dependent upon this one source of finance see the light. Large enough cuts in project assistance, together with a manipulation of the counterpart funds, could easily bring the whole development program to a halt, with far-reaching economic and political consequences.

THE INVISIBLE HAND IN ECONOMIC POLICY

The experts attached to the Pakistan Planning Commission are in a particularly strong position to influence our economic policy. It appears that they have played a determining role for some time. Professor Bell was for some time on the staff of the Pakistan Planning Board. His testimony before the Senate Foreign Relations Committee provides an interesting comment on the kind of relationship that exists between important organs of the Pakistan government and the U.S. Mission. He was asked: "How closely did your organization [i.e., the Pakistan Planning Board] work with the FAO, FAS, and the ICA ?" i.e., the U.S. Mission. Professor Bell replied:

> The ICA Mission members we knew very well personally, of course. Officially they consulted the Planning Board of the Pakistan government regularly in two main kinds of things: first of all we were an excellent source of information for them on economic conditions in general in Pakistan, and on specific problems they might be encountering.
>
> Secondly, after a while—although not in the beginning, but after a while, when the Planning Board began to have reasonable views as to what sort of things made sense to be done in Pakistan and what sort of things did not make sense—the ICA Mission began to use this information to guide them in making their own decisions as to what they wanted to put their money into and what they did not. I do not mean to imply that they followed without review the opinions of the Planning Board; but they gave them heavy weight.

This testimony is revealing in many ways. First of all, it shows the extent to which the U.S. has special access to most vital information and matters before important government departments such as the Planning

Board. But what is even more revealing is the casual way in which the statement reveals the fact that the key decisions are taken not by the Planning Board on the advice of the Aid Mission but rather the other way around.

The quotation also reflects how, after the firm hand of Zahid Hussain was removed from the Planning Board, it abandoned the independent national approach to planning, which obviously did not "make sense" to the Aid Mission. It is no longer Pakistanis who determine the pattern of development projects and then seek ICA or other aid to finance them. It is the ICA which lays down the priorities in the plan, and the Planning Board is reduced to little more than an adjunct of the ICA Mission.

In addition to all this, vast amounts are spent upon propaganda. A huge organization for this purpose is kept in Pakistan; there has been a flood of cheap literature; an extensive program of translation into the local languages has been undertaken, and subsidized books and pamphlets are made available at a very low cost. An example is Rostow's *The Prospects for Communist China*, which was sold for 10 cents. Much of the money spent upon propaganda is supplied from the counterpart funds established by the sale of commodities provided under the Mutual Security Act and P.L. 480. The equivalent of $8.8 million was provided from the sale of commodities under P.L. 480 alone for this purpose. The aid agreements also bind the Pakistan government to inform the people of the aid given by the U.S. and the purpose of such aid. Naturally it is to be expected that this does not mean giving all the facts about its operation, as that would hardly bring much credit to either government. So the result can only be that the Pakistani money is spent on extolling the aid and the donor.

Education Exchange and allied programs of providing training in America also help in this. The rationale for these programs is summed up very well in a study prepared by Brigadier General Shingler and the staff of the President's Committee to Study Military Aid: "Hardware wears out or becomes obsolete," the study says. "Man, and the impact of training on his capability and the way he thinks, does not." Great emphasis is therefore put on giving scholarships and facilitating the exchange of teachers. Between 1950 and 1959, more than 100,000 foreigners received training in the U.S. under the Military Aid Program, 46,000 under the ICA and its predecessors, and another 42,000 under the International Educational Exchange. For the military and civilian trainees these programs have provided more than just skills of military and civilian value. A majority of them has acquired, the report says, "an orientation in consonance with the objectives of the U.S. national policy." The impact of these activities in influencing opinion in the receiving countries can be imagined, especially in countries like Pakistan where a responsible and free press is not allowed to exist.

All of this together forms a fairly tight network of controls and pressures by which Pakistan is made to follow policies along lines favored by the State Department. He who pays the piper calls the tune.

AID AND DEVELOPMENT POLICY

There is a fundamental difference between the approach to economic development adopted, for instance, in India's Second Five-Year Plan, which laid down a basis for effective industrial development, and the policy favored by the typical U.S. expert in Pakistan, which discourages industrialization and exerts pressure for a plan which would develop our economy along lines complementary to and subordinate to the economy of the United States.

The U.S. has about 10 percent of the world's population. It uses up about 50 percent of the world's raw material output. This is a conclusion reached by the Paley Commission on Resources for Freedom appointed by President Truman in 1951. The Paley Report provides the basis on which U.S. foreign economic policy is based. The Paley Commission estimated that by 1975 the U.S. will have to depend upon imports for 35 percent of its requirements in iron ore, and 25 to 40 percent of its requirements in copper. The U.S. import requirements for most commodities will go up. Therefore, the Commission recommended that the U.S. should take steps to insure an increase in raw material production to meet U.S. demands. This remains a major objective of the foreign aid program. In the case of U.S. private investments abroad, it was found in a Report of the Committee for Economic Development entitled "Economic Development Abroad and the Role of American Foreign Investment" that the U.S. corporation which had invested abroad in underdeveloped countries had pursued two specific objectives: to open up new sources of raw materials (e.g., petroleum, copper, iron ore, etc.) mainly for export and, secondly, to establish assembly and packaging factories abroad in order to gain an advantage in foreign markets. Neither of these assists very greatly the process of industrialization.

In Pakistan there has been a steady move away from a policy of industrialization. The First Five-Year Plan stepped down industrial investment under the excuse of "consolidating" the development which had already taken place. The Second Five-Year Plan has carried the anti-industrialization policy still further. The proportion of resources devoted to industry has been reduced even further. In this change of policy, local feudal interests as well as the monopoly interests of a few big businessmen are involved. But the most important influence in this direction has been the "advice" of the "experts" and the directions that the ICA Mission has been able to give the Planning Board. Mr. G. Faruque, who was the head of the Pakistan Industrial Development Corporation until he was removed by the present regime, once said that at one time our foreign experts were trying to advise us against developing the jute industry. But this was when American aid had not provided Americans with a hold on the country; the industry was developed, and has done well.

It is not difficult to see that the central point—the development of a balanced economy—becomes distorted by the pressures which are brought to bear upon the planners. The allocation of resources to agriculture and industry is no longer decided freely by the Pakistanis but according to the wishes of the aid donors.

Besides these objectives there is the important one of insuring the privileges of American capital in the aid-receiving countries. This must be of considerable interest to the U.S. government in view of the increasing need of American corporations to set up plants and facilities in the countries where their manufactures are sold and the relative decline in direct exports from the U.S. Much of such investment is in assembly or packaging plants which seek to evade restrictions on imports and establish outlets for U.S. manufactures imported as "raw materials." Very often investments by giant foreign corporations are in the most profitable fields from which Pakistani enterprise is driven away, thus inhibiting our own development. But if their greater competitive power does not suffice, they are able to bring much pressure, through their aid-giving government, to obtain preferential treatment in Pakistan vis-à-vis Pakistani concerns. Contradicting textbook theories, foreign investment, instead of producing a catalysis of Pakistani development, brings about instead a paralysis of our business enterprise in the most profitable areas of investment.

But foreign investment can be justified only if it stimulates and supports our own development. As applied it serves only to drain our potential for growth, in the form of its current profits, which are remitted abroad. In the course of economic development profits are the source of capital accumulation. If all investment in our country was undertaken by foreign enterprises and all profits remitted out, our growth potential would be reduced to nil. And, in fact, very little of these profits *is* left behind. Moreover, in most cases the bulk of the working capital of foreign concerns is raised from local borrowing. Thus it is profits earned by utilizing Pakistani resources which are remitted out and which constitute a drain on our foreign exchange resources. In addition to this, a substantial part of the "foreign aid" is earmarked for providing loans to American concerns operating in Pakistan and to Pakistani firms engaged in marketing American goods. From one source alone, P.L. 480 counterpart funds, the U.S. gave (up to June 1959) rupees equivalent to $28.7 million for this purpose.

Our analysis of U.S. aid to Pakistan is not intended to be an argument against foreign aid as such. Countries like Pakistan, which suffer from the consequences of two centuries of stagnation and economic disintegration and which face a terrible battle against the most abject poverty, will certainly welcome and be most grateful for such assistance as they can get. But this is precisely the kind of aid which we are not getting from the U.S. at the present time. We hope that by exposing the hypocrisy and cynicism with which the aid is administered we shall have helped Pakistanis and our friends in the U.S. to strive for a more just and more enduring relationship. Our first step in that direction must be an end to the ties which bind and the restoration of our national independence. Only through a free and democratic government in Pakistan can the egalitarian ideals of foreign aid and our objective of national development be realized.

A Brief Bibliography

Lieuwen, Edwin. *Arms and Politics in Latin America*. Rev. ed. New York: Praeger, 1961. (A pioneering study of the social and political role of the armed forces.)

Munkman, C. A. *American Aid to Greece*. London, 1958. (A first-rate, first-hand account by a member of the U.S. Mission staff.)

President's Materials Policy (Paley) Commission. *Resources for Freedom*. Washington, D.C., 1952. (The original basis of U.S. foreign aid policy. See especially Volume 1, Chapter 11.)

U.S. Senate, Special Committee to Study the Foreign Aid Program, 1956–1957. *Report and Hearings of the Special Committee*. Washington, D.C., 1957. (See also the large number of studies commissioned by the special committee.)

Wolf, C. *Foreign Aid: Theory and Practice in South Asia*. Princeton, N.J.: Princeton University Press, 1960. (A very useful survey overlaid with bad theory.)

5

Philip Reno

Aluminum Profits and
Caribbean People

When Arthur Vining Davis, long-time head of the Aluminum Company of America (Alcoa), died last year, he left behind $400 million. Of this, $1 million went to his secretary, about $100 million to the United States in taxes, and $300 million to two Arthur Vining Davis foundations. Income of the foundations—more than $13 million a year if the principal were simply banked—is to be used "for such charitable, scientific, literary, and educational purposes within the United States and its possessions as the trustees shall see fit." A princely legacy, bequeathed to uses of broadest latitude.

The bequest does, however, stipulate one restraint of substance: its use is limited to the United States and its possessions. Lands from which much of this fortune was derived, lands in urgent need of help, were not remembered in the will. Nor could these lands recover through inheritance taxes (as the United States could and did) any part of the huge block of wealth that their people and their resources had helped provide. This limitation on spending the foundations' income might be hopelessly shrugged off—"To him who hath, etc."—if it were not related to the struggle by the countries that produce aluminum ore for a share in the wealth extracted from their lands.

Bauxite, the ore from which aluminum is refined, is found in high grade and in quantity in a dozen emerging and half a dozen industrialized countries. Major among these primary producers are various Caribbean islands and lands bordering them to the south. The North American aluminum industry obtains over 90 percent of its ore from this area, and out of this ore produces half the capitalist world's aluminum. Jamaica, Surinam, and British Guiana are the major bauxite sources, Jamaica alone

---

This essay originally appeared in the October 1963 issue of *Monthly Review*. Copyright © 1963 by Monthly Review, Inc.

supplying one-fifth of the bauxite of the world. The Dominican Republic and Haiti mine fair quantities, and extensive exploration is going on in Costa Rica, Panama, Puerto Rico, and French Guiana.

Historically, one crop—sugar—dominated the Caribbean economy, raised on great estates first by slaves, then by indentured labor, and now by "free labor"—free in the classic, Marxist sense. Sugar, British-owned, is still the Caribbean king, but American-owned aluminum has moved quietly in beside the throne. And around the rich sugar and aluminum holdings, the slogan of the slaves of the 1830's— "Massa day done"—again agitates the Caribbean air. This time the people, more sophisticated, are adding a question, or implied purpose, about the new day that will replace the old, "Massa's," day. "Massa day done," they say, "but it for who?" Foreign exploitation of mineral resources is an important aspect of this ultimate question.

ALUMINUM'S BIG FOUR

Aluminum operations in the Caribbean area have grown steadily since 1922, when Alcoa began to ship bauxite from Surinam and British Guiana. Alcoa, then worth under a hundred million dollars, grew to a capitalization of one and a quarter billion by 1961, and in the meantime had set up a Canadian subsidiary, Aluminium, Ltd. (Altd), to take over most of Alcoa's foreign operations. Altd was itself capitalized in 1961 at over a billion dollars. As the most accessible Arkansas bauxite was depleted, the bauxite of Surinam and British Guiana, high grade and moderately low cost, became basic to the industry's prodigious growth.

By the mid-1920's, the aluminum industry had taken on monopoly form—probably the most perfect monopoly in America. By the end of that decade, Alcoa and Altd had organized an international aluminum cartel—a prototype of international cartels. In accord with monopoly economics, prices were maintained by restricting output.

The Second World War at last set off a vast expansion of aluminum production—in France, Germany, and most of all, in North America. In 1939, Alcoa and Altd were the only American producers of aluminum ingot. Reynolds took advantage of war demands to force its way into the production field, and after the war Kaiser also entered. Within ten years, Reynolds and Kaiser had grown to giant size, in large part through opening rich Jamaican mines.

In spite of the newcomers' successes, Alcoa and Altd still dominate world aluminum. Their combined capacity includes 54 percent of North American capacity, and they also have refineries in Brazil, Italy, United Kingdom, Norway, Sweden, Japan, and India, as well as fabricating plants in other countries. Their 1961 production totaled over 40 percent of capitalist world output, and exceeded that of the socialist world. A 1951 court decree divorcing the stock ownership of Alcoa from that of Altd did not disturb their working relationship.

The following few statistics may help assay the resources of the four great aluminum companies (the figures are from 1961 company reports, and are in millions of U.S. dollars):

	Alcoa	*Altd*	*Reynolds*	*Kaiser*
Total invested capital	1,160	1,088	814	654
Sales and operating revenue	853	521	478	424
Return on capital (profits after taxes plus interest paid)	135	109	80	86

Other North American producers in 1961 were Ormet Corporation, Harvey Aluminum, and Anaconda Aluminum. The total capacity of these three companies was 325,000 tons, compared to 446,000 for Reynolds, lowest-tonnage producer of the big four in 1961.

THE CARIBBEAN PRIMARY PRODUCING COUNTRIES

What of the Caribbean countries that produce the ore for half the capitalist world's aluminum? Not one has a Gross National Product of all goods and services as large as Alcoa's sales and operating revenues. The total expenditure of all combined for health, education, and welfare is far less than the big four's net profits. Their per capita income is barely one-tenth that of the United States.

Out of every four of their urban workers, at least one is unemployed. In their countrysides, underemployment is universal and chronic. On the islands, refugees from eroded highlands have flooded the already overcrowded cities. General population growth will double their working force in fewer than forty years, so that a large part of any increase in their national incomes must go just to hold their own.

The most cursory review brings out that the countries are in fact not holding their own, at least in terms of the living standards of their people. In Haiti, a corrupt government has let the economy degenerate into chaos. In British Guiana, an honest and enlightened government is beleaguered by American and British imperialisms, and its valiant efforts cannot stretch meager resources enough to cover broad social needs. In Jamaica, Surinam, and the Dominican Republic, national income has been expanding significantly, but the increase seems to go simply to growing numbers and rising living standards of the middle and upper classes. These countries' many poor are actually, as well as relatively, growing poorer, while the few rich grow richer.

The essential thing, as in all developing countries, is capital investment and social planning. Government resources for investment are limited, although an adequate tax structure could raise them substantially. The upper class is not inclined to invest its money locally, but sends it to the United States or England or Canada, and joins it in flight as soon as possible. Sugar and aluminum have invested very little in relation either to what they could invest or to what is needed. American aid has bypassed the European colonies; while England, with four hundred years of plunder and profit safely stowed away, pleads poverty itself and offers little development capital.

Within the Caribbean countries, the people who mine and process bauxite are relatively well off. The aluminum companies pay wages which are about twice the going Caribbean rates (that is, they pay about one-third of North American rates) and provide hospitals, trade schools, and housing. There are also other islands of well-being rising from the general sea of poverty and discontent—the islands of middle-class life.

An important section of the Caribbean middle class, the decisive section in certain countries, is made up of government employees. In Jamaica and British Guiana this section was recruited and trained by the British, and in Surinam by the Dutch. Advancement and other advantages went to individuals whose attitudes and loyalties promised the defense of colonial economic empires after the political empires were dissolved. The middle-class political organizations, as well as the individuals who made up the middle class, responded predictably. And increasingly, the income of the government employee section of the middle class depends on government revenues that the aluminum companies supply.

Government revenues have more than doubled over the past ten years.

Taxes on bauxite have made an increase of this magnitude possible. Nevertheless, what the aluminum companies can and should pay in taxes beyond what they now pay is the first issue the countries face in dealing with the companies. How the additional revenue may be used for the countries' welfare is a correlative issue.

ALUMINUM PROFITS AND HOW THEY ARE TAXED

Taxes on bauxite have been set in bargaining between each country and the aluminum companies. In the course of this bargaining, the countries have established tonnage export duties and royalties on bauxite. These yield a regular, if minor, contribution to government revenue. Each Caribbean country also has an income tax, and each began by trying to fit the aluminum companies into the general income-tax structure. This proved all but impossible.

That the aluminum companies do make high profits from their Caribbean operations cannot be doubted. Total return on capital for the big four was over $400 million in 1961, and to this affluence the Caribbean countries must have contributed substantially. There are, however, but few reports to indicate just how large this Caribbean contribution may have been.

The U.S. Commerce Department's *Survey of Current Business* does report 1961 profits amounting to $64 million for U.S. mining companies' operations in Western Hemisphere dependencies of European countries. Over 90 percent of these profits would certainly have come from aluminum operations in Jamaica (independent by 1962), Surinam, and British Guiana. If Altd earnings are added, total aluminum company profits would have been $70 to $75 million on an investment of between $220 and $270 million (the companies can write off investment rapidly through heavy depreciation allowances). Profits as a percent of investment would thus amount to somewhere between 26 and 34 percent, and as a percent of value of product (about $200 million), to at least 35 percent. These figures suggest that this could well be among the most profitable U.S. investment structures in the world.

It should be possible to check these profit figures by estimating individual company earnings in the various producing countries. Such estimates, however, run into difficulties, study of which brings out that actual profits are even higher than any reported figures. The less significant of these difficulties concerns company bookkeeping.

Commerce Department reports, for example, give certain breakdowns of U.S. company operations in Jamaica, Surinam, and British Guiana. These show current costs of aluminum company operations in 1957 as amounting to $81 million, divided as follows: materials and services—$31 million; wages and salaries—$19 million; depreciation and depletion—$13 million; taxes—$14 million; other—$4 million. How materials and services could account for almost 40 percent of the costs, and so much more than wages and salaries, is hard to see in this kind of operation. The suspicion of padding naturally arises, and of payments to U.S. shipping, insurance, and other interests that permit a transfer of payments to hide profits.

A more serious difficulty arises from the fact that these great aluminum operations extend vertically from mining in various countries, through intermediate processing and transshipping in other countries, to smelting in the mother country, and on to fabrication often in yet other countries. The companies operate in the primary producing countries either directly or through wholly owned subsidiaries. Practically all metal grade bauxite produced by a subsidiary is taken by the parent company, and at a price set by the parent.

The price thus set on bauxite need not permit a profit by the subsidiary since the only matter of consequence to the industry owners is that the overall operation make money. The lower the bauxite price, the less the taxes paid to the primary producing country, and the more the profit after taxes left over for the companies. As a result, bauxite prices have been kept down with a rigidity singular even within the controlled price mechanisms of American monopoly.

From 1938 to 1959, the general U.S. price level rose by 138 percent. During these years, the price of the bauxite produced in the United States doubled. Yet the price of bauxite imported from Surinam and British Guiana was almost the same in 1959 as it had been in 1938. That the companies were holding the price of imported bauxite at a dead level did not prevent them from raising the price of aluminum, which went up by 78 percent between 1948 and 1959.

The prices set on bauxite from all the Caribbean countries except British Guiana did finally begin to rise a few years ago. The explanation lies with the law granting tax concessions to U.S. companies operating in other countries of this hemisphere through what are called Western Hemisphere Trade Corporations. Instead of a 52 percent corporate income tax, Western Hemisphere Trade Corporations pay the U.S. only 25 percent. By raising the price of bauxite, U.S. companies could now reduce their total income taxes. The price of bauxite began to rise for the first time in twenty years, except for British Guiana bauxite mined by Altd, Canada based and unaffected by Western Hemisphere Trade Corporation maneuvers.

Prices of bauxite imported into the United States in 1960, as reported by the Bureau of Mines, varied from $6.85 for British Guiana bauxite to $12.50 for Dominican Republic bauxite. Yet British Guiana bauxite is higher grade, and hence worth more, than Dominican Republic bauxite. If the value of British Guiana bauxite in 1961 had been equal to that of Surinam bauxite (of approximately the same high grade), British Guiana would have gained more than $1.5 million in income taxes from Altd's British Guiana subsidiary.

Because of the difficulty of determining profits, the aluminum-producing countries, with the exception of British Guiana, have turned increasingly toward a fixed tax per ton of bauxite produced. The trouble with this method is that the countries do not benefit from the companies' high-profit years. Reynolds, for example, reported U.S. taxes (the sum of current and deferred taxes for purposes of this comparison) of just under $5 million in 1961, and state and foreign taxes, no doubt largely to Jamaica, of $3.4 million. In 1958, Reynolds' U.S. taxes had been almost $28 million, state and foreign taxes $4.4 million. Reynolds' high-profit years mean little to Jamaica.

ALUMINUM'S WAVE OF THE FUTURE

The aluminum companies have, in the standard imperialist pattern, kept the Caribbean countries simply as sources of raw material, and have refined and fabricated aluminum in Canada, the United States, and England. Now at last, economic compulsions reinforced by political pressures are impelling the companies toward processing and refining operations in the primary producing countries.

The economic compulsions derive primarily from the opening of markets for aluminum products in the developing countries. Aluminum's resistance to corrosion suits it for use in tropical climates. The ease with which it can be formed and fabricated makes it attractive to economies without extra capital. Its high electrical conductivity and light weight give it a market in countries embarking on electrification programs. Yet even in the most advanced of the industrializing countries, such as Argentina, per capita aluminum consumption is less than one-tenth of that in the United States. Both Kaiser and Reynolds have projected smelters in Argentina, each with a capacity of 20,000 tons annually.

Aluminum smelting is important to underdeveloped countries not only because of the consequent gains in national income and industrial skills, but also because of the high electricity consumption in the smelting process—nearly seven kilowatt-hours per pound of aluminum. Electric power can be the key to any country's industrialization. An example of how electrification for aluminum smelting can aid an emerging country is Ghana's Volta River Project, undertaken by Kaiser, with a 10 percent Reynolds interest, in cooperation with the Ghana government. Aluminum capacity of 100,000 tons is scheduled by 1965. Aluminum reduction will be provided by a hydro-electric development partly private, partly government financed. Half of the power will go to the Ghana government, and will make possible a qualitative change in the Ghanaian economy.

The Brokopondo Project being undertaken by Alcoa in Surinam is a far more conservative enterprise than the Volta River project, and far less favorable to the development of the area. The Surinam government is to get 10 percent of the power generated by the project. A 60,000-ton aluminum capacity is expected in 1965, making this the largest producer in South America.

Ghana and Surinam are two instances of the remarkable expansion going on in the aluminum industry. Larger developments are in Australia where Alcoa, Kaiser, and Pechiney of France, major concern outside of North America, are each engaged in large-scale expansion. Alcoa has also joined Mexican interests to build Mexico's first aluminum smelter, and Reynolds has contracted with Venezuela to build a $30-million smelter. In Africa, Ormet and Pechiney have combined in the $150-million Fria development in Guinea. In India and Indonesia refineries are going up, the Indonesian complex being built by the Indonesian government with technical and financial aid from the USSR. These and other projects will double the aluminum capacity outside of North America within the next few years.

Whether world aluminum consumption will grow fast enough to take up the new production is very doubtful—one of the doubts that cloud the future in unplanned capitalist society. When retrenchment sets in to allow consumption to catch up, small nations, like small businesses, will be left at the mercy of the great combines. Another dubious factor for the aluminum future is the U.S. "strategic" stockpile, swollen now to more than a two-year supply of bauxite needed for all U.S. production, and including excessive quantities of alumina and aluminum as well.

In fact, nowhere more than in aluminum is the whole frenetic, Cold War, capitalist world more startling, and nowhere are the evil consequences of its planlessness as unnecessary. For the aluminum industry in the developing countries is the last word in industry which is social in form while private in ownership. The Demba (Altd subsidiary) operations in British Guiana are more or less typical. Competent managers and technicians directing skilled workers (an increasing number of whom are Guianese) smoothly run a complex process to make profit for faraway and largely unknown owners. These profits, which go and stay in foreign lands, are derived from the diminishing natural resources of a people whose present is one of urgent need, and whose future is at the mercy of planless, conflicting economic forces.

A few conclusions seem obvious. One is that the aluminum industry can easily afford a more substantial contribution to Caribbean development. Practically, this means higher taxes on bauxite operations, and insistence on more processing, refining, and fabricating in the Caribbean countries.

Another conclusion is that as long as the great companies can play one primary producing country off against another by granting or witholding investments, the countries cannot cope with the companies. Furthermore, even with sound planning within the primary producing countries, the sporadic development of the capitalist world can catch these small countries in an economic cul-de-sac from which they will not be able to escape. The consequences to Jamaica, for example, of a not unlikely cutback in aluminum production in 1966 could be desperate. A common front of the primary producing countries, perhaps with UN technical aid, could set standards of taxation, industrialization, etc., and could even take steps to soften the economic blows resulting from capitalist planlessness.

Finally, without effective economic planning, much of any increased income from taxes, or from loans or any other sources, will not go into capital development, but into goods and services for the middle class, and into deposits by the upper class in foreign banks.

It is widely accepted in the Caribbean that for economic planning to mean anything for the masses of the people, it must be planning for socialism. Manley in Jamaica, Bosch in the Dominican Republic, and others who lead or have led or hope to lead governments, promise socialism. But it is abundantly clear in the Caribbean and throughout the emerging world that middle-class and business-dominated governments, just as feudal and gangster governments, will not plan for anything except individual and class advantage. This is the kind of planning that the United States and Britain understand and approve of. There are, however, an increasing number of Caribbean people who are determined to have socialism whether we approve or not. The hope for the Caribbean is in their hands.

6

Andre Gunder Frank

On the Mechanisms of Imperialism:
The Case of Brazil

*It is madness for one nation to expect
disinterested help from another.*
—George Washington

The United States does not have friends; it has interests.
—John Foster Dulles

In an article which appeared in *The Nation* of April 27, 1964, entitled "Brazil in Perspective," I examined the official Brazilian and U.S. views of economic relations between the two countries as presented by Roberto de Oliveira Campos, then Brazilian Ambassador in Washington and now the minister in charge of economic policy in the military dictatorship which took power in April, and by Lincoln Gordon, then and now American Ambassador to Brazil. My conclusions were that both official views are wrong: the United States does not help Brazil a lot (Gordon) or a little (Campos), but rather exploits Brazil unmercifully and stunts and distorts its economic development. In this article I propose to probe more deeply into these questions, especially in the hope of throwing light on a few of the numerous and often hidden mechanisms of which the imperialist countries make use in their relations with the colonial and semicolonial countries of the underdeveloped world.

THE FLOW OF CAPITAL FROM BRAZIL TO THE UNITED STATES

It is widely believed that the United States and other developed capitalist countries contribute more capital to the underdeveloped

---

This essay originally appeared in the September 1964 issue of *Monthly Reveiw* and is included in *Latin America: Underdevelopment or Revolution* (New York and London: Monthly Review Press, 1969). Copyright © 1964 by Monthly Review, Inc.

countries than they receive from them. Nonetheless, all available statistics, including those compiled by the official agencies of the developed countries themselves, show precisely the opposite. Between 1947 and 1960, the flow of investment funds on private capital account from the United States to Brazil was $1,814 million, while the capital flow of amortization, profits, royalties, interest, and other transfers from Brazil to the United States totalled $3,481 million. For the seven largest Latin American countries (Argentina, Brazil, Chile, Peru, Venezuela, Colombia, Mexico), the United States Department of Commerce's conservatively calculated figures for the years 1950 to 1961 indicate $2,962 million of investment flows on private account out of the United States and remittances of profits and interest of $6,875 million; adding in American public loans and their Latin American servicing between the same years still leaves a conservatively calculated net capital flow of $2,081 million *to* the United States.

My present purpose, however, is not to dwell further on the amount of this capital transfer from Brazil and other countries to the United States. Instead it is proposed to inquire into some of the reasons for and sources of this—for Brazil and others—so prejudicial capital flow. When the facts finally force American business, political, and unfortunately also academic, spokesmen for American capital to admit the existence of this capital flow from the poor underdeveloped countries to the rich developed ones, they often try to defend it in the following terms: either it is said that the direction of the flow is the result of the accidental or deliberate choice of a year or set of years in which the return flow on past investment happens to be greater than the outflow of new investment; or it is said instead (and sometimes in addition) that this drainage of capital from the poor underdeveloped countries really helps them to develop and that it is normal and logical that the capital flow into the investing and lending country—in this case into the United States—should be greater than the capital flow out of it because, after all, profits and interest legitimately earned abroad must be added to the amortization and repayment of the original investment.

The facts of economic life completely vitiate this American logic. If the disparity between capital inflow from and outflow to Brazil is as normal and legitimate as its defenders claim, then why is it that according to the late President John F. Kennedy the capital inflow to the United States from the underdeveloped countries in 1960 was $1,300 million and the capital outflow from the United States to the same countries $200 million, while in respect to the advanced countries of Western Europe the outflow from the United States ($1,500 million) exceeded the inflow ($1,000 million) by a wide margin?[1] Why does *U.S. News & World Report* (December 25, 1961), using Department of Commerce data, find the same pattern to obtain for the five-year period 1956-1961, that is, a ratio of inflow to the United States to outflow from the United States of 147 percent for Latin America, 164 percent for the underdeveloped world as a whole, and 43 percent for Western Europe? To eliminate still further the possibility that this disparity may be due to accidentally comparing years of low current outflow and high return flow of previous outflows, we may add up (as the Department of Commerce never does) the officially registered capital flows into and out of the United States for each year from 1950 to 1961 as reported in the *Survey of Current Business* and find that the total capital outflow is $13,708 million and the "corresponding" inflow $23,204 million, or an inflow/outflow ratio of 177 percent.[2] Are we to believe that it is normal and legitimate that profits and interest earned by the United States in weak underdeveloped countries are very much greater than in the strong developed ones, the United States included?

The disparity between capital inflows and outflows is more realistically explained by examining, as I propose to do in the paragraphs following, the source and composition of these flows than by appeal to any simplistic theories. In the first place, the argument that it is only logical for capital inflows to the United States to exceed outflows because, after all, the latter must earn a profit is premised on the unstated but erroneous assumption that official capital inflows into the United States are earnings on capital the United States previously sent abroad. As a matter of fact, much of the capital on which Americans "earn" profits in Brazil is Brazilian in origin and American only in ownership, control, and earnings. The Brazilian origins of "American" capital are manifold. We here take note of only those which fall under the titles of loans, concessions, and foreign exchange privileges.

Direct loans from the government's Bank of Brazil to American firms and to mixed American-Brazilian consortia are common in industry, commerce, and agriculture. The two giant American worldwide cotton merchants, SANBRA and Anderson & Clayton, in 1961 received $54 billion cruzeiros in loans from the Bank of Brazil, or 47 percent of that bank's entire agricultural and industrial loan portfolio.[3] By re-loaning this money (at higher interest rates, of course) to wholesalers and producers of cotton whom they thereby control; by buying up harvested stocks, storing them in government provided bins, and speculating with them later; by monopolizing important sectors of organization and distribution—these American firms use *Brazilian* capital to control much of the Brazilian domestic and export cotton market (as they also do that of many other countries) and to ship the profits therefrom home to the United States. Swift, Armour, and Wilson (recently involved in a public scandal for having partly exported and partly held back for a higher price the meat consigned to them by the government for storage and sale to the public), the A. & P.'s subsidiary American Coffee Company and other American monopolies similarly derive fat profits from using Brazilian capital to monopolize critical sectors of the domestic and export markets. American banks like the ubiquitous National City Bank of New York, insurance companies, and other financial institutions evidently work almost entirely with Brazilian capital, loan much of it to American nonfinancial firms in Brazil, and then serve as a channel to send their own and others' profits on this Brazilian capital "back" home.

In the public utility sector especially, the ownership and earnings of so-called American capital are based not on original investment of capital, but on concessions, exorbitant use rates, and other privileges. The capital is provided by Brazil. The São Paulo Light Co. (now merged with the Rio Light, Rio Gas, Brazilian Telephone, and other companies in the Brazilian Traction Co.), in 1907 took over a concession already granted to two Brazilian individuals until 1950 and then got it extended to 1990. By engaging an ex-president as its lawyer to fight a legal battle through several courts up to the Supreme Court—still staffed by the ex-president's appointees—the company in 1923, contrary to the stipulations of its contract, obtained an extension of the concession for its telephone subsidiary. Later the concession of the gas subsidiary was also extended. For its starting capital São Paulo Light issued bonds for $6 million. It then took over the already existing streetcars and associated properties. Following the usual procedure, the various light companies financed expansion of service to new areas by assessments on, and more recently by loans from, the communities to be served, while equipment was purchased out of earnings from exorbitant public utility rates. Even so, as any user can testify, service always lags far behind demand (electricity rationing is now normal in Rio and sometimes reaches blackouts of five hours daily). Through political influence and bribery, the company managed to delay the construction of competing facilities for fifteen years at one site. In 1948 the company received $90 million in loans from the International Bank for which it obtained a guarantee from the Brazilian government. Part of this foreign exchange was used, of course, not to import new equipment, but to convert cruzeiro earnings into dollars for remittance to the United States. To avoid showing exorbitant profits, the company increased its registered capital base by issuing stock dividends to its owners. Between 1918 and 1947, Brazilian Traction made profits of $550 million, of which $165 million were sent home. Now that public utilities have become unprofitable relative to other industries and that the Brazilian government wants to take them over in order to permit the expansion of needed service, the American owners bring all possible diplomatic and other pressure to bear in usually successful attempts to obtain once again the remaining equipment's value several times over through "expropriation."[4]

Addressing the Brazilian Senate in 1953, President Vargas' Treasury Minister said: "I have to declare that foreign capital ... demands guarantees to enter the country, greater guarantees to remain in it, and still greater ones to withdraw from it. Therefore, it does not seem desirable for any country and still less for Brazil."[5] After the establishment of a state petroleum company and threatening to do the same with electric power, the government of Vargas was, owing to foreign and domestic pressure, replaced by one which proposed the "creation of a climate favorable for the investment of foreign capital in the country." To this end the Superintendency of Money and Credit (SUMOC) issued Instruction 113 according to which, in the words of the President of the Federation of Industries of the State of São Paulo, "foreign firms can bring their entire equipment in at the free market price ... national ones, however, have to do so through exchange licenses established in import categories. In this way there was created veritable discrimination against national industry. We do not plead for preferential treatment but for equal opportunities."[6] Moreover, foreign firms were permitted to import used equipment (often already depreciated for tax purposes at home), while Brazilians could import only new machinery. As a result, Brazilians who on this basis were unable to compete with foreign firms and/or who were unable to get assignments of foreign exchange from the

Central Bank, were forced to combine with non-Brazilians who, though they might not contribute much of any capital to the common enterprise could contribute and capitalize on special privileges as foreigners. Ten years after Vargas, President Goulart was still forced to observe:

> In fact it is incomprehensible—and much less justifiable—that in this time of renewed heavy burden for the people, innumerable superfluous or easily dispensable products which are consumed mainly by the richer classes continue to enjoy the benefits of an exchange rate of 475 cruzeiros [the market rate was then 800 cruzeiros]. The same exchange rate as for petroleum products and other basic goods is enjoyed by extract of whisky and of Coca-Cola. . . . The disappearance of our scarce foreign exchange resources occurs not only through imports. The concession of exchange privileges to remit foreign exchange destined for the payment of unessential services causes the same harmful effects to our balance of payments.[7]

It is worthy of note that, "fascist" or "communizing" or not, as Presidents Vargas and Goulart respectively have been termed by the foreign press, the effective power of these Presidents was evidently insufficient to combat the forces, inside and outside their own governments, which benefit from and fight to maintain those privileges which accrue to small but powerful foreign and domestic interests at the cost of national development. There are, of course, influential Brazilian interests which willingly cooperate in this provision of Brazilian national capital to American firms so long as, in association with this powerful ally from the North, they can participate in some of the spoils.

Effects on Brazilian Economic and Industrial Structure

Spokesmen for the supposed advantages for Brazil of American investment often claim that the distribution of American investments and loans among productive sectors in the receiving country contributes to that country's economic development, and that the resulting import substitution is converting the Brazilian economy into one capable of self-sustained overall economic growth. The facts support neither of these contentions.

We have already noted in part what kind of contribution American owned, *but not supplied*, capital makes to Brazilian development in the trade and public utilities sectors which, according to the Department of Commerce, absorb 43 percent of the total. Of the 791 American firms in Brazil in 1960, we must certainly call into question the allegedly essential contribution to the development of its economy made by the 125 import, export, and other commercial houses; the banking, insurance, real estate, and other financial institutions, which are 64 in number; petroleum distribution (by the worldwide petroleum monopoly of notorious fame); retailing (such as Sears and Roebuck which outside the United States is a luxury chain); and publishing, advertising, hotels, cinema, and other services (including towel supply), which account for 77 more dubious contributions to a solid basis for Brazilian economic development.[8] Coca-Cola at least built or equipped a manufacturing plant.

As for the 54 percent of American capital which the Department of Commerce attributes to manufacturing, no detailed breakdown is given. In 1959, light consumer goods industry accounted for 48 percent of foreign, including American, manufacturing in Brazil, of which approximately 20 percent was in the food and beverage sector, including 17 bottling and ice cream firms.[9] Even the 40 percent of United States investment which the Department of Commerce attributes to basic industry is not telling. To serve as a base for self-sustained industrialization and growth, investment must, all will agree, produce the materials and equipment—steel, machinery, trucks, tractors—necessary for expanded production. But the bulk of this investment is in the automotive industry, and there it does not produce primarily trucks and tractors which are needed for development purposes but which are not immediately profitable; rather, it seeks maximum profits in the production of passenger cars for the high-income market.

In general, then, American enterprises in Brazil tend to produce nonessentials, and they do so largely with Brazilian capital.

But this is not all. The composition of foreign investment and its effects on the structure of the Brazilian economy are crucial to the maintenance of underdevelopment there. It is often claimed that American investment in Brazil results in import substitution which creates Brazilian capacity for autonomously directed and self-sustained economic development. Examining only American investment in the most basic sectors, we find, unfortunately, that the facts demonstrate largely the opposite. It is characteristic of American investment in Brazil and elsewhere that the giant investing corporations set up only a part of a particular productive process abroad and keep a critical, though it may be a smaller, part under their immediate control at home. The archetype of this arrangement is the Brazilian assembly plant of an American corporation which is made to depend on the import from the parent corporation of the basic equipment needed, later of its spare parts and replacements, often of critical components, especially the highly tooled ones, of critical raw materials, associated patents, technicians, transport, insurance, and above all, of the technical and organizational schema of the productive process.[10] Significantly, this arrangement also serves to eliminate any existing or potential Brazilian markets for inventive engineering and ties Brazilian technological development to the American economic structure; the reason is, of course, that the solutions to technical problems are already engineered into the productive process in the United States and are exported to Brazil in the form of the technological organization established there.

The Brazilian economy is tied still further to the stronger American economy when American interests "cooperate" with Brazilian capital in joint enterprises, or when American firms farm out part of the productive process to local suppliers of components. While the propaganda has it that the United States is stimulating private enterprise and economic development, the reality is that American corporations use Brazilian capital for their own purposes, transferring part of the risk and cost of demand fluctuations to the local supplier, channeling Brazilian capital into the provision of goods and services which maximize the American corporations' profits, and binding the Brazilian economy increasingly to themselves in particular and to the American economy in general. Moreover, American influence thus increases not only in the Brazilian economy but also in Brazilian political life; and, interestingly, in view of the claims about import substitution, this process results in increasing American determination of the composition even of Brazilian imports. Brazilian exports, of course, have been largely in American hands. Thus, what to Americans may appear as "the natural process of import substitution" appears to Brazilians, other than those directly cooperating in the process, as what it is: the progressive domination of the Brazilian economy and the strangulation of its capacity for national development.

The problem of imports is compounded by that of exports which are not keeping pace. The United Nations Economic Commission for Latin America (ECLA) notes that, subtracting petroleum, Latin America exports have risen only 40 percent since 1938, while world trade has doubled and the trade of the developed countries has tripled. ECLA notes further that "the deterioration of Latin America in world trade is one of the most important points of strangulation of its economic and social development."[11] Add to this the drain of capital out of Brazil and the misuses of its own resources engendered by foreign investment, and the result is Brazil's chronic balance of payments deficit. Now come the foreign loans.

These loans, we are asked to believe, are also development-producing. The fact is that to an increasing extent they are deposited in New York banks to cover the dollar needs of Americans in Brazil. As Simon Hanson has repeatedly pointed out in his *Latin American Letter* (for American businessmen) and in *Inter-American Economic Affairs* (Summer 1962), Alliance for Progress dollars are destined to serve as the source of the foreign exchange needed by Brazil to buy out American-owned (but as we saw, not supplied) capital in Brazilian public utilities, and to pay for imported equipment, materials, technicians, and service "needs" that (as we also saw above) American corporations have built into the Brazilian economy's underdeveloped structure. As these loans come with economic and political strings attached, Brazil thus loses control of critical sectors of its economy to foreign interests on foreign investment, domestic production, export, import, and loan accounts. These levers of control integrate the weaker Brazilian economy ever more into the stronger American economy, render the oligarchic Brazilian allies of American interests ever more dependent on the United States, and structure *under*-development all the more firmly into the very foundations of Brazilian society.

Beyond these considerations, some observations about recent features of American aid in Brazil may be illuminating. It is well to note that, though included in the dollar totals of aid, loans under Public Law 480, euphemistically called "Food for Peace," do not supply a single dollar but consist rather of cruzeiros derived from the sale in Brazil of American surplus wheat which, like all other "dumping," competes unfairly with and inhibits the development of Brazilian wheat production.

The major American-financed capital project in Brazil, the Volta Redonda steel mill, was, in fact, built by the United States during the Second World War to provide steel in Brazil for the United States' own wartime needs: Brazilians have been paying for the mill ever since. As for the much-heralded aid for the development of the "depressed Northeast," the governor of one of its states has publicly pointed out that with a population of 25 million and one of the world's lowest standards of living, this area received $13 million from the Alliance for Progress while the state of Guanabara (including the city of Rio de Janeiro), with four million inhabitants and the highest per capita income among Brazil's twenty-two states, was allocated $71 million. The governor of this latter state, it just so happens, is the presidential candidate of the ultra-right economic interests, the Brazilian Barry Goldwater, who spends his American-supplied dollars on parkways marked "works of the government of Carlos Lacerda" and on other projects such as forcing slum dwellers to move out to "John Kennedy village" located twenty miles out of town, while burning down their houses in the center of town to make room for a new tourist hotel. That's development!

UNDERDEVELOPMENT, INDUSTRIALIZATION, AND FOREIGN INVESTMENT

Finally, we may briefly broach what is undoubtedly the most difficult but the most important matter of all, the economic history of under-development and development, and the role of foreign trade and invest-ment therein. The events in this history which are critical for the under-standing of the problems under discussion are universally known, albeit all too conveniently forgotten in certain circles.

The expansion of metropolitan mercantilism and capitalism to Latin America, Africa, and Asia wrought the destruction of productive and viable agricultural and also industrial economies on these continents and most notoriously in Mexico, Peru, West and East Africa, and India. Arriving mostly by force of arms and establishing alliances in these societies (and in newly established ones such as Brazil) with old and newly created exploitative oligarchies, the metropolitan economies reduced the large bulk of the world's people to levels of abject poverty that they had never suffered at the hands of their previous own or foreign masters. In our times, it has become fashionable to call these societies "under-developed," as though they have always been this way. The developing metropolitan powers pillaged the peoples in these political and economic colonies of capital which they used to industrialize their own economies. By incorporating them into what is now known euphemistically as the world market, they converted these now *underdeveloping* economies into appendages of their own. As we have seen above, this process continues unabated in our day.

Lest it be thought that the United States is only a newcomer to this exploitative process which produces development for some at the expense of underdevelopment for others, it is well to remember that the initial industrial capital of the northeastern United States was derived largely from the slave trade and from the products of Southern slavery. Though the forms have been modernized, the content and the effects of the expansion of capitalism in contemporary times remain essentially what they always have been; the level of living of the majority of the people is still *falling*. The United Nations Food and Agricultural Organization (FAO) supplies part of the evidence. Taking per capita food production in 1934-1938 as 100, in the three crop years 1959/60, 1960/61, and 1961/62, it was 99, 100, and 98 in Latin America, Africa, and Asia (excluding the socialist countries) respectively; while it was 113 for the world as a whole, and 145 for the countries universally known for the failure of their agriculture, the Soviet Union and Eastern Europe.[12] But these figures tell only part of the story. The other part lies in the combination of low or negative economic growth rates with the increasing *inequality* of the distribution of income in countries for which estimates are available such as Brazil, Argentina, Mexico, and India. The result is that while foreign and domestic exploiters enrich themselves, the masses of the people in the underdeveloping countries are suffering an absolute decline in their per capita incomes.

This article has been an attempt to report on a few of the mechanisms of imperialist exploitation of underdeveloped countries. It is not, and is not intended to be, a substitute for inquiry into the structure and transformation of the imperialist system. But even these structurally derived mechanisms of imperialism in action, though no doubt familiar to practising imperialist and allied businessmen and diplomats, are all too unfamiliar to many of those who would combat imperialism. Yet an understanding of contemporary imperialism in action is essential to the theoretical base necessary for any successful struggle against the system. And there are many more such mechanisms of imperialism in action.[13] But even where reports of economic mechanisms of imperialism exist, they are usually studies of individual firms, industries, incidents, etc. Not only do these make tedious, if necessary, reading, as those who have followed this report this far will have found out; but in the absence of more inclusive and quantitative information on such matters as real profit rates and totals, concessions, financial control, imperialist-nationalist joint ventures, etc., we can reach only a very inadequate understanding of even these mechanisms of imperialism. It is hoped, therefore, that students in the underdeveloped countries, as well as in underdeveloped regions and sectors of the industrialized nations, will increasingly report on the hard facts of imperialism.

Notes

1. Cited in *O Estado de São Paulo*, April 12, 1963.
2. These totals can be computed from the following issues of the *Survey of Current Business*: November 1954, pp. 9, 13; August 1955, pp. 18, 20; August 1957, p. 25; August 1959, p. 31; August 1961, pp. 22, 23; August 1962, pp. 22, 23.
3. Reported by Congressman Jacob Frantz in Congressional debate and cited in *O Semanario*, May 30–June 6, 1963.
4. See Paulo F. Alves Pinto, *Antologia Nacionalista*, vol. 2, cited in Barbosa Lima Sobrinho, *Marquinas para transformar cruzeiros em dolares*, and Sylvio Monteiro, *Como Atua o imperialismo ianque?*
5. Quoted in Osny Duarte Pereira, *Quem faz as leis no Brasil?*, p. 97.
6. Quoted in Jocelyn Brasil, *O Pao, O Feijao, e as Forzas Ocultas*, p. 125.
7. *O Semanario*, September 26, 1963.
8. Barbosa Lima Sobrinho citing Editora Banas, in *O Semanario*, September 26, 1963.
9. Editora Banas, *Capital extranjero no Brasil*.
10. Much the same pattern in Latin American petroleum, mining, steel, automotive, machine building, and other industries was noted and criticized by the American observer John Gerassi in *The Great Fear* (New York: Macmillan and Company, 1963).
11. *Jornal do Brasil*, January 22, 1964.
12. FAO, *The State of Food and Agriculture*, 1962, p. 15 of Spanish edition.
13. Hamza Alavi has recently reported on some others. See his article, pp. 62–78 above.

7

James O'Connor

The Meaning of Economic Imperialism

THEORIES OF IMPERIALISM

There is still much controversy, and more confusion, about the meaning of economic imperialism. Monopolistic privileges and preferences, plunder of raw materials, seizure of territory, enslavement of local peoples, nationalism, racism, militarism—all of these phenomena have been closely identified with imperialism. Only on the association of imperialism with expansion—economic, political, cultural, and territorial expansion—has there been any general agreement. But if imperialism means "the extension of political power by one state over another, [then] all through the sixty centuries of more or less recorded history" it has been a principle feature in human relations.[1] Beneath the undergrowth of over half a century of historical, theoretical, and polemical writings, however, three general doctrines can be distinguished. Two of these reflect the period of European expansion which began during the 1880's and ended in 1914. The third is an interpretation of contemporary world capitalism, and, in particular, United States expansionism.

Imperialism : A Political Phenomenon

The first doctrine disassociates capitalism from imperialism. For Joseph Schumpeter, the leading exponent of this view, imperialism is "a heritage of the autocratic state . . . the outcome of precapitalist forces which the autocratic state has reorganized . . . [and] would never have been evolved by the 'inner logic' of capitalism itself."[2] The "inner logic" of capitalism consists of nothing more or less than free trade and "where free trade prevails *no* class has an interest in forcible expansion as such . . .

This essay was originally printed as a Radical Education Project pamphlet.

citizens and goods of every nation can move in foreign countries as freely as though those countries were politically their own." Only the "export monopolist interests"—in particular, monopolies in the metropolitan countries which dump surplus commodities abroad behind high tariff walls—profit from imperialism. Schumpeter was confident that these interests would not survive capitalism's "inner logic." His confidence was, of course, misplaced; as we will see, the national and regional economic policies of the advanced capitalist countries today rightly merit Joan Robinson's label—the New Mercantilism. The reason is not hard to find: Schumpeter selected one characteristic of capitalism, "rationality," which he considered central, to the exclusion of other features.

The vast majority of bourgeois economists in the past and present adopt a position similar to Schumpeter's, even though few today would share his optimism in connection with the revival of free trade. The generally accepted "comparative advantage" theory of Ricardo and Mill holds that all parties in international commodity trade under competitive conditions benefit in accordance with the strength of the demand for their respective commodities. Nationalist economic policy and monopoly restricted free trade and inhibited the growth of income and economic well-being, but these barriers have been lowered by the breakup of the European empires. The trademark of this doctrine is that exploitive economic relations between the advanced and backward capitalist countries cannot survive in a world of politically independent countries. According to this line of thinking, the real problems of world capitalism today spring from the misplaced faith of the ex-colonies that nationalist economic policies which have created new and higher barriers to international investment and trade can put the backward countries on the path of self-sustained economic growth.

Schumpeter and other bourgeois writers uncritically disassociate capitalism from imperialism for three reasons: First, because their criteria for distinguishing and identifying imperial and colonial relationships are ordinarily political and not economic (for example, Hans Kohn has developed the most sophisticated typology of imperialism, which he understands in terms of the distribution of political power[3]); second, because they do not consider capitalism as such to be an exploitative system; third, because imperialism historically has contained certain features identified with the theme of expansionism which have not been uniquely associated with any given economic and social system. Thus bourgeois writers have concluded not only that imperialism predates capitalism, but also that imperialism is essentially an anachronistic system. For this reason, there have been few investigations of the specific features of capitalist imperialism.

In connection with economic expansionism, pre-capitalist and capitalist societies differ in five general ways: First, in pre-capitalist societies economic expansion was irregular, unsystematic, not integral to normal economic activity. In capitalist societies, foreign trade and investment are rightly considered to be the "engines of growth." Expansion is necessary to maintain the rhythm of economic activity in the home, or metropolitan economy, and has an orderly, methodical, permanent character. Second, in pre-capitalist societies the economic gains from expansion were windfall gains, frequently taking the form of sporadic plunder. In capitalist societies, profits from overseas trade and investment are an integral part of national income, and considered in a matter-of-fact manner.

Third, in pre-capitalist societies plunder acquired in the course of expansion was often consumed in the field by the conquering armies, leaving the home economy relatively unaffected. In capitalist societies, exploited territories are fragmented and integrated into the structure of the metropolitan economy. Imperialism, in effect, potentially emancipated space-bound and time-bound man. Fourth, in pre-capitalist societies debates within the ruling class ordinarily revolved around the question whether or not to expand. In capitalist societies, ruling-class debates normally turn on the issue of what is the best way to expand.

Last, in relation to colonialism, pre-capitalist and capitalist societies also differ in a fundamental way. In the former, colonialism (land seizure, colonist settlement, or both) was the only mode of control which the metropolitan power could effectively exercise over the satellite region. As we will see in detail later, capitalist societies have developed alternative, indirect, and more complex forms of control.

Not only do pre-capitalist and capitalist expansion depart in significant ways, but also the character of expansion (especially the nature of trade and colonialism) in mercantile capitalist societies differs from that in industrial capitalist societies. To be sure, the definition of colonialism adopted by some writers—monopolistically regulated trade and investment at higher rates of profit than those obtaining in the home economy—applies with equal force to both the mercantilist and industrial capitalist eras. In fact, the term "neo-mercantilism" has frequently been used to describe nineteenth-century imperialism, and, as we have mentioned, mid-twentieth-century nationalist economic policy has been labeled the "new mercantilism." In addition, throughout the history of capitalism businessmen and traders have followed the same rule—extract capital from areas where the cost is lowest, invest where anticipated returns are highest.

The differences between mercantilism and nineteenth-century imperialism, however, outweigh the similarities.[4] First, the resemblance between monopolistic commercial organizations in the two political-economic systems is only superficial. Mercantilist monopoly trading companies did not spring from the prevailing modes of production. They were formed to minimize physical and commercial risks along uncertain and distant trade routes. As "normal" patterns of trade were established, risk and uncertainty were reduced and the great monopoly companies met increasing competition from other nationals and foreign companies. The East India Company, the last of the great monopolies, was dissolved early in the nineteenth century. From then until the last quarter of the nineteenth century, British manufacturers and merchants adopted free trade on principle because their control over advanced methods of production gave them a decisive competitive advantage. But Britain's foreign investments in Europe and the United States and the diffusion of industrial technology eliminated this advantage. And further advances in technology which were not consistent with small-scale enterprise led to the cartelization and monopolization of industry. Latter-day monopolies, unlike their forerunners, have proven not to be transitory.

A second important difference between mercantilism and imperialism is related to the character of trade. Early mercantilism was commercial capitalism in its purest essence, middlemen exchanged goods for goods in a lively entrepôt trade, and mercantilist wars were mainly trade wars—the Anglo-Dutch wars of the seventeenth century were the purest commercial wars in history.[5] It is true that, as early as the first decades of the seventeenth century, the East India Company purchased raw materials in exchange for British manufactured goods. But this was not typical. It was only in the late mercantile and early industrial capitalist periods that Britain increasingly exported manufactured commodities for agricultural raw materials and minerals.[6] As late as 1800, for example, British ships took woolens and hardware to India and returned with cotton and silk products. Then, as the nineteenth century wore on, a new dimension was added to trade: capital goods financed by foreign loans and invest-ments, as well as consumer manufacturers, exchanged for foodstuffs and industrial raw materials.

Finally, there are superficial similarities between mercantilism and imperialism in the sphere of state economic policy. Both systems of political economy relied on active state participation in the direction, organization, and character of trade or investment. But the nature of state policy was fundamentally different. In England, after the prohibition on the export of bullion was abolished in 1663, the state employed commod-ity import and export controls with the aim of maintaining a favorable balance of trade, or export surplus, with *each* of Britain's trading partners, colonies and noncolonies alike. Gradually, a system of multilateral trade replaced the more primitive bilateral trade patterns. It was this system of multilateral trade which the imperialist states of the late nineteenth century inherited. Imperialist state policy revived the older technique of export promotion and import restriction (and invented new tech-niques, as well) with the aim of maintaining a favorable balance of trade *with the world as a whole*, not with any specific trading partner.

These contrasts between mercantilism and imperialism give rise to important differences with respect to colonization. In the first place, it is certainly true that the leading late mercantilist and imperialist powers discouraged both subsistence production and the manufacture of com-modities in the colonies. But mercantilist industry was technologically primitive, small-scale, and, most important, not vertically integrated. Thus the exploitation of raw materials under mercantile impulses, and colonization itself, were of necessity *national* policies, and generated fierce national rivalries. From the late nineteenth century down to the present, however, national rivalries have increasingly given way to struggles between fully integrated corporations based in the metropolitan countries. These struggles have typically been resolved in compromise. The sharing out of oil resources between the great oil monopolies in the Middle East is an excellent example of cooperation between integrated corporations (and, by extension, imperialist nations). To make the point slightly differently, in the mercantilist era it was impossible to conceive of an international ruling class; in the contemporary imperialist period, an international ruling class is an accomplished fact.[7]

Secondly, colonial conquest in the sixteenth and seventeenth centuries had as its chief purpose the mitigation of the hazards of trade and the preservation of monopoly control. The mercantilist powers established factories, trading bases, and forts where regional trade was already established.[8] By contrast, the seizure of territories in the late nineteenth century was motivated less to preserve commercial positions which had already been won by peaceful methods than to open up possibilities for trade and investment where none had existed before. Colonialism under mercantilism was therefore defensive in nature and required a passive state presence, while latter-day imperialism in comparison exhibited an aggressive character which stood in need of active state participation.

Mercantilism and imperialism departed in still another important respect. The doctrine used to support rigid trade restrictions, and an important element of the theory which the mercantile colonial system was based on, was that the maximum inflow of bullion required a favorable balance of trade with each colony. This doctrine limited the scope of territorial conquest and seizure, as well as the development of commercial relations with other colonial powers. In the late mercantile era, however, the state gradually realized that an expansion of output was the key to maximum trade and therefore the nursing of home industry and creation of employment became central goals of state policy. Thus were created the preconditions for the growth of complex, multilateral trade patterns, which in turn awakened the interests of the imperial powers in any and all underexploited regions.

In sum, industrial capitalist expansionism distinguished itself in the following important respects: it exhibited a more aggressive attitude toward the underexploited lands; it was less particular, and more universal, in character; it more fully integrated underexploited economic regions into the structure of the metropolitan country; it required the active participation of the state; and, finally, internecine warfare between the economic monopolies tended to be less acute. Imperialism thus contained the important contradiction which has afflicted the advanced capitalist countries down to the present day. On the one hand, the *national* power elites seek to advance the economic interests of their respective countries; on the other hand, the integrated, multinational corporations, or the *international* ruling class, extend their sway irrespective of the interests of the countries in which they are based. This contradiction is heightened by the aggressive, universal character of modern imperialist expansion.

(In our comparison of mercantilism and imperialism we have neither surveyed the differences between the early, middle, and late mercantilist era, nor reviewed satisfactorily the relation of the free trade period to either mercantilism or imperialism. One school of thought sees a great deal of continuity between mercantilism and early industrial capitalism. M. Barratt-Brown, for example, argues that the decades after 1815 saw the expansion and consolidation of the British Empire based on the need to conquer and secure markets and keep trade routes open in the face of rivalries from developing European and United States capitalism and the first outbreaks of nationalism and anti-imperialism in the colonies. D. Fieldhouse, on the other hand, asserts that Britain's industrial supremacy after 1815 meant that the colonies and monopolistic privileges involved few benefits and large costs. He claims that the acquisition and defense of colonies were motivated chiefly for reasons of military security and administrative efficiency.)

Imperialism : An Aspect of Monopoly Capitalism

Against the view that dissociates capitalism and imperialism, Marxist economists have put forward many variations on the same fundamental argument. The second doctrine of imperialism, also inspired by European expansionism in the late nineteenth and early twentieth centuries, holds that monopoly capitalism, imperialism, and colonialism are basically the same phenomena. Perhaps it is more accurate to call this view "neo-Marxist," because those who hold it have inherited few clear theoretical guidelines from Marx himself. In the three volumes of *Capital*, apart from the brief concluding chapter in Volume 1, there are only two or three references to the economics of colonialism, the gist of which is that commodities produced under conditions of high labor productivity and sold in countries where labor productivity is low will command an abnormally high rate of profit.[9] Marx's relative silence on the economics of imperialism may have handicapped the development of Marxist theory, or it may have been a blessing in disguise. The absence of any theoretical precedent has forced (and continues to force) Marxists back on their own experiences and intellectual resources. Thus older interpretations of imperialism as far apart as those of Lenin and Rosa Luxemburg, and modern theories as disparate as those of Paul Baran and Joseph Gillman, have arisen from basically the same critical tradition.

Nothing succeeds like success, however, and Lenin's ideas have dominated the field. Yet Lenin owed much to John A. Hobson's *Imperialism*, published in 1902, a book which is frequently (and legitimately) read as the precursor of Lenin's study. Thus we will begin by sketching out the main ideas of Hobson and Lenin, later subjecting them to analysis on the basis of theoretical and historical studies published in recent years.

Hobson and Lenin wrote about imperialism during the heyday of colonialism (1885-1914), which naturally enough appeared to be *the* most significant economic-political phenomenon of the time. By making colonialism their focal point, however, both men equated imperialism and colonialism and thus failed to understand the significance of the "imperialism of free trade"—an expression coined to describe British economic expansion from the 1840's to the 1880's. Moreover, they barely acknowledged United States expansion and could not anticipate future modes of imperialist controls which have proved to be even more effective than formal colonial rule.

The distinctive feature of Hobson's theory is his conception of colonialism as the reflection of the unfulfilled promise of liberal democracy. As Hobson saw it, inequalities in the distribution of wealth and income in Britain dampened the consumption power of the British working classes, which in turn made it unprofitable for capitalists to utilize fully their industrial capacity. Unable to find profitable investment outlets at home, British capitalists subsequently sought them abroad in the economically underexploited continents. Britain therefore acquired colonies as a dumping ground for surplus capital. The end of imperialist conquest and de-colonization would come about only when the British working classes acquired more economic and political power through trade unionism and parliamentary representation, which would set the stage for a thoroughgoing redistribution of income and hence the development of a home economy in which the volume of consumption corresponded more closely to the volume of production.

Hobson supported his thesis not only by his faith in the promise of liberal democracy, but also by reference to changes in Britain's trade and investments. He tried to show that the expansion of empire during the last two decades of the nineteenth century, when most of the world not already independent or under European rule was carved up among the European powers, resulted in a *decline* in British trade with her colonies in relation to trade with noncolonies.[10] He also underlined the obvious fact that the new colonies in Africa and Asia failed to attract

British settlers in significant numbers. Through a process of elimination Hobson thus hit on what he considered to be the crucial element in British imperialism—foreign investments. He linked the vast outflow of capital from Britain during this period—British overseas investments rose from 785 million pounds in 1871 to 3,500 million pounds in 1911 and annual net foreign investments were frequently greater than gross domestic fixed investments—with the frantic struggle by the European powers for colonies, and inferred that the former caused the latter. The political struggles between the major European powers were thus dissolved into struggles for profitable investment outlets, and the explorers, missionaries, traders, and soldiers of the period were seen as the puppets of London's financial magnates.

Lenin agreed with Hobson that the prime cause of capital exports was the vast increase in the supply of capital in the metropolitan countries, especially Britain, and played down the role of the demand for capital in the underdeveloped regions. He also, like Hobson, causally linked foreign investments with the acquisition of colonies. The distinctive element in Lenin's theory related to the *cause* of the surplus of capital.

Lenin understood that imperialism is a *stage* of capitalist development, and not merely one possible set of foreign policy options among many. In particular, imperialism is the monopoly capitalist stage, and exhibits five basic features:

(1) The concentration of production and capital, developed so highly that it creates monopolies which play a decisive role in economic life.

(2) The fusion of banking capital with industrial capital and the creation, on the basis of this financial capital, of a financial oligarchy.

(3) The export of capital, which has become extremely important, as distinguished from the export of commodities.

(4) The formation of the international capitalist monopolies which share out the world among themselves.

(5) The territorial division of the whole earth completed by the great capitalist powers.[11]

The key element is the formation of local and international monopolies behind high tariff barriers in the metropolitan countries. Monopolistic organization develops "precisely out of free competition" in essentially four ways. First, the concentration (growth in absolute size) of capital leads to the centralization (growth in relative size) of capital. Second, monopoly capital extends and strengthens itself by the seizure of key raw materials. Third, financial capital, or the investment banks, "impose an infinite number of financial ties of dependence upon all the economic and political institutions of contemporary capitalist society," including nonfinancial capital. Fourth, "monopoly has grown out of colonial policy. To the numerous 'old' motives of colonial policy, the capitalist financier has added the struggle for the sources of raw materials, for the exportation of capital, for 'spheres of influence,' i.e., for spheres of good business, concessions, monopolist profits, and so on; in fine, for economic territory in general." In short, the new colonialism opposes itself to the older colonial policy of the "free grabbing" of territories.

The cause of the surplus of capital and capital exportation, and of monopolistic industry, is the tendency of the rate of profit to fall.[12] Two underlying forces drive down the rate of profit in the metropolitan country. First, the rise of trade unions and social democracy, together with the exhaustion of opportunities to recruit labor from the countryside at the going real wage, rule out possibilities for increasing significantly the rate of exploitation. Second, labor saving innovations increase the organic composition of capital. Monopoly is thus in part formed in order to protect profit margins. At the same time, economies of large-scale production (internal expansion) and mergers during periods of economic crises (external expansion) strengthen pre-existing tendencies toward monopolistic organization.

Meanwhile, in the economically underexploited regions of the world, capital yields a substantially higher rate of return. For one thing, the composition of capital is lower; for another, labor is plentiful in supply and cheap; and, finally, colonial rule establishes the preconditions for monopolistic privileges. Rich in minerals and raw materials required by the development of metals, automotive, and other heavy industries in the metropolitan powers, the underexploited regions naturally attract large amounts of capital. Consequently, foreign investment counteracts the tendency for the rate of profit to fall in the metropolitan economy. On the one hand, high profit margins in the colonies pull up the average return on capital; on the other hand, the retardation of capital accumulation in the home economy recreates the reserve army of the unemployed, raises the rate of exploitation, and, finally, increases the rate of profit.

Pushing this thesis one step forward, the precondition for a truly "favorable" investment climate is indirect or direct control of internal politics in the backward regions. Economic penetration therefore leads to the establishment of spheres of influence, protectorates, and annexation. Strachey suggests that the backward regions assumed a dependency status (the last step before outright control) in relation to the metropolitan powers chiefly because the former were in debt to the latter. What was significant about the shift from consumer goods to capital goods in world trade was that the colony-to-be needed long-term credits or loans to pay for the capital goods, and that, finally, the relationship between the backward country and the metropolitan country became one of debtor and creditor. And from this it was but a small step to dependence and domination.

Whatever the exact sequence of events which led to colonialism, Lenin's economic definition of colonialism (and imperialism) is monopolistically regulated trade and/or investment abroad at higher rates of profit than those obtaining in the metropolitan country. "As soon as political control arrives as handmaid to investment," Dobb writes, "the opportunity for monopolistic and preferential practices exists." The essential ingredient of colonialism therefore is "privileged investment: namely, investment in projects which carry with them some differential advantage, preference, or actual monopoly, in the form of concession-rights or some grant of privileged status."[13]

The criticisms of Hobson's and Lenin's theories, and the alternative views which have been put forward, do not constitute a new theory so much as a catalogue of historical facts which are not fully consistent with the older theories. These criticisms bear on three key aspects of Lenin's theory, two of which also figured importantly in Hobson's thought.

One line of criticism is that Lenin ignored the theme of continuity in European expansionism and was too eager to interpret the partition of Africa and the Pacific as a qualitatively different phenomenon. Alexander Kemp has shown that throughout the *entire* nineteenth century British net capital exports in relation to national income amounted to just over 1 percent during recession periods and about 6 to 7 percent during boom years.[14] Pointing to a similar conclusion is Richard Koebner's judgment that British "imperial responsibilities were enlarged step by step by a hesitant government."[15] Gallagher and Robinson also reject the idea that there were important qualitative differences between British expansionism in the first and second parts of the nineteenth century. In both periods the formula was "trade with informal control if possible; trade with the rule if necessary."[16] In Egypt and South Africa, for example, they maintain that Britain was only responding to internal upheaval and that traditional controls could no longer be relied upon.

Lenin was aware of the continuity in European expansionism but maintained that the development of monopoly capitalism led to a break in this continuity. In principle Lenin had solid earth under his feet because the generation of business savings and their absorption by new investments are governed by different laws in a competitive capitalist society than under monopoly capitalism. But in practice it is by no means certain that Lenin was right when he asserted that at the beginning of the twentieth century, monopolies have acquired complete supremacy in the advanced countries.[17]

In the most powerful imperialist country, Great Britain, there were few trusts or cartels of any consequence in 1900.[18] One highly qualified economic historian maintains that the British economy failed to enter the monopoly stage until the early 1930's.[19] Lenin was aware that British capitalism was far from a model of monopoly domination, but slurred over the problem by referring to a "monopoly" of a few dozen companies and by interpreting Chamberlain's Imperial Preference System as Britain's reply to the European cartels. The German economy was not thoroughly trustified until after 1900, even though bank control of industry was established at a much earlier date. As for the United States economy, recent research has thrown doubt on the received idea that the great merger movement around the turn of the century resulted in the cartelization and trustification of heavy industry, and has substituted the thesis that the economy was more competitive in the first decade of the twentieth century than in the last decade of the nineteenth.[20]

The same line of criticism developed from a different perspective also casts doubt on Lenin's major thesis. The truth is that British capital exports to Africa were mobilized by small-scale speculators, not mainly by the big London banking houses. For the former, although not for the latter, foreign lending was a precarious undertaking. One of the first of the African companies, The Royal Niger Company, "had to . . . enlist subscribers in order to make certain that the Company would be equal to its administrative undertaking."[21] Similarly, subscribers to the Imperial British East Africa Company and Cecil Rhodes' South African Company were mainly small-scale savers, such as pensioners and retired military officers. If monopoly capitalism is essentially a post-Lenin phenomenon, it is readily understandable why the African companies were financed by small capital. The interesting point in this connection is that capital exports to the underdeveloped regions today conform closely to the Leninist vision. It is not the small investor attracted to an empire builder like Rhodes who provides the savings for foreign investment, but the giant multinational corporations such as Standard Oil, General Motors, and General Electric.

The second line of criticism challenges directly the thesis of Hobson and Lenin that vast amounts of capital from Britain flowed into new colonies. As Cairncross has shown in his definitive study, the great mass of British foreign investments penetrated India and what Ragnar Nurkse has termed the regions of recent settlement—the United States, Canada, Australia, Argentina, and South Africa.[22] These areas contained primary commodities, chiefly agricultural goods, which Britain required and which in turn needed a steady flow of foreign capital, mainly to finance railroad construction, to exploit. This analysis lays great stress on the increase in the demand for capital (and is sometimes called the capital-pull thesis) and plays down the significance of the capital surplus which Hobson and Lenin saw piling up in the metropolitan countries.

Maurice Dobb has countered this reasoning with the observation that Britain's need for foodstuffs and raw materials was specific to Britain and in no sense characteristic of the other imperial powers. Thus while the demand for British capital may have increased more rapidly than the supply, the same conclusions cannot be applied to France or Germany. What is more, repatriated interest and dividend payments on investments "pulled" from Britain in the early years of the colonial epoch may have been during later decades "pushed" out into both the old and new colonies. Fieldhouse has pointed out that there were no important differentials between home and foreign interest rates during the pre-World War I colonial era, concluding that capital could hardly have been attracted by colonial superprofits.[23] Taken at face value, this conclusion supports the Nurkse-Cairncross "capital-pull" thesis. But the conclusion is fallacious because it was precisely the vast outflow of capital which depressed interest rates abroad and kept them firm at home.

The new colonies did fail to attract many investments during the period directly before and after their conquest. Egypt's indebtedness to Britain was a factor, to be sure, but it was the collapse of the Egyptian government which led Britain to occupy that country in 1882 in order to protect Suez and the routes to the east.[24] As for the rest of Africa, British enterprise in the nineteenth century was restricted mainly to the palm oil trade on the west coast, and moderate investment activity in the Transvaal and Rhodesia. As Robinson and Gallagher have shown, Africa provided little trade, less revenue, and few local collaborators, and Britain supplied little capital and few settlers. Certainly, until the twentieth century British ruling-class opinion held widely that there was no real economic reason for the partition of Africa.[25] In the Pacific, large-scale investments in Malayan tin and rubber were made considerably after the annexation of that country, and other late nineteenth-century conquests in Asia and the Pacific failed to attract new investments in any significant quantity. This of course does not prove that these acquisitions were not economically motivated, but only that investors may have had over-optimistic expectations.

Lenin's description of the chief characteristics of the new colonial era—foreign investments, seizure of territories, monopolistic preferences—was therefore largely accurate. A single, or simple, theoretical pattern, however, cannot be imposed on the complex sequence of events which revolutionized the world capitalist system between the 1880's and World War I. More often than not, in Robinson and Gallagher's words, the "extension of territorial claims . . . required commercial expansion." Certainly the attitudes expressed by the German Colonial Congress in 1902 suggest that in point of time investment and trade followed the flag, rather than vice versa: "The Congress thinks that, in the interests of the fatherland, it is necessary to render it independent of the foreigner for the importation of raw materials and to create markets as safe as possible for manufactured German goods. The German colonies of the future must play this double role, even if the natives are forced to labor on public works and agricultural pursuits." Similar sentiments were expressed in one form or another by Joseph Chamberlain, Theodore Roosevelt, and a host of lesser leaders and ideologists of imperialism.

We have finally to discuss a criticism of Lenin's thesis which arises from the experiences of Britain in the period directly after World War II. Although domestic investment had been considerably in excess of foreign investment (thus reversing the pre-1914 ratio of home to foreign investment),[26] capital exports did not come to a complete halt with the political independence of Britain's colonies. It has been inferred from this that formal colonial rule was really not necessary to provide profitable investment outlets. In defense of Lenin, the argument has been raised that

British economic stagnation in the immediate postwar era can be attributed to the decline in repatriated earnings from foreign investments, and therefore a decrease in the rate of profit, in turn due to the removal of British economic interests from their monopoly over trade, banking, agriculture, and other branches of politically independent ex-colonies.[27] The empirical work published by Michael Barratt-Brown tends to confirm this line of reasoning: Brown estimates that after deducting payments to foreign owners of property, net earnings from overseas investments in the postwar period amounted to only 1 percent of Britain's national income.[28]

These estimates, and the conclusion implicit in them, have been questioned by Hamza Alavi, who argues that informal economic control exercised by the advanced capitalist countries can be as effective, and as profitable, as formal political rule.[29] In our subsequent interpretation of contemporary imperialism we lay great stress, and develop in detail, this idea. Alavi challenges the estimates on three grounds. First, he maintains that the gross return, not net return, on capital invested abroad is the relevant figure on the grounds that Britain incurred her liabilities independently. Second, he rightly stresses that profit remittances represent but a portion of the return flow on foreign investments. Although it proved impossible to arrive at any accurate estimates, income remitted in the form of monopolistic prices, "services" such as commission royalties, and head office charges, should be included in the return flow. Lastly, Alavi states that income remissions in relation to the domestic economic surplus (and not relative to national income) is the relevant comparison for measuring the impact of foreign investments on the metropolitan economy. Alavi calculates that gross income from overseas investments in the postwar period (excluding the disguised income remissions listed above) amounted to 3.3–4 percent of the national income and 40–55 percent of domestic net investment. Clearly, if Britain financed perhaps one-half of her home investments from overseas profits, foreign asset holdings must have been a decisive element in the maintenance of the rate of profit at home.

Neo-Imperialism: Control Without Colonialism

A brief sketch cannot even begin to resolve the many theoretical and historical questions which run through the two major contending doctrines of nineteenth-century imperialism. It is clear, however, that two features of imperialism are not in dispute. The first concerns the general description of economic organization and economic policy. As we have seen, Dobb considers the essential ingredient of imperialism to be "privileged investment . . . investment in projects which carry with them some differential advantage." This feature must be placed in a wider frame of reference, as in Paul Sweezy's description of imperialism as "severe rivalry [between advanced capitalist countries] in the world market leading alternatively to cutthroat competition and international monopoly combines."[30] Schumpeter's view of imperialism is very similar. Cutthroat competition and international monopoly combines are seen as "protective tariffs, cartels, monopoly prices, forced exports (dumping), an aggressive economic policy, and aggressive foreign policy gener-ally . . ."[31] A second general area of agreement (generally implicit in the writings of both Marxists and non-Marxists) is that modern imperialism, whatever its causes, depends on colonial rule as the main form of eco-nomic and political control of the economically backward region and that political independence would significantly reduce, or eliminate entirely, exploitative imperialist relations.

Opposed to these doctrines is what may be called the neo-Leninist, or modern Marxist theory of imperialism. The increasing economic domina-tion exercised by the United States in the world capitalist economy and the failure of the ex-colonies to embark on sustained economic and social development have caused older Marxist economists to rework original doctrines and have given rise to a new theory of neo-colonialism. Many of its outlines are still indistinct, but there is broad agreement that a sharp distinction should be made between colonialism and imperialism, while the original Leninist identity between monopoly capitalism and im-perialism should be retained. In this view, which we adopt throughout this study, monopoly capitalism remains an aggressively expansionist political-economic system, but colonialism is seen as merely one *form* of imperialist domination, and frequently an ineffective one at that.

The phrase "neo-colonialism" was first used in the early 1950's. Anticolonial leaders in Asia and Africa focus on the element of control—in the words of Sukarno, "economic control, intellectual control, and actual physical control by a small but alien community, within a nation."[32] To cite a specific illustration of economic neo-colonialism, Nkrumah denounced as "neo-colonialism" the economic association of France's African colonies with the European Common Market. An example in which the political element was in the fore was France's claim to the right to suppress the revolt against the puppet ruler of Gabon in February 1964 in order to defend French economic interests in that country. A comprehensive summary of the chief manifestations of neo-colonialism was made at the Third All-African People's Conference held in Cairo in 1961:

> This Conference considers that neo-colonialism, which is the survival of the colonial system in spite of formal recognition of political independence in emerging countries, which become the victims of an indirect and subtle form of domination by political, economic, social, military, or technical [forces], is the greatest threat to African countries that have newly won their independence or those approaching this status . . .
>
> This Conference denounces the following manifestations of neo-colonialism in Africa:
>
> (a) Puppet governments represented by stooges, and based on some chiefs, reactionary elements, antipopular politicians, big bourgeois compradors, or corrupted civil or military functionaries.
>
> (b) Regrouping of states, before or after independence, by an imperial power in federation or communities linked to that imperial power.
>
> (c) Balkanization as a deliberate political fragmentation of states by creation of artificial entities, such as, for example, the case of Katanga, Muritania, Buganda, etc.
>
> (d) The economic entrenchment of the colonial power before independence and the continuity of economic dependence after formal recognition of national sovereignty.
>
> (e) Integration into colonial economic blocs which maintain the underdeveloped character of African economy.
>
> (f) Economic infiltration by a foreign power after independence, through capital investments, loans, and monetary aids or technical experts, of unequal concessions, particularly those extending for long periods.
>
> (g) Direct monetary dependence, as in those emergent independent states whose finances remain in the hands of and directly controlled by colonial powers.
>
> (h) Military bases sometimes introduced as scientific research stations or training schools, introduced either before independence or as a condition for independence.[33]

This description supports two broad generalizations. First, modern imperialism requires the active participation of the state in international economic relationships; imperialist nations cannot singly or collectively implement a neo-colonialist policy—via agencies such as the European Common Market, for example—without state capitalism. Secondly, neo-colonist policy is first and foremost designed to prevent the newly independent countries from consolidating their political independence and thus to keep them economically dependent and securely in the world capitalist system. In the pure case of neo-colonialism, the allocation of economic resources, investment effort, legal and ideological structures, and other features of the old society remain unchanged—with the single exception of the substitution of "internal colonialism" for formal colonialism, that is, the transfer of power to the domestic ruling classes by their former colonial masters.[34] Independence has thus been achieved on conditions which are irrelevant to the basic needs of the society, and represents a part denial of real sovereignty, and a part continuation of disunity within the society. The most important branch of the theory of neo-colonialism is therefore the theory of economic imperialism.

The definition of economic imperialism which we employ is the economic domination of one region or country over another—specifically, the formal or informal control over local economic resources in a manner advantageous to the metropolitan power, and at the expense of the local economy. Economic control assumes different forms and is exercised in a number of ways. The main form of economic domination has always been control by the advanced capitalist countries over the liquid and real economic resources of economically backward areas. The main liquid resources are foreign exchange and public and private savings, and real resources consist of agricultural, mineral, transportation, communication, manufacturing, and commercial facilities and other assets. The most characteristic modes of domination today can be illuminated by way of contrast with examples drawn from the colonial period.

Examples of control over foreign exchange assets are numerous. In the colonial era the metropolitan powers established currency boards to issue and redeem local circulating medium against sterling and other metropolitan currencies. In its purest form, the currency board system required 100 percent backing of sterling for local currency. The East African Currency Board, for example, was established in 1919, staffed by British civil servants appointed by the Colonial Office, and at one time exercised financial domination over Ethiopia, British and Italian Somaliland, and Aden, as well as the East African countries.[35] The Board did not have the authority to expand or contract local credit, and therefore expenditures on local projects which required imported materials or machinery were limited to current export earnings, less outlays for essential consumer goods, debt service, and other fixed expenses. Measures to expand exports were thus necessary preconditions of local initiatives toward economic progress. In this way, British imperialism indirectly controlled the allocation of real resources.

This mode of control still survives in modified form in the Commonwealth Caribbean economies and elsewhere.[36] The Jamaican central bank, for example, has limited power to influence the domestic money supply, but sterling and local currency are automatically convertible in unlimited amounts at fixed rates of exchange. The local government is thus prohibited from financing investment projects by inflation, or forced savings; nor are exchange controls and related financial instruments of national economic policy permitted. The structure and organization of the commercial banking system aggravates the situation. Local banks are branches of foreign-owned banks whose headquarters are located in the overseas financial centers and are more responsive to economic and monetary changes abroad than in the local economy; specifically, local banks have contracted credit at times when foreign exchange assets have been accumulating. This combination of monetary and financial dependence has caused artificial shortages of funds and prevented the Jamaican government from allocating local financial resources in a rational manner.

A more characteristic form of control over foreign exchange today is private direct investment. In the nineteenth and early twentieth centuries, backward countries were often able to attract portfolio investments and local governments and capitalists were thus able to exercise some control over the use of foreign exchange made available by long-term foreign investment. Today direct investment constitutes the great mass of long-term capital exported on private account by the metropolitan countries. Foreign exchange receipts typically take the form of branch plants and other facilities of the multinational corporations—facilities which are difficult or impossible to integrate into the structure of the local economy. What is more, satellite countries which depend on direct investment ordinarily provide free currency convertibility and hence foreign-owned enterprises which produce for local markets have privileged access to foreign exchange earned in other sectors of the economy.

Another feature of economic domination is the control of local savings, which assumes two forms. First, economic rule means that local government revenues, or *public* savings, are mortgaged to loans received from the metropolitan powers. An extreme example is Liberia—a country with an open door policy with regard to foreign capital—which in 1963 expended 94 percent of its annual revenues to repay foreign loans.[37] In the nineteenth century, persuasion, coercion, and outright conquest often insured that tariffs and other taxes were turned over to foreign bond-holders. In the absence of direct colonial rule, however, foreign lending was frequently a precarious undertaking. Latin American countries, for example, had an uneven history of bond payments.[38] Foreign loans today are secured in more peaceful and more effective ways. The international capital market is highly centralized and dominated by the agencies of the main imperialist powers—the International Bank for Reconstruction and Development, the International Monetary Fund, and other financial institutions. No longer is it possible for borrowing countries to play one lending country off against another, or to default on their obligations or unilaterally scale down their debt without shutting the door on future loans. That no country has ever defaulted on a World Bank loan, or failed to amortize a loan on schedule, is eloquent testimony to the ability of the advanced capitalist countries to mortgage local tax receipts to foreign loans.

Secondly, *private* savings are mobilized by foreign corporations and governments in order to advance the interests of foreign capital. Foreign companies float local bond issues, raise equity capital, and generally attempt to monopolize available liquid resources in order to extend their field of operations and maximize profits. World Bank affiliates finance local development banks which scour the country for small and medium-size savings to funnel into local and foreign enterprise. The United States government acquires a significant portion of the money supply of India and other countries through its policy of selling surplus foodstuffs for local currencies which it makes available to United States corporations. In these and other ways foreign interests today exercise control of local private savings.

A final feature of economic domination is the control of mineral, agricultural, manufacturing, and other real assets, and the organization and management of trade by foreign corporations. In Africa, for example, French bulk-buying companies in the ex-colonies monopolize the purchase and sale of coffee, peanuts, palm-oil products, and other commodities produced by small and medium-sized growers. In Mexico, one foreign corporation organizes the great part of cotton production and exportation. Frequently control of commerce necessitates financial domination. The United States, for example, has penetrated Mexico's financial structure with the aim of restricting Mexican-Latin American trade in order to insure control of Latin American markets for itself.[39]

Control of iron, copper, tin, oil, bauxite, and other mineral resources is in the hands of a handful of giant corporations. In some countries, foreign interests dominate the commanding heights of the economy—transportation, power, communication, and the leading manufacturing industries. These examples should suffice to show that foreign control of real, as well as of liquid, assets extends into all branches of local economies and penetrates every economically backward region in the world capitalist system.

These examples of specific kinds of economic domination illustrate most of the main features of contemporary imperialism and can be summarized as follows:

(1) The further concentration and centralization of capital, and the integration of the world capitalist economy into the structures of the giant United States-based multinational corporations, or integrated conglomerate monopolistic enterprises; and the acceleration of technological change under the auspices of these corporations.

(2) The abandonment of the "free" international market, and the substitution of administered prices in commodity trade and investment; and the determination of profit margins through adjustments in the internal accounting schemes of the multinational corporations.

(3) The active participation of state capital in international investment; subsidies and guarantees to private investment; and a global foreign policy which corresponds to the global interests and perspective of the multinational corporation.

(4) The consolidation of an international ruling class constituted on the basis of ownership and control of the multinational corporations, and the concomitant decline of national rivalries initiated by the national power elites in the advanced capitalist countries; and the internationalization of the world capital market by the World Bank and other agencies of the international ruling class.

(5) The intensification of all of these tendencies arising from the threat of world socialism to the world capitalist system.

WHY IMPERIALISM?

The general features of contemporary imperialism are much better understood than the sources of economic expansion—the specific contradictions in the metropolitan economies which drive the multinational corporations to extend their scale of operations over the entire globe. As we have seen, Hobson explained nineteenth-century British imperialism by way of reference to inequalities in the distribution of income, while Lenin rested his case on the declining rate of profit in the home economy. Neither of these explanations is very useful today, at least in the form which they have come down to us. In the first place, the advanced capitalist economies have become mass consumption societies; secondly, savings have become concentrated in the hands of the government, financial intermediaries, and trust funds, as well as a relatively few giant corporations; thirdly, the concept of "the" rate of profit is out-of-date. In the overcrowded competitive sector of the advanced capitalist economies, the profit rate remains a datum, a given, but in the oligopolistic sector, profit margins are themselves determined by corporate price, output, and investment policies.

Economic Surplus

Some contemporary Marxist economists have proposed an alternative approach to the problem of identifying the important economic contradictions in advanced capitalist societies. These approaches are based on the elementary concept of economic surplus, which Baran and Sweezy define as the difference between total national product and socially necessary costs of production.[40] Total product is the aggregate value of all commodities and services produced in a given period of time, or, alternatively, total business, worker, and government expenditures. Nowhere in the literature is there a satisfactory discussion of the meaning of socially necessary costs. A working definition is the outlays which are required to maintain the labor force and society's productive capacity in their present state of productivity or efficiency.

Economic surplus consists of outlays which either augment productive capacity and increase labor skills and efficiency, or are used for economically wasteful or destructive ends. Any specific expenditure item which can be reallocated from one use to another without affecting total production (e.g., military expenditures to foreign gifts), falls into the general category of economic surplus. An expenditure item which cannot be reallocated from one employment to another (e.g., wages of workers in basic food industries to military expenditures), without reducing total production can be defined as a necessary cost. Unlike total output, neither necessary costs nor surplus is easily quantifiable, particularly since many outlays, highway expenditures for example, comprise both costs and surplus. Hence it is not possible to calculate with any great precision the proportion of total product which is constituted by surplus, nor can the relation between total product and surplus over a span of time be known with absolute certainty. Nevertheless, there is powerful indirect evidence that the surplus in relation to total product in the advanced capitalist countries tends to increase historically.

Provisionally identifying surplus with corporate profits, sales expenditures, and taxes, Baran and Sweezy demonstrate easily that corporate price and cost policies result in an absolute and relative increase in the surplus. In a nutshell, the corporations stabilize prices around an upward secular trend, while constantly seeking to increase efficiency by reducing production costs. Cost reductions are not transmitted to consumers in the form of lower prices, but rather are channeled into new investment, sales expenditures, and taxes.

The questions thus arise: What are the various ways available to advanced capitalist countries to absorb the increasing economic surplus, or raise the level of demand, and what are the limits on their absorptive capacity? These are obviously large and complex questions the answers to which we can do no more than suggest here.

Within the metropolitan economy the economic surplus is absorbed in three distinctive ways.[41] Expenditures on productive investment in both physical and human capital are the first, and historically most important, mode of surplus utilization. Investment outlays are made on both private and government account. In the private sector of the economy, investment opportunities are available in two distinct spheres: oligopolistic industries, dominated by the giant conglomerate corporation, and competitive industries, characterized by relatively inefficient, small-scale enterprise. In the former, technological change, which was at one time the most important outlet for investment-seeking funds, no longer can be relied upon to absorb more than a tiny fraction of the surplus. In the first place, in the few older, stabilized industries where competition between firms for larger shares of the market is at a minimum, there is a tendency to suppress new technologies in order to preserve the value of the existing productive capacity. There is, in Dobb's words, "an increasing danger of the ossification of an existing industrial structure owing to the reluctance or inability of entrepreneurs to face the cost and the risks attendant upon such large-scale change."[42]

Secondly, Baran and Sweezy have shown that in industries in which firms struggle to increase their share of the market and hence are under considerable pressure to lower costs, the rate of introduction of new technology is reduced, thus limiting the amount of investment-seeking funds which can be profitably absorbed during any given period. Lastly, as Gillman and others have demonstrated, there has been a historic rise in fixed capital stock per employed worker, and a decline in business fixed investment and producer durable equipment expenditures in relation to total national product. Thus technological change—independent of the rate at which it is introduced into the production processes—tends increasingly to be capital-saving.[43] To put it another way, oligopolistic enterprises favor input-saving, rather than output-increasing innovations when (and if) the industrial structure becomes relatively stabilized and a provisional market-sharing plan has been agreed upon. For their part, competitive industries are overcrowded, the turnover rate is high, profit margins are minimal, and they offer few incentives to corporations with investment-seeking funds.

Productive investment outlays are also made on government or state account, but most of these are merely special forms of private investment and hence are determined by the rhythm of capital accumulation in the private sector. The costs of these complementary investments—water investments in agricultural districts, for example—are borne by the taxpayer, while the benefits are appropriated by private capitalists. The state also finances investments which aim to create future profitable opportunities for private capital—examples are industrial development parks—but these discretionary investments are limited by the need on the part of the state bureaucracy to justify the extra tax burden (due to the absence of long-term investment horizons generally shared by capitalist class and state officials), as well as by the lack of new markets for final commodities.

Expenditures on private and social consumption over and above economic needs, or in excess of outlays on necessary costs, constitute the second mode of surplus utilization. These expenditures, like all economically wasteful outlays, are limited to the degree that they can be rationalized within the logic of capitalist economy—that is to say, insofar as they lead to greater profits. The proportion of current earnings which the corporation can channel into advertising expenditures, product differentiation, forced obsolescence, and other selling expenses, as well as other socially wasteful uses of the surplus, is limited to the extent to which these outlays increase commodity demand, sales, and profits. There are also limits on the absorption of the surplus via borrowing private consumption demand from the future—that is, by the expansion of consumer credit—which are determined by the relation of current consumer income to loan repayments.[44]

Consumption outlays are also made by local, state, and federal government bodies. A greater or lesser portion of education, transportation, recreational, and cultural expenditures—in general, spending on social amenities—constitutes social consumption, a special form of private consumption. Socially necessary costs make up a large part of social consumption, while much of the remainder comprises economic waste. Again, government expenditures are limited by the ability of the political authority to rationalize waste within the framework of private profit-making. In addition, there are political limits on the expansion of spending destined for public housing, health, and other socioeconomic activities which are inconsistent with the hierarchy of rank and privileges in a capitalist society, or which compete with private capital. The same conclusion can be drawn in connection with the possibilities of re-distributing income with the aim of raising the wage and salary share of total product—and hence private consumption expenditures—at the expense of private profits. The only major type of discretionary state expenditure consistent with private ownership of the means of production, social and economic inequality, and other central features of a capitalist society is military spending.

Imperialism as a Use of Surplus

The preceding sketch in no sense substitutes for a full-dress analysis of the surplus absorption capacity of the advanced capitalist countries, in particular the United States, but rather provides a general background for the detailed exploration of the possibilities of utilizing the economic surplus in the backward capitalist countries and the other advanced capitalist societies. Our general conclusions are twofold: First, the multinational corporations are under unceasing pressure to extend their field of operations outside the United States. Economic prosperity in the United States during the two decades since World War II has increasingly depended on military expenditures and overseas expansion. Between 1950 and 1964, United States commodity exports, including the sales of overseas facilities of United States corporations, rose nearly 270 percent, while commodity sales at home increased only 126 percent. Expectedly, earnings on foreign investments make up a rising portion of after-tax corporate profits—10 percent in 1950, and 22 percent in 1964. In the strategic capital goods sector of the United States economy, military and foreign purchases account for a surprisingly large share of total output—between 20 and 50 percent in 21 of 25 industries, and over 80 percent in two industries.[45] Our second general conclusion is that overseas expansion since World War II has not weakened, but intensified the antagonism between the generation and absorption of the economic surplus.

Close examination of the two modes of surplus utilization overseas is required to substantiate these claims. Foreign commodity trade is the first, and, until the era of monopoly capitalism, the only important way of absorbing the surplus abroad. Contemporary state policies which seek to promote commodity trade encounter a number of crippling handicaps. For one thing, low-cost supplier credits and other forms of export subsidies provided by state agencies such as the Import-Export Bank merely export the surplus absorption problem abroad and hence meet with resistance from other advanced capitalist countries. A comprehensive system of export subsidies is almost guaranteed to result in retaliation in kind. The widely adopted "most favored nation" clause in international trade agreements was an expression of the willingness to "give and take" on the part of the advanced capitalist countries in the immediate postwar period. Second, in recent decades United States commodity exports have run consistently ahead of imports, limiting the ability of the United States to wring tariff concessions from other countries without offering even greater reductions in return. Third, United States penetration of Europe, regions in the sphere of influence of the European imperialist powers, and the semi-independent backward capitalist countries which employ tariffs, import quotas, and exchange controls to conserve foreign exchange by reducing imports is increasingly restricted by a revival of economic nationalism, as well as by the birth of a new economic regionalism—that is, by what Joan Robinson has termed the New Mercantilism.

Private foreign investments and state loans and grants constitute the second, and today far and away the most important, mode of surplus absorption. Capital exports may increase demand in one of two ways: first, by borrowing demand from the future and directly expanding the market for capital goods; second, by raising production and income abroad and therefore indirectly increasing imports in the recipient country or in third countries.

In recent years there have been three new tendencies in capital exporting which support the conclusion that it will become increasingly difficult to find outlets abroad for the investment-seeking surplus generated by the multinational corporations. These tendencies are: first, increased collaboration between foreign and local capital; second, the shift in the composition of foreign investments against primary commodity sectors and in favor of manufacturing and related activities; and third, the shift in the composition of capital exports against private investment and in favor of state loans and grants. All three tendencies are related to the development of anticolonial and national independence movements in the backward capitalist countries. A brief review of the general implications of national independence for foreign investment opportunities is therefore in order.

Political Independence and Foreign Capital

Gillman and others have put forward two arguments which support the view that national independence reduces opportunities for the penetration of foreign capital. In the first place, it is asserted that public ownership of the means of production in the ex-colonies encroaches on the traditional territory of private capital and limits investment opportunities available to the international monopolies. This line of reasoning is not only at odds with the facts—in the backward capitalist countries joint state-private ventures are more characteristic than state enterprise—but also pushes aside the critical question of the control of capital. In a number of countries, including many European capitalist nations, the state is the nominal owner of many heavy industrial and infrastructure facilities, but control rests with an autonomous bureaucracy which is highly responsive to the needs of private capital. The vast majority of state and joint enterprises in the backward countries are market-oriented, integrated into the structure of the private market. Far from discouraging foreign investors, one task of state enterprise in many countries is to attract new private investment.

Secondly, there is the argument that anticolonial sentiment and the urge for an independent field of economic action lead to exchange controls, restrictions on profit remittances, higher business taxes, more costly social legislation, and other policies which are repugnant to foreign capital. Against this view it should be stressed that the economic autonomy of politically independent countries is itself a question for analysis. Military coups in Brazil, Indonesia, and Ghana, to cite only three recent counterrevolutionary movements, provide dramatic evidence for the view that political autonomy must be insured by economic autonomy. Again, seven long-independent Latin American countries with such disparate attitudes toward foreign capital as Chile and Peru—historically the former has been less permissive than the latter—collectively signed the Treaty of Montevideo (1960) which favored foreign investment, and recognized the need for foreign capital in economic development.[46] On the other side China, Cuba, and other countries which have abandoned the world capitalist system obviously hold little promise for foreign capital.

In reality, there are a number of reasons to believe that politically independent, economically underexploited countries will continue to welcome private foreign capital. First, and perhaps most important, local financiers and industrialists are eager to participate in profitable economic activities initiated by the multinational corporations based in the advanced countries. Joint ventures and other partnership arrangements are looked upon with great favor by local business interests.[47] Tariff policy is designed to encourage assembly, packaging, and other final manufacturing investments, not only to promote the development of national industry but also to increase the flow of foreign capital and open up profit opportunities for the local bourgeoisie.

Secondly, the Latin American countries, as well as the ex-colonies in Asia and Africa, are under great pressure from the masses to initiate and promote economic and social development. In these nonsocialist countries local sources of capital are dissipated in luxury consumption and other wasteful expenditures, or cannot be mobilized in the absence of fundamental agrarian and other economic reforms, and hence local governments increasingly depend on foreign capital, private as well as public. Most ex-colonial governments are desperately searching for ways to conserve foreign exchange and actively seek foreign investments and loans. Third, British and French foreign investments are welcome in backward countries which belong to one or the other of these metropoles' currency blocs—where exchange controls are minimal or entirely absent— because there are few if any ways to acquire private foreign capital from other advanced capitalist countries. British investments, for example, are more and more oriented to Sterling Area countries.[48] Fourth, backward countries which have no ambition beyond expanding exports of primary commodities require active foreign participation in the export sector because of the difficulties of independently acquiring and maintaining distribution channels and marketing outlets. After Bolivia nationalized the tin mines, for example, planning of production and sales was partly thwarted because the government "remained beholden to the same big companies for processing and sale."[49]

On the other side, there are at least two reasons for believing that political independence has discouraged some foreign investment, although it is difficult to even guess how much. In the first place, foreign corporations hesitate to invest in the absence of political controls which prevent local firms from using unpatented production processes to invade third-country markets or to pass on to competitors.[50] Second, the ex-colonies have eliminated or reduced in many spheres of the economy the special privileges and exclusive rights which corporations based in the colonial power once took for granted. The increased risk and uncertainty which face foreign capital have discouraged investments by small-scale enterprises which are unable to finance multi-plant, multi-country operations.[51]

The Reduction of Surplus Absorption Capacity: Use of Local Savings

Anticolonialism, political independence, and the elimination of the colonial powers from many formal economic command posts have contributed to three new tendencies in foreign investment which reduce the surplus absorption capacity of the backward capitalist countries. There is overwhelming evidence of the first tendency, the growing mobilization of local savings and capital by foreign corporations which diminishes the need for capital exports from the advanced countries. In Latin America, local capital is the most important source of financing for wholly owned subsidiaries of United States corporations.[52] One-half of American and Foreign Power Company's $400 million postwar expansion program in eleven countries was financed from local savings, the other half from retained earnings.[53] A $72-million investment in Argentina by five oil companies illustrates the character of modern overseas finance; the corporations' investment amounted to only $18 million; debentures raised $30 million in Argentina; and the United States government and local investment corporations supplied the remainder.[54]

In the capitalist world as a whole, roughly one-third of total U.S. corporate financing overseas in 1964 comprised foreign borrowing or equity financing, and foreign supplies of capital made up two-thirds of the increase in financing over 1963 levels.[55]

The multinational corporations mobilize local savings and capital in a variety of ways: bonds and equities are sold in local capital markets; joint ventures and mixed enterprises mobilize private and state capital, respectively; local development and investment banks acquire local savings directly, and indirectly via local governments;[56] foreign and domestic banks, insurance companies, and other financial intermediaries have access to pools of local savings. To cite one example, Morgan Guarantee Trust Company's sixteen correspondent banks in Venezuela hold 55 percent of privately owned commercial bank resources, and help foreign firms raise local funds. Morgan is also part owner of a large Spanish investment bank which in a two-year period raised $40 million for local and foreign companies.[57] The World Bank pioneered in the organization and contributes to the financing of local development banks, develops and integrates capital markets in countries where monetary institutions are weak, and acts as a wedge for private foreign capital's entrance into established capital markets.[58]

The growing demand by the international monopolies for local capital is prompted by both political and economic factors. First, and probably most important, both the multinational corporations and local bourgeoisies are eager to form partnership arrangements, the former to exercise indirect control over, and politically neutralize, the latter; the latter in order to share in the profits of the former.[59] In Nigeria, for example, "foreign investors are beginning to realize that their presence constitutes a political problem and that it is in their interest to encourage Nigerian participation in the structure of their firms to enhance acceptability."[60] Joint ventures and partnerships are up-to-date versions of the colonial policy of creating a dependent, passive local bourgeoisie; British capital, to cite perhaps the most important instance, allied itself with the largest and best-organized Indian monopolies, such as those dominated by the Tatas and Birlas, as a hedge against possible discriminatory action by the Indian government.[61]

Second, the alliance between foreign and local capital inhibits potential economic competition and paves the way for the diversification of the foreign operations of the international monopolies, and extends their control over related product fields in the local economy.[62] Even in countries such as Mexico, where the government refuses to extend its cooperation to foreign corporations which compete with local business or displace local capital, foreigners often have "decisive influence" over company policy because domestic equity ownership is dispersed and minority stock ownership is concentrated in the hands of one or two United States corporations.[63] Extending the sphere of corporate operations opens up opportunities for increased profits in the form of royalties and fees for technical services, patents, and brand names. What is more, the use of local capital reduces the risk of conducting operations in foreign countries; local capital is smaller and less diversified than foreign capital and therefore is more vulnerable and assumes a disproportionate risk. In addition, local businessmen are valuable for their knowledge of domestic product and labor markets, government contacts, and other information which insures secure and profitable operations overseas. Finally, the international monopolies profit by spreading their capital thin in branches of production characterized by economies of large-scale production.

Growth of Investment in Manufacturing

The growth of private foreign investment in manufacturing industries, and the relative decline of agricultural and mining investments, is the second new tendency in capital exporting. The development of synthetic fibers, the rise in agricultural productivity in the advanced countries, the inelastic demand for foodstuffs, the reduction in the mineral component in production (e.g., nonferrous metals), and tariff walls erected by the advanced capitalist countries against imports of primary commodities have reduced the demand for investment funds abroad in mining and agriculture. Tariffs, quotas, and other measures to protect manufacturing industries in the backward countries and regional marketing arrangements in Europe and elsewhere have compelled the large corporations in the United States to construct or purchase manufacturing facilities abroad to retain traditional markets. In turn, the expansive impulses of the multinational corporation have affected worldwide capital flows and the production and distribution of commodities.

Accurate comparable statistics covering long spans of time are not available, but the benchmark data shown in Table I below suggest the general order of magnitude of change.

Table I
Book Value of United States Direct Foreign Investment by Industry
(*millions of dollars*)

	1929	1940	1946	1950	1955	1959
Total	7,528	7,002	8,854	11,787	19,313	29,735
Agriculture	880	435	545	589	725	662
Mining and smelting	1,185	782	1,062	1,129	2,209	2,858
Petroleum	1,117	1,278	1,769	3,390	5,849	10,423
Manufacturing	1,813	1,926	2,854	3,831	6,349	9,692
Public utilities, comm. & transportation	1,610	1,514	1,277	1,425	1,614	2,413
Trade	368	523	740	762	1,282	2,039
Other (excludes insurance in 1929)	555	544	607	661	1,285	1,648

Source: Raymond Mikesell, "U.S. Postwar Investment Abroad: A Statistical Analysis," in Mikesell, *U.S. Government and Private Investment Abroad*, p. 54, citing U.S. Department of Commerce, Office of Business Economics, *Balance of Payments Statistical Supplement;* U.S. Department of Commerce, *U.S. Business Investments in Foreign Countries, 1960* (for 1959 figures); *Survey of Current Business* (December 1951), p. 13 (for 1946 figures).

Between 1940 and 1964 United States direct manufacturing investments in Latin America (which absorb about 60 percent of U.S. manufacturing investments in all backward regions) increased from $210 million to $2,340 million, or from 10 percent to 25 percent of total Latin American holdings. In the same period, agricultural investments remained unchanged, mining investments doubled, and the value of petroleum holdings rose from $572 million to $3,142 million. A similar trend is visible in connection with British investments in India. In 1911, about three-quarters of all direct private investments were in extractive industries, utilities and transportation accounted for roughly one-fifth, and the remainder was divided between commerce and manufacturing. In 1956, manufacturing investments made up over one-third of the total, commerce another one-fourth, and plantation investments only one-fifth. As Hamza Alavi has written, "this is a complete contrast from the old pattern" of investment holdings.[64] Of all British direct foreign investments (excluding oil) in 1965, Kemp has estimated that manufacturing investments constituted about one-half, the great part located in other advanced capitalist countries.[65]

Turning again to the United States, Table II below summarizes the distribution of direct investments by region and industry in 1964.

Table II
Value of Direct Investments Abroad by Region and Industry, 1964 (preliminary)
(millions of dollars)

	Total	Mining smelt.	Petro-leum	Manuf.	Pub. util.	Trade	Other
Total	44,343	3,564	14,350	16,861	2,023	3,735	3,808
Canada	13,820	1,671	3,228	6,191	467	805	1,458
Latin America	8,932	1,098	3,142	2,340	568	951	832
Other Western Hemisphere	1,386	250	569	166	49	89	263
Common Market	5,398	13	1,511	3,098	45	551	180
Other Europe	6,669	43	1,575	3,449	8	921	674
Africa	1,629	356	830	225	2	93	122
Asia	3,062	34	2,014	535	55	238	186
Oceania	1,582	100	444	856	2	87	93
International	1,865	—	1,038	—	827	—	—

Source: U.S. Dept. of Commerce, *Survey of Current Business* (September 1965), Table 2, p. 22.

Most United States manufacturing investments in backward countries are concentrated in consumer goods fabrication, assembly and packaging, and light chemicals. The pattern is roughly the same in the advanced capitalist economies, with the single exception that investments in industrial equipment facilities are more common. During 1958-1959, of 164 U.S. investments in new or expanded manufacturing enterprises in Latin America, 106 were located in the chemical and consumer goods sectors; in other backward regions, the number of facilities were 34 and 24, respectively.[66]

In connection with opportunities for capital exporting, and the significance of capital exports for absorbing the economic surplus, nineteenth-century and mid-twentieth-century imperialism differ in a number of profound respects. In the earlier period, foreign investments were concentrated in raw material and mineral production, and the economic satellites were no more than extensions of the metropolitan economies. Overseas capital expenditures opened up cheap sources of productive inputs, and lowered the costs of production in manufacturing industries in the metropoles. In turn, home and foreign demand for manufactured goods increased, prompting an expansion of output and fresh rounds of foreign investment. To the degree that capital exports were channeled into railroad and other transportation facilities, there were favorable indirect effects on the availability of raw materials, and hence manufacturing costs in the metropoles. For nineteenth-century Great Britain, this cumulative, expansive system worked to perfection. Income generated in the satellites by the inflow of capital was expended on British manufactured exports. During periods of rising foreign investment, British exports rose faster than imports, and a consistently favorable balance of payments was maintained.[67]

To be sure, contemporary imperialist powers continue to import many raw materials, and petroleum needs expand at a rapid pace. The economic relationships between the metropolitan economies and their satellites, however, differ in important respects. Petroleum production is concentrated in the hands of a few oligopolists which maintain rigid price structures and fail to pass on reductions in exploration, drilling, and production costs to consumers. The same conclusion can be drawn with regard to other raw materials (iron and copper, for example) for which the ratio of imports to U.S. production is higher than in the prewar era. Moreover, in comparison with other regions, imports have increased more rapidly from Latin American countries, which have met the expansion of demand for copper, tin, manganese, cocoa, and other commodities largely by diverting sales from other markets, rather than by expanding supplies. The basic reason is that Latin American raw material production is today highly monopolized, and, in addition, operates under conditions of decreasing returns to large-scale production. Thus neither new capital outlays nor modernization investments have significantly reduced the costs of production of primary commodities, and, unlike investments in the earlier period, are not self-perpetuating. What is more, international commodity agreements and regional marketing arrangements reduce competition between raw material producing countries, and tend to maintain prices at relatively high levels.

Manufacturing investments in backward countries fall into one of two categories. Tariff-hopping investments, quantitatively most significant, are defensive moves which enable the international corporations to retain established export markets, and merely change the locale of investment from the metropolis to the satellite. These outlays fail to expand commodity demand, and hence do not provide growing outlets for the economic surplus. Opportunities for other manufacturing investments in backward countries are also generally limited to import-substitute activities because domestic markets are typically oriented toward middle- and upper-class consumption patterns which are imitative of those in the advanced countries. Export markets for satellite manufactured goods are weak because national and regional monopolies operate behind high tariff walls, and, in addition, monopoly controls which the multinational corporations exercise over international distribution systems and marketing outlets place insurmountable barriers to large-scale satellite manufacturing exports. For these reasons, the United States has shown a growing interest in new regional marketing groupings such as the Latin American Free Trade Area and the Central American Common Market. One of the chief objectives of the Common Market during its formative period (1958-1962) was to attract fresh supplies of foreign capital. There are two important barriers, however, to flourishing regional marketing arrangements in economically backward areas. First, less productive, entrenched local monopolies put up a tenacious struggle to retain their privileged market positions—in comparison with the giant, integrated European cartels and monopolies which promoted the European Common Market. Secondly, the new preferential trading areas in backward regions are too small to compete effectively with Britain's Sterling Area or the European Economic Community. In sharp contrast to the upsurge of United States investment in Canada after the expansion of the Imperial Preference System in 1932, to cite one example, dollar flows of fresh investment to the new trading areas will be limited.[68]

We have finally to consider opportunities for manufacturing investments in other advanced economies. As we have seen, in recent years the great mass of United States manufacturing investments have been in Europe and Canada. Most of these investments have been tariff-hopping operations, or have been channeled into the purchase of existing facilities. Moreover, United States corporations have increasingly been compelled to penetrate lines of production which are competitive with United States exports. Similar to the effect of British reconstruction investments in Europe following World War I, United States capital flows to other advanced capitalist countries tend to be self-defeating in the long run. An excellent illustration is provided by one study of the impact of 112 British subsidiary companies in Europe on British exports; only 5.6 percent of the subsidiaries' capital outlays was expended on British capital goods.[69] Only investments in distribution facilities, specifically motivated to expand foreign sales, can be expected to significantly increase commodity exports.

These lines of analysis suggest that the surplus absorption capacity of both the advanced and backward countries—in both traditional and newer branches of the economy—will in the future be limited to replacement demand, together with the modest flow of new investments necessary to keep pace with expanding incomes abroad. Reflecting the marginal impact of foreign investments on United States commodity exports is the continuing, although muted, crisis in the United States' balance of payments.

State Loans Replace Private Loans

Roughly the same conclusion can be drawn in connection with public and international loans. The third, and perhaps most striking, tendency in capital exporting is the substitution of state loans for private capital outflows. About two-thirds of all capital exports are on state or international (public) account. As Table III shows, nearly three-quarters of all loans and investments destined for backward capitalist countries originate in the public or international sector. In 1964, the net outflow of resources to satellite countries and multinational agencies (which in turn loan funds to the satellites) amounted to nearly $8 billion, of which less than $2 billion was private.

Table III
Net Outflow of Resources to Backward Countries and Multinational Agencies, 1964
(*millions of dollars*)

		State Flows			Private Flows	
	Total	Total	Bilateral	Multi-lateral agencies	Total	Bilateral	Multi-lateral agencies
1960	7,177	4,572	3,982	590	2,605	2,420	185
1961	8,109	5,617	4,803	814	2,492	2,390	102
1962	7,533	5,676	5,031	645	1,857	1,627	230
1963	7,351	5,704	5,294	410	1,647	1,685	−38
1964	7,854	5,698	5,271	427	2,156	1,999	157

Source: United Nations, Department of Economic and Social Affairs, *The Financing of Economic Development, World Economic Survey, 1956*, Part I, New York, 1966, Table II-1, p. 45.

The relationship between private and public capital flows is highly complex, and a brief analysis inevitably runs the risk of oversimplification. Reduced to essentials, however, state loans serve two main purposes.

First, public funds which build up the infrastructure of backward countries frequently complement private capital flows and represent merely a special form of private investment, the costs of which are borne by taxpayers in the lending country. With regard to surplus absorption capacity within the infrastructure sectors of backward countries, the same conclusion reached in our discussion of private investment can be applied *a fortiori*.

Second, the character of U.S. "aid" programs underlines their growing importance as projected points of entry for private capital. Many Export-Import Bank loans are made with the purpose of encouraging the flow of private investment—since 1960 the Bank has offered long-term loans of up to five years.[70] Provisions of Public Law 480, the "Food for Peace" program, are "designed almost entirely for the purpose of stimulating the flow of U.S. private investment to the less-developed countries."[71] Under this program, the United States government loans local currencies acquired from the sale of surplus agricultural commodities to American corporations in order to finance the local costs of investment projects. The greatest portion of both the interest and principal is reloaned either to private investors or local governments. "How useful to our own foreign aid and foreign development programs could it be," the president of one multinational corporation has written, "if these funds, in local currencies, were to be loaned on an increasing scale to competitive private borrowers—either Americans or others—for local investment . . ."[72] Finally, the United States Agency for International Development grants survey loans to American corporations, paying one-half of the cost of feasibility studies in the event it is decided not to proceed with the investment.

The international agencies, in particular the World Bank, are also beacon lights for private investment. Originally regarded by the leading imperialist nations as a way to restore private international capital movements by guaranteeing private loans, the World Bank has been compelled to centralize and rationalize the world capital market. The Bank has eliminated many of the anarchic features of international capital movements, supervises vast amounts of capital which penetrates the backward countries, and acts as a funnel for private capital in search of safe, profitable returns—banks and investment houses participate in World Bank loans, and the Bank frequently floats bond issues in United States and European money markets. In part dependent on private

money market conditions, most Bank activities are financed by sub-
scribed or borrowed government funds. The Bank is thus relatively autonomous, and allocates vast amounts of capital for large-scale infrastructure projects in order to clear the way for private investment flows.

MODERN IMPERIALISM'S FOREIGN POLICY

Whether or not private capital responds to the incentives held out by
national governments and international agencies depends on a host of
factors, chief among which are the investment "climate" in the satellite
economies and the character of other state political-economic policies.
Suffice it for now to note some of the major differences between imperialist foreign policy in the nineteenth and mid-twentieth centuries.

First, and most obvious, modern imperialism attempts to substitute
informal for formal modes of political control of countries in the backwash
of world capitalism. The methods of establishing political control are
varied. The use of old economic and political ties is practiced whenever
possible; these include the relationships formed within the British
Commonwealth and the French Community, closed currency zones,
preferential trading systems, military alliances, and political-military
pacts. Economic, political, and cultural missions, labor union delegations,
joint military training programs, military grants, bribes to local ruling
classes in the form of economic "aid," substitute for direct colonial rule.
Only when indirect policies fail are the older instruments of coercion and
force brought into play, and the principle of continuity in change applies.
An excellent example is the U.S.-instigated and supported counter-
revolution in Guatemala in 1954, the accomplishments of which the
State Department listed under four headings:

1. "The conclusion of an agreement with a United Fruit Company subsidiary
   providing for the return of property expropriated by the Arbenz Government."
2. "The repeal of the law affecting remittances and taxation of earnings from
   foreign capital."
3. "The signing of an Investment Guarantee Agreement with the United
   States."
4. "The promulgation of a new and more favorable petroleum law."[73]

Within Guatemala, the Armas regime in the post-1954 period was maintained in office via contracts with United Fruit, Bond and Share, and other monopolies.[74]

Secondly, contemporary imperialist states enjoy relatively more financial, and hence political, autonomy. In the nineteenth century, imperialist countries regarded themselves as dependent on the private capital market for raising funds for discretionary state expenditures and were compelled to pursue economic and fiscal policies designed to make it possible for their colonies to meet their private debt service. The dominant state capitalist countries today are financially independent and can follow a more flexible policy toward their satellites. The reason is that both the potential and actual economic surplus are comparatively large. The potential surplus is large because the normal tendency of monopoly capitalist economies is stagnation and unemployment of labor and capital, attributable to a deficiency of aggregate demand. State expenditures—including military expenditures and foreign loans and grants—normally increase not only aggregate demand but also real income and output, and hence the tax base. A rise in expenditures thus increases revenues, even if tax rates remain unchanged. State expenditures are partly self-financing and virtually costless in terms of the real resources utilized. The actual economic surplus constitutes a relatively large portion of national product because of technological and productivity advances. For these reasons, taxes (and state expenditures) make up a large share of national product with few serious adverse effects on economic incentives, and thus on total production itself.

The significance of the financial independence of the contemporary imperialist state for foreign policy lies in its ability to export capital—or absorb the surplus overseas—without a quid pro quo. The Marshall Plan, the extensive program of military aid and grants, and the low-cost loans extended to backward countries by AID are the main examples of this mode of surplus absorption. The surplus absorption capacity of satellite countries which are closely tied to the United States' political-military bloc is for practical purposes unlimited. Two factors, however, circumscribe state grants without a quid pro quo. First, low-cost state loans and grants-in-aid, or capital exports which are not extended on normal commercial principles, compete "unfairly" with private loans and are resisted by private capitalist interests in the metropolitan economy. Second, metropolitan governments are unable to discipline their satellites effectively unless there are economic strings attached to international loans. Moreover, state bilateral and multilateral loans financed in private capital markets in the advanced countries must earn a return sufficient to cover the cost of borrowing and administration. Opportunities for capital exports extended on commercial principles are limited by the availability of profitable investment projects.

Nineteenth- and mid-twentieth-century imperialism depart in a third important respect. In the nineteenth century there were few important antagonisms between Great Britain's role as the leading national capitalist power on the one hand, and as the dominant imperialist power on the other. Policies designed to expand Britain's home economy extended capitalist modes of production and organization to the three underexploited continents, directly and indirectly strengthening the growing British imperial system.[75] For this reason, foreign policy ordinarily served private foreign investors and other private interests oriented to overseas activity. Only occasionally—as in the case of Disraeli's decision to purchase Suez Canal shares in 1875[76]—was foreign investment employed as a "weapon" of British foreign policy. Even less frequently did Britain promote private foreign investments with the purpose of aiding global foreign policy objectives.[77]

By way of contrast, the national and international ambitions of the United States in the mid-twentieth century are continually in conflict. In the context of the limited absorption capacity of the backward capitalist world and international competition from other advanced capitalist economies and the socialist countries, the United States is compelled to employ a wide range of policies to expand trade and investment. To further national ends, a "partnership" between "public lending institutions" and "private lenders"—with the former "leading the way" for the latter—has been formed.[78] Underlining the role of the state in the service of the multinational corporations, in 1962 Secretary of State Rusk described the newer government policies which extend beyond state loan programs; investment guarantee programs in forty-six backward capitalist countries which cover currency inconvertibility, expropriation, war, revolution, and insurrection; instructions to local embassies to support business interests by making "necessary representations to the host governments . . ."; the creation of a new Special Assistant for International Business in the State Department in order to insure that private business interests receive "prompt representation" in the government.[79] Especially in the case of disguised public loans or special forms of private loans (see above), the commitment of the United States government to national capitalist interests inhibits state policies which seek to strengthen the industrial bourgeoisie and ruling classes in other advanced countries and the national bourgeoisie in the backward nations. Perhaps this is the most important limit on capital exports on public account.

As the leading international power, the United States is under constant and growing pressure to strengthen world capitalism as a system, including each of its specific parts. Policies which aim to recruit new members for local comprador groups, stimulate the development of capitalist agriculture and the middle farmers, reinforce the dominance of local financial and commercial classes, and reinvigorate local manufacturing activities—these general policies pose a potential or real threat to the interests of United States' national capital. Alliance for Progress funds destined for the middle sectors of Latin American agriculture, Export-Import Bank loans to foreign commercialists, loans and grants to foreign governments dominated by the urban bourgeoisie, loans and subsidies to the Indian iron and steel industry, Mexican industry and agriculture, and other branches of production in countries which are slowly industrializing—these and other stopgap and long-range measures help to keep the backward countries in the imperialist camp in the short run, but directly or indirectly create local capitalist interests which may demand their independence from United States' capital in the long run.

United States' private capital increasingly requires the aid of the state, and the state enlists more and more private and public capital in its crusade to maintain world capitalism intact. Specific and general capitalist interests serve each other, finally merging into one phenomenon, a certain oneness emerges between them. This must have, finally, its institutional reflection. The multinational corporation has become the instrument for the creation and consolidation of an international ruling class, the only hope for reconciling the antagonisms between national and international interests.

SURPLUS ABSORPTION OR SURPLUS CREATION?

The preceding analysis supports the conclusion that the surplus absorption capacity of the backward countries, and, probably to a lesser degree, the other advanced economies, and hence opportunities for utilizing investment-seeking funds overseas, are circumscribed in a variety of ways. Opportunities for "enterprise," or profit-making, however, show few signs of weakening. We have touched on some of the reasons. First, the multinational corporations increasingly mobilize and utilize local and state savings and capital, undertake more ambitious investment projects, and profit from economies of large-scale production and more efficient intracorporate planning. Second, a larger share of the retained earnings of corporation branch plants and subsidiaries is absorbed by modernization investments, which reduce costs and raise profits. Third, the multinational corporations monopolize patents, brand names, and production processes in the greatest demand, and are able to establish control over national and international markets via licensing and similar agreements which require relatively small capital outlays. Fourth, the giant international corporations are more and more integrated and diversified, and production and sales are subject to less risk and uncertainty. Lastly, the international monopolies can count on the active participation and aid of the state.

For these reasons, the multinational corporations command growing profit margins on their overseas operations. Small amounts of capital are sufficient to penetrate, control, and dominate the weaker, less productive national economies. The price of disposing of a given amount of economic surplus this year is the creation of even more surplus next year—hardly a high price for the individual corporation to pay, but from the standpoint of the metropolitan economy as a whole, the problem of surplus absorption becomes increasingly severe.

The United States government, the European powers, and the United States-dominated international agencies are thus under growing pressure by the international monopolies to formulate and implement political-economic policies which will create an "attractive" investment climate abroad, in particular in the underexploited countries. Looked at from another angle, the imperialist powers are increasingly compelled to "promote economic development" overseas or, to put it differently, to integrate the backward areas even more closely into the structure of world capitalism. In effect, the advanced countries are desperately seeking to expand outlets for the economic surplus. To be sure, the imperialist powers view the problem as one of surplus creation (or profit-realization), rather than of surplus absorption—their line of vision generally corresponds in this respect with the perspective of the corporations themselves.

These are merely different sides to the same coin: by promoting profitable opportunities abroad for private capital, the state lays the basis for the absorption of a portion of this year's surplus, and, simultaneously, for the creation of additional surplus next year.

For U.S. economic, political, and foreign policy this line of analysis has a number of important consequences. In the first place, national economic development programs in the backward countries which seek the participation of the socialist countries and other advanced capitalist countries have been and will continue to be opposed by the United States. Secondly, investments in lines of industry which are noncompetitive with U.S. products, especially those which increase demand for these products, have been and will continue to be encouraged.

Thirdly, the participation of U.S. capital in the European economy (as well as the participation of European capital in the backward countries) will increasingly be discouraged because these investments will eventually compete with U.S. commodity exports. Fourth, the United States will continue to initiate anti-socialist, anti-communist military and political pacts and alliances with both backward and advanced capitalist countries— for the international monopolies the basic importance of state loans and aid lies in the long-run impact on the demand for arms, capital equipment, and consumer goods in those satellites which have developed intimate political and military bonds with the United States.

More generally, because the expansion of commodity exports, as well as capital exports, generates even more surplus in the future—because the process of surplus creation and absorption is a cumulative one—the United States is increasingly compelled to follow the policies of a militant, expansive imperialist power, all in the name of economic development for the underdeveloped countries. The task facing the United States in relation to the backward countries is truly Herculean.

At one and the same time, the United States must convince the backward countries that the growing penetration of U.S. capital, and the growing control of the multinational companies over local economies, are useful and necessary for their economic growth and development, at a time when politically oppressive policies which aim to create more favorable conditions for private investment are followed. Thus economic development is oriented by the multinational companies, and where there are national development plans which on paper assign a certain limited role to private investment, in fact private investment assigns a role to the plan. The underdeveloped world becomes bound up even more closely in a new imperialist system in which investments in consumer goods industries replace investments in raw materials and minerals; in which the backward countries are compelled to deal with a unified private capital-state capital axis; in which political control by the World Bank and the other international agencies, together with the political arm of the official labor movement, the giant foundations, and other quasi-private political agencies, replace colonial rule; and in which the national middle classes in the underdeveloped countries are slowly but surely transformed into a new class of clients and compradors, in every important respect equivalent to the old class of traders, bankers, and landlords which for centuries bowed and scraped before their imperial rulers in China, India, Latin America, and elsewhere. A new era of imperialism is just beginning, an era which holds out contradictory promises to the imperial powers and their clusters of satellites. Whether or not the advanced capitalist countries can deal with this crisis of their own making depends on two basic factors: first, the power of peoples in the underexploited continents to resist; and, secondly, the flexibility of the structure of the imperialist system.

Notes

1. Margery Perham, *The Colonial Reckoning* (London, 1963), p. 1.
2. Joseph Schumpeter, *Imperialism and Social Classes* (1919; reprint ed., New York: Augustus Kelly, 1951), pp. 98, 128. It should be stressed that the above paragraph fails to capture the subtleties and complexities of Schumpeter's thesis, and aims chiefly to provide a point of comparison with the other two doctrines.
3. Hans Kohn, "Reflections on Colonialism," in Robert Strausz-Hupe and Harry W. Hazard, eds., *The Idea of Colonialism* (London, 1958). The different kinds of political control are as follows: (1) The metropolitan power can grant the subject people full autonomy, with the exception of foreign relations. (2) Subject peoples can be granted full citizenship, and assimilated into the foreign culture. (3) Indigenous peoples can be annihilated or expelled. (4) Subject peoples can be maintained in an inferior status. (5) The metropolitan power can tacitly claim the right to oust an unfriendly government.
4. An excellent review of mercantile thought and practice is provided by Eric

Roll, *A History of Economic Thought*, 3rd ed. (Englewood Cliffs, N.J.: Prentice-Hall, 1957), Chapter II.

5. Charles Wilson, *Power and Profit: A Study of England and the Dutch Wars* (London, 1957).

6. This changeover set the stage for the ruin of Indian manufacturing industries, and can be roughly dated from the abolition of the East India Company's trade monopoly in 1813. The East India Company had provided an umbrella for India's weaving industry, which could not survive the massive importation of British cotton manufactures.

7. This is not meant to imply that there are no important conflicts between international-minded capitalists and national-minded power elites.

8. This, of course, does not exhaust the motives for colonial conquest. In the conquest of Mexico and Peru, the search for precious metals was of foremost importance. The east coast of Africa was at first seized for strategic reasons. But the characteristic sequence was followed in India and West Africa. In the latter region, Portugal had acquired a monopoly over trade based on coastal fortifications. Cloth, metal, and glass were exchanged on favorable terms for gold, ivory, and, above all, slaves. In the middle of the seventeenth century Portugal's monopoly was broken by the Dutch, and then by the British and French.

9. *Capital*, Kerr ed., Volume III, pp. 278–279.

10. Cairncross has shown on the basis of more and better data than those available to Hobson that there was a relative increase in empire trade, most of it, however, with the older colonies such as India. See J. Cairncross, *Home and Foreign Investments, 1870–1913* (Cambridge: Cambridge University Press, 1953), p. 189. Cairncross's findings refine but do not contradict Hobson's argument.

11. V. I. Lenin, *Imperialism: The Highest Stage of Capitalism* (New York, 1926), pp. 71–76. By comparison, Rosa Luxemburg's *The Accumulation of Capital* bases its analysis of capitalist expansion abroad on Marx's models of expanded reproduction which assume a *competitive* economy. Luxemburg saw imperialism as a necessary result of competition between capitalist enterprises which drove capitalism outward in search of new markets in areas which were not incorporated into the world capitalist system. Lenin, as we have noted, stressed the export of capital, not commodity exports. Moreover, Lenin viewed imperialist rivalries over areas already integrated into world capitalism as extensions of the struggles between the European powers over the underdeveloped continents.

12. In the following paragraph we will rely not only on Lenin's theory of the causes of imperialist expansion, but also on Maurice Dobbs' and John Strachey's readings of Lenin. See "Imperialism," in *Political Economy and*

Capitalism (London, 1937); *The End of Empire* (New York: Praeger, 1960).

13. Dobb, *Political Economy and Capitalism*, pp. 239, 234.

14. Alexander Kemp, "Long-Term Capital Movements," *Scottish Journal of Political Economy*, vol. 13, no. 1 (February 1966), p. 137.

15. R. Koebner, "The Concept of Economic Imperialism," *Economic History Review*, 2nd series, II (1949), p. 8.

16. Nevertheless, these historians believe that reasons must be found to explain the *pace* of colonial conquest from the 1880's on. Fieldhouse's explanation—that there was an overriding need for military security after 1870 because Europe had become an armed camp—they consider inadequate by itself. To the spillover from rivalries in Europe, they add the following reasons: the collapse of Western-oriented governments under the strain of previous European influences; the changing importance of Africa for British geopolitical strategy; and the need to relieve economic depression, especially relief from tariff increases by Germany in 1879 and France in 1892. As we have seen, the final "reason" itself was explained by Lenin. See R. Robinson *et al.*, *Africa and the Victorians* (New York: Doubleday, 1968), p. 181.

17. See Lenin, *Imperialism: The Highest Stage of Capitalism*, p. 24.

18. D. K. Fieldhouse, "Imperialism: A Historiographical Revision," *Economic History Review*, 14 (1961), *passim*.

19. Richard Pares, unpublished manuscript.

20. Gabriel Kolko, *The Triumph of American Conservatism: A Reinterpretation of American History, 1900–1916* (Chicago: Quadrangle, 1967).

21. Koebner, "The Concept of Economic Imperialism," p. 12. The evidence brought to light by D. C. M. Platt suggests that with regard to Latin American loans, only the small lender, not the large financial interests, bore great financial risks. "British Bondholders in Nineteenth-Century Latin America—Injury and Remedy," *Inter-American Economic Affairs*, vol. 14, no. 3 (Winter 1960).

22. Cairncross, *Home and Foreign Investment*, p. 185.

23. Fieldhouse, "Imperialism: A Historiographical Revision," p. 198.

24. Robinson, *Africa and the Victorians*.

25. *Ibid.*, p. 15.

26. Kemp, "Long-Term Capital Movements." In 1964, a year of high capital outflow, long-term capital amounted to only 9 percent of gross domestic investment.

27. Palme Dutt, *The Crisis of Britain in the British Empire* (London, 1953).

28. Michael Barratt-Brown, *After Imperialism* (London: Heinneman, 1963).

29. Hamza Alavi, "Imperialism Old and New," *Socialist Register 1964* (New York: Monthly Review Press, 1964), pp. 108–109.

30. Paul M. Sweezy, *The Theory of Capitalist Development* (1942; reprinted, New York: Monthly Review Press, 1964).

31. Schumpeter, *Imperialism and Social Classes*, p. 110.

32. Kenneth J. Twitchett, "Colonialism: An Attempt at Understanding Imperial, Colonial, and Neo-Colonial Relationships," *Political Studies*, vol. 13, no. 3 (October 1965).

33. "Neo-Colonialism," *Voice of Africa*, vol. 1, no. 4 (April 1961), p. 4.

34. Pablo González Casanova, "Internal Colonialism and National Development," *Studies in Comparative International Development*, vol. 1, no. 4 (Washington University, St. Louis, Social Science Institute, 1965).

35. J. W. Kratz, "The East African Currency Board," International Monetary Fund *Staff Papers* (July 1966), p. 13(2). In 1960, three new members were added to the board, one from each of the three East African states. The board was also granted the power to extend credit by fiduciary issues.

36. C. Y. Thomas, "The Balance of Payments and Money Supplies in a Colonial Monetary Economy," *Social and Economic Studies*, vol. 12, no. 1 (March 1963), pp. 27, 35; William G. Demas, "The Economics of West Indian Customs Union," *Social and Economic Studies*, vol. 9, no. 1 (March 1960). According to Thomas, the inability of the Commonwealth Caribbean economies to control their money supply is due not only to their monetary arrangements with Britain, but also to the dependent nature of their "open" economy. The pre-revolutionary Cuban economy was also characterized by monetary dependence. Henry C. Wallich, *Monetary Problems of an Export Economy: The Cuban Experience, 1914–1947* (Cambridge: Harvard University Press, 1950), *passim*.

37. K. Brutents, "Developing Countries and the Break-Up of the Colonial System," *International Affairs* (January 1966), p. 67.

38. Platt, "British Bondholders in Nineteenth-Century Latin America."

39. James Schlesinger, "Strategic Leverage from Aid and Trade," in David M. Abshire and Richard V. Allen, eds., *National Security: Political, Military, and Economic Strategy in the Decade Ahead* (New York: Praeger, 1963), *passim*. In the past, the United States could discipline a satellite country by threatening to cut off supplies of needed commodities. Today, substitutes from other sources are ordinarily available. Thus the United States must threaten to damage other economies by curtailing access to markets which it controls.

40. Paul A. Baran and Paul M. Sweezy, *Monopoly Capital* (New York: Monthly Review Press, 1966), *passim*. See also Shigeto Tsuru, ed., *Has Capitalism Changed?* (Tokyo: Iwanami Shoten, 1961), *passim*.

41. The scheme developed below is a greatly modified version of that of Tsuru in *ibid.*, pp. 197–198.

42. Quoted in *ibid.*, p. 143.

43. Joseph Gillman, *The Falling Rate of Profit: Marx's Law and Its Significance to Twentieth-Century Capitalism* (New York: Cameron, 1958).

44. In general, a consumer will not be able to borrow in order to finance new consumption when economically necessary outlays (costs), together with loan repayments, equal current income.

45. Harry Magdoff, *The Age of Imperialism* (New York: Monthly Review Press, 1968), pp. 180, 182.

46. United Nations, Department of Economic and Social Affairs, Consultant Group Jointly Appointed by the ECLA and the OAS, *Foreign Private Investment in LAFTA* (New York, 1961), pp. 18–19.

47. *Ibid.*

48. Kemp, "Long-Term Capital Movements," p. 145.

49. Allen Young, "Bolivia," *New Left Review*, no. 39 (September/October 1966), p. 66.

50. Raymond Vernon, "The American Corporation in Underdeveloped Areas," in Edward S. Mason, ed., *The Corporation in Modern Society* (Rev. ed.; New York: Atheneum, 1966), p. 254.

51. J. Behrman, "Promotion of Private Investment Overseas," in Raymond Mikesell, ed., *U.S. Government and Private Investment Abroad* (Eugene, Oregon: University of Oregon Books, 1962), pp. 174–175.

52. J. Behrman, "Foreign Associates and Their Financing," in *ibid.*, p. 103.

53. H. W. Balgooyen, "Problems of U.S. Investments in Latin America," in M. Bernstein, ed., *Foreign Investment in Latin America* (New York: Alfred Knopf, 1966), p. 225.

54. John McLean, "Financing Overseas Expansion," *Harvard Business Review*, (March–April 1963), p. 64.

55. Samuel Pizer and Frederick Cutler, "Financing and Sales of Foreign Affiliates of U.S. Firms," *Survey of Current Business* (November 1965), p. 26.

56. William Diamond, "The Role of Private Institutions in Development Finance: Service-Oriented Profit Making," *International Development Review* (March 1965), p. 10.

57. *Wall Street Journal*, February 23, 1966, advertisement. Morgan Guarantee has eighteen correspondent banks in Spain with resources equal to 85 percent of privately owned commercial bank resources.

58. Industrial finance institutions in East Africa are typical. "National development corporations" were established before political independence to promote and direct new ventures and to participate in existing enterprises by subscribing to equity capital issues. "Development finance corporations," in which British and German capital are deeply involved, were established more recently; they specialize in loans and grants and promote partnerships

between African and European capital. Economic Commission for Africa, Conference on the Harmonization of Industrial Development Programs in East Africa, "Industrial Financing in East Africa," Lusaka, October 26–November 6, 1965 (E/CN. 14/INR/103).

59. There is some evidence that monopolistic corporations are more interested in acquiring local partners than competitive firms. See Wolfgang Friedman and George Kalmanoff, *Joint International Business Ventures* (New York: Columbia University Press, 1961).

60. Douglas Gustafson, "The Development of Nigeria's Stock Exchange," in Tom Farer, ed., *Financing African Development* (Cambridge, Mass.: MIT Press, 1965).

61. Nural Islam, *Foreign Capital and Economic Development: Japan, India, and Canada* (Rutland, Vermont, 1960), p. 175.

62. McLean, "Financing Overseas Expansion."

63. Mario Ramón Beteta, "Government Policy Toward Foreign Investors," *The Statist* (London), January 8, 1965.

64. Alavi, "Imperialism Old and New," p. 118.

65. Kemp, "Long-Term Capital Movements," p. 148.

66. Behrman, "Promotion of Private Investment Overseas," Table VII–I, pp. 168–169.

67. Kemp, "Long-Term Capital Movements," p. 139.

68. Vernon, "The American Corporation in Underdeveloped Areas," p. 249,

69. Kemp, "Long-Term Capital Movements," p. 153.

70. Raymond Mikesell, *Public International Lending for Development* (New York: Random House, 1966), p. 30.

71. *Ibid.*

72. Harvey Williams, "New Dimensions for American Foreign Operations," in International Management Association, *Increasing Profits from Foreign Operations* (1957).

73. *State Department Bulletin*, no. 6465, April 1, 1957.

74. Alfonso Bauer Paíz, *Cómo opera el capital Yanqui en Centroamérica: El Caso de Guatemala* (Mexico City, 1956).

75. The argument that Britain's home economy suffered because it was deprived of capital which was absorbed abroad is fallacious. On the one hand, given the prevailing distribution of income and industrial organization, there were few profitable opportunities to absorb the surplus at home; on the other hand, the return flow on foreign investments more than offset the original capital exports.

76. Leland Jenks, *The Migration of British Capital to 1875* (New York: Alfred A. Knopf, 1927), p. 325.

77. It has been suggested by one expert, however, that private investments

were made to serve specific foreign-policy objectives more frequently than it is ordinarily believed. Herbert Feis, *Foreign Aid and Foreign Policy* (New York: St. Martins, 1964), pp. 33–40.

78. Mikesell, *U.S. Government and Private Investment Abroad*, p. 7.
79. Dean Rusk, "Trade, Investment, and U.S. Foreign Policy," *Department of State Bulletin*, November 5, 1962.

Part II

The Underdeveloped Economy and Economic Policy

Introduction

Most of the underdeveloped countries are primary producers. They obtain foreign currencies through the production of agricultural goods and/or the extraction of minerals. What this implies in terms of a country's economic and political organization and its links with the former colonial power is outlined by Terence K. Hopkins in his article "On Economic Planning in Tropical Africa." Hopkins discusses the steps required for a primary producer to develop, and delineates the far-reaching political implications of such a development strategy. He argues that development will require a basic reorientation of the colonial economy which, in turn, will require a radical change in the political and economic positions of various groups in the newly independent country.

Dudley Seers' analysis, "The Stages of Economic Growth of a Primary Producer in the Middle of the Twentieth Century," may be considered an extension of Hopkins' thesis. Seers describes the economic stress which pushes the primary producer toward the import-substitution phase of development and deals with a country which has been successful in its attempt to substitute consumer and light capital goods of home manufacture for those produced abroad, and which then tries to diversify its exports and become a modern industrial nation. Like Hopkins, Seers shows that barriers to development can be understood only when studied within the context of internal political conflicts and the contradictory interests of the developed capitalist nations.

Each of the following four articles deals with a more limited aspect of economic planning.

In "Mineral Development and Economic Growth," Charles E. Rollins argues that mineral development will not lead to development. As he suggests, his analysis may, with some reservations, also be applied to countries which rely on agricultural rather than mineral exports. Rollins suggests there is a conflict of interest between the extractive industries' desire for low-cost labor and limited taxation on the one hand, and the development needs of the underdeveloped nation on the other, and discusses the implications of this conflict.

In "Agricultural and Economic Development," Thomas Balogh presents a strategy for agrarian change. He argues that an increase in agricultural productivity and the utilization of underemployed rural manpower is essential if development is to take place. He points to the Chinese as an example of what can be accomplished, but he rejects both Chinese (dictatorship) and agricultural reforms based on fiscal measures. Instead, he suggests the establishment of rural marketing boards and cooperatives which would carry out public works and encourage greater agricultural productivity. These measures, Balogh points out, would necessitate the defeat of "vested interests desperately anxious to prevent a diminution of their privileges."

Hans O. Schmitt's thesis in "Foreign Capital and Social Conflict in Indonesia" may have much broader application. He argues that "additions to the capital stock concurrently enhance the power of those who control it, and thereby induce them to forego consumption. Those who do not share in the control of capital have not the same incentive to save." He goes on to relate this thesis to the social conflicts in Indonesia and the likely consequences of these conflicts.

Giovanni Arrighi's article, "International Corporations, Labor Aristocracies, and Economic Development in Tropical Africa," traces the complex interrelations among a number of technological, social, and political variables. He argues that the lack of skilled labor and the impact of managerial and technological factors encourages the development of capital-intensive industry in tropical Africa. The consequence is the creation of a small, semiskilled, but highly productive and highly paid labor elite. In contrast with labor-intensive industry, the expansion of capital-intensive production does not lead to the rapid expansion of internal markets for either agricultural goods or goods manufactured locally. The lack of a rapidly expanding internal market, and the bias that modern oligopolistic industry has against investment in the capital-goods sector, discourage the growth of this sector. Arrighi goes on to point out the implications this has for rural-urban ties and class structure. Arrighi, like Schmitt, concludes with the view that economic development implies the creation of forms of class structure very different from those that now exist in the areas which they examine.

I

Terence K. Hopkins

On Economic Planning in Tropical Africa

THE COLONIAL ECONOMY

The characteristics of a tropical African economy are well known:

—Its modern sector is organized around the production and export of one or a few raw materials and engages a few people full time, some people part time, and many people almost none of the time. It thus leaves to a large number of locally organized subsistence economies the provisioning of the majority's food, furnishings, and housing.

—Dominating the modern sector is an over-elaborate, inefficient mercantile network: at its center, in the country's principal city, are fairly large-scale wholesale import/export operations; out along the strands that spread into the countryside is a large number of small-scale, partly wholesale, partly retail units; and at the numerous end points of the network is a very much larger number of miniscule, marginal units distinguished for their pathetically low turnover, dishonest produce-buying practices, and exorbitantly high markups on the few items they sell. Expatriates ordinarily control the central operations, alien resident traders control the medium levels, and even those who run the most marginal places often differ by tribe, region, or religion from their customers.

—Private capital, if invested by its expatriate or alien owners rather than hoarded or exported, goes almost entirely into mercantile or extractive operations, is well serviced by foreign-owned banks, and nets handsome profits that usually leave the country. Public capital goes predominantly

---

into nonproductive investments or infrastructure needed by the commercial and extractive operations.

—Manufacturing is virtually nonexistent, the principal plants being easily enumerable (one cement factory, two textile mills, a brewery, say). The factory labor force, consisting largely of unskilled, temporary migrant workers, is thus small, being far outnumbered by the even more temporary and unskilled agricultural wage laborers.

—Paralleling the mercantile network, and functioning largely as a supplement to it, is an administrative system or civil service in which the great majority of white-collar jobs are to be found. Its employees, although forming the bulk of the educated population, often lack desired levels of experience and training, and its salary structure is seriously distorted for reasons to be mentioned shortly.

—It goes without saying that the levels of investment, productivity, and living are all low, although sharply marked differences in level of living between a tiny minority of well-to-do, a not much larger middle group, and a very large majority, are readily discernible, being perhaps most pronounced in the differences between those living in the central city and administrative centers and the 90-odd percent living in the countryside.

DE-COLONIZATION AND PLANNING

The reason an economy of this sort came into existence is equally well known. It was never supposed to constitute the economy of a separate society at all. Its modern sector was to form an integral part of the metropolitan country's economy, and each of its several, territorially distinct, subsistence economies was to remain the principal provisioner of a tribe. Labor or its produce was encouraged to flow from the subsistence to the modern sector, and some imports, social services, and administration were permitted to flow in the opposite direction; and that was about it.

When the former colony became politically independent, this definition of the scope and purpose of such an economy changed, at least in the minds of some, and there exist at present two rather different conceptions of how its development should proceed. Among the group usually associated with those who formerly held power in the now independent country, the economy of the area is identified with its modern sector, and its development with two kinds of change in that sector. First, the modern sector as presently organized is to be extended into the hinterland and to encompass in due time the remaining subsistence areas; second, it is to be incorporated still further into the economy of the metropolitan power, or into the particular international economy this power takes part in. Political independence in this view is seen as signaling little more than a certain degree of political decentralization, whereby the polity of the area that was once a colony gains some autonomy from the metropolitan polity. The economy of the area, in contrast, is to develop not by becoming more coherently related to its own polity but by becoming more closely integrated with the metropolitan economy. (The kind of society implied by such contrasting directions of development is not usually touched upon.) Among another group, usually associated with the new national leaders, the economy is defined more inclusively as the economy of the emerging national society, and its development is seen in the context of the task of creating a reasonably integrated national society from the fragmented structures that made up colonial society, that is, as the development of a national economy. Political independence here is viewed as eventually signaling economic independence as well, and hence the economy's integration with the metropolitan economy is to be reduced and its integration with the rest of its own society, particularly with the political and stratification systems, increased.

This difference inevitably gives rise to different conceptions of economic planning. The first proposes arrangements whereby the economic activities in the developing country are to be kept as free from local social and political constraints, and as responsive to externally located economic sanctions, as is consistent with the country's social and political stability. The second proposes arrangements whereby the activities are to be as integrally related to the evolving political and stratification systems of the country as is consistent with the simultaneous growth of a viable, integrated, self-generating economy.

Thus the one stresses the balance-of-payments problem and derives a program designed to increase agricultural and extractive productivity, maintain the mercantile structure largely intact, and finance such industrialization as seems feasible through capital market operations. The derived program is less important than the basic emphasis. For in a society exporting from a half to three-fourths of its nonsubsistence output and importing about the same proportion of its commodities, such emphasis can only result in externally formed prices, with the relative values they reflect becoming the principal determinants of the planning decisions within the nascent economy. In this way, what will determine the nature and frequency of the country's economic activities will not be the values the people themselves place on the activities, but the values of outsiders. And in time, owing to the intimate relations among a society's economy, polity, and stratification system, these external valuations will pull the evolving social structure out of its path, and an independent national society may simply fail to emerge. Those concerned with the creation of a national economy focus on means-of-production problems, particularly on problems of capital accumulation, credit conditions, and investment in industries manufacturing instruments of production. Hence they stress the need to evaluate projects less in terms of their money costs, as determined by externally formed prices, and more in terms of their contribution to the progressive emergence of a diversified modern economy built around a basic industrial complex; and their programs, which have a much longer time perspective, give eventual priority to industrial over agricultural development, heavy over light industry, and capital-intensive over labor-intensive operations.

The positions of the two groups are equally contrasting on the matter of integrating structures and mechanisms. The first group envisages an economy where in due course all three major integrative functions will be performed by the emerging system of price-making markets, which by this time will be free of both traditional constraints, like communal land-holding patterns, and presently needed state controls, like produce-buying boards. Thus price-making markets will, first, mediate between the economy as a whole and other economies; second, provide the interconnections both among the diverse sectors within the expanding economy and among the units within each sector; and third, articulate the complex relations between the economy and its societal matrix, the most important being of course the markets for land, labor, and consumers' products. The second group envisages an economy where the independent significance of price-making markets will be practically nil and state agencies will perform the several kinds of integrating functions. The state's present role, far from receding as the economy grows, will expand, partly because, as the interconnections become more numerous, more state action will be required, and partly because, as the conditions for effective large-scale planning come into existence, which they do only as an economy develops, more state action will be possible.

PRIVATE POWER

The tasks of planning differ depending upon the part of the economy under consideration. With respect to the modern sector proper, planning concentrates on problems of capital accumulation and investment. With respect to the sector transitional to the modern one, whose participants combine specialized activities with subsistence production, planning concentrates on problems of productivity and specialization. With respect to the subsistence sector proper, whose participants are integrated into the national economy hardly at all, it concentrates on providing for them various services—medical treatment, education, transportation, technical advice—and of developing a regular supply from this sector of some product or labor.

Increasing the rate of capital accumulation, preventing the export of capital, and directing investments away from mercantile operations and toward industry are, given the present structure of interests in these economies, difficult and complex tasks. In part the difficulty is technical: there is seldom either an adequate supply of reliable information on which to base plans or adequate machinery for constructing and executing plans.[1] But the difficulty is also political: there exist in most of these countries substantial vested interests which stand to lose considerably should any basic reorganization of the economy be undertaken.

At the present time, the integration of flows among the units of the economy is performed in the first place by prices. These prices are determined in many different ways, but not, generally, through the market mechanism. To list a few: governmentally administered prices set by state agencies or boards, such as prices for agricultural exports; competitively determined prices, such as for agricultural staples disposed of domestically, usually in local markets; bargained prices between sole suppliers and sole or dominant users, such as some utility and transport rates; privately administered prices set by holders of governmentally licensed monopolies, such as on some imported manufactured goods; privately administered prices set through agreements—for example, commercial bank rates; communally administered prices set through trade associations composed of people from one ethnic or religious group—for example, prices for many consumption goods.

There are, in short, a number of private individuals and groups having a considerable amount of power in these economies as they are now organized. Occupying strategic positions which for one reason or another have been legally guaranteed in the recent past, or virtually so, they have determined to a large extent the direction of the economy's development and in the process have appropriated to themselves very considerable profits. To date most of these appropriated profits have been exported rather than reinvested in the country, and the small portion that has been reinvested has gone into activities unrelated to the development of an integrated industrial base. Furthermore, in the absence of planning that deals directly with the internal organization of the economy, the likelihood of this pattern continuing in the future is high—the existing interests can be counted upon to continue to set and administer prices, and thus to exert a profound influence on the process of accumulation, all in ways that insure the preservation of their own positions.

To advocate reliance on the emergence of price-making markets is, under these conditions, utopian; those now having economic power will not permit such markets to emerge. Rather, in order to increase internal accumulation, and in particular in order both to prevent capital from leaving the country and to divert it from mercantile and into industrial operations, a substantial reorganization of the modern part of the economy is necessary.

Any such attempt comes up against a number of difficulties. In particular, the existing interests have many ways in which they can, in effect, convert their economic power into political power and thereby threaten not only the success of a particular plan but the fruition of the national revolution. For example, owing to their prominence in the economy and the liquidity of their assets, they can and do attempt to buy protection. The very substantial and rapid change which most African political leaders have experienced in their social standing makes them particularly prone to anomie, to a condition of normlessness regarding what they can and cannot legitimately aspire to.[2] Some among them are susceptible to bribery, and corruption is often a serious problem. An alternative kind of strategy consists of forging various links among the interests, so that a government which attacks one interest finds itself doing battle with them all. Thus, trading communities in many countries, particularly immigrant trading communities, have taken out substantial mortgages with banks that are owned by residents (or the government) of the former metropolitan power, with the result that a government which attempts to regulate the structure of trading operations begins to experience difficulties in securing foreign-aid grants.

Nevertheless, it should be remembered that corruption will certainly not recede with time and, indeed, is rather more likely to increase. Its elimination at the source, through a reduction in the economic power of those liable to use it, would appear to be a condition not only of economic development but of the success of the national revolution as well. And although the interrelation of interests is likely to mean for a government which moves against them that its ability to survive is put to the test, foreign-financed, right-wing revolutions or secessionist movements have not, at least to date, proved successful in tropical African countries.

Notes

1. Jozef Bognar, "Economic Planning in Ghana," *The New Hungarian Quarterly*, vol. 3, no. 7, p. 15. This is an admirable analysis of socialist planning in an African country.
2. ". . . as the conditions of life are changed, the standard according to which needs are regulated can no longer remain the same . . . The scale is upset; but a new scale cannot be immediately improvised. Time is required for the public conscience to reclassify men and things. So long as the social forces thus freed have not regained equilibrium, their respective values are unknown and so all regulation is lacking for a time. The limits are unknown between the possible and the impossible, what is just and what is unjust, legitimate claims and hopes and those which are immoderate. Consequently, there is no restraint upon aspirations . . . The state of de-regulation or anomie is further heightened by passions being less disciplined, precisely when they need more disciplining." Emile Durkheim, *Suicide*, Book II, Chapter 5, Section II.

2

Dudley Seers

The Stages of Economic Growth of a Primary Producer in the Middle of the Twentieth Century

The growing foreign exchange problem in Ghana is by no means unique. Many other underdeveloped countries face similar difficulties. It may help us to understand what has happened in the past and to anticipate future developments if we set it in the context of the general patterns of change in primary producers in recent years.

The most useful procedure is to see if there are identifiable stages of economic development with common characteristics at each stage—and a mechanism which can carry countries along from one stage to the next. The advantages of a successful classification (a sort of morphology) of development would not merely be that it would show where any country stands in the process of economic change; it would also be a step toward the badly needed general theory of development appropriate to modern economic conditions.

What is proposed below is not the only classification possible. Rostow has provided a well-known system, which is however subject to the common criticism that it is not concrete enough. The "take-off" is in the end little more than the period at which growth starts to accelerate. Another scheme, that of Karl Marx, has also proved in many ways inadequate to present-day needs. Feudalism is supposed to evolve into

This essay originally appeared in *The Economic Bulletin* (Ghana), vol. 7, no. 4 (1963).

Author's note: It was Professor Giersch, a fellow visitor at Yale in 1962, who suggested that a classification I had developed for Latin America could yield a stage-by-stage analysis. I am also grateful to my colleagues at the Economic Commission for Africa, Mr. Nypan, Mr. Singer, and Mr. Stamenkovic, for helpful criticisms of an earlier draft. I ought to make it clear that the views expressed here are my own, and not necessarily those of the United Nations.

capitalism and then socialism, but the last step has clearly not occurred on a world scale in the time span Marx envisaged, and many hybrid forms have developed that do not fit easily in the Marxist scheme.

Both these theories suffer from attempting to be all-inclusive. It seems preferable to be more modest and limit the construction of a development model to primary-producing countries, and to the middle of the present century; it is then possible to discern patterns of growth more clearly, and to be more specific about the institutional features (foreign exchange systems, industrial patterns, types of planning, political structures) typical of each stage.

The first part of this paper proposes a general scheme of stages of development; the second discusses how the theory fits the experience of Latin America; and finally, some conclusions are indicated.

A GENERAL SCHEME OF DEVELOPMENT

I. (a) *The Open Economy in Its Pure Form*

A starting point is one elementary fact. A large number of countries exporting primary products show all of the following characteristics:

(1) The currency is highly backed, and is held at parity with, and fully convertible into, the currency of a major international power;

(2) There are few quantitative restrictions on imports;

(3) Tariffs are relatively low.

This type of economy can be called "open," because it responds readily to external influences.

The main feature of the performance of this sort of economy is that the long-period rate of growth is very largely determined by one exogenous variable (exports), and one structural relation (the income-elasticity of demand for imports). As exports rise, government revenue and personal income climb, the precise mechanism depending on the organization of the export sector. The income-elasticity of demand for imports links the trends in national income and in imports, which in turn must rise, in the long run, parallel to exports, unless there are very large capital flows from abroad. Capital inflows are themselves largely induced either by the growth of exports or by the expansion of the internal sector—so that even allowing for these flows, the economy still depends ultimately on the two determinants cited.

Let us examine the factors affecting the size of each determinant.

Exports depend mainly on the rate of growth of the main customer countries, or, in the cases of a colony or neo-colony, on one country. (The monetary system of an open economy is merely an appendage of the dominant power with which it is linked. Consequently, even if it has its own central bank, its development is also affected by the monetary policy of the latter. Because of the absence of exchange control the interest rate cannot for example become significantly lower than that of the dominant power or there will be a serious outflow of funds.)

The average income-elasticity of demand for imports, taking a primary-producing economy as a whole, is not likely to be less than unity, because high elasticities are common for imported goods. There are many reasons for this. Certain luxuries are not made in such countries—for example, motor cars, household durables, processed foods. It is well known that expenditure on these tends to rise more quickly than income. This is particularly likely to happen if there are expatriate communities setting fashions in consumption habits. In addition, the propensity to import is raised by the shift of population toward the districts where imports are customary purchases and very probably by the increasing inequality of income distribution because labor is in surplus supply.

In practice we may have to drop our assumption that imports rise parallel to exports. Where there is a rapidly rising capital inflow from abroad, imports may be able to climb more quickly than exports. (We must of course take account of the fact that capital inflow in the form of private direct investment is associated with imports of equipment, so that it is not fully available to finance the imports of the rest of the economy.) If, however, the inflow of capital is in the form of private direct investment, the profits of overseas companies will probably absorb an increasing proportion of export proceeds, so that the *net* total of foreign exchange receipts available to finance imports, the figure which is the next relevant one, rises more slowly than exports.

In addition, there may be a leakage through the banking system; the overseas assets of foreign banks (e.g., their deposits with their head offices) may grow. (It is a common feature of an open economy that the banking system is largely in the hands of foreigners.) Or people may invest increasingly in foreign shares.* A capital outflow of this type makes it

*By definition, there is nothing to prevent this in an open economy, and the very tendency of such an economy to fluctuate encourages such outflows, especially if investment possibilities are not expanding at home.

possible for exports to grow consistently faster than imports; if there were no such leakage, any export surplus would tend to cause an expansion of the supply of money in the territory, leading to easier credit and a rise in income, until imports were once more equal to exports.

Finally, there is one development that may alter this deterministic set of relationships and permit income to grow faster than imports (in the long run reducing the dependence on external trade). This is import substitution. But here we must allow for the political context of an open economy. If we look at such economies, we notice that many of them are, if not colonies, then usually very much under the influence of one of the great powers. This power will try to keep the door open for the sale of its products and will discourage or prevent the establishment of high tariffs or import quotas. Moreover, a colony, or neo-colony, is typically in a comatose state; few political leaders realize the need for an aggressive policy of import substitution, or could mobilize sufficient support to carry it through in the face of opposition from importers, landowners, bankers, and the dominant foreign power.

One point should be stressed before we go on any further. This is that we have had to introduce social and political factors in order to explain the operation of this type of economy. Moreover, there are clearly common social and political characteristics to be found in countries of this type. Consequently, any theory of development must attempt to incorporate such factors—a purely economic growth model is of very limited usefulness.

(b) The Open Economy Under Stress

Where the open economy has disappeared, this has been due to its destruction by two forces. In the first place, political pressures for development (in the form of protests against unemployment, demands for higher wages, etc.) have been too strong. Secondly, exports of its primary commodity have run into a stagnant or declining phase.

Pressures for development are being stimulated in the third quarter of this century by the great acceleration in the population increase due mainly to a decline in death rates and by what is commonly known as the "revolution of rising expectation." This revolution in turn draws its force from the growing contrast between the state of the underdeveloped economies and that of the industrial countries of Western Europe and North America and the growing realization of this contrast. (These two aspects are not always clearly distinguished.) It has acquired additional impetus from the example of Soviet experience and from the general emergence from colonial rule. At the same time export proceeds from most commodities are ceasing to rise rapidly.

This does not mean that open economies are all disappearing. Some economies (especially petroleum exporters) have had consistently rising exports. In others, new export products have emerged. Moreover, commodity markets recover from time to time, with war scares, crop failures in other countries, etc., enabling the economy to move forward again.

Various devices can be used to prolong the open stage. The government can run down reserves, raise the rates of taxation on foreign mineral companies, or make mild increases in tariffs. A certain amount of import substitution can be achieved without much protection because of the cost of ocean freight; the government may encourage this by such measures as setting up industrial development institutions. For any of these reasons, income can grow for some years more quickly than exports without an economy essentially ceasing to be open. Then again, foreign exchange receipts may be deliberately sustained by foreign governments which wish to keep the economy open, through payments of special prices for some export commodities or through financial assistance or the grant of preferential tariffs. (For instance, the United States made such concessions to Cuba, among other Latin American countries, in return for agreements not to impose obstacles on U.S. products entering the economy.)

Even if the economy fails to make progress, political pressures for development can be contained by force so long as it is a colony, or the government is armed by one of the great powers, or the poorer classes are very backward. (This explains why, in Africa and Asia, economies remained open during the Great Depression, or else returned rapidly to open status after a brief lapse.)

One of the most interesting developments of the past decade has been that, whereas in the early 1950's few economies were under strain, now many only keep their economies open with the help of some form of foreign aid or suppressive policies or both.

II. (a) *The Closed Economy: The Period of Easy Import Substitution*

Despite the temporary reliefs which have just been described, the period of stress cannot be endured indefinitely. Whereas the pressure for economic development persistently mounts, the markets for primary products show a chronic tendency to sag, while countries supplying financial assistance do not provide it at a fast enough rate. Moreover, in the current political climate of the world, it is becoming increasingly difficult to suppress by violence political demands for economic development. After a while, the forces acting to close the economy become cumulative. Governments may concede general wage increases to reduce political tensions, but such rises in cost may hamper exports (by making production in marginal farms or mines too expensive), and at the same time they are bound to stimulate imports.* Official measures to encourage local industries involve an increase in outlays for imported equipment. Furthermore, as the foreign exchange crisis deepens, it is found that loans are harder to float in overseas markets, foreign private capital may become more reluctant to enter, and domestic private capital tends to seek safety overseas. These developments are especially likely if revolutionary upsurges, even though unsuccessful, are frequent.

At a certain point the open economy loses its capacity to cope with the socioeconomic demands on it, and a crisis develops, triggered off perhaps by some quite small event (such as a dip in the price of a leading export or a change of government). The symptom is a fast decline in reserves of foreign exchange.

What happens next depends on the balance of political forces in the country. Conservative factions will argue that international confidence in the country has been lost, that this must restored, and that the government should cut down on expenditure, limit bank credit, etc. They will be supported in a constrictionist attitude by financial institutions (national, foreign, and international), to which the government may have to turn in the crisis, and perhaps by the great powers that still retain influence on policy.

In other quarters, other conclusions will be drawn. Labor unions and local industrialists will argue that what is needed is to press ahead with development so that the economy becomes less dependent on imports.

---

* In petroleum economies, and to some extent in economies exporting other minerals, periodic wage rises in the export sector are conceded without great resistance and then union action spreads them to the rest of the economy. This is a potent force undermining a type of open economy that is otherwise quite viable because of the rising demand for its products.

Politicians who anticipate the serious social consequences of cutting government expenditures will favor a solution to the foreign exchange crisis by import restriction, to block purchases of nonessential goods; the inadequate supply of foreign currency can thus be preserved to satisfy the rising needs for equipment and materials (including in most cases fuel). It may also be urged that expenditure on imported luxuries should be restrained by taxation, that imports of staples should be held in check by rationing, and that prices of essential commodities should be controlled. The same political forces will probably also press for an autonomous banking system, with a central bank that regulates the commercial banks, so as to prevent capital leakage and reduce dependence on the monetary policy of a foreign country. Moreover, the necessary stimulus to the economy can hardly, in the circumstances predicated, be given without a budget deficit or a policy of easy credit (or both).

The question really is not whether any particular economy is better "open" or "closed," or whether a restrictive or expansionary monetary policy should be followed. The point is that the various forces tending to close the economy are growing all the time, while the forces acting to keep it open are not. Similarly, the preservation of high backing for currency eventually appears to the political leadership more dangerous than increasing the fiduciary issue. These tendencies must result sooner or later in controls on the use of foreign exchange, in high tariffs, and in a reduction in backing for the currency.

Since a large proportion of foreign exchange is spent by open economies on consumer goods of various kinds, increases in imports of capital equipment and industrial materials can now take place without a sharp rise, or even any rise, in total expenditure of foreign exchange. To some extent the goods previously imported appear to be not really essential, in the new political climate, and to some extent substitutes for them can be produced without great difficulty: cigarette manufacture, beverage and confectionery industries, cement production, shirt-making and tailoring, etc. Many of these industries may have appeared in the "open" stage of economic growth, although they will have been hampered then by competition from imports.

This stage should be considered in some ways as a period of schooling. The administration grows accustomed to operating controls. The banking system acquires experience in its new role. Statistical collection is improved in response to the growing demands of policy-makers. Industrialists and labor unions become stronger pressure groups in the protectionist camp, whereas the influence of foreign banks and businesses grows weaker. It gradually becomes widely recognized that every pound (or franc or dollar) spent on imports means less employment and less income at home. Economic nationalism grows conscious, expressed in political statements, government reports, and the writings of local professional economists. The political structure, too, changes so that it can contain and channel the acute tensions of such a period; perhaps, typically, a form of coalition emerges, covering a range of nationalistic views and more or less permanently in office.

The most conspicuous change, however, is the development of machinery for planning. A "plan" may well have existed earlier, but during the "open" phase of the economy it can be little more than a collection of long-term expenditure plans of government departments, together with some rather vague aspirations for social progress and nonquantitative statements of policy in various fields. A declining expenditure is probably shown in the later years of the "plan," because of the failure of some departments to foresee their capital requirements any further ahead than the immediate future. This is a typical symptom of pseudo-planning; its implications would be intolerable to a government with a serious development policy. There may be "targets" or "target rates of growth" for the productive sectors, but in the absence of means for seeing that they are achieved (or even of a sense of urgency in reaching the targets), they have little significance.

The essential difference is that the shortage of foreign exchange introduces a constraint which limits the number of possible growth processes, and to a considerable extent the government is compelled to choose between them when it takes the basic decisions on import licensing. (In mineral and marketing-board economies, a great deal of the savings for investment arises in the public sector; the question of how to use these funds also prompts governments to think in terms of planning economic development, especially when the external stimulus weakens.) Planning, therefore, becomes more comprehensive, and the trend in this direction is reinforced by the growing political determination to mobilize the resources of the country for development. The choice of targets for different sectors actually affects the allocation of resources, which are now partly under government control.

(b) The Closed Economy : The Phase of Difficult Import Substitution

Whereas it is more or less clear when an economy ceases to be "open" (because by some means the import of luxuries is suddenly reduced), there is no such recognizable symptom of its passing to the next stage, where import substitution involves the establishment of industry to make intermediate products and light capital goods. One reason why this boundary is hazy is that the sequence of industrialization varies from country to country. A factory to make pharmaceuticals may come before or after a cotton-spinning mill. What is perhaps the clearest symptom is the slowing down in the change of the composition of imports as between finished consumer goods and other commodities. For at that point, the manufacture of intermediate products (heavy chemicals, pulp and paper, and particularly steel) becomes the main means of achieving a fast rate of growth.

The economy is propelled in this direction by the growing political pressure from the unemployed. Attracted by the establishment of factories, people swarm into the towns and the urban labor force grows more quickly than employment opportunities, which turn out to be disappointingly small at the beginning of industrialization. But how rapidly the economy is forced to embark on new secondary products depends on a number of factors, particularly on how pressing is the foreign exchange shortage. (The very acceleration in the shift of population to the towns due to industrialization means, for the reasons explained above, an acceleration in the rising demand for imports.) And how far it *can* go depends also on local circumstances, particularly the size of the local market. The smaller this is, of course, the more restricted are the possibilities of extending import substitution, especially into the field of intermediate products. The possibility of further progress depends in addition on such physical limitations as the educational level of the labor force; one must bear in mind that the typical open economies have large numbers of unskilled, illiterate people, and there may not have been sufficient time, even though education has been expanded in the previous stage, to change the quality of the labor force very greatly.

This push forward into new areas of industrialization during a period of acute foreign exchange shortage, and before the human factor has been much improved, is a great strain on the administration. There are likely to be conspicuous failures in planning, scandals of corruption, and nepotism. Smuggling may arise on an economically significant scale. There may prove to be too few capable organizers and these are too hard worked.

There are also physical strains in this period. Electric power and transport facilities may prove inadequate for their new role in supporting the extension of the domestic economy. Particularly dangerous is the possibility that the food supply to the cities may fail to keep pace with the growth of urban income. If it does fail, the consequence will be a rise in food prices, now that these are no longer kept in check by imports of foodstuffs on a large scale. Labor costs tend to be pushed up anyway, especially for skilled grades, because the wage rates paid by the new factories tend to influence those paid in other sectors, and because the shortage of various types of labor affects efficiency. Other further reasons why the prices of import substitutes are probably high are that the market is small and the number of factories is limited to one or two, which enjoy a more or less monopolistic position.

There are therefore upward pressures on prices. The heavier industries require a good deal of capital (per unit of value produced); this has to be provided in whole or in part out of local savings, and it takes time before new factories add significantly to supplies. The exchange rate is only held at parity with difficulty, especially if exchange control is less than fully effective. Physical shortages may hasten devaluation, through hampering the export sector. Thus inflation becomes a threat if not a reality. (It is of course true that inflation can only be mild so long as a high proportion of the currency is backed by foreign exchange reserves. But, for reasons given above, legal or customary limitations on the backing for the currency will by this time have proved hard to tolerate.)

This stage also involves a corresponding advance in planning. The purposive development of intermediate products implies the adoption of some form of input-output projections covering the economy as a whole, in order to estimate the likely trends in demand. The perspective of plans may also become longer, reflecting the realization that the needed structural changes, especially raising the educational level of the population, cannot be achieved hurriedly.

There are a number of reasons now why friction may arise (or increase) between an underdeveloped country in this position and any great power which is in a dominant trading relation with it. The performance of foreign companies in the export sector may prove slower than is needed for growth; foreign landowners may be leaving large areas of potentially useful land idle; foreign importing or processing companies may insist on buying from their own subsidiaries instead of in the cheapest markets (this has been particularly a feature of petroleum company policy); foreign utilities may insist on higher prices for basic services. So in its attempt to accelerate growth, the government may search for means of increasing taxes on foreign companies or controlling in some way their performance; and there may be acts of nationalization of foreigners' property. The possibility of conflict with foreign interests is inherent in planning. The realization of this, perhaps largely subconscious, helps explain why in some instances the governments of the great powers, and their associated financial organizations, try to prevent the adoption of exchange control and an expansionist policy; these involve, particularly in the long run, raising issues of the treatment of foreign companies which the latter would prefer not to be on the agenda of public discussion.

Any of these measures may create friction and affect the flow of private and public capital. The government may therefore turn to the socialist countries as alternative sources of finance. This may be associated with internal political shifts and with votes in international bodies which the great capitalist countries consider unfriendly. Such a sequence of events may (or may not) cause further friction with these countries, changing the whole setting of the development problem. Whether this happens or not depends very much on the flexibility of the great powers.

There are also quite different reasons why internal political tension rises. During this period of hard structural change, there is a shake-up in society. Where land is scarce and unequally distributed, and where food output is sluggish, the demand for land reform becomes strong. Since a government in this position is dependent in some degree on popular support, it can hardly avoid being egalitarian. Indeed, the appearance of a homogeneous market is a condition of the development of industry after a certain stage. The structure of retail prices becomes more unfavorable to the rich; direct taxes are raised, or more efficiently collected. The real incomes of the upper classes fall, while on the other hand a "new elite" appears. The basic reality of this situation is that not much change is possible in per capita consumption, so the rise in the living standards of some has to be balanced by a decline for others, including probably the old rentier class. What may be more serious a cause of friction is that, with the shifting values of a society undergoing structural change, the status of the traditional upper classes, and of old people in all classes, is lowered.

This period of forced industrialization can hardly, by its very nature, be one in which there is a great diversity of open political pressures. If an effective open opposition exists (drawn in part from the well-to-do, and those linked to the former dominant power), its only means of gaining office lies in encouraging popular resentment at the sacrifices involved. From the point of view of the authorities, this endangers the process of structural change.

Yet it cannot be assumed that there would be greater political diversity if other paths were followed. To refrain from industrialization also leads to political trouble in time, because it implies the failure to solve economic and social problems, or even to hold out hope of their solution. The consequences in the end might well be a regime that was considerably less liberal than one which vigorously promotes economic development; a government bent on development is more likely to enjoy enough political support, from those who see the possibilities of advancement opening for them (and their children), to permit a certain diversity of views.

III. (a) Export Diversification

As the limits of feasible substitution are reached for any size of economy, only one solution to economic difficulties still lies open: to become an exporter of manufactures. A possible way of doing that is to achieve economic integration with other underdeveloped countries, so as to widen markets and realize some of the economies of scale. This involves institutional change ranging from some type of common market organization to political federation or even union. Then industries not previously feasible can be created, especially engineering industries. It is worth paying a certain price for this, such as an income transfer or accepting imports from the new trading partners, not merely of materials, but also certain types of secondary products.

When exports of manufactures have become significant, growth is dependent once more on foreign demand, but the collection of export commodities is much more varied and probably more promising. Moreover, the economy becomes in some degree "open" again, though import controls are probably retained on purchases from countries which are not members of the new trading community. (In a way, the process of import substitution continues, but it can best be seen now as a change in the composition of imports, not of a single country, but of a group of countries.)

In time, these possibilities too become exhausted, at least for the economies which have made most progress in industrialization; the long-term solution can only lie in selling manufactures to the *developed* countries (the Japanese route) unless, of course, an international fiscal system that effectively redistributes income is established. This is a very difficult step, if the industrial countries themselves do not facilitate such imports.

A question may bother the reader: how were today's industrial countries able to grow without going through periods of import control and high protection? The answer is twofold. In the first place, the political pressures for growth were far less compelling in the eighteenth and nineteenth centuries, so the pace could be much more leisurely. There were few richer countries to be envied or emulated; these were not very much richer, and in any case communications were not good enough to make people aware of international contrasts. Population growth was also slower.

The time element is crucial, because economic development implies transforming a labor force which is largely illiterate and unskilled, and perhaps also racially divided, into one with the necessary proportions of professional people and skilled workers, with social cohesion and with the habits typical of the producers and consumers of an industrial society. To do this in a couple of centuries is very much easier than to do it in a couple of decades. It is noteworthy that when these countries were under the stress of structural change, namely in wartime, their economies too suffered inflationary pressures and adopted controls.

The other part of the answer is that the first countries to industrialize were innovators with their manufactures. Consequently, they faced little foreign competition on their home ground at the start, and later they could shift the emphasis in their export trade from primary to secondary products without encountering entrenched obstacles in other countries. It was therefore feasible to construct a world system in which their exports could rise parallel with their imports of foodstuffs and raw materials. As a general rule, controls on trade were against their interests. This was accordingly the period when the free trade doctrine emerged (though it is worth noting that the later arrivals on the scene, Germany and the United States, did make quite extensive use of tariffs). Today, those who want to industrialize have first to close their own markets and then to battle their way into the corridors of trade in manufactures, corridors which are already filled.

For these reasons, the political climate of growth is now quite different from what it was in the nineteenth century. The degree of liberalism which can be expected in developing countries depends very much on the extent to which the governments of the countries already developed ease tensions by providing financial assistance, sustaining the markets for primary products, acquiescing in nationalization of their property, and—what is becoming increasingly important—preparing to buy imports of manufactures on a large scale from the rest of the world.

(*b*) *The Latin American Experience*

Of course, these five stages are not automatically reached one after another in sequence. A country may become "stuck" at some stage. It may be prevented by the political strength of one or more developed countries, or by internal pressures, from raising barriers against imports and progressing beyond the open economy. If the internal market is very small, and nothing is done to widen it by commercial policy, progress in import substitution will be limited. The push through into the final stage, when the country exports manufactures, requires an aggressive search for big new markets overseas, which means overcoming not merely the technical difficulties of satisfying foreign buyers, but also the obstacles raised by manufacturing interests in the developed countries, interests which are, of course, politically very powerful. Such failures to move on are quite common.

In fact, efforts may be made, through a combination of external and internal pressures, to force an underdeveloped country back to an earlier stage in its development. Foreign loans may be made conditional on measures such as the abandonment of exchange control, the reduction of public expenditure (especially subsidies), and the restriction of credit. These measures are, on occasion, perfectly justifiable steps. However, they are being widely urged on governments which are experiencing the natural foreign exchange difficulties of growth, often without any deep economic analysis. This line of advice is therefore in effect, if not in intention, an attempt to block the structural change of primary-producing countries. It also normally involves an increase in the equality of living standards. The result may well be dictatorship, to compel acquiescence in this deterioration of social conditions.

The clearest examples of this whole process in the last few decades can be found in the experience of Latin America. In 1929, all the countries of that region were on the gold standard and technically "open." During the Depression they all broke the rules of this system to some extent (with the exception of Panama). But eleven of them (Cuba, Venezuela, Ecuador, the Dominican Republic, Haiti, and the countries of Central America) became fully open economies once more when recovery came at the end of the 1930's with currencies convertible and highly backed. They continued to depend on exports, and suffered mounting political pressures. These pressures were severe in the two largest countries of this group, Cuba and Venezuela, where they were only contained by repressive dictatorship. The next largest country of these eleven, Guatemala, has also experienced great political turmoil. Eventually, political revolution in each led to the adoption of policies of rapid industrialization. Cuba moved quickly through to a closed economy (and plans to establish heavy industries in the years after 1965, with exports of manufactures at a not much later date, though the actual realization of these plans will depend on the solution of currently severe organizational problems). The measures taken, including a far-reaching land reform and nationalization of foreign companies, aroused great American hostility, and led to a fast transformation of internal and external policy, involving dependence on the socialist countries and a high degree of central planning. In Venezuela, petroleum revenues eased the transition and the country moved more slowly to a situation with characteristics often found in a closed economy (import control, high tariffs, more than one exchange rate, a sizeable fiduciary issue, planned industrial development, etc.), though political stability has not yet been achieved. Some of the other countries of this group have had their problems eased by gaining part of the export markets lost by those which have moved on to later stages (notably the Cuban sugar market in the United States, but also to some extent the world market for Brazilian coffee). Nevertheless, they are by now mostly under some strain, depending rather heavily on the United States and the International Monetary Fund to meet their foreign exchange obligations, but lacking both the political independence and the economic size to close their economies. The moves being made toward economic integration in Central America hold out some hope that further economic growth can be achieved there through a measure of diversification.

The other nine countries of Latin America closed their economies more completely in the 1930's and kept them closed thereafter, but found difficulties of another sort. The two smallest, Bolivia and Paraguay, lacked the markets for much import substitution, and have suffered severe economic crises (which were not helped by the fact that they fought each other in a war), including the fastest rates of inflation in the region. They have, so to speak, hovered between an open and closed economy, enjoying many of the disadvantages of both stages.

The larger economies of the region fared more successfully, although in cases where the growth of the national income was faster than exports, it was accompanied by quite rapid inflation. Argentina moved into the heavy-industry stage and was followed by Chile, Brazil, Mexico, Colombia, Peru, and Uruguay in about that order. (Peru made partly successful efforts to open its economy up once more in the 1950's.) The central problem of these countries is that they became stuck at this stage and have not gone on to export manufactures on a significant scale, as Japan did.

Even the Latin American Free Trade Area has as yet been of only limited impact, and not much effort has been made to develop attractive industrial products that would penetrate overseas markets. In my view, the great historical error of Argentina in the early part of the Peron regime of 1945-1950, was not (as is widely believed among economists) that the government allowed domestic consumption of meat to rise at the expense of meat exports. This was certainly a serious mistake, which aggravated the country's problems, but the government's real failure was that it did not take the chance to build industries which would supply manufactures to other Latin American countries, or even hold on to its wartime markets in the region. Mexico and Brazil have not been so severely hampered so far by their failure to develop such exports. Fairly satisfactory rates of growth have been achieved in Mexico with the help of tourism and a reasonably dynamic group of exports; Brazil has had the advantage of big internal markets, and it has maintained growth by various short-period devices for primary imports.

Another weakness is that all these countries have not fully accepted the logic of a closed economy. They have been slow to accept planning by comparison with others suffering from comparable structural problems, or even to coordinate economic policy in different fields. Both cause and effect of this administrative weakness is the failure to carry out social reforms which would raise the educational and economic levels of the great majority of the people. The region's problems (especially inflation) do indeed look intractable if one has to take these archaic social structures as given for policy discussion.

The stabilization programs which have recently been attempted in several countries can be considered in the class of attempts to force them back to earlier stages, rather than to tackle tasks set by the current stages of development. In Argentina and Chile especially, but to a lesser extent in Colombia and Uruguay as well, the results have been unsatisfactory, even though they were accompanied by large foreign loans. National products fell, and unemployment and poverty became more acute; when growth was resumed it was accompanied by price inflation once more and also by a deficit in foreign payments. Despite a rising inflow of capital under the Alliance for Progress (which is also trying to stimulate planning), political conditions appear to be deteriorating.

IV. Conclusion

There are still some loose ends in the above discussion. For example, there has been no attempt to link the stages of growth to income levels. Indeed, while the move from one stage to the next may be described as being motivated (largely unconsciously), by the demand for higher incomes, the attempt may be fruitless because of adverse conditions, such as a deterioration in export markets, limited internal markets, poor resource patterns, high birth rates, etc. (Chile is a good example of a country which moved from an open economy to a closed economy producing intermediate products without a significant improvement in living standards.) However, there might well be correlations, if the association were explored, between the stage of growth and one or more of the following variables: income level, population, and the date.

There appear to be few obvious exceptions to the general theme outlined above, i.e., few economies where the rate of development has greatly exceeded the rate of growth of exports without the tensions described developing, and movements toward a controlled economy taking place. Apart from Latin America, this account seems to fit the experience of Ghana quite well; this economy moved into stage I(b) in about 1955, and II(a) in 1961.

It is, I am afraid, a rather controversial doctrine. For one thing, I have introduced social and political factors which our profession usually prefers to ignore. The test is a pragmatic one—does their introduction make it easier or more difficult to understand what is happening? If the former, then it would be not merely inappropriate but also unscholarly to leave them out.

I have also—and this may be counted a more serious transgression—given an appearance of inevitability to a process which many would ascribe to policies they consider wicked or foolish. The key question here is whether one views the existence of a chronic balance-of-payments crisis as a normal feature of economic development of a primary producer under modern conditions. This depends in turn on three questions. Are commodity markets dynamic enough to permit an adequate rate of growth? Are economies of this type flexible enough to adapt themselves automatically (without state intervention), to adverse movements in the terms of trade? How powerful are the social pressures for development? On these matters everyone makes up their own mind and my views will no doubt be evident to the reader already.

3

Charles E. Rollins

———

Mineral Development and Economic Growth

Of the possible ways in which economic growth of the underdeveloped areas of the world might be furthered, one that has received considerable recent attention is via the inflow of capital from the advanced nations to develop the supplies of raw materials which have not, as yet, been intensively utilized in many of these areas. This attention has grown out of an increasing awareness, particularly in the United States, that the industrialized nations are faced with rising raw-material costs in many important lines unless alternative cheap sources of supply are developed. It has been reinforced by prolonged discussion of the poorer countries' need for an inflow of foreign capital if their growth is to proceed, and the realization that raw-material production is the area in which private capital has in the past been most readily interested and in which it remains interested, given an appropriate investment climate.

Little attention has been given, however, to making explicit the manner in which the development of raw materials can be expected to lead to economic growth in the source country. The present paper presents a

This essay originally appeared in *Social Research*, vol. 23, no. 3 (Autumn 1956). Copyright © 1956 by the New School for Social Research.

Author's note: The ideas expressed in this paper are the result primarily of rather detailed studies of developments in Bolivia during the years of extensive tin-mining operations in that country, and of developments in Venezuela since the country became an important oil producer. I wish to thank the Stanford Committee for the Study of Social Change and the Social Science Research Council for their generous financial assistance. Of the many individuals, both in this country and in Latin America, who aided in the collection and preparation of the data, I should like particularly to acknowledge the contributions of Professors Paul A. Baran and Bernard F. Haley of Stanford University. Responsibility for remaining shortcomings is, of course, my own.

hypothesis in answer to this question, and discusses some of the obstacles to its realization in today's world.

The paper will be restricted in several ways. First, it will consider only the results of investment in nonagricultural raw materials; while the conclusions reached are largely applicable to agricultural developments, the transference cannot be made without further analysis, since in general the proportion of agricultural raw-material output that is supplied by small local producers is very much greater than is the case with mineral or petroleum operations. Second, I shall consider only the "old" under-developed economies; the relatively recently populated countries that might also be regarded as to a large extent underdeveloped, such as Canada or Australia, will be excluded. Finally, I am primarily concerned with private growth; the prospects for centrally controlled advance are not considered.

Within these restrictions the general conclusion reached is that pro-jects of this type are not likely to lead to the economic development of the source country. Integration of such undertakings into the domestic economy tends to be too incomplete, and the revenues made available too small, given prevailing conditions, for development to result.

THE HYPOTHESIS

The ways in which mineral projects might be expected to contribute to economic growth will be grouped in two general categories: direct influences and fiscal influences. The first includes all those influences that result from direct contact of the mineral project with other sectors of the economy, and the second includes those elements that enable the state to contribute to the growth process.

Direct Influences

Probably the most important of the stimulating secondary effects to be expected from a mineral-development project is the expansion of markets and incomes. The increase in economic activity represented by the establishment of the enterprise means an expansion of markets: any item used in the operations can conceivably be supplied from internal sources. The employment of local workers in the undertaking will create new incomes, which will further broaden the domestic market. To the extent that the newly created incomes are saved rather than spent, new sources of investment funds will be made available.

An important consideration is that these benefits are entirely net: new markets are created and no attempt is made to enter established ones; new incomes are created and no internal funds are required to pay them. Further, the nature of the operations, which makes this so—the fact that the original capital comes from abroad and the product is sold abroad—has an important contributing characteristic for the prospects of growth: the accrual of foreign exchange. All receipts will be in foreign currency, and to the extent that costs consist of local expenditures such currency will be placed at the disposal of the country concerned. The means are thereby provided to obtain those goods required for growth which are not available in the internal market.

Stimulation may also be forthcoming from the supply side. The mineral project will provide a new, presumably lower-cost, source of supply of the material concerned. This will represent a cost-reducing factor, and also open up the possibility of various processing activities designed to place the product on the export market at a more advanced stage of transformation.

Local workers may be expected to provide the major portion of the working force, and these workers, through experience as a part of a rationalized operation, will to a greater or lesser extent acquire the industrial discipline required by such undertakings. Insofar as they receive specialized training in the operation of the machinery employed or with regard to modern methods of operations, they will acquire higher skills. In this manner a pool of skilled labor may be established which will then become available for use in other types of developments within the country.

There may in addition be a favorable influence on the social structure. The institution of a mineral-development project in an underdeveloped area transplants a representative sample of an economically progressive culture into an economically less progressive culture, and insofar as the raw-material development becomes an integrated part of the source community's economy, a culture or set of values more favorable to economic advance may be adopted.

Fiscal Influences

Yet even if it does not become an integrated part of the economy, the mineral exploitation still may contribute to further economic growth in a less direct manner by the channeling of funds through the fiscal authorities. The enterprise will be required to pay various taxes for the privilege of carrying out its operations, and the funds thus collected may be used by the state to stimulate further growth quite independent of the mineral development.

With the funds thus made available, conditions can be made more favorable to the expansion of private investment activity by, for example, improving market conditions and developing external economies. Some of the external economies can be directly provided: roads can be built, power facilities expanded, labor skills trained, and such activities can be undertaken largely with domestic resources, thus providing additional effective demand. In addition, or alternatively, the capital itself can be funneled into the hands of private persons or enterprises, through the establishment of industrial and agricultural banks that will loan the funds to individuals willing to undertake desirable investment projects.

The two channels set forth, through direct economic contact with the domestic economy and through the agency of the fiscal authorities, are not of course mutually exclusive; they can perfectly well operate concurrently. But the considerations involved in determining the probability that the process as described will actually materialize are quite different in the two instances, and in any actual development process one or the other is likely to be clearly dominant. Therefore, in the remainder of this paper, devoted to examining the practical probabilities of these possibilities, the two types of influences will be considered separately.

DIRECT INFLUENCES

With regard to those influences that result from direct contact of the mineral scheme with other sectors of the economy, the conclusion is that such undertakings are not likely to lead to general economic growth in the way described, because they do not become integrated into the economy of the source country to the extent required.[1]

One of the most commonly encountered characteristics of economically underdeveloped regions is the existence of a relatively small, rather highly developed monetary sector (frequently organized around foreign enterprises of the type under consideration, and practically always oriented toward the export market), in the midst of a much larger "native" economy that continues to be organized on the old semifeudal or tribal basis, and to be but little affected by the monetary sector.

Bolivia is a good example. The mining operations there are quite self-contained; special mining communities have been erected to accommodate those working in the mines, and these settlements are in many respects quite isolated from the rest of the internal economy. The United Nations Mission of Technical Assistance to Bolivia, in its Report (1951), takes note of the establishment of a market economy around the mines, largely as a result of the undertaking of these operations, and then observes (p. 85) that "this new trading economy remained divorced to an extraordinary degree from that of the rest of the country." Four-fifths of the populace continued to find their subsistence in feudally organized agriculture, remaining quite untouched by the intrusion of the mining companies.

Although to a lesser degree, the Venezuelan oil fields present the same picture. Special oil camps have grown up, and these have relatively little contact with the rest of the economy. Were it not for the government revenues paid, the petroleum operations could more properly be considered a part of the economy in which the investing companies are domiciled than of Venezuela itself.[2]

In Africa and Asia the split appears to be even sharper than generally prevails in Latin America, since the nonmonetized sector of the economy has in general been undisturbed by direct outside intervention for a longer period, and therefore has more completely retained its old forms and customs.[3]

From the present point of view, the most important manifestation of this lack of economic integration is that expenditures within the country, aside from tax payments, tend to be limited to a rather small percentage of the value of output. Mining operations are capital-intensive, and therefore wage payments, the chief item of local expenditure, are less there than in many lines. The capital equipment used in the operations is almost certain to be purchased abroad, since it is unlikely to be produced in the underdeveloped areas. These two items, along with transport costs (which again tend to be paid either to the government or to a foreign concern), make up the bulk of costs. An extractive industry is likely to use relatively little of the crude materials produced in an economically backward area, the chief possible exception being domestically produced fuels. Resulting profits will, of course, be paid abroad, since the project is financed with foreign capital.

Figures in this area are difficult to obtain, but some estimates have been made. In Venezuela, local-currency expenditures of the oil companies (exclusive of government payments) have not exceeded 20 percent of the value of exports;[4] some seven-eighths of these expenditures have gone to meet wages and salary payments, with the remainder used to make purchases within the country. Judging from an unpublished study of the International Monetary Fund, the comparable figure applicable to the Chilean copper operations is also about 20 percent; the share of labor and material costs in this figure cannot be determined. For the Bolivian mines it has been estimated that during the last half of the 1940's about 25 percent of total receipts were required to meet wage payments, but this is undoubtedly high because the low official rate of exchange was used to compare dollar sales figures with Bolivian wage figures.[5] It is estimated that less than 5 percent of Middle East oil revenues is paid out as wages, while in recent years from one-fourth to one-third of total mining receipts has gone toward wage payments in the Northern Rhodesian mines;[6] it seems probable that the high Rhodesian percentage results from the fact that Europeans make up an important part of the mine labor force in that country, and the wage scale of this group is substantially higher than that of Rhodesian workers.

This failure to spend extensively in the internal economy has a bearing in two important ways on the possibilities of self-generating growth. In the first place, the extent to which a mineral development scheme will actually provide new markets for domestic products is considerably smaller than the possibilities envisioned in the hypothesis outlined in the preceding section. Even the stimulus provided by the wage payments is less than might appear at first glance, for the raw-material operations are often removed from established production centers, and, since transport facilities to the exterior must be established to sell the product, it may well prove easier and cheaper to bring even consumption goods from abroad than to purchase them within the economy. To the extent that this is so the wage payments do not add to the internal market, since they leave on the very first spending round. This effect is very noticeable in the case of the Bolivian tin companies, for example. For many years the companies maintained stores that were largely stocked from abroad, and although in recent years (since the mines have been nationalized) efforts have been made to change this situation, shelves remain stocked to a significant degree by foreign goods.

Secondly, the prospects of an accrual of domestic capital in the private sector are also rather slight under these conditions. The major item of local expenditure is wage payments, and in a poor country it is very unlikely that these will provide a source of capital. These wage payments are certain to go almost entirely for consumption goods, in an attempt to raise the very low standard of living; further, the higher officials of the company (and therefore those receiving the highest wages) are normally brought in from abroad, their salaries are paid in foreign currency, and such savings as they may make seldom remain in the raw-material-producing country. Savings result largely from profits, and since these are paid abroad this source is eliminated.

It is also easy to exaggerate the extent to which the labor force is likely to be provided with new skills. The bulk of the more skilled technicians and practically all the professional and managerial staff are commonly brought in from abroad. The majority of the local labor employed is unskilled, and it is doubtful whether most of such skills as are acquired can be readily transferred to other types of industrial employment. The imposition of industrial discipline is likely to make the workers significantly more suitable for other nonskilled industrial work, but here one must recognize that the proportion of the working force so affected is likely to be very small. In Venezuela 3 percent of the labor force is engaged in the petroleum sector, in Bolivia about 5 percent in the tin mines, in Chile less than 1 percent in the large copper mines, in Malaya in recent years about 2 percent in the tin mines, in Iraq and Iran probably less than 2 percent in the oil operations. In some countries with very small populations and large developments the percentage is of course higher (for example, about 10 percent in the Northern Rhodesian copper mines, and certainly much higher proportions in the territories of Kuwait and Bahrein, where the oil industry has been responsible for about 90 percent of the national income in recent years); but these cases are rare. When we consider that not all these workers are available to shift to other activities, but only those amenable to change, the importance is further decreased. While a small group of skilled workers might be able to exert considerable economic influence, it is unlikely that an unskilled, even though disciplined, group will be able to do so.

Possibilities of stimulation from the supply side are likewise slight, and have not in fact been realized to any significant degree. The best possibilities have existed in the case of petroleum, which may make available to a rather wide segment of industry a lower-cost source of fuel and power. In addition, refineries have been established in some of the underdeveloped producing countries, thereby making possible a new industry on the basis of the raw-material operations; but trends are toward the establishment of refining plants in the consuming countries, except where legal enactments require refining to be undertaken in the source country.

In other lines prospects are less good. Steel mills have in some cases been constructed in underdeveloped countries on the basis of iron-ore deposits, but the causal relation has more often than not been in reverse order; that is, the iron-ore deposits were developed because a steel mill was desired. Other metals offer much less promising prospects: tin, copper, lead, and the like tend to be used in rather advanced manufacturing processes and are consumed almost entirely in the leading industrial countries. Even the concentrating of the ore takes place abroad in many cases, and in no case has any metal-fabricating industry expanded to major proportions.[7] The growth of processing or fabricating plants on the basis of a raw-material supply in an underdeveloped economy would require the production of materials to be sold very largely abroad, and therefore in a market where the most that could be hoped for would be equal treatment in such matters as tariffs. It is highly unlikely that many such undertakings could be successfully established in the face of the competition of established producers in the advanced nations.

Superimposed on all these difficulties is another rather general characteristic of the underdeveloped countries: not only are they not developed, but even now they are not developing very rapidly. In most of them there does not exist a sufficiently vigorous entrepreneurial class to take advantage of these new opportunities, even to the extent that they do arise. Prevailing social structures, value systems, and monopolistic tendencies all militate against the undertaking of any considerable investment activity. It is not, for example, as though there were actual or potential business enterprises eagerly awaiting the availability of new members in the industrial labor force; in most of the larger cities of the underdeveloped world there are already more laborers than can be occupied in the existing state of affairs, and the problem of urban unemployment is a serious one. Many skills are lacking, to be sure, but these, as was pointed out above, are unlikely to be made available by mineral projects.

The second and more important way in which a mineral project might lead to economic growth is through the agency of the fiscal authorities. There are here three stages of the envisioned process at which difficulties might arise and which must be investigated. First, is capital in fact likely to accrue to the governments concerned in sufficient magnitude to provide an effective base for a program of development? Second, is such capital as does accrue likely to be utilized in a manner calculated to stimulate development? Third, if both the first and the second question are resolved favorably, are such actions likely to succeed in stimulating the required investment activity in the private sector? Each of these questions must be answered in the affirmative if growth is to result.

The Magnitude of Funds

A good idea of the order of magnitude of the funds likely to accrue to the governments concerned can be obtained by examining the recent history of the leading raw-material producers among the underdeveloped countries. I shall here consider Bolivia, Venezuela, Chile, Mexico, Northern Rhodesia, the Belgian Congo, Malaya, Indonesia, Iran, and Saudi Arabia. These countries as a group dominate the production, as far as the underdeveloped areas are concerned, of oil, rubber, and nearly all the important minerals, if importance is determined by the value of output.

Thus figures computed from the *American Bureau of Metal Statistics Yearbook* indicate that Bolivia supplies over 20 percent of the world's tin and nearly 30 percent of the antimony, ranks behind only the United States and Portugal with 10 percent of the tungsten, and turns out significant quantities of copper, lead, silver, zinc, and wolfram. Venezuela accounts for some 30 percent of the petroleum produced outside the United States. Chile has in recent years produced 20 percent of the world copper supply (nearly half originates in the United States and Canada), and is the only important source of natural nitrates. Mexico turns out 16 percent of the total lead produced (again about half comes from the United States and Canada), 11 to 12 percent of the zinc (between

50 and 60 percent from United States and Canada), over 20 percent of the antimony, some 30 percent of the silver, 3 percent of the copper, and minor amounts of some other nonferrous metals. Northern Rhodesia supplies over 11 percent of the copper, about 10 percent of the cobalt, and around 1 percent of the lead and zinc. The Belgian Congo produces nearly 8 percent of the copper, 3 percent of the zinc, 9 percent of the tin, about 75 percent of the cobalt, and small amounts of lead. Malaya and Indonesia jointly supply the bulk of the world's natural rubber, and one-third and one-fifth respectively of the tin output. Iran, prior to the nationalization dispute, ranked third (after only the United States and Venezuela) in the production of petroleum, and Saudi Arabia is now third.

Estimates of the fiscal receipts that have resulted from these operations are, unfortunately, available in only a few cases, and less direct methods must be used. In determining these magnitudes an upper limit is obtained from data on the value of the product produced; fiscal accruals will depend, of course, on the profitability of the operations and the manner in which the "profits" are divided between the companies and governments concerned.

Table I
Raw-Material Export Values, 1948–1953, and Population, 1950

| | *Average annual exports, 1948–1953* | | *Population, 1950* | |
	Total (million $)	*Per capita (in $)*	*Total (millions)*	*Per sq. kilom.*
Venezuela	$1189.1	$237.8	5.0	5
Malaya	781.2	150.2	5.2	40
N. Rhodesia	168.2	88.5	1.9	2
Saudi Arabia	415.0[a]	63.8	6.5	3
Chile	242.5	41.8	5.8	8
Bolivia	97.7	32.6	3.0	3
Iran	610.5[b]	32.5	18.8	12
Belgian Congo	151.1	13.1	11.5	5
Mexico	160.8	6.3	25.4	13
Indonesia	388.2	5.3	73.5	49

[a] Estimate.
[b] 1948–1950 average.

Sources: United Nations, *Yearbook of International Trade Statistics;* International Monetary Fund, *Balance of Payments Yearbook* and *International Financial Statistics;* United Nations, *World Demographic Yearbook.*

Table I shows, for the years 1948-1953 inclusive, the average annual value of exports of the above-enumerated raw materials from each of the countries listed. The figures cannot be regarded as exact, since the problem of conversion between currencies is involved, but they are sufficiently accurate to give a good idea of the relative magnitudes. Also shown are population figures and per capita export values. The countries are listed in order of per capita exports.

The Venezuelan per capita export figure is far above any other, the decline thereafter being so rapid that the Venezuelan figure is nearly six times that for the fifth-ranking country, Chile. All indications are that if fiscal-receipt figures were available the disparity would be even greater; the Venezuelan petroleum industry is a very profitable one, and the government share of the gains has been relatively large. Just how profitable these operations have been can be seen by observing the "profit" that has been available to be shared in one manner or another between the companies and the government; the figures are given in Table II. It is unlikely that this situation is equaled in many other instances. The

Table II

Gross Income, Taxes, and Profits of the Venezuelan Petroleum Industry, 1943–1952

(*in million* $)

	Gross income	Tax payments	Net profits	Total "gross" profits	
				Million $	% of gross income
1943	$ 195	$ 26	$ 32	$ 58	30
1944	270	85	84	169	63
1945	343	101	89	190	55
1946	473	135	143	278	59
1947	755	194	246	440	58
1948	1112	329	377	706	64
1949	956	349	343	692	72
1950	1183	287	369	656	56
1951	1413	407	407	814	58
1952	1486	436	408	844	57

Sources: Figures for gross income and net profits, 1943-1949, from H. J. Struth, *Venezuela Holds Key to Needed Oil Supplies* (mimeographed; Caracas, 1953); reprint of three articles from *World Petroleum* (February, March, April, 1952); for 1950-1952 from Banco Central de Venezuela, *Memoria, 1953* (mimeographed edition), p. 4-C-19. Tax figures were compiled by author, and do not include payments to the government for specific goods or services used in production.

"gross" profit percentage earned by the large Chilean copper mines is less than 50 percent, that of the Bolivian tin mines is probably less than 40 percent, and in neither case do the "costs" include social investments like those carried out in Venezuela.

Actual fiscal payments can be obtained in a few cases, and indications of probable magnitude in others. The figures for Venezuela, Chile, and Bolivia are given in Table III, which shows that the disparity between Venezuela and the other two producers is, on the average, even greater

Table III

Tax Payments in the Postwar Period, Venezuela, Chile, Bolivia

	Venezuelan oil		Chilean copper and nitrates		Bolivian minerals	
	Total (million $)	$ Per capita	Total (million $)	$ Per capita	Total (million $)	$ Per capita
1945	$101	$20	$25.7	$ 4.4	$14.1	$4.7
1946	135	27	22.7	3.9	13.3	4.4
1947	194	39	53.4	9.2	11.6	3.9
1948	329	66	60.4	10.4	20.5	6.8
1949	349	70	40.5	7.0	21.2	7.1
1950	287	57	37.4	6.4	15.2	5.1
1951	407	81	60.6	10.4		
1952	436	87				
1953	460	92				

Sources: Venezuelan and Bolivian figures compiled by author; Chilean figures from unpublished International Monetary Fund study. All figures must be taken as only approximate, especially because of the difficulty of selecting a "correct" exchange rate.

in regard to tax payments than in regard to per capita export values. In recent years tax payments in Venezuela have amounted to more than the total per capita income of some underdeveloped areas.

From fragmentary data regarding fiscal receipts in Iran and Malaya it is clear that there the disparity is even more marked. Oil revenues in Iran, including the tax implicit in the low rate of exchange applied to the purchase of foreign exchange from the oil companies, appear to have amounted to about $60 million in 1948–1949 and again in 1949–1950, and to perhaps $80 million in 1950–1951.[8] This means that some 10 to 12 percent of the value of petroleum exports accrued to the Iranian government; in Venezuela the corresponding figure is over 25 percent. Thus the disparity between the two countries' per capita fiscal receipts is much greater than that between their per capita export values.

The same is true of Malaya. There it appears that a maximum of 15 percent of the tin and rubber export receipts may have been paid to the state at the height of the boom in 1951–1952; in the half-dozen preceding years the percentage was perhaps half that figure, and it has fallen again in the last few years.[9]

The funds received by the Venezuelan government from petroleum development have, then, been quite out of proportion to those received by other governments as a result of the exploitation of industrial raw-material resources within their borders. The only countries with any prospects of achieving levels comparable to the Venezuelan are some of the more sparsely populated Middle East oil producers. In the overwhelming majority of instances the revenues have been only a fraction of the Venezuelan returns, and it is not likely that the future will change the existing picture appreciably. A study of nineteen Latin American countries[10] has shown, on the basis of the expanded consumption foreseen by the President's Materials Policy Commission, that only seven of these countries can be expected to have even as large a volume of raw-material exports per capita in 1975 as prevailed in 1950. Of the seven, only one is expected to show a substantial increase—Venezuela, where by 1975 the figure is expected to be almost 45 percent higher than that of 1950. The next country is El Salvador, which is expected to show an 11.3 percent increase.

Not only is there, in Venezuela, a very much larger volume of available funds, but the purely economic obstacles to development are less serious there than in many instances. The country is sparsely populated, and the natural-resource endowment, even aside from oil, is high. It is clear that Malaya, for example, with a population density eight times as great, has a more difficult problem with which to contend. It is important to recognize the exceptional position held by Venezuela in these respects, for the Venezuelan experience is sometimes held up as an example of what can be accomplished—for instance in the 1952 report of the President's Materials Policy Commission (Vol. 1, p. 61). In view of the differences in the magnitudes of the funds involved, the Venezuelan case cannot be legitimately used as an example of the results to be expected in other instances.

THE UTILIZATION OF FUNDS

Having obtained a reasonably good idea of the magnitude of funds likely to result from raw-material developments, we have still to consider whether these funds will be used to promote growth. It is sometimes implied (as in the report of the President's Materials Policy Commission) that such funds will be regarded as distinct from "general revenues," that everyday government functions can and will be financed with "normal" receipts, and that the returns from raw-material projects can be applied to special projects—in order to stimulate growth.

Of central importance in this connection is the magnitude of the payments in relation to the accustomed budget, and the speed with which the volume of payments changes. If the payments are small, and if they increase gradually, they are likely simply to be incorporated into the general revenue and never to be treated in a special way, even if they should eventually grow to be the basis of the entire revenue system. On the other hand, if the payments are large in relation to existing income, and if they increase in sudden spurts, they are much more likely to be regarded as something available over and above what is required to meet operating expenses; special attention is then likely to be given (and somewhat different criteria applied) to their disposal, and the possibility that they will be devoted to developmental expenditures is correspondingly increased.

For example, there is no evidence that Bolivian tin revenues were ever regarded as in any way a distinctive segment of general receipts. The tin revenues never, in absolute terms, reached really large magnitudes; they increased rather slowly up to the late 1930's, and from that point on remained approximately steady. Normal administrative expenses grew along with receipts, and at no time was there a significant volume of revenues over and above the level of immediately preceding years the disposal of which had to receive conscious consideration. The mining operations did, it is true, come to be regarded as the central source of fiscal receipts, but this meant only that the normal operating budget was prepared on the basis of how much this sector was expected to yield. The mining receipts were not regarded as a marginal payment that could be utilized for development spending.

In Venezuela, on the other hand, the oil revenues were large (in relation to a relatively adequate level of receipts), and they increased at a very rapid rate at several points. Ordinary administrative expenses showed a steady tendency to increase, but considerable funds remained available for other types of activity. Special attention was perforce given to their disposal. Concern arose in some quarters as to what would happen should these large receipts stop. It was realized that the oil was in fact an exhaustible resource, and the slogan "sow the petroleum" was phrased— the funds should be invested in order to prepare against the day of exhaustion. In Bolivia there has never been similar concern, in spite of the fact that tin is an equally exhaustible resource and that exhaustion is a very much more imminent possibility than is the case with Venezuelan oil.

In general, revenues received by governments of oil-producing countries have tended to accrue in bursts and to be of considerable size, and their disposal is therefore likely to receive more conscious attention. Almost all the important oil-producing countries seem aware of the desirability of financing a development plan with their oil receipts— although this does not in all cases lead to its actual undertaking. This is not, however, likely to be the case in most raw-material-producing countries; materials other than oil are likely to yield a much lower volume of revenue.

The degree to which these revenues, if they are indeed regarded in a special light, will be expended on projects designed to promote growth will depend on the set of values of the particular government concerned. Although the extent to which most governments in the underdeveloped world have devoted their attention and resources to promoting growth is disappointing, it is not appropriate to extrapolate these experiences into the future. It may be expected that as the desire for economic advance throughout the underdeveloped areas continues to increase, governments will become more concerned with this aspect of their spending programs.

A study of the manifold social and economic forces which together will determine government policy as to development is quite beyond the scope of the present investigation. But it is relevant to investigate the extent to which mineral development in itself is likely to add to or detract from the probability of particular governments adopting a vigorous development policy. There are several factors indicating that such influence as is exerted is likely to be adverse.

To begin with, the establishment of an important export industry in the midst of an underdeveloped economy, an economy that is likely to be dominated by a semifeudal type of organization, is likely to focus interest to an unwarranted degree on this sector and on dealings with the external world, with a consequent slighting of the internal economy. The extent to which attention is centered on the mineral sector will depend on several things. The more important the new project is within the monetary sector of the economy, the greater will be the attention it receives, for it is from the monetary sector that the state derives its revenues and with which its activities are primarily concerned, except insofar as these activities may be directly aimed at stimulating development in the non-monetized sectors. Also, the closer the operations are to the center of government in a geographic sense, the greater is the attention likely to be given them. And finally, the extent to which the industry is able or willing to provide its own external economies will be an important factor.

The Bolivian tin-mining operations provide an excellent example of the importance that such a negative influence can attain. The tin mines were established in an economy very largely dominated by feudal agriculture. Within this economy they created a monetary sector (the cities and mines of the *altiplano*) whose chief interests were oriented toward the advanced Western nations where the tin was sold, and which remained to an extraordinary degree separated from the bulk of the populace, who continued in their old ways. Government functions were almost entirely concerned with city activities, and the government itself was controlled by the city populace. (Until 1952 voting rights were restricted to the literate, and this provision, given the prevailing system of education in the country, automatically eliminated practically all the rural populace. Further, governments have been superseded by revolt with much greater frequency than by ballot.) Although the legal capital of the country is Sucre, the de facto capital has long been La Paz, the center of the commercial and financial dealings of the mining sector, and in actual fact control of La Paz has meant control of the country.

In the first quarter of this century, when the need for modern means of transportation became apparent, government attention and funds were devoted for many years to the construction of a rail network, and this network was almost exclusively designed to serve the needs of the mining industry. Not only did it fail to serve as an effective stimulus to the rest of the economy but actually it was a detriment, since it provided much better transportation facilities with the outside than with the other sectors of the internal economy and therefore facilitated the competition of foreign agricultural and industrial goods with Bolivian production. Again, at the end of the 1930's, when there was talk of aiding various sectors of the domestic economy, the first action was the establishment of the Mining Bank, designed to aid the small miners, who represent an insignificant part of the whole, in terms both of numbers and of potential contribution to the national economy.

The Venezuelan petroleum operations present a quite different picture in this respect. When oil entered the Venezuelan economy the country already had a well-developed export trade in coffee and cocoa. These crops were grown in the higher lands that follow the Andean chain and were transported along this chain to Puerto Cabello or Caracas, where they were shipped to the exterior, and it was in this area that the political and social control of the country was centered. When the oil operations were begun they were located not here, but in the lowlands bordering Lake Maracaibo, and the oil was shipped out and supplies entered through Maracaibo; it was here that the effect of oil was felt, while the center of government was well removed in Caracas. And, finally, the industry not only has provided its own transport facilities but has carried out significant social spending which would normally be considered a government responsibility. The composite result has been that the Venezuelan government has been substantially free from pressure to concentrate on the petroleum sector at the expense of the rest of the economy.

It is not likely that many countries will be so fortunate in this respect. Venezuela, by Latin American standards, was a relatively prosperous country, and had a correspondingly highly developed monetary sector, prior to the arrival of the oil companies; and Latin America in turn appears to be somewhat better off economically than the bulk of Asia and Africa. In addition, the petroleum industry in Venezuela is an extremely profitable undertaking, and it is unlikely that many other operations will be so well situated in this respect and thus so able to provide completely for themselves.

In addition to this possibility of distortion, introduced by the mere presence of the mineral development, there is the further probability that, insofar as the companies concerned exert influence in the political affairs of the country, this influence will militate against the adoption of a vigorous development policy by the state. This is so for a variety of reasons: mineral-development projects have little or nothing to gain and much to lose by the economic growth of the source country, and many of the development policies of the state are likely to be against the immediate interest of the companies concerned.

Insofar as economic growth of the source country affects the price of the raw material at all, this effect will be favorable to the private company's profit, since such growth will represent a growth in demand. This, however, is likely to be a negligible effect in most cases, for the internal use of the product will become significant only when the country has reached a rather advanced stage of development. Although petroleum, for example, may be sold in significant quantities to the internal market at a relatively early stage in the growth process (in Venezuela at the present time from 4 to 5 percent of total production is internally consumed), most of the products under consideration are utilized only in rather advanced stages of manufacture.

The effect of growth on costs of production for the mineral industry is much more immediate, and is detrimental. As productivity increases in other sectors of the economy, wages tend to rise. While in the industrial and agricultural sectors these increased costs can be offset (and indeed are made possible) by the adoption of improved techniques, and the squeeze on profits may therefore not be felt, this solution is possible to a much smaller degree in the mineral-production sphere. Mining and petroleum operations carried on by foreign companies in underdeveloped areas in general utilize roughly the same methods of production as are in use in the advanced economies in which these companies are based.

Mineral producers have, then, in a very real sense, a vested interest in the continued backwardness of the economy in which their production operations are carried on. Growth of this economy would be unlikely to increase the price at which the product could be sold, and would be certain to lead to cost increases, the net result being a fall in profits.

If raw-material producers have a long-run interest in avoiding the economic growth of the country in which they operate, they have an even greater immediate interest in avoiding the adoption of many governmental policies of the type likely to be necessary to bring about such growth. The requirement of additional revenue to finance a development program will immediately affect the mining companies, for, being at the center of the monetary sector, they represent the logical target for new impositions. The promotion of local industry or agriculture through restricting imports, while it *may* in the long run result in cheaper products, will certainly in the short run raise costs insofar as the products concerned are utilized by the mineral producers. The use of foreign-exchange controls to allocate available exchange in a manner conducive to growth will again in no way aid the mineral producers; insofar as they are affected at all, their freedom of action will be restricted, since they are important suppliers of exchange. These are only a few of the more general measures that might be undertaken. That they are recognized as contrary to the interests of raw-material producers is evidenced by the frequency with which complaints against such measures are voiced.

The fact that economic growth in general and some specific measures that may accompany it are not in the interest of mineral producers does not necessarily mean that these groups will offer open or strong opposition to a development program. While their attitude will clearly depend on all the circumstances of each particular case, one important factor is certain to be the present profitability of the operations and their long-range prospects. For example, the Venezuelan oil companies have not openly opposed government actions of this sort (the actions taken have been relatively mild), and an important reason is undoubtedly the fact that the profit position of these companies and the long-run prospects of the industry are excellent; under such conditions it would be most unwise to voice strong protests at the risk of arousing ill will.

It is unlikely that many industries find themselves in such a fortunate position. That individuals do not always react so wisely as have the Venezuelan companies, even in rather similar situations, is suggested by the recent history of Anglo-Iranian Oil in Iran, where the timely making of a concession might have salvaged most of what was lost. That some industries do not consider themselves to be in a position where they can afford such magnanimity, and that they may not hesitate to exert considerable political pressure when government measures threaten to affect their costs adversely, can be illustrated by the attitude of the large tin-mining companies in Bolivia. Government taxation, social requirements, and exchange regulations were clearly considered excessive by the mining interests; there is good evidence that reinvestment was held to a low level after the late 1930's because of this; and the companies took political measures in an effort to change the adverse government policies.

Thus while we cannot say whether a particular government is likely to utilize funds made available to it by a raw-material industry in order to promote the economic development of the country, we can say that the presence of the mineral scheme may well prejudice such a possibility; and a situation in which its presence would be a positive factor is difficult indeed to conceive.

Response of the Private Sector

We come finally to the third area of possible difficulty: is it likely that private investment will respond to the stimulus provided by an appropriate government-spending policy? This is the most difficult question to answer, and perhaps the crucial point in the whole matter, for what is involved is whether there are in the country individuals or institutions in the roles of capitalist entrepreneurs; and if not, whether the provision of external economies and direct assistance to the degree made possible by the funds available will be sufficient to activate such a group. If such an institutional structure already exists, then government assistance of the type discussed will quite clearly result in a speeding of the growth process. It is where such institutions are not already established that difficulties will probably be encountered, for in these cases rather strong measures are likely to be required to establish them.

There is first of all the broad issue of the role of nationalism in the development of an economic and social structure conducive to a high level of domestic investment, and the compatibility of foreign-owned raw-material schemes with strong national feeling. It is beyond the scope of the present paper to consider this issue, but it is suggestive that of the Latin American nations, Brazil, Mexico, and Argentina appear to have progressed farthest in establishing a functioning entrepreneurial class—and it is in precisely these countries that nationalism has been an important feature and that opposition to the establishment of foreign-owned mineral and petroleum undertakings has been most insistent.

But quite apart from the possibility that developing nationalism and a developing domestic capital market may go hand-in-hand, the measures likely to be required for the establishment of the desired institutional structure are difficult to carry out. A well-functioning investment structure must do two things: it must accumulate income, and the income, once accumulated, must be directed to productive investment. The first of these functions is performed only too well in most underdeveloped economies (as is evidenced by the extreme inequality in income distribution which generally prevails); it is the second which is defaulted. Those individuals who receive the accumulated income too frequently prefer to spend it on consumption goods (many of which are imported), or to hoard it (often abroad for greater safety). If investment is to take place this group must be induced to change its spending pattern, or the income must be transferred to another group that has been induced to adopt the desired values—unless, indeed, the sums of money available for the investment program (especially foreign exchange) are so large that the new group can be given sufficient income and none need be taken from the old.

In such circumstances "positive" incentives are unlikely to be sufficient. The achievement of an adequate investment level in the private sector is likely to require also the imposition of "negative" measures. That is, it will prove necessary not only to offer inducements, in the form of external economies and low-interest loans, to those willing to undertake the desired investment projects, but also to place obstacles in the path of those who wish to utilize the available resources for other purposes. And this will be especially true of foreign exchange, since the desire for imported goods, particularly on the part of the well-to-do who cling to the old spending habits, and the necessity of importing an important part of the goods required for the investment program, will make the pressure especially severe in this area. In a word, private investment is likely to respond to the stimulus of an appropriate government-spending policy only if this is carried out in conjunction with other measures designed to force private expenditures into the desired channels; and these latter measures are, in general, of the type contrary to at least the short-run interest of the raw-material producers.

Developments in Venezuela are of interest in this connection. The economic measures adopted there have without an important exception been of a "positive" nature. Assistance has been offered to those who chose to invest funds in industry or agriculture; penalties have not been attached to choosing otherwise, nor have obstacles been erected to make choosing otherwise particularly difficult. It is not possible to state with conviction that this program has brought into existence a native entrepreneurial class. Local funds and initiative have gone into commercial activity on a considerable scale, but attempts to promote advance in agriculture have met with almost complete failure, and there is strong doubt regarding success in the industrial sphere, where growth has been substantial but heavily concentrated on a few items, and where foreign initiative and capital have played a central role in the erection of nearly all of the new industries that have come into existence.[11]

It must be borne in mind that in Venezuela the period of really large-scale government expenditures began only a decade ago, that some success has been realized, and that with the passing of more time it is probable that an institutional framework will evolve which will result in a quickening of the growth process. But the magnitude of the sums involved in Venezuela compared with what can be expected to be available else-where, in relation to population and resources, makes this last considera-tion not too consoling. During recent years an annual sum of $300 million has been spent there on what may be termed developmental expenditures. Even if it is assumed that this figure includes an important amount of waste, it still represents a sum that not many other countries are likely to manage.

CONCLUSIONS

Is it probable that the development of a mineral resource in an under-developed country will lead to general economic growth? We may first recognize one group of countries for which the answer is yes. This group comprises those countries in which an institutional structure conducive to investment is already in existence; here the provision of additional funds will clearly speed the development process. It is for this reason that the "new" countries, such as Canada or Australia, have not been considered in this paper. These countries have long had advancing Western European capitalism as a social and economic background, and they have no important indigenous population to convert. An institutional framework favorable to growth is present in these areas, and in Canada, for example, the undertaking of mineral development schemes has undoubtedly speeded the country's economic advance.

In the "old" underdeveloped areas the situation is quite different. In Central and South America the colonizing powers were Spain and Portugal, the part of Western Europe where the economic growth of capitalism has even now not materialized, and in most Latin American countries there are important Indian populations to be converted. In Asia the institutional structure is again quite different, and the European populace a tiny part of the whole. The same is true of Africa, with the important exception of the Union of South Africa (where a large Euro-pean population dominates the economy and where considerable eco-nomic growth has taken place, aided to an important degree by the deve-lopment of the gold and diamond mining operations). In these "old" underdeveloped areas the country that already has an institutional basis fostering economic growth can with justification be regarded as quite exceptional.

For these countries the answer to our question will generally be no. These countries are at an early stage in the development process. Income levels are low, and a large part of the economy remains on a semifeudal basis. In such a situation the establishment of an important mineral project will loom large, and, as was discussed above, the dangers of an unwarranted focusing of attention on this sector are considerable. If this danger is overcome another conflict is faced. The funds obtained by underdeveloped countries from mineral schemes will, in most cases, be sufficiently small to require the most careful husbanding if they are to finance an economic advance of significant size; and the measures required to insure that the funds are so used will be of a type regarded as contrary to the interests of the mineral producers.

If, prior to the consideration of a raw-material-exploitation possibility, there were in power a government willing and able to take the measures necessary to promote development, it is unlikely that large-scale investments would be made, for the country would be regarded as one in which a "hostile" investment climate prevailed. If such a government came to power after the scheme had begun, the companies involved could be expected to oppose the adoption of the necessary measures. If the companies prevailed there is little chance that development would result; if they did not, a variety of solutions might result, depending on the exact complexion of the government and the degree to which the concerns involved chose to carry their opposition. The solution might be an uneasy truce, such as now prevails between the copper companies and the government in Chile, where the companies have lost much of their freedom of action in the disposal of both copper and the foreign exchange received, yet still maintain a strong bargaining position, largely because of their ability to withhold investment funds. Or the companies might oppose these measures so strongly that if the government eventually prevailed they would lose everything; this has been the result in Bolivia.

It must be recognized, I think, that the exploitation of an industrial raw material by foreign capital does not involve the community of interest often envisioned. The desire for development on the part of the source country will in most cases necessitate measures that conflict with the desires of the private investor for an appropriate investment climate. If the funds involved are sufficiently large, as has been the case in Venezuela, the flood of dollars may be sufficient to dissolve the difficulties: the country can achieve considerable development while still leaving the investor a relatively free hand. In the vast majority of cases, however, this will not be a possibility; rapid development will have to be sacrificed or the investor must forgo some of his prerogatives, as these are presently conceived.

Notes

1. This has been recognized in a general way for some time. Singer, for example, argued in 1950, in a somewhat broader framework, that the integration did not take place and that the raw-material project had better be regarded as a part of the investor's economy, since it was here that the main secondary effects occurred. See H. W. Singer, "Distribution of Gains Between Investing and Borrowing Countries," in American Economic Association, *Proceedings*, vol. 40 (May 1950), pp. 473–487.

2. United Nations, Economic Commission for Latin America, *Recent Facts and Trends in the Venezuelan Economy*, mimeographed for presentation at the Fourth Session of the United Nations Economic and Social Council, Mexico City, May 1951, pp. 6–7.

3. See, for example, Julius H. Boeke, *Economics and Economic Policy of a Dual Society* (New York, 1953).

4. Banco Central de Venezuela, *Memoria, 1950*, p. 36.

5. M.D. Pollner, "Problems of National Income Estimation in Bolivia" (Master's Thesis, New York University, 1952), p. 39.

6. United Nations, *Development of Mineral Resources in Asia and the Far East* (Bangkok, 1953), p. 40.

7. *Ibid.*, p. 38.

8. See United Nations, Department of Economic Affairs, *Public Finance Information Papers, Iran* (New York, 1951), and Bank Melli, Iran, *Annual Report*.

9. See Federation of Malaya, Department of Statistics, *Monthly Statistical Bulletin;* Great Britain, Board of Trade, *Malaya* (London, 1952); United Nations, *Statistical Yearbook*.

10. See Inter-American Economic and Social Council, *Secretariat Report on the Long-Term Prospects of Latin American Exports to the United States* (Washington, D.C., 1953).

11. For a discussion of recent developments in Venezuela see my "Economic Development in Venezuela," in *Economic Development and Cultural Change* (October 1955), pp. 82–93.

Thomas Balogh

Agricultural and Economic Development

LINKED PUBLIC WORKS

Even the most recent schemes or theoretical models of economic development tend to be based on the twin assumptions that the productivity of agriculture cannot be increased except by investment using resources obtained from outside, and inversely, that the pace of industrialization is in some sense dependent on the extent to which supplies can be extracted from agriculture and the agricultural population, helped only by this "outside" investment.

Agriculture in most of the poor countries is notoriously sluggish if not completely stagnant. This, indeed, is the main reason for the primeval poverty, as it represents the greater part—up to 80–85 percent—of employment. The standard of life of the peasant is near or at starvation levels. There is thus, in this view, a double limitation on the pace of development, especially in democratic countries, which, unlike the totalitarian systems, cannot exact the means of development from a poverty-stricken peasant.

A drastic reform of taxation of the well-to-do urban classes is held to be one of the ways, if not the sole way, in which the deadlock can be broken.[1] This is, however, politically difficult in countries where political power is dependent on electoral success, unless all-party agreement can be reached. The consequent failure is said to explain the ill success in most underdeveloped areas of the world in starting a self-sustained growth embracing the whole of the economy and not merely some small sector, in which foreign capitalists are interested for the sake of supplying foreign markets.

I shall try to show that neither of these assumptions is correct and that, therefore, a great deal of the theoretical work which proceeds from them will lead to conclusions which might be inimical to the most effective mobilization of the potential economic power of underdeveloped areas outside the Soviet orbit.

The most important brake and limit on the potential expansion of productive activity in underdeveloped areas is represented by the defective operational framework of agriculture.[2] With few exceptions, represented by a few imaginative landlords in Spain and some of the French settlers in North Africa, and a few, often foreign, enterprises in other countries, land, whether held in vast latifundia or broken small-holdings, is incapable of giving adequate returns.

The insufficiency of the agricultural framework may be due to a number of reasons and take various forms. Models of, or plans for, economic growth which do not take due account of the existence of these hindrances to economic development are likely to go awry even if, in Keynesian terms, "savings" (including taxation) and investment seem to balance. *Institutional reforms* eliminating these hindrances, or at least modifying and improving the defective agricultural framework, and *direct controls* which can discriminately deal with certain acute bottlenecks without having to cut income, would seem indispensable.

The great dormant potentialities of these improvements should be emphasized: they probably represent by far the most hopeful avenue of development, both in respect to the utilization of the vast idle manpower of all these countries and also as one of the most fruitful and productive ways of employing scarce capital resources. They are well demonstrated by the amazing achievements of the Yugoslav State Farms, based on relatively small expenditure of capital in terms of technical knowledge, implements, seed, and fertilizers. Nothing could be more promising than the fact that these farms were, in relative terms, *more* successful in resisting bad, than in making use of good, weather. The contrast with the productive performance of individual small-holding peasants is painful.

In the case of the vast feudal or tribal landholdings exemplified from Spain and Morocco to Iraq, Persia, or even farther east, landowners have no interest in improving the land. Their interest is to be able to derive an income with as little trouble from, and subject to as little fraud by, their tenants or farm workers as possible. Thus, in a large part of the Afro-Eurasian area, as well as of South America, there is a heavy concentration on crops or animals needing relatively little supervision and enabling the holder to absent himself for the maximum of time. This is so whether the owner works his estate with farm workers or lets it out in small fractional units to sharecroppers. The political desire to keep the peasantry from becoming too knowledgeable contributes to the stability of this anachronistic setup. As Professor Dumont has conclusively demonstrated,[3] in these cases land reform dividing the vast estates, far from being merely a welfare measure, is necessary from a *purely economic point of view* in order to create incentive to land improvement and more intensive cultivation on the small area which remains to the estate owner, who will want to retain his accustomed standards. The organization of the surrendered area into viable units will present problems in some cases. One possible solution could be found in the formation of compulsory co-operatives on the model of the Gezira scheme, with a closely supervised system of cropping and cultivation pattern. This has been the policy followed by Egypt. The success will, as in the Gezira, depend on the training of adequate technical supervisory staffs and on obtaining willing cooperation from the peasants.

In a number of areas, the latifundist does not himself work his land. He lets it out at varying—mostly extortionate—terms, terms which have steadily worsened against the peasants as the pressure on land increased with growing numbers. Thus the large ownership unit is de facto already broken up into small operational units. Iraq before the recent revolution was a particularly crass example of this type of land tenure. Neither the landlord nor the peasant has much incentive to improve agricultural productivity, though the basic unified ownership would permit the introduction of large-scale intensive production methods. This is prevented by the fact that the owner is content with his income, the magnitude of which depends not on efficiency but on inequality of ownership. In these cases again, the maintenance of the traditional system of land tenure, and its very inequality, is the main obstacle to full mobilization of resources.[4]

In those areas where estates are broken into small-holdings—among which India presents an especially difficult case—the problem is even harder to solve. The operational unit is unfit for much improvement in the technique of exploitation. The partitioning of ownership hinders improvements, as single owners are incapable of dealing with technical problems such as irrigation or drainage. The elimination of the larger feudal landlords left in being a vast agglomeration of smaller landlords, or even hierarchy of landlords, often absentee. These "landlords" or lease-owners, or even the owners of the "superior" rights, might themselves be miserably poor.[5] Their ownership rights, together with social tradition (connected with religion), magnify the operational defects of the system. The existence of a large licensed and subsidized class of leisured poor, prevented by status or caste considerations from working, renders economic mobilization difficult. The great number of these "landlords-merchants-moneylenders" confers upon them an important voting power in a democratic system, magnified by their oppressive influence on the lower strata of the village society. It is this system of land tenure and traditional behavior which creates underemployment.

Finally, it should be added that in the absence of a large-scale re-organization, piecemeal attempts at improvement might not merely not be effective but actually do more harm than good. Thus irrigation without drainage in very large parts of the Eurasian continent poisons the soil by salting; the provision of fertilizers without water and drainage might result in a total failure of crops through burning, while some poor crops might survive without fertilizers even under the same conditions. The peasants' resistance to new techniques is therefore not as irrational as is often thought.

Due to these deeply imbedded impediments arising out of the traditional system of land tenure and social arrangements, there is an immense amount of underemployment. It does not seem exaggerated to claim that success in planning development for self-sustaining economic growth will mainly depend on the success achieved in mobilizing this reserve—practically the sole hidden asset of most underdeveloped areas. Given the overwhelming numerical preponderance of the agricultural sector in the whole economy of these countries, a decisive increase in its productivity could make all the difference. A failure in this sector would condemn the greatest success on the industrial front alone to relative ineffectiveness for long periods, as in Soviet Russia, in lifting average productivity and thus the standard of life. Foreign aid, invaluable as it may be, is no substitute for such effective mobilization. Indeed, its value might mainly consist in permitting this mobilization to take effect over time, thus reducing the scope and severity of the compulsive measures needed for any given achievement.

The magnitude of the possible effect of a successful mobilization of idle manpower has been consistently underestimated. This failure of appreciation has been mainly due to the assumptions about the shape which development programs ought to take. It has been implicitly assumed that development would, in the main, have to take the form of industrial growth absorbing the unemployed or underemployed of the rural areas, of a removal of surplus labor from the land. Elaborate calculations have been made, therefore, to determine how much "true" underemployment existed. This was defined as that part of the labor force the removal of which would not affect output. As primitive agriculture is highly seasonal in character, this severely limits the availability of labor. In the context in which some of these calculations were made (e.g., Professor Rosenstein-Roden, for southern Italy), these assumptions were legitimate. Certainly, a reduction in the absolute numbers on the land, and not merely their proportion in total employment, is an essential part of the effort to increase national income. What is more justified is to assume that this is to be the main or sole means of rural improvement. Two considerations especially have been, I think, consistently neglected in shaping these programs.[6]

The first is that the demand for labor in modernized agriculture based on irrigation increases very rapidly, while even after the removal of the "true underemployed" the seasonal character of the traditional methods of agriculture would leave unemployment which can be estimated at between one-third and one-half of the remaining labor force. Thus productivity in agriculture would still remain so low and so inflexible as to render any development planning difficult, if not hopeless, because of the potential inflationary threat if a program of expansion is superimposed on this type of economic system.

The second consideration is that agriculture presented at one and the same time not merely an investment opportunity with exceedingly high marginal productivity, which was not utilized only because of the structural and institutional impediments to development, but one which could use manpower for intensive methods of construction. Thus there was here a chance for the seasonal utilization of unemployed rural labor, the only reserve and, at the same time, the greatest curse of underemployed areas. In this way, fuller employment could be attained without incurring the extra cost of transportation and the necessary urban rehousing investment which is so great an obstacle to national economic planning in these areas. At the same time, the capital investment in dams, irrigation canals, drainage, and roads would increase permanent employment opportunities and productivity.

The problem was exhaustively discussed in the *Interim Report* of the FAO *Mediterranean Development Project*.[7] We concluded there that development planning would have to base itself on creating in strategic sectors a "creative" unbalance, a new level of demand, while at the same time widening the basic bottleneck of agricultural production.[8] In peasant, and even more in tribal, societies it is difficult to introduce far-reaching changes on a voluntary basis of popular participation, since the benefits of these are not apparent sufficiently soon to make their causal connection unmistakably evident. Yet it is obvious that the only way in which the large mass of idle manpower can effectively be used without scarce and costly implements (or other scarce materials) is agricultural improvement.

The Chinese Communists—unlike the Soviet leaders at the time of the inauguration of the first Five-Year Plan—clearly recognized this fact. After several different starts, which were soon abandoned,[9] their answer was an increasingly wide and tight organization of the peasant masses, first in work teams, subsequently in the so-called communes. These permitted the mobilization of the workless without disrupting their nexus to their localities, which were obliged to continue to maintain them. This performed the vital task of keeping consumption level steady until production had increased. The communes were used for creating, without any modern capital equipment, important capital projects, such as dams, irrigation, drainage, canals, nonchemical fertilizer production, yielding in most part phenomenal returns, and social substructure investment, such as roads, schools, and hospitals, as well as industrial ventures (often of an extravagantly unsuitable type soon to be abandoned).

If we bear in mind that unemployment must have amounted to at least 150 million man-years in pre-revolutionary China, the colossal size of the potential capital investment becomes apparent. No doubt a great deal was misdirected. No doubt a lot could have been better allocated, and its effectiveness improved by different techniques. What should be remembered is that it was a *net* addition, *potentially of the order of magnitude of more than a quarter of the national income*, and a large part of it probably with a capital-output ratio possibly as low as two or below. The mechanism of the expansion is not difficult to understand. It is dependent on complete ruthlessness and either total compulsion or fanatical enthusiasm. It is, needless to say, also dependent on the absolute liquidation of legal obstacles in the way of the physical reorganization of production, especially the removal of the integument of obsolete land-tenure systems, and all traditional social-behavior patterns inimical to increases in productivity.

In democratic countries, such direct mobilization of rural manpower is hardly feasible. The only direct compulsion which could be contemplated is general service in the army, or in special labor corps for education, and the undertaking of investment. Even if no money were paid, such organization of labor would disrupt the connection between the individual and his rural base. This means that his maintenance would fall on the state, an appreciable burden which necessarily limits such direct methods outside the village or district framework.

An alternative would be to organize community development on the basis of liability for a number of days' service from which individuals could free themselves by payment of sufficient tax to maintain a worker. In some countries, the introduction of a poll tax might be easier, with the alternative of serving a number of days in work teams.

Beyond such devices to utilize labor service, the mass of the population would have to be provided with appreciable immediate incentives, making them eager to try out new methods of rural organization and production. A drastic reform of obsolete land-tenure systems would also be necessary. As a minimum, the formation of productive cooperatives has to be envisaged. These can, with due compensation, possibly guaranteed by the government, take over rights over land which, in scattered hands, or in the hands of stagnant latifundia owners, prevent a rational solution of technical problems of agricultural production.[10] Fortunately, compensation is not prohibitive, as present landowners' rights are based on (as they are also responsible for) an extraordinarily low production. Rural reorganization might easily enable a doubling, trebling, or more of yields.[11] Thus, it is economically feasible to pay adequate compensation for existing rights without overburdening the state. This should facilitate reform even in the countries where there has been no revolution.

In cases where a once-for-all, large-scale land reform is not possible, an alternative would be to impose a progressive land tax on family holdings. This tax should be based on a (high) average yield in the district according to each class of land (irrigated, dry-farmed, and varying soil structure). This would force the owners of larger holdings to consider whether to improve their farming methods or to sell. The state, through the cooperatives, ought to reserve the right of first refusal to acquire any land sold. This would reduce the mass of land to be dealt with but increase the difficulty of rational land-use reform, as the cooperative holdings would be scattered and no rational production plan could be imposed.

The organization of cooperatives would enable the rational use of land and water, and the carrying through of infrastructure and agricultural investment. The story of the Gezira scheme shows what can be accomplished through adequate organization, education, and leadership in assimilating scientific methods and obtaining a substantial yield in an originally primitive environment within a relatively short period. The first requirement would be the training of inspectors to take charge of such cooperatives, as it is essential to give a new leadership in the villages, a leadership divorced from existing feudal or tribal restrictiveness. This has been shown to be far less time-consuming or educationally difficult than was thought even a short time ago.[12]

Resistance to innovation has been fierce. It might be overcome if the reorganization itself is made immediately attractive.

Two parallel lines of action would seem to be needed. The first is the organization of marketing boards so as to cut out the usury dealings of merchants. Land reform in a number of Asiatic countries (including some parts of India) came to naught because the landlord-merchant-money-lender remained in effective control of the peasant. As the West African marketing boards have shown, the most important function of a reform of marketing is to enable the peasant to receive something resembling the current consumer price for his produce and not a price distorted by interest deductions or by deductions administered in view of possible seasonal fluctuations. The net effect on consumption of such increase in peasant income would be slight as the landlord-merchant did not save much.

The second line of action is to assure the peasant some immediate increase in his income through the cooperative, but in such a way as to minimize inflationary dangers by increasing production. This could be achieved by *linking public works in infrastructure investment to rural reorganization schemes and by channeling paid employment through the new cooperative organization.* Thus membership of cooperatives could and would be made immediately profitable because peasants would only receive employment and income if they joined the cooperative.[13]

Most of the *linked public works* could, as in China, represent undertakings which do not need implements or material. The wages need be no more than the *average* income of peasants and landlords from their unreformed holdings. This is of course far below the urban wage rates. This gap is one of the main reasons for the existing maldistribution of resources, causing an overconcentration on primary production by creating a large-scale divergence between social and private cost in industry to the detriment of the terms of trade and the average real productivity of the country.[14] Thus the "monetary" capital-output ratio in this type of public works would be even more favorable than it would be in "real social" terms because the money wage cost is far below that ruling in industry. Accordingly, the threat of inflationary consequences would be less.

Another, hardly less important, argument strengthens this conclusion. There is in most of these countries a substantial unused productive capacity for handicraft or primitive industry, the products of which cannot compete qualitatively with large-scale industry. As public works could bring purchasing power to the village population, which is not accustomed to buy high-quality products, it would be fairly simple to divert this purchasing power toward these products.[15] The argument that redistribution of purchasing power inevitably leads to an increase in demand and thus to a worsening of the balance of payments is incorrect in a large number of underdeveloped countries. Not only do the rich not save much, if at all; their demand is concentrated on foreign products and products with high import-content. Redistribution toward the lower-income classes might actually help rather than hinder the achievement of balance-of-payments equilibrium.

Most of these public works can be suitably timed to coincide with the seasonal slack in rural areas. They can, therefore, make use of workers who could not, without costly replacement in terms of machines, be utilized in industrial development. Moreover, the output created is a net gain in the additional sense that it does not require large and costly additions to urban capital, houses, water, etc., for its materialization.

A program of rural works could, moreover, help in redressing the balance in development programs in favor of giving employment. This is more essential, as it is likely that, mainly because of the balance-of-payments consideration, the nonrural program will have to be concentrated on basic industries producing intermediate products and capital goods, which, due to technical considerations, are likely to be capital-intensive in the sense of providing relatively few employment opportunities.

Rural reorganization, if linked with public works programs, might be accepted with less resistance, as it might help with the initial stages by assuring due compensation for old rights. Their being channeled through cooperatives (together with the marginal increase in income) might weaken the stranglehold of tribal or feudal relations which have in the past widely prevented—even in India—the effectiveness of community development schemes.[16] A new source of income placed in the hand of "outsiders" might—as in the Gezira and in some regions of Egypt—provide that loosening of the impediments to rural reform and progress which is essential if a new deal is to be introduced.

Linked public works programs can thus fulfill an essential role in a plan for integral development. They could be useful in helping to achieve social change without prior violence and subsequent compulsion. They might speed up development and reduce the danger of eventual failure when foreign aid is diminished. Conversely, they probably represent one of the most effective uses of foreign aid. Together with technical assistance, they might become the main weapon helping to eliminate the formidable food bottleneck which constricts expansion. They might provide the framework in which technical knowledge and administrative capacity can be infused into the countryside. Thus the development impulse given to the original industrial sector might receive an adequate and expansive response instead of either causing inflationary pressure and hoarding or slowly petering out. Given the inevitably accelerating growth of population, they might make the difference between success and failure of efforts to achieve reconstruction without revolution. A failure of rural reorganization, should Chinese reconstruction succeed, would spell an inevitable victory for the totalitarian approach.

It might be asked why such schemes have not been adopted when their advantages are so obvious. The answer to this question is not difficult. It lies partly in the resistance of vested interests which feel menaced, partly in the shortage of manpower to which leadership could be entrusted. These two factors, however important they may be, do not explain the extent of the failure. This cannot be really understood without realizing that instead of *channeling foreign aid toward cooperatives, and insisting on their accelerated organization, the administrators of foreign aid resolutely set their face against them.*

In some cases, the use of resources derived from foreign aid through cooperatives (especially of bilateral aid) has been prohibited, instead of being made a condition of the grant. This discrimination is presumably due to the fact that the Soviet system also makes use of this form of agricultural organization. The difference in the content is ignored because of the similarity of form, and the resistance of the feudal vested interests, instead of being combated by the foreign experts, is strengthened.

Without radical rethinking of the strategy and tactics of international aid it is difficult to avoid pessimism about the chances of success in promoting self-sustained growth in non-Soviet areas. The use of foreign resources without reorganization would merely raise rural incomes temporarily but (as the case of Iraq prior to 1958 shows) would not generate a multiple expansion of national income.[17] Once disappointment sets in, and the flow of aid diminishes, little permanent improvement would remain from the initial impetus. Change cannot be effected without the wholehearted cooperation of the mass of the rural population.[18] Incidentally, only cooperative organization and marketing could prevent an increase in food production from generating an exactly corresponding income and thus exerting increased demand on productive capacity.[19] There is urgent need for a reversal of the opposition by governments in control of aid resources to the formation of cooperatives.

A word needs to be said about proposals which are based on the belief that fiscal measures, a general tax reform, would render more direct reform, especially agricultural reform, unnecessary. In this view, the rate of progress, and even of providing new employment, depends on the "ability and willingness to tax," which is taken to be synonymous with "the Government's willingness or ability to redistribute consumption sufficiently in favor of the newly or more intensively employed."[20]

If this statement of the case means that tax measures of a sufficient harshness must be taken up to a point where a redistribution of consumption is achieved, it is self-evident but not very helpful. If it means that taxes will bring about the required decrease in the consumption of certain goods in scarce supply, instead of causing unemployment among the producers of other, less necessary, articles, it is incorrect. As the bottleneck is food and certain specific products for which the demand is extremely stubborn, taxation might have to be a multiple of the monetary equivalent of the desired specific effect in terms of a redistribution of the consumption of these foods. Nor would it be safe to assume that the displaced producers of the unintended cuts in consumption (e.g., producers of silk saris, or domestic servants) will be readily available for more useful work.

A further objection against attaching an exaggerated importance to the fiscal aspect of the problem of development is that the administration and enforcement of a complex tax reform, including capital, capital-gains, and expenditure taxes, would absorb a great deal of scarce skilled manpower. Damage would be done by diverting entrepreneurial ability and drive from building up new enterprise to tax evasion.

There can be no question whatever that a decisive increase in production would very much facilitate the extraction of additional supplies.[21] The creation of a sufficient collective (budgetary) saving must come as a by-product of the organization of increased production. It is one thing to restrict people's consumption, and quite a different one to prevent their consumption from rising exactly in proportion to their productivity. This goes for the urban as much as for the rural sector, for rich and poor alike.

In this connection, it should also be remembered that practically the only way in which rural supplies can effectively be mobilized is through cooperatives which organize marketing and can extract the taxes while carrying out these duties. Inasmuch as the cultivators at present are oppressed by extortionate marketing practices, the weight of the taxes might not be felt by them but by the displaced merchants whose activities benefit no one but themselves. Thus tax collection becomes a by-product of the drive for higher production, and skilled administrators are not wasted on purely negative tasks in this vital sector. But unless the formation of cooperatives leads to a substantial increase in production, an attempt to use them for taxation would result in a revulsion of feeling which would certainly prevent rapid development without compulsion of the utmost harshness. It explains the tribulations of cooperatives and the hatred with which they are regarded in the Soviet orbit. On the other hand, the Yugoslav cooperative experiments with improved seeds, fertilizers, and cultivation techniques show equally conclusively the scope and rapidity of improvement.

Fortunately—and in complete contrast to the attitude with which the preparation of the second Indian Five-Year Plan was received by the "Western powers"—both the importance and the extent of the needs of the poor areas, and especially of India, are now fully realized. There is, moreover, a large (and still growing) surplus in the West of practically all those products for which demand might be expected to rise in the intermediate period of reform and reconstruction, prior to the rise in production and the establishment of an effective organization to handle the increase in crops. This, providentially, facilitates the policy of linked works. As rural reorganization would lead to a more rapid increase of output than could otherwise be contemplated, a more rapid use of the foreign food supplies might be permissible. Thus a shock effect might be achieved, tempting rather than coercing peasants and "landlords" to cooperate.

No illusions must be fostered about the difficulties which would face any government in implementing a program of organizing a cooperative increase in production through linked public works. Traditional behavior patterns are stubborn. They are stiffened by the existence of vested interests desperately anxious to prevent a diminution of their privileges, however miserable the absolute level of existence to which the system condemns even them. What might be claimed is that a "linked" public works program might sufficiently diminish the resistance to enable the successful launching of rural reform. Without such reform it is very questionable whether the best efforts on the industrial front will not prove insufficient to bear the increasing burden of a fast-growing population. If persuasion and incentive do not work, compulsion, however repellent, will prove inevitable.

Notes

1. See for example, the "Introduction" of the report by Mr. N. Kaldor on Indian tax reform, p. 1.
2. See FAO, *Mediterranean Development Project* (Rome, 1959).
3. René Dumont, *Lands Alive* (New York: Monthly Review Press, 1965).
4. Traditionally "Western" economists seem to equate inequality and growth. See, for example, Professor Kindleberger's *Economic Development*, 2nd ed. (New York: McGraw Hill, 1965), p. 225.
5. See V. M. Dandekar and G. J. Khudanpur, *Working of Bombay Tenancy Act, 1948* (Poona: Gokhale Institute, 1957). Their social superiority, however, has prevented effective land reform. Often they were able to get their tenants to renounce the new rights conferred on the cultivators. They frequently combine the function of landlord, merchant, and moneylender and exact an extortionate price for each.
6. This neglect, however, has not been permitted to mar the programs elaborated for the Mediterranean countries by FAO. See FAO, *Mediterranean Development Project, Interim Report* (Rome, 1957); *Final Report* (Rome, 1959).
7. This report was prepared by a team headed by myself. I must acknowledge my indebtedness especially to Mr. Ergas, Mr. Holland, and Professor Nagi. See paragraphs 111–112, 118–124. The strategy of purposive unbalance has since received impressive support.
8. An alternative has been elaborated by Mr. Sushil Dey when Development Commissioner in Western Bengal (see his book *Industrial Development—A New Approach* [Calcutta, 1955]). It had striking success in the province so long as it was pressed energetically (see *The Village Exchange—A Programme for Industrial Extension in Western Bengal by the Development Department of the Government of West Bengal* [Calcutta, 1954]). This approach encourages production by the villagers of food and simple handicraft products for exchange through special village centers. In this way additional products are created beyond the level which the village could buy from the organized market sector. The saving in purchases from the town was to be used for the purchase of capital goods. The scheme has been likened to the combination of discrimination, internal liberalization, and aid which was adopted by Western Europe after the war to get production going without having to restrict it as a result of inability to balance dollar imports and exports. If pushed with vigor, it might give an invaluable impetus to community developments on a primitive level and thus smooth the path for voluntary popular participation in more elaborate schemes. The difficulty may possibly be in the transition period when

peasants have to be persuaded to buy and use modern tools (including fertilizers). Its advantage is that the improvement is simultaneous with, and a consequence of, individual effort. This has great moral impact.

9. T. J. Hughes and D. E. T. Luard, *The Economic Development of Communist China 1949–1958* (New York: Oxford University Press, 1959), especially pp. 35–71.

10. The Third Indian Plan, which came to hand when this had been completed, envisages some such reform.

11. See FAO, *Country Report* for Iraq (Rome, 1959).

12. There is little doubt that despite the shocking neglect of agricultural training colleges by the British and even the Indian government, there is more expertise at hand than is being made use of at present. The professional unemployment acts as a terrible deterrent to progress.

13. The organization of Egyptian cooperatives in the areas affected by land reform was compulsory. The grant of additional incentives might be wise.

14. See my article "Welfare and Freer Trade," *Economic Journal*, 1951, pp. 76–80; and for an estimate of the degree of distortion see the two FAO *Country Reports* on Iraq (1957) and Rome (1959), for which I was responsible.

15. Possibly in conjunction with the village-exchange scheme initiated by Mr. S. K. Dey (see note 8).

16. See, for example, the FAO *Report of the UN Committee on the Evaluation of Community Development Schemes* (New York, 1959), IND/31.

17. This has been demonstrated in Iraq, despite the extremely favorable conditions for successful development: abundance of foreign income, water, and land. See *Country Report* for Iraq.

18. Thus it would be wrong to think that a diversion of industrial investment toward agricultural investment without basic reorganization could bring about a radical improvement in production (see, for example, Ford Foundation Agricultural Team, *Report on India's Food Crisis and Steps to Meet It*, 1959).

19. But see above on the existence of unused productive capacity to meet an increase in demand for simple goods.

20. I. M. D. Little, "The Strategy of Indian Development," *National Institute Economic Review*, May 1960.

21. Professor Galbraith's belief to the contrary (*Affluent Society*, pp. 178–179, 215) contradicts his own basic thesis, which I believe to be correct and important, that utility decreases as available supplies in general increase.

5

Giovanni Arrighi

International Corporations, Labor Aristocracies, and Economic Development in Tropical Africa

The emergence of the large-scale corporation as the typical unit of production in advanced capitalist economies has had momentous implications for the process of development in the still underdeveloped lands. Implicitly or explicitly, this is generally acknowledged by all but those who continue to base their theories on the competitive model, thus assuming away the problem. It is also agreed that such implications are, on balance, negative. There is no agreement, however, concerning the nature of the relationship between the growth of oligopoly in the advanced capitalist countries and the permanence of underdevelopment.

All theories that emphasize the size of the market and its growth and/or technological discontinuities as important factors in hampering development are, to some extent, implying the relevance of the increased scale of capitalist production and of oligopolistic behavior.[1] However, this relationship between oligopoly and underdevelopment is often seen in purely technological terms, that is, as having little to do with the political-economic systems obtaining in the advanced and underdeveloped economies. Perroux has made the point explicitly:

> The organization of nations on a one-by-one and separate basis goes against technical and economic requirements which do not depend on democracy or dictatorship, communism or capitalism, but which are the direct and unavoidable consequence of techniques used in industry in the twentieth century.
>
> The conflict between the exigencies of the political and territorial organization of the social life of peoples and the exigencies of the multinational administration of the large-scale industries is a continuing reality.

This essay was written in 1967.

220

It may be doubted whether Marxism has yet accurately and sufficiently grasped this fact.[2]

An emphasis on oligopolistic behavior, rather than on technological factors, can be traced in Prebisch's[3] argument that the terms of trade between the "industrial centers" and the "periphery"[4] of the world economic system have behaved in the opposite way than one would expect from the competitive model. In that model the faster technical progress in the industrial centers, relative to the periphery, ought to result in falling prices of industrial products relative to primary products. However, the market power of workers, in pressing for higher wages, and of oligopolists, in resisting a squeeze on profit, in the industrial centers is considerably greater than the market power of capitalists, workers, and peasants in the periphery. As a consequence, in the centers the incomes of entrepreneurs and of productive factors increase relatively more than productivity, whereas in the periphery the increase in income is less than that in productivity.

Marxist theorists have, of course, been far more explicit in tracing the inability of contemporary capitalism to promote development in the non-industrialized lands to the oligopolistic structure of advanced capitalist countries. The argument has been succinctly expressed by Lange:

> With the development of large capitalist monopolies in the leading capitalist countries, the capitalists of those countries lost interest in developmental investment in the less developed countries because such investment threatened their established monopolistic positions. Consequently, investment in under-developed countries of capital from the highly developed countries acquired a specific character. It went chiefly into the exploitation of natural resources to be utilized as raw materials by the industries of the developed countries; and into developing food production in the underdeveloped countries to feed the population of the developed capitalist countries. It also went into deve-loping the economic infrastructures . . . needed to maintain economic relations with the underdeveloped countries.
> . . . the profits which were made by foreign capital . . . were exported back to the countries where the capital came from. Or if used for investment . . . they were not used for industrial investment on any major scale, which, as we know from experience, is the real dynamic factor of modern economic development. . . .
> Furthermore . . . the great capitalist powers supported the feudal elements in the underdeveloped countries as an instrument for maintaining their economic and political influence. This provided another obstacle to the economic development of these countries. . . .[5]

With regard to Africa, Nkrumah[6] has emphasized another aspect of the problem by pointing out that the "Balkanization" of Africa has created a superstructure that makes it impossible for individual nations to cope with the bargaining power of the international corporations which, by means of interlocking directorships, cross-shareholding, and other devices, effectively act on a Pan-African scale.

The purpose of this essay is to analyze the relationship between capitalist centers and periphery in order to assess the validity of these assumptions. The analysis will be limited in two ways. In the first place, it will be concerned with Tropical Africa and, within that region, with East and Central Africa in particular. The main reason is that, while it may be legitimate to deal with an "ideal" or "average" type of underdeveloped country when the interest of the analysis is centered on the advanced capitalist countries, the procedure may be misleading when the interest is focused on the periphery.

The discussion is limited in another direction. The pattern of relationships between centers and periphery is changing and considerable confusion concerning such relationships stems from the fact that different conclusions are drawn according to whether the "old" or the "new" pattern is emphasized. The relative importance of the two is difficult to assess, though the former is still predominant. Notwithstanding this, we shall focus our attention on the new pattern, i.e., that emerging from the relative decline in importance, not only of foreign portfolio investment in colonial government and railway stock, but also of foreign capital attracted to Tropical Africa by the combination of rich natural resources and cheap labor, on the one hand, and the growing relative importance of direct investment by large-scale oligopolies, on the other.[7] By limiting the study in these two ways we shall be in a position to gain an insight into the developmental potential of the emerging pattern of center-periphery relations under conditions of embryonic class formation in the periphery itself.

The advantage of an analysis of center-periphery relations under conditions of embryonic class formation is that it enables us to examine the position of the "intelligentsia" and the proletariat in the political economy of the periphery in the absence of "conservative" classes. The alliance of foreign interests with conservative elements in the periphery (feudal elements, landowning classes, some sections—or the whole—of the national bourgeoisie, upper ranks of the armed forces, corrupted bureaucrats, etc.), is usually thought to be the most powerful factor determining the stability of center-periphery relations.[8] The working class and the "intelligentsia" are left in a rather equivocal position. While it is sometimes acknowledged that the exploitation of cheap labor no longer represents an important determinant of foreign investment in the periphery,[9] suggestions that the interests of the proletariat proper and of the intelligentsia may conflict with those of the peasantry (often semi-proletarianized) have called forth some strongly worded criticism:

> [The working class is] the object of systematic defamation, to which some European idealists, infatuated with agrarian messianism, have unconsciously lent themselves. It is true that the wages of the workers are incomparably higher than the income of the African peasants; it is true that their standard of living is higher . . . it is normal that the bourgeoisie in power should use this state of affairs to set the peasants against the workers by presenting them as the privileged. It is, on the other hand, aberrant to find the same arguments coming from the pens of socialist theoreticians. The Russian workers in 1917 also formed a privileged minority with regard to the mass of mouzhiks, but what does that prove?[10]

In East and Central Africa in particular, the classes or groups usually singled out as likely to form alliances with foreign interests are economically and/or politically too weak to compete successfully for power with the intelligentsia (normally in bureaucratic employment), the wageworkers, and the peasantry. We shall, therefore, have to look for some other factor contributing to the stability of the present center-periphery relations.

We shall proceed as follows. In Section I we shall analyze the emerging pattern of foreign investment in Tropical Africa with particular reference to the choice of techniques and of sectors implicit in that pattern and to its developmental potential. In Section II we shall analyze the changes in the class structure of Tropical African societies associated with that pattern. In Section III we shall examine the implications for growth and development of the conclusions reached in the previous two sections, and finally, in Section IV, we shall discuss the limitations of state action in the light of the political economy of Tropical Africa.

I

The growth of oligopoly as the dominant structure in the advanced capitalist countries has been accompanied by a relative decline in importance of rentier capital as an independent center of economic and political power, and of competitive capitalism as a dynamic factor of growth. Small competitive firms still exist but in a subordinate position with respect to the large manufacturing or distributive corporations.[11] The latter, on the other hand, are increasingly able to take care of their investment needs from internal financing (especially depreciation allowances),[12] thus freeing themselves from outside financial control. The reciprocal recognition of strength and retaliatory power on the part of competitors, suppliers, and customers, characteristic of oligopolistic structures, enables the corporations to protect their profit positions through adjustments in prices, techniques, and employment. The long time-horizon in investment decisions that the financial independence of the corporations makes possible, and the greater calculating rationality of corporate managers enable the oligopolies to approach new developments with care and circumspection and to calculate more accurately the risks involved.[13] These changes in the competitive structure of the industrial centers have, since World War II, been reflected in the pattern of investment in the periphery.

The declining relative importance of rentier capital has been matched by a decline in portfolio investment in the periphery relative to direct investment on the part of the corporations.[14] At the same time, the vast financial resources available to the corporations favored further vertical integration while oligopolistic behavior encouraged the formation of consortia in mineral extraction and processing.[15] These tendencies were strengthened by the process of "decolonization." The "colonial preserves of European imperialism" were opened up to American capitalism,[16] in which the oligopolistic corporation plays a more central role than in French or British capitalism. More important still was the outflow of small-scale, competitive capital that accompanied independence. In fact, de-colonialization was, among other things, the result of a conflict between the dynamic elements (the big companies) and the backward elements (marginal enterprises, small planters, small trading houses, small semiartisanal workshops) of colonial capitalism.[17] Independence favored the outflow of the latter. For example, the accession to independence of French-speaking Africa was accompanied by capital outflow in the sector of small colonial enterprises and trading houses and a capital inflow in mining, manufacturing, and industrial agriculture.[18] Similar tendencies were at work in English-speaking countries: the flight of small-scale colonial enterprise was undoubtedly an important factor in the drastic fall of British private investment in Sterling Africa from £30 million in 1960 and £33.4 million in 1961 to £8.8 million in 1962, £2.5 million in 1963 and *minus* £9 million in 1964.[19] The upshot of these changes has been the emergence of a new pattern of foreign investment in which financial and merchanting interests and small-scale capital (mainly in agriculture but also in secondary and tertiary industries) have declined in importance relative to large-scale manufacturing and vertically integrated mining concerns. The typical expatriate firm operating in Tropical Africa is more and more what has been called the "multinational corporation" [20] or the "great interterritorial unit," [21] i.e., an organized ensemble of means of production subject to a single policy-making center which controls establishments situated in several different national territories.

An analysis of the factors determining the investment policies in the periphery of such multinational corporations is therefore necessary in order to assess the impact that foreign investment is likely to have on the process of development of Tropical Africa. It is useful to break down the analysis into two problems: (1) The sectoral distribution of investment; and (2) the type of techniques adopted in each sector. As we shall see, the two problems are interrelated but, as a first approximation, their separate treatment is analytically convenient.

There is a lack of basic quantitative evidence on the *sectoral distribution of foreign investment* in Tropical African countries. Most of what exists is aggregated in such a way as to be of little use for our purposes. There is, however, considerable agreement on a few broad generalizations:

1. The colonial pattern of capital investment in production for export has basically remained unaltered: investment in mining and petroleum absorbed the preponderant amount of private funds in the last decade.[22] What has changed in this respect is that complementary investment in the infrastructure, which used to be undertaken by private interests, is now the responsibility of the public sector. Private capital is now invested in more directly productive enterprises.[23]

2. Industrial investment other than in mining has been almost entirely concentrated either in primary products processing for the export market [24] or in import substitution in the light branches of manufacturing such as food, beverages, textiles, clothing, footwear, furniture, soap, and other consumer goods. More recently, the development of import substitution has begun to move gradually into branches of manufacturing industries

producing intermediate goods (cement, nonmetallic mineral products, and, less often, fertilizers and chemical products).[25]

3. Notwithstanding these developments, heavy industry in Tropical Africa is either nonexistent or, being export-oriented, is totally unrelated to the structure of the national and supranational African economies in the sense that it can hardly constitute a basis for the production of the capital goods required for the industrialization of the areas in which it is located. Rhodesia is possibly the only exception to the generalization. This situation is in sharp contrast with that of South Africa, where metallurgy, chemicals, and rubber are relatively advanced, and, to a lesser extent, with that of some North African countries, where chemicals and some basic metal and metal products industries have been developed.[26]

This sectoral pattern of foreign investment is likely to change slowly or not at all for reasons that are partly technological and partly political-economic. The sectors in question (mainly heavy engineering and chemical industries) are those in which economies of scale and the advantages of operating in an industrial environment (low costs of buying, erecting, maintaining, and operating machinery) are greatest. Hence the very underdevelopment and the "Balkanization" [27] of Tropical Africa hinder the development of an organic capital-goods industry.

However, as Barratt-Brown[28] has pointed out, there are more fundamental reasons than these:

> The main reason for the failure of capitalism to invest more in the industrialisation of the less-developed lands has arisen from a real doubt about the possibilities of success, and, therefore, of a profitable return. Investment in heavy industry is a big business, on which a return may only be seen in the very long term. There must be good reasons to believe that the whole overseas economy will develop in such a way as to nourish a market for capital goods. . . . It is not surprising that capitalist firms and financiers . . . should prefer to wait and see how the establishment of light industries and the development of power supplies and a marketable surplus of food goes, before wishing to sink their capital in heavy industry.

Bearing this in mind it would seem that the greater calculating rationality and the greater care and circumspection in approaching new developments of the modern international corporations, relative to competitive capital and to chartered companies and finance capital of old, are an important obstacle to the development of capital-goods industries in the periphery. The oligopolistic structure of advanced capitalist countries, however, plays a more direct role in favoring the bias of investment in the periphery against the capital-goods industry. As we have seen, oligopoly favors the reciprocal recognition of strength and retaliatory power. This means that when a large-scale manufacturer is deciding whether to invest in a new area, he will take into consideration, among other things, the effect of the decision on: (1) his own export interests, (2) his competitors' export interests, and (3) his customers' export interests, if any.[29] A textile manufacturing concern, for example, will take into consideration only (1) and (2). A manufacturer of capital goods, on the other hand, will also consider possible effects on his customers' interests which may be impinged upon by the growth, in the periphery, of a competing industry induced by the local production of capital goods. In consequence, quite apart from its effects on the level of investment to be discussed later on, the oligopolistic structure of the industrial centers strengthens the other factors mentioned above in producing in Tropical Africa a sectoral pattern of foreign investment biased against the capital-goods industry.

With regard to *choice of techniques*, it seems fairly well-established that foreign investment in Tropical Africa has a capital-intensive bias.[30] This bias is sometimes due to technological constraints. In mining, for example, the nature of the deposits may be responsible for differences in capital intensity. The scattering of Rhodesian gold deposits favored labor-intensive techniques while the concentration of high-grade copper deposits in Zambia favored capital-intensive techniques.[31] In the latter case, even if highly labor-intensive techniques exist, such as those used by Africans prior to European penetration, the technological gap is too great for such techniques to develop the industry on a significant scale.[32] However, even in extreme cases like the one in question, alternative techniques are always available,[33] though within a relatively limited range. Thus technological constraints are only one factor in determining the capital intensity of investment, and, in the case of many industries (e.g., light industries) in which foreign investment shows an equally strong bias toward capital-intensity,[34] they are rather unimportant. Other determinants have to be sought. Somewhat related to technological factors, management constraints have to be mentioned. Techniques of management, organization, and control have evolved in the technological environment of the industrial centers and cannot be easily adapted to the conditions in the periphery.[35] Often, therefore, either the conditions in the periphery can be modified, at least partially, to make capital and skill-intensive investment possible or no investment at all will be undertaken by the multinational corporations.[36] In other words, the spectrum of techniques taken into consideration by the multinational corporations may not include labor-intensive techniques.

There is another reason, probably more important than management constraints, why labor-intensive techniques may be disregarded.

As Perroux and Demonts[37] have pointed out, the multinational firm applies to all its branches technical methods corresponding to its capital, whatever the importance of the factors at work in the territories where it settles. There is a tendency in discussions of underdevelopment to overlook the fact that a shortage of finance is an important impediment to the growth of the small enterprise and of the public sectors of African economies, but it is no problem for the multinational firms. The latter not only have access to the capital markets in the industrial centers,[38] but, as we have mentioned, they are in a position through their pricing and dividend policies (in the industrial centers as well as in the periphery) to build up large accumulated reserves of capital for their investment programs. Financial strength makes the large firm adopt capital-intensive techniques, not only in the industrial centers but also in the periphery.[39]

In a way, capital intensity is favored also by the qualitative characteristics of the labor force in Tropical Africa. The problem is too often overlooked because of insufficiently clear definitions of the various categories of labor.[40] Let us classify labor as follows:

1. *Unskilled labor*, characterized by versatility (in the sense that it can be readily put to varied unskilled activities), and by lack of adaptation to the discipline of wage employment.

2. *Semi-skilled labor*, characterized by specialization, regularity, and identification with the job.

3. *Skilled labor*, characterized by relative versatility (in the sense of having complex skills), e.g., carpenters, mechanics, supervisors, etc.

4. *High-level manpower*, characterized by specialization and by educational qualifications other than, or besides, training on the job, e.g., maintenance and production engineers, purchase and sales experts, designers, cost and accounting personnel, etc.

Capital-intensive techniques will not only require less labor for each level of output, but they will also require a different composition of the labor force than labor-intensive techniques, as they make possible the division of complex operations, which would need skilled labor, into simple operations that can be performed by semiskilled labor. In other words, labor-intensive techniques are associated with a pattern of employment in which labor of type (1) and (3) predominates whereas capital-intensive techniques are associated with a pattern of employment in which labor of type (2) and (4) predominates. As we shall see in the next section, provided that employers take a sufficiently long time-horizon in their wage and employment policies, it is easier, under African conditions, to provide the remedy for a shortage of the latter types of labor than it is to do so for a shortage of skilled labor. Thus, from this point of view as well, the longer time-horizon of the multinational corporations favors the adoption of capital-intensive techniques.

These two biases of the pattern of investment emerging in Tropical Africa (i.e., in favor of capital-intensive techniques and against the capital-goods sector) reinforce each other. The choice of capital-intensive techniques within each industry favors the use of specialized machinery and consequently restrains the growth of demand for capital goods that could be produced in the periphery. The lack of investment in the capital-goods sector, in turn, prevents the development of capital goods embodying a *modern* labor-intensive technology which may reduce the bias in favor of capital intensity. This double bias has many implications for growth, development, and class formation in Tropical Africa that will be examined in the following sections. What must be considered here is *the relationship between the pattern of investment* just discussed and *the size of the internal market* that is a key determinant of foreign investment in the region.

The development of the capital-goods sector performs the double function of expanding both the productive capacity of the economy and the internal market. The latter function was emphasized by Lenin in a controversy with the Narodniks on the subject of the possibility of the *"internal* expansion of capitalism." The development of the internal market, Lenin argued, was possible despite the restricted consumption by the masses (or the lack of an external outlet) because to expand production it is first of all necessary to enlarge that department of social production which manufactures means of production, and it is necessary to draw into it workers who create a demand for articles of consumption. Hence, "consumption" develops after "accumulation." [41] The crucial assumption in the argument is that the demand for capital goods is largely autonomous, i.e., that it is not induced by the pre-existing size of the market and its growth. However, this autonomous development of the

capital-goods sector presupposes a type of behavior which may character-
ize competitive capitalism, but which cannot be expected from the modern
corporations.[42] These corporations tend to expand productive capacity
in response to market demand and in consequence restrain the endogenous
generation of growth stimuli.

In the case of Tropical Africa and the periphery in general, the position
is made worse by the fact that the multinational corporations (whenever
the nature of the productive process permits it) usually prefer to expand
productive capacity in the industrial centers where they are more secure
and where they can take advantage of operating in an industrial environment.[43] Expansion in the periphery is usually undertaken by a foreign
concern in response to protectionist policies on the part of national government in order either to protect its own export interests, or to establish
itself anew in the area.[44] In other words, the existence of a local market
for the production of the foreign concern, though a necessary condition,
is not sufficient for the actual establishment of a plant. This presupposes
the ability of individual governments either to set up production in
competition with foreign interests or to play one oligopoly off against the
other. The fact that this ability on the part of the governments of Tropical
Africa is most limited in the case of capital-goods industries is an additional factor strengthening the bias of the emerging pattern of investment
against such industries.

It follows that the emerging pattern of investment is unlikely to reduce
the basic lack of structure of the Tropical African economies. Growth
in these economies continues to depend on the growth of outside markets.
In fact, the dependence is even greater than it used to be in view of the
fact that industrialization tends to take a capital-intensive path which
presupposes the importation of specialized machinery. For this reason the
integration of the modern sectors of Tropical Africa (due to the need of
the multinational concerns to operate on a supranational scale) is accompanied by their greater integration with the industrial centers. We shall
return to these conclusions in Section III where their implications for
growth and development are discussed. We must now analyze the impact
of the emerging pattern of foreign investment on the class structure
of Tropical African societies.

II

The analysis in this section will be focused on wage and salary workers and their direct and indirect relationships with other classes and interests. *Wage employment in Tropical Africa* is at a low stage of development. Table I[45] gives no more than an idea of the order of magnitudes involved.

Table I
Estimated Population Labor Force and Total Nonagricultural Wage Employment in Africa
(*by region, around 1960*)

Region	Population in millions	Labor force		Total wage employment		Nonagricultural wage employment	
		in millions	*as per-cent of pop.*	*in millions*	*as per-cent of labor force*	*in millions*	*as per-cent of labor force*
East Africa	67.6	24.7	36.5	3.8	15.4	2.5	10.1
Central Africa	32.8	13.8	42.1	2.1	15.2	1.6	11.6
West Africa	71.8	32.9	45.8	2.0	6.1	1.7	5.2
Tropical Africa	173.2	71.4	41.2	7.9	11.1	5.8	8.1
North Africa	65.4	22.6	34.6	7.5	32.2	4.6	20.4
Southern Africa	16.9	6.0	35.5	3.8	63.3	3.0	50.0
All Africa	254.5	100.0	39.3	19.2	19.2	13.4	13.4

As will be pointed out below, this small participation in wage employment is matched by qualitative characteristics of the wage-labor force which reduce even further the relative importance of the proletariat proper in Tropical Africa. Equally important is the fact that wage employment has been relatively static over the last ten–fifteen years,[46] though in almost every country there have been periods, coinciding with heavy investment in infrastructure and with installation investments, during which the proportion of the labor force in wage employment temporarily rose. This relatively static wage employment has been accompanied by rising wages; the average annual rate of increase in African wages during the 1950's, for example, appears to have been in the order of 7–8 percent.[47] In general, wages are not merely chasing prices but are running ahead of them, the rise often implying an increase in real wages considerably faster than that in real national product.[48] In consequence, the employees' share of national income rose sharply in many countries.[49] As Turner[50] remarks, "It seems rather hard to find a case where the general level of real wages has in recent years behaved as it theoretically ought in an underdeveloped economy—i.e., has lagged behind other incomes, and particularly profits." Thus the main characteristics of the wage working class are: relatively static numbers and rising incomes. With regard to the structural characteristics of wage employment, the table below[51] illustrates them for selected Tropical African countries.

Table II

Structures of Wage Employment in Selected Tropical Africa Countries

Country	Year	Nonagricultural wage employment		
		percent of total wage empl.	*percent employed in public sector*	*percent employed in services sector*
Kenya	1965	65	30	77
Uganda	1965	82	39	77
Tanzania (Tanganyika)	1965	62	32	75
Malawi	1961	65	—	61
Malagasy Rep.	1961	77	—	77
Nigeria	1962	98	34	46
Ivory Coast	1961	55	—	68
Ghana	1960	73	35	55
Sierra Leone	1963	95	—	53

It can be observed from the table that the public sector, as a rule, employs a substantial proportion of wage workers and that nonagricultural employment is heavily concentrated in the service sector. The underdevelopment of industry is an obvious determinant of that structure. Another important factor is that the colonial powers superimposed a complex administrative structure on near-subsistence economies which tended to control not only the public services but also many economic and social agencies, such as marketing boards. After independence, African governments have taken over these functions and expanded them in their attempts to step up economic growth and to enlarge social services (agricultural extension work, development corporations, education, etc).

Unfortunately, there are no data on the relative importance of wage employment in concerns to which the analysis of the previous section may apply (viz., in enterprises with international affiliations including the vertically integrated combines and mixed or state enterprises managed by international corporations). This lack of quantitative data, however, is only a partial obstacle to our analysis as our main concern is with the qualitative changes in the wage-labor force that can be associated with the pattern of investment discussed in the previous section. In this connection the first point that has to be emphasized is the heterogeneity of the African salary and wage-working class. We have already classified the labor force according to skills, singling out four categories: unskilled, semiskilled, and skilled labor, and high-level manpower. This classification only to some extent overlaps with two other classifications that are relevant in the present context. The first, to be discussed presently, concerns the degree of commitment to, or dependence upon, wage employment and gives rise to the two main categories of "proletariat" and "semi-proletarianized peasantry" (or, less frequently in Tropical Africa, semi-proletarianized artisans). The other classification focuses on status and prestige and distinguishes an elite, a sub-elite, and the mass of the wage workers.[52]

At a seminar of the International African Institute on the New Elites of Tropical Africa (Ibadan, July 1964) it was suggested that the term "elite" could be appropriately used to denote those who were Western educated with an annual income of at least £250.[53] The sub-elite, on the other hand, is made up of the less well educated, i.e., those with post-primary education or some secondary education (executive-clerical grades, primary school teachers, and skilled artisans).[54] The rapid growth of the African elite and sub-elite in the last decade can be traced to the expansion of educational facilities and of job opportunities for Africans in highly paid employment that accompanied and followed the accession to independence. This expansion has been phenomenal but it is still a fortunate few who manage to reach secondary school. In no African state does the proportion exceed 2 percent, though in some constituent regions this figure is exceeded.[55] The fast rate of expansion of highly paid job opportunities for Africans has been due mainly to the Africanization of the complex administrative structure inherited from colonial rule, the scope of which, as I have mentioned, was extended by the African governments. Another factor favoring this expansion, the Africanization policy of expatriate firms, is of lesser but growing importance as the top posts in government service are uniformly held by young men with decades of service ahead of them. Expatriate firms have become increasingly conscious of their "public image" and have quickly Africanized their office staffs, middle commercial posts, and some managerial posts, especially in personnel management and public relations. Production, engineering, and other technical and higher executive posts are still mainly in expatriate hands, though in a few instances Africans have been recruited to nominal directorships.[56] In the colonial period the private professions held great attraction for Africans who were subject to discriminatory practices in the civil service. These professions are still popular, but, though in general lawyers remain in private practice, most doctors are now employed in the public service.[57] Thus the overwhelming majority of the elite and the sub-elite in Tropical Africa is in bureaucratic employment, and, though employment in the public sector is predominant, the international corporations are becoming an increasingly important outlet for the newly educated African.

When we come to analyze what in the classification just discussed is lumped together as the "masses of wage workers," the distinction focusing on the commitment to, or dependence upon, wage employment becomes relevant. The mass of English migrants in the early nineteenth century were landless agricultural laborers. In Tropical Africa the mass of migrants are peasants with rights to the use of land. While the former were proletarians, the latter are peasants at different stages of proletarianization and therefore present a much greater heterogeneity. Labor migration in Africa[58] is compounded of various elements of "push" and "pull," the former relating to the maintenance of subsistence or essential consumption and the latter relating to the improvement of the pre-existing standard of living. "Push" factors are usually associated with a deteriorating relation of the population to the traditional means of subsistence (e.g., land shortage), or changes in the nature of essential consumption due to the penetration of the money economy. The improvement of the existing standard of living, on the other hand, can be achieved either directly or indirectly—directly when the aim of labor migration is a net addition to the consumption of the extended family; indirectly when the aim is the purchase of equipment to improve production in the traditional sector or the accumulation of sufficient financial means to enter some petty capitalistic activity (e.g., commercial farming, trade, contracting, etc). The two main characteristics of the labor force under the system of labor migration are low wages and high turnover. The wage rate is customarily based on the subsistence for the bachelor workers. Such wage may or may not allow some saving according to whether "pull" or "push" factors, respectively, predominate in the economy. Low wages strengthen the tendency for the participation in the labor market to be of a temporary nature which in turn accounts for the persistently unskilled character of the labor force. These factors interact, favoring the development of a poorly paid and unskilled labor force.[59] In addition, the lack of division of labor between agricultural and nonagricultural activities and between wage employment limits the internal market, especially for agricultural produce. Thus, by hampering the development of capitalist agriculture, it further entrenches the labor-migration system.

Under these conditions the complete *proletarianization of the wage workers*, i.e., the severance of the ties with the traditional sector, is largely optional. It occurs when the incomes derived from wage employment are high enough to make the worker uninterested in the maintenance of reciprocal obligations with the extended family in the traditional sector. More specifically, his income must be sufficiently high and reliable to allow him to support his family in the town and to save enough to insure himself against distress in periods of unemployment, sickness, and in his old age. The difference between this income and the low migrant-labor wage rate will normally be considerable. This differential is reflected in the high cost of semiskilled and skilled labor relative to unskilled labor. The time-horizon of the migrant worker is typically short and therefore as soon as his acquired skill commands remuneration in excess of that which he presently receives, he leaves the employer.[60] In consequence, either the employer is willing and able to pay the much higher wages that can induce greater stability of the labor force or he must adapt his techniques to the existing qualitative characteristics of the labor force rather than train the workers for more skilled activities. The nature of the typical enterprise in colonial times militated against a breakthrough in the vicious circle "high turnover–low productivity–low wages–high turnover" and therefore against the development of a semiskilled, relatively highly paid, stabilized labor force. Small planters, small trading houses, small work-shops could hardly be expected to take a long time-horizon in their invest-ment decisions. Similarly, the large enterprises engaged in primary production were either indifferent toward the use of mechanized tech-niques or positively against it in view of the instability of markets or, whenever technological constraints imposed capital intensity and the use of skilled and semiskilled labor, found it more convenient to resort to the importation of expatriate workers than to embark upon the expensive exercise of stabilizing the African labor force.[61] Thus traditional colonial employers relied on African migrant labor for their requirements of unskilled labor and on racial minorities (Europeans, Asians, Levantines) for their requirements of skilled labor. The demand for semiskilled labor remained, on the whole, very limited. In the 1950's important changes took place. As we have seen, the pattern of foreign investment altered, especi-ally in the immediate preindependence period when the importance of small-scale colonial enterprises declined and that of the multinational concerns increased. This change was accompanied by the slackening of the influence of the former interests and of the racial minorities on government policies, and by the correspondingly greater influence of the international corporations and of the African elite, sub-elite, and work-ing class. These two changes can be assumed to have been instrumental in bringing about the breakthrough in the vicious circle "low wages–high turnover–low productivity–low wages." Various factors were at work in producing the breakthrough and their relative importance is not only difficult to assess (given their interaction), but varies considerably from country to country. Let us first analyze some of the most important factors and later suggest what their relative contribution to the change might have been.

The salary structure of the independent African states remains a colonial heritage. As Africans gradually entered the civil service and the managerial positions in large foreign concerns, they assumed the basic salaries attached to the posts since, so far, the principle of equal pay be-tween African and expatriate for equal posts has generally been main-tained.[62] In consequence, Africanization brings about a huge gap between the incomes of high-level manpower (the African elite and sub-elite), and the incomes not only of unskilled labor but also of semiskilled and skilled labor. Thus the whole level of wages, from the unskilled laborer upward, comes into question.[63] The workers' capacity for industrial conflict may be negligible but their political influence is often considerable while increases in wages and salaries seem an easy route to prove the value of the recently acquired independence.[64] For these reasons governments in Tropical Africa are easily induced to steadily raise wages either through increases in legal minimum wages or, being major employers of labor, by acting as wage leaders. Thus the Africanization of high-level manpower and greater influence of the working class on government policies favored a gradual rise in wages at the lower levels.

Another important factor was the *emerging pattern of foreign investment* discussed in the previous section. As we saw, the greater capital intensity of production associated with that pattern requires a labor force in which semiskilled labor predominates. For the multinational concerns, therefore, stabilization of a section of the indigenous labor force is essential and actively sought after as the importation of skilled labor becomes impracticable and indeed unnecessary as complex operations are broken down into simpler operations that can be performed by semiskilled labor. Capital intensity of production (which makes wages a small proportion of total costs and requires labor stability), the ability to pass on to the consumer increased labor costs (in the periphery in the case of manufacturing concerns, in the industrial centers in the case of the vertically integrated companies operating in primary production), and the ability to take a long time-horizon in employment and investment decisions, make the multinational companies willing and able to pay sufficiently high wages to stabilize a section of the labor force. In other words, for the companies in question the exploitation of natural resources or of market opportunities in the periphery with capital intensive techniques is far more important than the exploitation of cheap labor. These factors are undoubtedly responsible for the observed tendency to pay relatively high wages and to experiment with modern training and management methods on the part of large expatriate firms.[65]

Governments' and international corporations' wage and salary policies interact and the ensuing steady rise in wage rates induces further labor saving, not only on the part of expatriate firms, but also on the part of those locally based enterprises which can afford it.[66] Capital intensity, in turn, generally means that labor is a lower proportion of costs to the enterprise than it would otherwise be, so that the individual concern's willingness to concede wage increases is higher; but this reinforces the tendency to capital-intensive (or labor-saving) development *and a* "*spiral*" *process* may ensue.[67] Some disagreement is bound to arise concerning the extent to which growing capital intensity in Tropical Africa is induced by the investment and employment policies of the international corporations. The question is largely academic as such policies, either as a casual or as a permissive factor, are undoubtedly a crucial element in the "spiral" process. The importance as a "prime mover," on the other hand, will vary from country to country. In Uganda, for example, it would seem that government policies have played a predominant role in bringing about the steady rise in wages and, in consequence, most mechanization has been "induced."[68] In Rhodesia on the other hand, African workers have hardly any power to influence government policies and the steady rise in wages in the 1950's and in the early 1960's seems to have been induced by the stable labor requirements of the large-scale expatriate firms. Thus, while African money wages rose between 1949 and 1962 at an average annual rate of 9 percent, the increase was largely concentrated in those sectors where labor stabilization mattered most (viz., manufacturing and services). In the sectors where stabilization mattered least (viz., agriculture), money wages rose at a rate not much higher than that of price increases.[69]

An assumption that seems unacceptable is that the rise in wages has been due, to any important extent, to "*monopolistic action*" on the part of African workers as distinct from their power to influence government policies. This is Baldwin's assumption concerning the rise of wages on the Zambian copperbelt:

> Since the war . . . African and European wages have been raised by monopolistic actions to levels considerably above the rates necessary to attract the numbers actually employed. The consequences of this wage policy have been the creation of unemployment conditions in the Copperbelt towns, especially among Africans, and the wide-spread substitution of machines for men in the industry.[70]

That European workers, in the colonial situation, were in a strong bargaining position is a generally acknowledged fact. But it is equally acknowledged that the prevalence of the migrant-labor system and related lack of skills and specialization among Africans militates against the workers' capacity for industiral conflict.[71] Moderately effective trade-union organization normally follows and does not precede labor stabilization and mechanization,[72] as witnessed by the fact that, apart from the public services, the most important instances where anything like normal collective bargaining has been established appear to be in large-scale enterprises under foreign ownership and management.[73] It is possible therefore that, though trade union organizations have in the past mainly played a dependent role in the spiral process of rising wages and mechanization, they may, with the growing stabilization of the labor force, become a partly autonomous factor. However, the effect, if any, will be felt primarily on the differential between the remuneration of stabilized skilled and semiskilled labor and that of the semiproletarianized unskilled labor whose market power is bound to remain negligible.

This consideration brings us to the question of the stratification of the working class. The conclusion that emerges from the foregoing analysis is that the changes in the pattern of capital investment and in government policies in Tropical Africa that have occurred in the last decade have resulted in a breakthrough in the vicious circle "low wages–high turnover–low productivity–low wages"; such a breakthrough, however, concerns only the small section of the working class that is being rapidly proletarianized by enabling it to earn a subsistence in the wage economy. The breakthrough is therefore achieved at the cost of a relative reduction of the overall degree of participation of the labor force in wage employment. Whether this relative reduction can be assumed to be a short-term phenomenon which leads in the longer run to faster economic growth and greater participation in wage employment is a problem to be discussed in the next section. Here we are concerned with structural problems. From this standpoint it is correct to assume that the spiral process of rising wages and mechanization tends to produce a situation of rising productivity and living standards in a limited and shrinking modern sector, while the wage employment opportunities in that sector for the unskilled, semiproletarianized peasantry (which increasingly becomes a noncompeting group vis à vis the semiskilled proletariat) are reduced.[74] To find out to what extent this tendency is a special aspect of a more general trend toward a growing cleavage between the modern capital-intensive sector and the rest of the economy we must analyze the impact of the emerging pattern of foreign investment on the other classes of Tropical African society.[75]

Let us begin by examining the implications of the emerging pattern of foreign investment for the rural sector. The first point that has to be made is that the sectoral distribution of such investment enhances the dependence of agriculture on world markets for its expansion. The bias against the capital-goods sector not only restrains, as we have seen, the growth of the internal market but also increases the dependence on foreign sources for the supply of the capital goods necessary for the transformation of traditional agriculture. This transformation comes, therefore, to be subject to balance-of-payments constraints which, as it will be argued in the next section, are likely to become increasingly severe. The bias in favor of capital-intensive techniques has equally important implications. There are two ways in which the African peasantry can participate in the money economy, i.e., through periodic wage employment and through the sale of produce. We have seen that the emerging pattern of foreign investment restrains the growth of wage-employment opportunities in the modern sector for the unskilled, semiproletarianized peasantry. But, in addition to this, the low income-elasticity of the demand for agricultural produce in general and local produce in particular implicit in the capital-intensive growth of the modern sector also restrains the growth of demand for peasant produce.

It would seem, therefore, that the emerging pattern of foreign investment tends to reduce both the complementary links between urban and rural sectors (i.e., to increase further the lack of structure of the economies of Tropical Africa), and the spreading of development stimuli from the modern to the traditional sector. These conclusions hold for whatever assumptions one may want to make concerning the type of development of the agricultural sector, i.e., whether the expansion of agriculture takes place through the formation of a kulak class employing wage labor, or through the formation of cooperatives, collectives, and communes, or through the expansion of production by self-employed producers.

It may, however, be argued that the *relative* impoverishment of the peasantry associated with the emerging pattern of investment will speed up the spreading of capitalist relations in African agriculture,[76] i.e., the simultaneous formation of a kulak class and a rural proletariat, that would enhance the growth of agricultural productivity. This argument, however, misses the point that the relative impoverishment of the peasantry is accompanied by the negative impact of the emerging pattern of investment on the growth of demand for local agricultural produce. Such a pattern, therefore, restrains the incentive for, and financial ability of, the emerging kulaks to expand wage employment so that, other things being equal, it tends to produce an impoverished peasantry without fostering its absorption in capitalist agriculture.

The last point we have to discuss in this section is the implication of the emerging pattern of investment for the national bourgeoisie in nonagricultural sectors. In the colonial period most commerce (not directly in the hands of expatriate companies), and small-scale industrial enterprise[77] was in alien hands—the Levantines of West Africa, the Indians of East Africa, the Europeans, and, to a lesser extent, the Indians of Central Africa. African traders were almost totally absent in Central and East Africa while part-time trading activities were widespread among West Africans, especially in Ghana and Nigeria. This pattern started to change with the approach of Independence. In East and Central Africa the Africans, with official support, began to challenge Asian dominance in the commercial sphere. In West Africa the large expatriate firms, while Africanizing their staff, began to let slip into African hands the less sophisticated types of trade, particularly the produce buying and the retailing of simple goods—many of the licensed buyers are in fact men trained by these companies.[78] In industry, on the other hand, locally based capitalist enterprises are still largely in the hands of racial minorities and, though there are exceptions,[79] they are generally small and managed by people whose background is commerce rather than industry.[80] Africanization in this sphere is proceeding more slowly than in petty trade but in Ghana and Nigeria Africans own businesses and workshops in a wide range of light and service industries.

There are various factors hampering the growth of a locally based capitalist class. Lack of specialization generally characterizes African petty capitalism: wage employment, trade, farming, and artisanal activities are often combined, though the combination of more than two occupations is rare.[81] This lack of specialization favors the dispersal of capital, labor, and managerial resources, and in consequence it hampers the growth of productivity and credit-worthiness in each line. The emerging pattern of investment in Tropical Africa creates additional and more powerful obstacles. The rise of an African elite, sub-elite, and proletariat proper, enjoying a relatively high standard of living both imposes consumption patterns which discourage accumulation,[82] and makes business unattractive relative to salary employment or even wage employment in the capital-intensive expatriate or mixed enterprises.[83]

The new pattern of foreign investment, however, has more direct repercussions on the supply and demand conditions facing existing or potential local capitalism. On the supply side, we must consider the effects of foreign investment on the labor force. We saw that large-scale foreign corporations contribute to the rising trend in wages. While those local enterprises which can afford it adapt themselves to the new market situation by stepping up labor-saving, the rise in labor costs tends to discourage the expansion of the smaller scale, financially weaker enterprises which cannot afford mechanization.[84] However, to the extent that a dual wage structure obtains, de jure or de facto, the possibility of survival or expansion of small-scale local capitalism depends on how effectively labor-intensive enterprise can compete, in quality and price, with capital-intensive, large-scale enterprises. The experience of advanced countries shows that, given a sufficiently large market in relation to the minimum scale which makes capital-intensive production economical,[85] it is difficult to think of industries, besides construction, some servicing industries, and the exceptions mentioned below, where small-scale, labor-intensive enterprise has a competitive advantage.

The pattern of consumption associated with the capital-intensive production of the wage sectors of Tropical Africa aggravates the position. The income elasticity of demand not only for agricultural produce but also for simple consumer and capital goods in the production of which small-scale industry may have a competitive advantage, is much smaller than it would be in the case of a labor-intensive type of growth of the money economy. This pattern of demand, therefore, makes it easier for modern manufacturing based on the latest technology to undersell, or to pre-empt, the market opportunities for local small-scale enterprises.[86] This possibility threatens the latter even when no competition from large-scale enterprises is expected in the short run; the greater risks involved in undertaking production may thus discourage the exploitation of profitable opportunities by small entrepreneurs.

In each industrial process, however, there are *operations* which can be profitably subcontracted to smaller, labor-intensive enterprises by the large-scale expatriate firms. It is not inconceivable, therefore, that investment by multinational corporations in Tropical Africa will encourage the growth of a satellite, small-scale national bourgeoisie. Such a subordinate role is all that this national bourgeoisie will, at best, play in the area. In other words, the polarization of the business world so aptly described in the following passage by Mills with regard to the industrial centers, can be expected to grow in the periphery as well:

> Roughly speaking the business world is polarized into two types: large industrial corporations and a "lumpenbourgeoisie." The latter is composed of a multitude of firms with a high death rate, which do a fraction of the total business done in their lines and engage a considerably larger proportion of people than their quota of business. . . .
>
> Their remarkable persistence as a stratum . . . should not be confused with the well-being of each individual enterprise and its owner-manager . . . [as there] is a great flow of entrepreneurs and would-be entrepreneurs in and out of the small business stratum. . . .[87]

The small businessmen are increasingly concentrated in the retail and service industries, and, to a lesser extent, in finance and construction. Their most important characteristic from the standpoint of our analysis is the subordinate role they come to play:

> The power of the large business is such that, even though many small businesses remain independent, they become in reality agents of larger businesses. . . .
>
> Dependency on trade credit tends to reduce the small businessman to an agent of the creditor. . . .
>
> [By means of] "exclusive dealing contracts" and "full line forcing" . . . manufacturers, who set retail prices and advertise nationally [internationally, in our context], turn small retailers into what amounts to salesman on commission who take entrepreneurial risks. In manufacturing, subcontracting often turns the small subcontractor into what amounts to a risk-taking manager of a branch plant.

The main implication is that the national bourgeoisie will be increasingly incapable of creating growth stimuli independently of international capitalism in the sense that its expansion comes to be almost entirely induced by the complementary growth of the multinational concerns. In consequence, the integration of Tropical Africa with the international capitalist system can be assumed to exclude the possibility of a national capitalist pattern of development.

III

In this section we will analyze the implications for growth and development in Tropical Africa of the main assumptions that have emerged in the previous discussion. A brief summary of the main conclusions so far reached is in order. In Section I we argued that the financial strength and managerial characteristics of the multinational concerns are reflected in the choice of capital-intensive techniques within individual sectors or industries. In addition, the oligopolistic behavior and greater calculating rationality of the multinational concerns are reflected in a sectoral pattern of investment which is biased against the capital-goods sector. Both biases (in favor of capital intensity and against the capital-goods sector), contribute to the low demand-generating potential of investment which is already implicit in oligopolistic behavior. We concluded that this pattern of investment tends to promote the integration of the modern sector in the periphery and of these with the industrial centers but does not contribute to the reduction of the lack of structure of the national and supranational economies of Tropical Africa. In Section II, where attention was focused on the changes in the class structure of Tropical Africa that can be associated with the emerging pattern of investment, we saw that the multinational corporation contributes to the reproduction of an environment in the modern sector of the periphery that suits its operations: a semiskilled proletariat, a white-collar elite and sub-elite, a dependent "lumpenbourgeoisie." This tendency deepens the cleavages between modern and traditional sectors for two main reasons; that is:

1. Because of the growing qualitative differences between proletarianized and semiproletarianized labor. The former, through relatively high income and consequent greater stability, acquires specialized skills, while the latter's dependence on the traditional sector is increased by the labor-saving development of the modern sector.

2. Because of the lessening of the links between the traditional sector and the modern sector as the capital intensity and bureaucratization of the latter minimizes the income elasticity of its demand for the output of the former.

Growing internal cleavages and greater external integration tend, of course, to reinforce each other in a process of circular causation. The various "demonstration effects" which influence the pattern of consumption, investment, technology, and administration in the modern sector, are strengthened by greater external integration and, in turn, deepen the internal cleavages.

It may be argued that whatever the outcome in the short run, the long-term development potential of the Tropical African economies is increased rather than reduced by this pattern of growth. The argument may seem to be implicit in those theories of development which uphold the advisability—in definite conditions, to be discussed presently, and from the standpoint of long-term consumption and employment maximization—of a choice of capital-intensive techniques in underdeveloped economies.[88] The argument is based on the consideration that each technique of production has a double impact on employment and consumption. There is a direct effect on output and employment in the short run, and there is an indirect effect in the long run as the technique of production, through its influence on income distribution and the size of the investable surplus, affects the rate of growth of output and employment. Labor-intensive techniques are associated with high levels of employment in the short run and with a large share of wages in output. Capital-intensive techniques, on the other hand, imply a smaller share of wages in output, and may therefore yield a larger investable surplus and a faster rate of growth of employment.

The argument, implicitly or explicitly, is based on a number of restrictive assumptions. We shall limit our discussion to the following crucial ones:

1. The real wage rate is fixed whatever technique of production is adopted and it is constant through time.

2. The reinvestment of the larger surplus associated with capital-intensive techniques is feasible in the sense that either the productive capacity of the capital-goods sector is sufficiently large to supply the capital goods required by such reinvestment, or foreign exchange is available to make up the deficiency of capital goods through purchases abroad.

3. The reinvestment of the larger surplus is not only feasible but desired by whoever controls its utilization.

Let us discuss the validity of these assumptions in the context analyzed in Sections I and II.

1. *The real wage rate is constant whatever the technique of production and through time.*

Both assumptions are generally untrue in the context of Tropical Africa. Capital-intensive techniques require a semi-skilled and therefore stabilized labor force committed to wage employment. As we saw, the "price" of stabilization, and therefore the differential in real wage rates according to whether capital- or labor-intensive techniques are used is considerable. In consequence, even though the share of output accruing to wages is smaller in the case of capital-intensive techniques, the size of the investable surplus (and therefore the rate of growth of output and employment) may be greater in the case of labor-intensive techniques. The case for capital-intensive techniques is further weakened by the fact that, either as a permissive or as a causal factor, they encourage a steady rise in wages. In consequence, capital-intensive techniques may foster the rapid growth of consumption on the part of employed workers rather than the rapid growth of employment.

2. *The reinvestment of the larger surplus associated with capital-intensive techniques is feasible.*

In a closed economy, if the capital-goods sector cannot supply the means of production necessary for the investment of the larger surplus associated with capital-intensive techniques, the ceiling to the rate of growth of output and employment will be determined by the capacity of that sector. We saw that the emerging pattern of investment in Tropical Africa has a double bias, i.e., in favor of capital-intensive techniques and against the capital-goods sector. The implication of this double bias for growth is that the positive impact of the former bias is counteracted by the latter. In other words, the bias against the capital-goods sector of the emerging pattern of investment reduces the problem of the feasibility of a faster rate of growth through capital-intensive development, to one of foreign exhange availability to purchase capital goods abroad.

The lack of structure of Tropical African economies makes them dependent for their foreign exchange earnings on the export of primary products. With the exception of the oil-producing countries and certain metal producers, underdeveloped economies relying on sales of primary products have, since the end of the Korean War boom, experienced a slowing down in the rate of growth of output and an actual fall in prices which has led to a decline in total earnings.[89] In the case of Tropical Africa, while the value of exports rose about 55 percent between 1950 and 1955, it rose only 15 percent between 1955 and 1960[90] and lately the position has probably worsened. In addition, it must be borne in mind that, in the case of many argicultural exports such as coffee, tobacco, short-staple cotton, oilseeds, sisal, etc., the position would have been seriously worsened in the absence of restrictive actions and/or lack of expansion in competing areas.[91] As Tropical Africa is principally an agricultural producer, though its world position is strongest in minerals, it is safe to assume that a steady and rapid expansion of exports in the future is highly unlikely. A few individual countries with important mineral deposits will, of course, represent the exception to the general rule.

Imports, on the other hand, have been growing faster than exports with the result that, in recent years, there seems to be no surplus in the trade account for Tropical Africa as a whole.[92] When investment income paid abroad and "services" are taken into account, Tropical Africa has a considerable deficit on current account.[93] Given this situation, the ability of Tropical Africa to sustain a high rate of capital-intensive investment will depend on the inflow of private and public capital from abroad.[94]

Let us first discuss foreign private investment. Such flow of capital has positive and negative effects on the balance of payments. The most obvious negative effect is the outflow of profits which, after a lag, the investment will bring about. It seems that returns of some 15–20 percent on capital, usually on the basis of an investment maturing in about three years, are required in order to attract foreign investment in Tropical Africa.[95] Table III gives the rates of growth of foreign investment, for different maturation lags and rates of profit, which must be maintained if the outflow of investment income is not to exceed gross foreign investment. The combinations denoted with a circle can be conservatively assumed to be the most relevant to our context. Rates of growth of foreign private investment in the order of 10–12 percent are very high from the standpoint, not only of past performance,[96] but, as we shall see later on, of future prospects. It seems, therefore, highly unlikely that a

Table III
Rates of Growth of Gross Foreign Investment Necessary to Offset the
Outflow on Investment Income
(*percent values*)

	Rates of profit (percent)			
Maturation period:	*10*	*15*	*20*	*25*
3 years	8	11	14	16
4 years	7	10	12	14
5 years	7	9	11	13

net inflow of private capital can, with occasional exceptions, be expected to ease the shortage of foreign exchange in Tropical Africa.

Let us now see whether we can expect a positive effect of foreign investment on the trade account. In the case of investment in mining, foreign investment can, in many cases, be expected to bring about a steady increase in the value of exports. These gains, however, may be offset by related effects of such investment on imports. As we have seen, the emerging pattern of foreign investment in Tropical Africa, in mining as well as manufacturing, favors (either as a permissive or as a casual factor), the development of a pattern of consumption and of production in the modern sector that weakens the links between the modern sector itself and the rest of the economy in the periphery. The pattern of demand for productive inputs and of consumption, associated with a capital-intensive and bureaucratized modern sector, tends to promote a pattern of derivative demand that will be mainly satisfied either by imports from the industrial centers or by production within the modern sectors of the periphery. In the former case the negative impact on the balance of payments is direct and immediate. In the latter case, on the other hand, it is indirect. In order to understand this more roundabout effect we must consider the impact on the trade account of the balance of payments of foreign investment in manufacturing. The biases of investment in Tropical Africa in favor of capital intensity and against the capital-goods sector are relevant in this connection.

They are in fact largely responsible both for the fact that import substitution has largely been self-defeating[97] and for the poor prospects for Tropical African economies to become competitive on the world markets for manufactures.[98] As a result, manufacturing tends to be undertaken to supply almost exclusively the national or supranational markets of Tropical Africa.[99] While a positive net impact on the trade account may obtain in the early stages of import substitution, the negative effects that we have earlier traced in the pattern of derivative demand associated with the emerging pattern of investment, become overwhelming in the longer run. If we take into account the fact that it is also in the early stages of import substitution, if ever, that foreign private investment is likely to attain the "critical" rate of growth of 10–12 percent discussed above, the general conclusion emerges that after that stage foreign private investment, far from easing the shortage of foreign exchange of Tropical African economies, increasingly worsens the situation.[100]

Let us now consider the possibility that the foreign exchange necessary for the capital-intensive development of Tropical Africa will be made available by the advanced capitalist countries through bilateral long-term financial loans, multilateral loans, and "aid." The inflow of finance from these sources is essentially a postwar phenomenon and has replaced private portfolio investment in financing expenditure in infrastructure. The net flow to Tropical Africa rose steadily in the 1950's[101] and, as the interest payments on loans credited to African countries has begun to rise rapidly,[102] it seems to have reached a ceiling of \$0.9–1.0 billion in the 1960's.[103] There is a strong possibility that these financial flows, other than for military purposes (which have no positive effect on the availability of foreign exchange), are, for the most part, a dependant factor, i.e., it is likely that they are determined by the flows of direct private investment. In the first place, this financial assistance is more and more made available on the basis of the "economic viability" of the projects which it is supposed to support. This, in general, means that private capital must be forthcoming to make use of the overhead capital financed by public capital. In the second place, as mentioned above, a large proportion of bilateral assistance aims at easing the balance-of-payments position of Tropical African economies in order to make possible either the importation of capital goods or the repatriation of profits and capital. For these reasons official flows of financial resources cannot but marginally be considered an independent variable in determining the availability of foreign exchange necessary for the capital-intensive development of Tropical Africa.

Such availability will ultimately depend on the level and growth of foreign private investment in the sense that public capital will in general reinforce whatever tendencies are favored by the inflow of private capital—in the case of a high propensity to invest in the area, it will provide the financial resources necessary for the materialization of that propensity; in the case of a low investment propensity it will ease the shortage of foreign exchange to make possible the outflow of capital, thus worsening the situation in the long run. In conclusion, the problem of the feasibility of the higher rate of growth made possible by the capital-intensive development of Tropical Africa is largely related to that of the propensity to invest in the area of private foreign capital. We must now discuss this propensity.

3. *The reinvestment of the larger surplus associated with capital-intensive techniques is not only feasible, but desired by whoever controls its utilization.*

In the present context the utilization of the surplus is controlled by the international corporations.[104] Thus, in order to assess the likelihood that the surplus will be reinvested in Tropical Africa, we must briefly discuss the determinants of their propensity to invest in the periphery. Three main considerations seem to be relevant in this context.[105]

1. The extent to which Tropical Africa is a "growth area," as it is in fast-growing economies that the profitable opportunities necessary to attract foreign investment will present themselves.

2. The extent to which Tropical Africa is affected by a shortage of foreign exchange which would restrain the freedom of foreign corporations to repatriate profits and capital.

3. The extent to which investment in Tropical Africa is subject to the risks of expropriation of assets and for nationalization without "full" compensation.

The last question is not particularly relevant in the present discussion as we assume that, in this respect, conditions favorable to foreign capital obtain. We shall return to it in the next section.

The fact that the propensity to invest in Tropical Africa is affected by its balance-of-payments position, on the other hand, gives rise to a problem of circular causation. Recalling what we said earlier in this section, if foreign private investment grows at a rate higher than the critical value of some 10–12 percent, then such investment eases the shortage of foreign exchange, and if other favorable conditions obtain, additional foreign investment will be attracted to the area improving further the balance-of-payments position. But if the rate of growth of foreign capital invested in the area falls short of that critical value, the opposite cumulative process of falling propensity to invest and growing shortage of foreign exchange will take place. As we have seen, the flows of official capital will, in general, strengthen these tendencies. This cumulative process is more likely to operate in a downward than in an upward direction, since in the latter case other conditions connected with the extent to which Tropical Africa is a "growth area" must obtain to make the process self-sustaining. Let us take the lower limit of 10–12 percent as the minimum rate of growth of foreign investment that would create the conditions for the reinvestment in Tropical Africa of the surplus accruing to foreign corporations. This rate seems of impossible attainment for two main reasons:

1. With the exception of a few countries with particularly rich mineral deposits, the prospects for a rapid rise of Tropical Africa primary exports, i.e., at a rate exceeding the present 3–5 percent per annum, are very poor.[106]

2. Given the bias of the emerging pattern of investment in the area against the capital-goods sector, the autonomous growth of the internal market is severely restrained.

The combination of these two factors makes it safe to assume that, given the behavioral and institutional framework we have been analyzing, Tropical Africa will not, in the foreseeable future, become a "growth area." In consequence, whatever the situation might be during the so-called phase of easy import substitution, foreign investment will increasingly become a mere device for transferring surplus generated in Tropical Africa to the investing country.[107] Under these conditions the higher surplus associated with capital-intensive techniques does not lead to faster growth of employment but to higher exports of profits.

We see therefore that none of the three crucial assumptions on which the argument for capital-intensive techniques is based apply to our context. In consequence, the bias of the emerging pattern of investment in favor of capital intensity and against the capital-goods industry cannot be expected to lead, in the long run, to a faster growth of wage and salary-employment; it will simply allow a larger outflow of surplus from the area and growing incomes for a small, and, in relative terms, constant or contracting section of the working population. This type of growth, which, as we have seen, already characterizes Tropical Africa,[108] we shall call growth without development. In the last section of this essay we must turn to discuss the reasons for the stability of this pattern of growth.

IV

The analysis in the previous sections has been carried out in some detail in order to show the complexity of the relationship between the integration of Tropical Africa with the international capitalist system and the obstacles to African development. The assumption of a connection between the persistence of underdevelopment and the evolution of oligopolistic structures in the advanced capitalist countries seems to be valid; we need, however, to qualify it in many ways to take into account various technological and behavioral factors that act independently of the form of ownership of the means of production in the periphery and in the industrial centers with which the former is integrated.

It should be clear that the mere participation of the state in stimulating or undertaking major industrial and marketing functions (a phenomenon that can be observed in many countries of Tropical Africa), or even the nationalization of foreign enterprises, does not necessarily alter the nature of the relations between periphery and industrial centers and among sectors and classes within the periphery itself. For example, it is normal in Tropical Africa for managerial control of enterprises wholly owned by the state (or in which the state holds a majority participation) to remain in the hands of international corporations.[109] Minority participation and management agreements insure the foreign corporations a regular flow of payments in the form of royalties, patents, licensing agreements, and technical assistance fees, etc., which to some extent replace the export of profits in affecting the balance of payments negatively.[110] But even if state ownership increases the share of the surplus retained in the periphery, the bias of investment in favor of capital-intensive techniques may remain unaffected not only because of the persistence of managerial constraints, but also because the managing corporations profit from the supply of equipment, components, materials, and technical services which embody capital-intensive techniques. Similar considerations apply to the bias against the capital-goods sector. In fact, though the state may have greater confidence in the future industrialization of the economy, which would justify the expansion of the capital-goods sector ahead of demand, the other obstacles discussed in Section I are not removed by the mere public ownership of the means of production. Indeed, if capital intensity is retained, the balance-of-payments problems, discussed in Section III, may be intensified.

Our analysis also implies that a disengagement from the international capitalist system and greater integration with the socialist economies of Eastern Europe and China may not in itself alter the pattern of growth without development. It is true that such reorientation of external economic relations, if it were possible,[111] might remove the various obstacles to development we have seen to be related to the existence of oligopolistic structures in advanced capitalist countries. It is also true that the integration of Tropical African countries with planned economies would make planning in the former less of a gamble. Yet the problems connected with the Balkanization of Africa which make the individual national economies inefficient planning units would persist. More important still is the fact that many technological and managerial constraints are independent of the mode of production obtaining in the industrial centers.[112]

In other words, there is no panacea for African economic development, and African unity is no such panacea either. The fact that international capitalism acts on a Pan-African—indeed on a world—scale undoubtedly reduces the bargaining strength and ability to plan of the small African nations. However, we have seen that the lack of development in Tropical Africa originates in a pattern of growth that is only partly due to the Balkanization of the area. Whatever the relative importance of these factors (i.e., ownership of the means of production in the Tropical African economies and in the industrial centers with which they are integrated, and the Balkanization of Africa) may be in determining the pattern of growth without development, none can be singled out as the crucial variable. Institutional changes alone cannot be expected to change that pattern.

African governments will have to face up to the problem of primary accumulation, a process that has not gone very far in Tropical Africa. Broadly speaking, this process has two related aspects: the mobilization of the saving potential implicit in the underutilized productive resources of the pre-capitalist economies; and the reallocation of the surplus from export of investment income and from conspicuous or nonessential consumption to serve the requirements of that mobilization. In this connection two patterns of growth of the modern sector seem to confront each other. The existing pattern is characterized by a high capital intensity of production within each sector and by a sectoral distribution of investment implying a low "implicit capital intensity."[113] We have seen that this pattern has a very low development potential because it restrains the growth of the internal market and (being associated with a high income elasticity of imports), it creates balance-of-payments problems which frustrate the further expansion of productive capacity. An alternative pattern of growth would be one characterized by a lower capital intensity within each sector but a higher "implicit capital intensity."[114] This pattern would have greater developmental potential because it would foster the autonomous growth (i.e., independent of external stimulants) of the internal market and would reduce the dependence of steady increases in productivity upon the availability of foreign exchange.

The importance of this last point warrants some detailed discussion. Increases in productivity involve a "learning process" that enhances the rationality of productive combinations. The existing pattern of growth not only restrains the spreading of the learning process over large sections of the population; in addition, even in the state-owned enterprises, it limits considerably the range of experiences that can be undergone in the periphery as crucial economic and technological decisions are made in the industrial centers. Furthermore, the bureaucratization and narrow specialization that capital-intensive, large-scale enterprises entail limit the number of different arrangements and situations in which learning can take place.[115] The use of labor-intensive techniques would not only spread the learning process to larger sections of the African population but also make it more complete and varied. The use of labor-intensive techniques is also more likely to make possible the mobilization of the underemployed labor of the African pre-capitalist system. Disguised unemployment in Africa is typically seasonal and periodic since no general population pressure on the land exists. The labor migration system (an adaption to African conditions of the "putting-out" system that has characterized primary accumulation in the now advanced economies), however inefficient, performed the function of mobilizing this type of disguised unemployment for productive purposes. As we have seen, the emerging pattern of investment is displacing the system but no alternative way of mobilizing underemployed labor has emerged. The main failure of the labor migration system in colonial times was that it did not create the conditions that would have made it obsolete. In other words, migrant labor was employed in primary production for export which, with some marginal exceptions, did not lead to industrialization and to the transformation of traditional agriculture that would have enabled the African economies to supersede the system. This consideration leads us to a fundamental question. As Nurkse[116] has pointed out, the state of disguised unemployment implies a disguised saving potential as well. The emerging pattern of growth with its bias in favor of capital intensity and against the development of a sector producing the capital goods most suitable for the modernization of the African economies makes the mobilization of that potential unlikely if not impossible.[117] In consequence, it leads to reliance on outside finance which, as we have seen, frustrates development in the long run. Labor-intensive techniques and the development of a capital-goods industry would, on the other hand, make possible the mobilization of the disguised saving potential of Tropical Africa and therefore the internal generation of the surplus necessary for long-term growth and development.

It is, however, important to bear in mind that the question of a shift toward more labor-intensive techniques within sectors and toward a different allocation of the investable surplus among sectors cannot be divorced from the second question mentioned above, namely, that of the distribution of the surplus among classes. We shall presently turn to this question; at the moment it is sufficient to point out the obvious incompatibility between the absorption of the surplus by the export of profits and by the conspicuous or nonessential consumption of a small section of the population, on the one hand, and its utilization to step up capital accumulation and to provide incentives for the transformation of traditional agriculture, on the other.

Thus, changes in techniques of production and in the sectoral distribution of investment, like the institutional changes discussed above, are only necessary and not sufficient conditions for the development of Tropical Africa. In other words, development must be seen as a total process in which technical, behavioral, and institutional factors are interrelated. This does not mean, of course, that institutional, technical, and behavioral obstacles to development all have to be tackled at the same time; it certainly means, however, that changes in each of the various factors can only make sense *as tactical moves in a strategy which aims at some special transformation in the total situation.* In concluding this essay we must attempt to find out why such strategy has failed to emerge in Tropical Africa.[11]

The emphasis is usually put on external obstacles. By not dealing with such obstacles it is not our intention to belittle them. We disregard them because, whatever the retaliatory power of foreign capital, it is more important to understand the causes of the failure to evolve a valid strategy of development, which are rooted in the political economy of Tropical Africa itself, namely in the power base of the African governments. As pointed out in the introductory section, in most countries of Tropical Africa feudal elements, landowning classes, and national bourgeoisies are either nonexistent or not sufficiently significant, politically and/or economically, to constitute the power base of the state. The implication is that the stability of the existing system of internal and external relationships must be sought for in a consistency between the interests of international capitalism and some classes other than the abovementioned. Our analysis has suggested that such classes are, in all likelihood, the African elite, sub-elite, and *proletariat proper* (i.e., excluding migrant labor), which we shall collectively refer to as the "labor aristocracy" of Tropical Africa.

The "labor aristocracy," as we have seen in Section II, owes its very emergence and consolidation to a pattern of investment in which the international corporations play a leading role. The displacement costs involved in the disengagement from international capitalism therefore have to be borne mainly by the "labor aristocracy" itself. The most important consideration, however, concerns the reallocation of the surplus that is necessary for the mobilization of the disguised saving potential of Tropical Africa. Such a reallocation directly hits the "labor aristocracy," which has most benefited from the present pattern of growth without development,[119] and whose consumption therefore has to be significantly curtailed. State ownership and management of the means of production is not sufficient to prevent the present unequal distribution of incentives. As we saw in Section II, the steady rise in wages and salaries of the last ten to fifteen years is only partly due to the investment and employment policies of the large-scale foreign corporations. Governments' wage and salary policies have also played a leading role. It follows that even though the "labor aristocracy" may not be opposed to state ownership and management of the means of production, it can be expected to resist that reallocation of the surplus on the part of the state which must be an essential component of the strategy for the transformation in the total situation of the societies of Tropical Africa.

It may be argued that there is no real conflict of interests between the semiproletarianized peasantry and the "labor aristocracies" as growth without development is, in the long run, self-defeating. The argument is ambiguous because the definition of class interests without a time dimension does not make much sense. Of course, we can always take a point in time distant enough to be able to show that the "labor aristocracy" can only gain from the organic development of the economies of Tropical Africa. However, in defining class interests one must make assumptions not only about the benefits derived by a class from a certain pattern of growth and development at a point in time, but also on whether that point in time lies within the time horizon that can be realistically expected from that class. Disregard of the time dimension may lead both to a kind of "proletarian messianism" and to unrealistic assumptions concerning the class interests that can be attributed to international capitalism. The view that international corporations have an interest in the development of the periphery is held by most non-Marxist economists and, to some extent, seems to have influenced some Marxist scholars. Barratt-Brown,[120] for example, in answering the question: "What chance is there of the great corporations embarking upon the policies of worldwide industrial expansion?" argues that since wider markets, rather than cheap labor, represent the most important interest of international capitalism:

> This gives rise to the hope that capitalist firms and governments will see . . . that economic development in the as yet underdeveloped lands is very much in their interest. . . . It seems hardly to be in the nature of capitalism to undertake such development, but British capitalism did it once for the lands of European settlement and we must consider the possibility of continuing the job in the less developed lands of Asia and in Africa.[121]

That international capitalism is made up of heterogeneous sectional interests and that some of its sections have an interest in the industrialization and development of the periphery is widely accepted. The point, however, is that the "freedom of action" of what we may call the "progressive" section of international capitalism and of the governments of capitalists countries are severely limited, in the case of the former, by the oligopolistic structure of the international capitalist system and, in the case of the latter, by their power base in which the "progressive" capitalist element is normally of little consequence. These two factors considerably curtail the time-horizon of international capitalism so that its long-term interests in the industrialization of the periphery are irrelevant to the determination of its behavior.

Proletarian and bourgeois "messianism" seem therefore to be closely related, both being rooted in the competitive models of capitalism of, respectively, Marx and Smith. A shift in the focus of attention from competition to oligopoly is most needed to understand both contemporary capitalist systems and the problems of development and socialism in their periphery.

Notes

1. Individual, small-scale, competitive producers assume that, at the ruling price, the market demand for their output is unlimited. Furthermore, under competitive conditions the flexibility of the rate of profit insures the expansion of demand to match supply. See below.

2. F. Perroux, "La nation en voie de se faire et les pouvoirs industriels," *Les Cahiers de la République* (July–August 1959), p. 51.

3. R. Prebisch, "The Role of Commercial Policies in Underdeveloped Countries," *American Economic Review Papers and Proceedings* (May 1959).

4. The terms "periphery" and "industrial centers" will be retained throughout to designate the underdeveloped and the industrial countries with which the former are economically integrated.

5. O. Lange, *Economic Development, Planning, and International Cooperation* (New York: Monthly Review Press, 1963), pp. 10–11.

6. Kwame Nkrumah, *Neo-colonialism: The Last Stage of Imperialism* (New York: International Publishers, 1965).

7. See below.

8. Cf., for example, Lange's passage quoted above and also Paul A. Baran and Paul M. Sweezy, *Monopoly Capital* (New York: Monthly Review Press, 1966), p. 205, and Hamza Alavi, "Imperialism Old and New," *The Socialist Register 1964* (New York: Monthly Review Press, 1964), p. 124.

9. Cf., for example, Alavi, "Imperialism Old and New," p. 116.

10. E. R. Braundi, "Neocolonialism and Class Struggle," *International Socialist Journal*, year 1, no. 1 (1964), p. 66.

11. Cf. C. Wright Mills, *White Collar* (New York: Oxford University Press, 1956), pp. 23–38.

12. Baran and Sweezy, *Monopoly Capital*, pp. 102–105; S. Tsuru, ed., *Has Capitalism Changed?* (Tokyo: Iwanami Shoten, 1961), pp. 51–53.

13. Baran and Sweezy, *Monopoly Capital*, p. 50.

14. R. Vernon, "The American Corporation in Underdeveloped Areas," in E. S. Mason, ed., *The Corporation in Modern Society* (Cambridge: Harvard University Press, 1959), pp. 238–239; W. A. Chudson, "Trends in African Exports and Capital Inflows," in M. J. Herskovits and M. Harwitz, eds., *Economic Transition in Africa* (London: Routledge and Kegan Paul, 1964), pp. 349–350; Michael Barratt-Brown, *After Imperialism* (London: Heinemann, 1963), Chapter 8; Baran and Sweezy, *Monopoly Capital*, pp. 196–197.

15. Cf. Nkrumah, *Neo-colonialism*.

16. *Ibid.*, pp. 58–60.

17. Braundi, "Neocolonialism and Class Struggle," pp. 55–56.

18. *Ibid.*, p. 60. See also the staff paper by G. Benveniste and W. E. Moran, Jr. (Stanford Research Institute, International Industrial Development Center), quoted in S. F. Frankel, "Capital and Capital Supply in Relation to the Development of Africa," in E. A. G. Robinson, ed., *Economic Development for Africa South of the Sahara* (London: Macmillan, 1964), pp. 431–432.

19. D. J. Morgan, *British Private Investment in East Africa: Report of a Survey and a Conference* (London: The Overseas Development Institute, 1965), p. 6.

20. "Multinational Companies, a Special Report," *Business Week*, April 20, 1963.

21. Cf. M. Byé, "La Grande Unité Interterritoriale," *Cahiers de l'I.S.E.A.*, quoted by F. Perroux and R. Demonts, "Large Firms—Small Nations," *Présence Africaine*, vol. 10, no. 38 (1961), p. 37.

22. Chudson, "Trends in African Exports and Capital Inflows."

23. *Loc. cit.*

24. United Nations Economic and Social Council, *Policy Aspects of Industrial Development in Africa: Problems and Prospects*, E/CN. 14/AS/II/2/K/1, mimeographed, 1965, pp. 22–27. In some cases increases in manufacturing activities merely represent classification changes. Cf. R. E. Baldwin, *Economic Development and Export Growth: A Study of Northern Rhodesia, 1920–1960* (Berkeley and Los Angeles: University of California Press, 1966), p. 181.

25. UNESCO, *Policy Aspects of Industrial Development in Africa*. See also G. Hunter, *The New Societies of Tropical Africa* (London: Oxford University Press, 1962), pp. 161–162.

26. UNESCO, *Policy Aspects of Industrial Development in Africa*.

27. Intermediary and capital-goods industries generally require, especially in nonindustrialized countries, supranational markets. The possibility of using protectionist policies or setting up competing units in neighboring countries increases the risks of, and therefore discourages, investment in each country. This consideration points to the possibility of conflicts of interest within international capitalism concerning the "Balkanization" of Tropical Africa.

28. Barratt-Brown, *After Imperialism*, p. 419.

29. We are assuming that the new plants will not compete in the national market from which the investment originates. The argument holds *a fortiori* if this assumption is not made.

30. Cf. Hunter, *The New Societies of Tropical Africa*, pp. 60–61. See also H. A.

Turner, *Wage Trends, Wage Policies, and Collective Bargaining: The Problems of Underdeveloped Countries* (Department of Applied Economics, Occasional Paper No. 6; Cambridge: Cambridge University Press, 1965), p. 21; and below.

31. Baldwin, *Economic Development and Export Growth*, pp. 79–80.
32. *Loc. cit.*
33. *Ibid.* This is also shown by the fact that the copper mines of Uganda have a lower degree of mechanization than the Katangese mines. Cf. A. Baryaruha, *Factors Affecting Industrial Employment: A Study of Ugandan Experience, 1954–1964* (EAISR, Occasional Paper No. 1; Nairobi: Oxford University Press, 1967), p. 58.
34. Cf., for instance, Baryaruha, *Factors Affecting Industrial Employment;* and Hunter, *The New Societies of Tropical Africa*, pp. 60–61.
35. Cf. Vernon, "The American Corporation in Underdeveloped Areas," pp. 253–254.
36. See below.
37. Perroux and Demonts, "Large Firms—Small Nations," p. 46.
38. Cf. D. J. Viljoen, "Problems of Large-Scale Industry in Africa," in Robinson, *Economic Development for Africa South of the Sahara*, pp. 253–254.
39. Capitalist enterprises always tend to adopt those techniques which "maximize" the surplus. Such techniques are relatively capital intensive (see Section III). However, financial stringency prevents the smaller firms from taking a long time-horizon in their investment decisions and therefore from adopting capital-intensive techniques. The large corporation, on the other hand, is to a large extent free from financial constraints upon its investment decisions.
40. One notable exception is W. Elkan, *Migrants and Proletarians: Urban Labor in the Economic Development of Uganda* (London: Oxford University Press, 1960).
41. Quoted in Alavi, "Imperialism Old and New," pp. 106–107.
42. Degree of competition is not the only variable in this context. As already mentioned, the calculating rationality of the capitalist concerns is equally relevant, giving rise to the discrepancy in the behavior of the chartered companies and concessionaries of old and that of the modern corporations.
43. Cf. Alavi, "Imperialism Old and New," p. 121. This point is discussed more fully in Section III, where the determinants of corporate investment in the periphery are dealt with.
44. Cf. Vernon, "The American Corporation in Underdeveloped Areas," pp. 248–249; Barratt-Brown, *After Imperialism*, pp. 273–276; Morgan, *British Private Investment in East Africa*, p. 47.

45. Derived from K. C. Doctor and H. Gallis, "Size and Characteristics of Wage Employment in Africa: Some Statistical Estimates," *International Labor Review*, vol. 93, no. 2 (1966), p. 166. The estimates are very rough.
46. Cf. Turner, *Wage Trends, Wage Policies, and Collective Bargaining*, p. 14; D. Walker, "Problems of Economic Development in East Africa," in Robinson, *Economic Development for Africa South of the Sahara*, p. 123; T. L. V. Blair, "African Economic Development," *Présence Africaine* (English edition), vol. 28, no. 56 (1965), p. 34. That the rate of growth of employment has been considerably less than the rate of growth of the population is clearly shown in the following table which gives data for selected countries of East and Central Africa:

| Country | Annual rates of growth (compound) | | | Period |
	Employment	Population	Real Product	
Uganda	1.2 (a b)	2.5 (c)	3.5 (c)	1952–65
Kenya	.9 (d b)	3.0 (c)	4.8 (c)	1954–64
Tanzania (Tanganyika)	−2.1 (e)	1.8 (c)	3.5 (c)	1953–65
Rhodesia	1.3 (e)	3.3 (c)	5.4 (c)	1954–64
Malawi	.3 (e)	2.4 (c)	2.5 (c)	1954–64
Zambia	.4 (e)	2.8 (c)	2.5 (c)	1954–65

The data were calculated from: (a) Uganda Government, *1963 Statistical Abstract* (Entebbe: Government Printer, 1963), p. 89; (b) East African Statistical Department, *Economic and Statistical Review*, no. 20 (1966), p. 51; (c) OECD, *National Accounts of Less-Developed Countries* (Paris: OECD Development Center, 1967), pp. 5–9; (d) Kenya Government, *Economic Survey, 1964* (Nairobi: Government Printer, 1964), p. 39; (e) International Labour Institute (ILO), *Year Book of Labour Statistics*, (1961), p. 100; *Yearbook of Labour Statistics* (1966), p. 288.

47. Cf. Turner, *Wage Trends, Wage Policies, and Collective Bargaining*, pp. 12–13.
48. *Loc. cit.*
49. *Ibid.*, p. 14.
50. *Ibid.*
51. Sources: For Kenya, Uganda, and Tanganyika, see East African Statistical Department, *Economic and Statistical Review*, p. 51; data for the other countries have been derived from Doctor and Gallis, "Size and Characteristics of Wage Employment in Africa."
52. The terms "elite" and "sub-elite" have ideological connotations. They

are used in this essay for want of a better terminology and not because of any implicit agreement with the view that no conflict of interest exists between the "elite," on the one hand, and the "masses," on the other, or that there is a lack of class structure within the "non-elite." This view seems to justify the use of the terms by some writers. Cf. P. Lloyd, ed., *The New Elites of Tropical Africa* (London: Oxford University Press 1966), p. 60.

53. *Ibid.*, p. 2.

54. *Ibid.*, pp. 12–13.

55. *Ibid.*, p. 22.

56. *Ibid.*, p. 8; and Hunter, *The New Societies of Tropical Africa*, p. 8.

57. Lloyd, *The New Elites of Tropical Africa*, pp. 7–8.

58. What follows is based on my own unpublished research on the proletarianization of the Rhodesian peasantry (cf. Arrighi, "Labor Supplies in Historical Perspective: The Rhodesian Case," a paper presented at the Economic Research Bureau Seminar, University College, Dar es Salaam, 1967, mimeographed) and, unless otherwise specified, on standard works on the subject such as J. C. Mitchell, "Labour Migration in Africa South of the Sahara: The Cause of Labor Migration," *Bulletin of the Inter-African Labour Institute*, vol. 6, no. 1 (1959); W. Watson, *Tribal Cohesion in a Money Economy* (Manchester: Manchester University Press, 1958); and, especially, Elkan, *Migrants and Proletarians*.

59 Cf. W. E. Moore, "The Adaptation of African Labor Systems to Social Change," in Herskovits and Harwitz, *Economic Transition in Africa*, pp. 293–294 and 297.

60. Cf. Elkan, *Migrants and Proletarians*, pp. 52–54.

61. A distinction has to be made between stabilization in the sense of "long service in one type of employment" and stabilization in the sense of proletarianization or urbanization implying "a severance from rural ties combined with a tendency to settle down forever as a town dweller." Obviously employers in Africa have always been keen on the former type of stabilization. However, as they were not prepared to bear the costs (and the risks) involved in the latter type of stabilization, their interest remained purely hypothetical. Cf. Baldwin, *Economic Development and Export Growth*, p. 138.

62. Lloyd, *The New Elites of Tropical Africa*, pp. 10–11.

63. Hunter, *The New Societies of Tropical Africa*, pp. 230–231.

64. Turner, *Wage Trends, Wage Policies, and Collective Bargaining*, p. 20–21.

65. Cf. Hunter, *The New Societies of Tropical Africa*, p. 207; Elkan, *Migrants and Proletarians*, p. 85; Turner, *Wage Trends, Wage Policies, and Collective Bargaining*, pp. 17–18, 48.

66. Baryaruha, for example, shows that locally based enterprises also stepped up mechanization in response to the steady rise in wages.

67. Cf. Turner, *Wage Trends, Wage Policies, and Collective Bargaining*, p. 21.

68. Cf. Elkan, *Migrants and Proletarians*.

69. Arrighi, "Labor Supplies in Historical Perspective," pp. 26–27.

70. Baldwin, *Economic Development and Export Growth*, p. 105.

71. Cf. Moore, "The Adaptation of African Labor Systems to Social Change," p. 290; Elkan, *Migrants and Proletarians*, pp. 61–62.

72. Moore, "The Adaptation of African Labor Systems to Social Change," p. 290.

73. Turner, *Wage Trends, Wage Policies, and Collective Bargaining*, p. 48.

74. Cf. *ibid.*, p. 21.

75. The following analysis is rather cursory as the focus of our attention is on the wage-working class and foreign capital. Its only purpose is to bridge the gap that would otherwise arise between the foregoing discussion and the analysis of the next two sections.

76. Some rural economies of Tropical Africa are already some way along the roadto class formation. Those of southern Ghana, parts of eastern and western Nigeria, the Ivory Coast, and Buganda are examples. They still are, however, rather exceptional, particularly in East and Central Africa.

77. Enterprises are here defined as small-scale if they have no international affiliations and employ a relatively small number of workers.

78. Hunter, *The New Societies of Tropical Africa*, pp. 129–131, 156. New opportunities have also arisen in the field of gasoline service stations as the oil marketing companies have become some of the largest investors in sub-Saharan Africa.

79. The Madhvani Group of East Africa is certainly the most conspicuous exception. In Uganda, Kenya, and Tanzania it controls twenty-three enterprises, excluding subsidiaries and associates, in a wide range of industries: sugar, vegetable oil, beer, steel, textiles, glass, confectionery, matches, and others. Obviously groups such as this, though locally based, must be included in international capitalism.

80. Cf. Elkan, *Migrants and Proletarians*, pp. 111–112.

81. Cf. M. Katzin, "The Role of the Small Entrepreneur," in Herskovits and Harwitz, *Economic Transition in Africa*, pp. 179–180; Hunter, *The New Societies of Tropical Africa*, pp. 100–101, 137–140.

82. Hunter, *The New Societies of Tropical Africa*, pp. 137–140; S. Chodak, "Social Classes in Sub-Saharan Africa," *Africana Bulletin*, no. 4 (1966), p. 35. In Buganda, it is the consumption pattern imposed by a prosperous farming community which frustrated the accumulation of savings on the

part of would-be petty capitalists. See Elkan, *Migrants and Proletarians*, p. 47.

83. Cf. Katzin, "The Role of the Small Entrepreneur," p. 195; Lloyd, *The New Elites of Tropical Africa*, p. 8.

84. In addition to this, the advantage that small enterprises may derive from the imparting of skills among the population on the part of large-scale enterprises is considerably reduced by the use of highly capital-intensive techniques. The less capital-intensive small enterprises will generally need either unskilled labor or labor fully skilled in one of the traditional crafts. As we have seen, however, the large-scale corporations will tend to create a semiskilled, specialized force largely unsuitable for the local employers.

85. The obstacles of the small national market can be overcome by the large-scale corporation by means of multinational operations.

86. This is another reason for assuming that international corporations may benefit from rising wages and salaries. As we have seen, large numbers are employed by the public sector (see Table II above); in consequence, the increase in demand for the products of the corporations brought about by the rise in labor incomes makes it easier to pass the increased labor costs on to the consumer.

87. Mills, *White Collar*, pp. 23–28.

88. See, for example, Maurice Dobb, *An Essay on Economic Growth and Planning*, orig. pub. 1960 (New York: Monthly Review Press, 1969); W. Galenson and H. Leibenstein, "Investment Criteria, Productivity and Economic Development," *The Quarterly Journal of Economics* (August 1955); A. K. Sen, *Choice of Techniques. An Aspect of the Theory of Planned Economic Development* (Oxford: Basil Blackwell, 1962). Since implicitly or explicitly these authors assume a socialist economy, what follows does not represent a critique of their theories.

89. Barratt-Brown, *After Imperialism*, p. 354.

90. Chudson, "Trends in African Exports and Capital Inflows," p. 337.

91. *Ibid.*, p. 340.

92. A. M. Kamarck, "The Development of the Economic Infrastructure," in Herskovits and Harwitz, *Economic Transition in Africa*, p. 75.

93. *Loc. cit.* The "guesstimates" of the deficit on current account given by Kamarck are $1.0 billion for 1963 and $0.9 billion for 1964. These deficits amount to 24.4 and 19.2 percent, respectively, of the exports from Tropical Africa in the two years.

94. We are excluding for the time being reductions in imports of nonessential consumer goods. This possibility is discussed in section IV.

95. Cf. Morgan, *British Private Investment in East Africa*, pp. 15–16.

96. For the trend of private investment from advanced capitalist countries to the underdeveloped economies cf. "The Slow-Down on Aid" in the *Economist*, August 26, 1967, pp. 736–737. With regard to Tropical Africa, gross private foreign investment seems to have reached a peak of about $800 million per year sometime between 1950 and 1957 and to have since then fallen. See Frankel, "Capital and Capital Supply in Relation to Development in Africa," p. 428. The following table gives U.K. and American foreign direct investment (excluding oil) in Sterling Africa and Africa, respectively, for the period 1959–1964. It was derived from Morgan, *British Private Investment in East Africa*, p. 6 (for the U.K.), and Kamarck, "The Development of the Economic Infrastructure," pp. 266–267 (for the U.S.).

Private direct investment, excluding oil *(millions of $U.S.)*						
	1959	1960	1961	1962	1963	1964
U.K. (Sterling Africa)	81	83	83	25	7	−25
U.S. (Africa)	92	13	8	93	105	75
Total	173	96	111	118	112	50

97. In the sense that import substitution leads to a faster growth of imports of semi-finished goods, capital goods, and raw materials.

98. Kamarck, "The Development of the Economic Infrastructure," p. 155.

99. Chudson, "Trends in African Exports and Capital Inflows," p. 352.

100. This conclusion refers to Tropical Africa as a whole and to the majority of countries. There will probably be exceptions of two kinds: countries with particularly rich mineral deposits, such as Gabon, and countries in which foreign investment in manufacturing will tend to concentrate to take advantage of a relatively industrialized environment.

101. Cf. Chudson, "Trends in African Exports and Capital Inflows," p. 349.

102. Cf. Blair, "African Economic Development," pp. 29–30; Nkrumah, *Neo-colonialism*, pp. 241–242.

103. Kamarck, "The Development of the Economic Infrastructure," p. 202. As Braundi has pointed out in "Neocolonialism and Class Struggle," pp. 241–242, these flows of public funds have been instrumental in making possible the export of profits from Tropical Africa which would otherwise have been paralyzed by disequilibria in the balance of payments.

104. Problems connected with the investment of the surplus on the part of the state are discussed in section IV.

105. Cf. Morgan, *British Private Investment in East Africa*.

106. See p. 246 above.

107. Baran and Sweezy have shown, on the basis of official data, that in the case of the U.S. (the industrial center par excellence), foreign investment is in fact a most efficient device for transferring surplus generated abroad to the investing country. In the period 1950–1963, while the net direct investment capital outflow from the U.S. amounted to $17,382 million, the inflow of direct investment income amounted to $29,416 million. See *Monopoly Capital*, pp. 106–108.

108. Cf. fn. 46 above.

109. Cf. Hunter, *The New Societies of Tropical Africa*, pp. 183–184.

110. Cf. Alavi, "Imperialism Old and New," p. 119; Nkrumah, *Neo-colonialism*, p. 178.

111. For the feasibility of a strategy of development that includes the institutional changes under discussion, see below.

112. The experience of China is instructive in this respect. In the early and mid-1950's the rapid industrialization of China was made possible by Soviet assistance. However, the nature of this assistance tended to produce a pattern of growth without development which contributed to the difficulties of the late 1950's. Cf. Franz Schurmann, *Ideology and Organization in Communist China* (Berkeley and Los Angeles: University of California Press, 1966).

113. By "implicit capital intensity" is here understood the proportion of the labor force employed in the sector producing means of production.

114. It would be futile and quite beyond the purpose of this essay to give a detailed and concrete description of this alternative pattern of growth. While its broad characteristics can be perceived at the theoretical level, its concrete characterization can only emerge from the praxis of African development.

115. On this last point cf. H. W. Singer, "Small-Scale Industry in African Economic Development," in Robinson, *Economic Development for Africa South of the Sahara*, pp. 640–641. The spread of an organic "learning process" is particularly important in connection with the development of a *modern* labor-intensive technology which might very well be necessary for the development of Africa.

116. R. Nurkse, *Problems of Capital Formation in Underdeveloped Countries* (Oxford: Basil Blackwell 1953), p. 37.

117. Cf. Singer, "Small-Scale Industry in African Economic Development," pp. 641 and 653. The capital-goods sector must be understood in a broad sense to include, for instance, capital construction and land improvements in the rural sector.

118. Tanzania may turn out to be an exception to the general rule.

119. Turner, in *Wage Trends, Wage Policies, and Collective Bargaining*, pp

12–14, estimates that the whole benefit of economic development in Africa during the 1950's accrued to the wage and salary-earners. In fact, however, we have seen that the unskilled semiproletarianized peasantry (as a class) can have benefited but marginally from this rise in labor incomes because of the loss of employment opportunities ensuing from increased mechanization. Hence, not wage earners as such, but the labor aristocracy has gained from the present pattern of growth.

120. Barratt-Brown, *After Imperialism*, pp. 324–327.
121. From the conclusions of this study it would seem that Barratt-Brown deems possible a coalition between the British government and "progressive" giant corporations to promote the industrialization of the underdeveloped world.

6

Hans O. Schmitt

Foreign Capital and Social Conflict in Indonesia, 1950-1958

In December of 1957, after eight years of social and political turmoil following independence, Indonesia expelled Dutch economic interests from the dominant position they had retained from the colonial era. This action climaxed a trend toward economic stagnation which was in striking contrast to the hopes of rapid economic growth held by many Indonesians. The question posed in this essay is this: Was there perhaps some connection between survival of foreign economic dominance on the one hand, and political turmoil and economic stagnation on the other?

THE ECONOMIC STRUCTURE

The incentives that make people save and invest for economic growth have as yet found no single and consistent explanation in economic theory. One aspect that is sometimes overlooked is that additions to the capital stock concurrently enhance the power of those who control it, and thereby induce them to forego consumption. Those who do not share in the control of capital have not the same incentive to save. They may still make provision for contingencies, such as old age and accident, but for the economy as a whole, such savings are likely to be offset by

This essay originally appeared in *Economic Development and Cultural Change*, vol. 10, no. 3 (April 1962), published by the University of Chicago Press. Copyright © 1962 by the University of Chicago.

Author's note: The author is indebted for stimulus and criticism primarily to Dr. A. Baranski, Professor H. Feith, Professor B. H. Higgins, Professor A. Kraal, Professor G. J. Pauker, and Mrs. Joan Robinson; and for financial support to the Ford Foundation. Responsibility remains his own.

expenditures when the contingencies occur. On balance, therefore, the interests of the "property-less" lie with maximum consumption. Aggregate savings can in consequence be maximized only to the extent that income payments to the "property-less" are minimized.

The balance of power between those who do, and those who do not, control the capital stock may therefore be decisive in placing limits on the rate of accumulation. In Joan Robinson's terminology, it sets the "inflation barrier" beyond which further reductions in real wages are successfully resisted.[1] The rate of growth will be maximized when one group is firmly in control and sees its power enhanced by further accumulation. Until very recently, no Indonesian group has quite been in this position. According to one estimate, before the Second World War only 19 percent of nonagricultural capital was owned by indigenous Indonesians, while 52 percent was held by Dutch interests.[2] Agriculture is the only area in which Indonesian ownership of resources has been at all substantial, and the larger part of the Indonesian population is in fact peasant small-holders. As W. A. Lewis has pointed out, however, peasant societies "may be happy and prosperous," but are not likely to show rapid accumulation of capital.[3] The reason for this, he argues, can be found in the fact that in societies where power and prestige are based on land holdings, ambition expresses itself chiefly in additions to real estate rather than to capital, with capital expansion often opposed as a threat to the vested interests of the landowners.

It is at any rate clear that in traditional Indonesian peasant society, capital accumulation has been slow and technical innovation rare, so much so that one Dutch scholar felt justified in assigning "limited needs" and an "aversion to capital" to "Oriental mentality" as inherent traits.[4] He does not seem to appreciate adequately the inhibiting effect of Dutch colonial policy, however. At its best it was designed only to preserve a "happy and prosperous" peasantry—by indirect rule through traditional chiefs and by the prohibition of sale of land to aliens—while at the same time making any escape from traditional society by Indonesians very difficult indeed. Under Dutch rule in Indonesia there existed three distinct social strata.[5] The indigenous population constituted the lowest layer; the Western managerial personnel in government, business, and the army, the highest. An intermediate position was occupied by the Chinese, who largely controlled the collecting and distributing trades, acting as middlemen between the Western and the indigenous sectors of society. Social advancement from one of the three layers to another was all but impossible.

Nonetheless, not quite all Indonesians were peasants, even under Dutch rule. A small proletariat of wage laborers—about 500,000 by Communist count[6]—worked on the plantations, in the mines, in the factories, and in transport within the "Western" sector. The traditional aristocracy survived in the lower categories of the civil service that remained open to them, and a vestigial business group of pre-colonial origin was also able to maintain itself.[7] For a stagnant society to be transformed into a dynamic one, these groups would have had to acquire a vested interest in capital accumulation. It was precisely this development that foreign dominance in the nonagricultural sector effectively blocked.[8] Unfortunately, when Indonesia attained her independence in December 1949, the economic structure was not changed significantly. The nonagricultural groups, which assumed responsibility for the government, remained narrowly wedged between the traditionalist peasantry on one side, and the Western business community on the other.

The balance of power between economic sectors, however, was changed by the political revolution. Toward the peasantry, the new rulers lacked the weight of power that their colonial predecessors had enjoyed.[9] At the same time, they did not identify their interests with the growth of capital either. It would seem that whenever indigenous capital is restricted—by market forces or by government policy—from reaching proportions competitive with foreign enterprise, opportunism, if not fatalism and resignation, in economic activity are the natural consequences in any society in any part of the world. The development of a "capitalist spirit" cannot reasonably be expected under such circumstances. Even "business enterprise" will be consumption-oriented, as indeed it was.[10]

The economic consequences were virtually inexorable. In 1939 the proportion of national income accounted for in the modern sector was 32 percent; by 1952 it had dropped to 24 percent, with the trend continuing in succeeding years. One of the contributory causes was a shift in the burden of taxation between sectors, until in 1952 taxes claimed 29 percent of the income per gainfully employed in the modern sector, as compared with only 5 percent in the agrarian. The end result has been, if one can trust the figures, a level of disposable income per gainfully employed in 1952 of Rp. 3,000 in the agrarian sphere, compared with only Rp. 2,650 in the modern sector.[11] "The central fact of economic development," writes W. A. Lewis, "is that the distribution of incomes is altered in favor of the saving class."[12] The logic of Indonesia's economic structure, it appears, has moved in exactly the opposite direction. We turn now to trace the pattern of its political repercussions.

POLITICAL REPERCUSSIONS

Both the political and the economic dilemmas of the Indonesian leadership had the same root in the precarious position they occupied between the peasantry and foreign business interests. At the political apex stood a relatively small group often referred to as the intelligentsia, consisting largely of those Indonesians who had been permitted to benefit from Dutch education during the colonial period.[13] Their control over the mass of the population in the countryside was loose, as has already been pointed out. But, though the peasantry was difficult to govern, it was not sufficiently well organized for effective participation in political decision-making, either. Politics therefore reflected primarily the interests of nonagrarian population groups, more particularly of the bureaucracy, the trading interests, and the working classes. These groups can perhaps be described as occupying positions of "intermediate" leadership between the intellectual elite and the peasantry.[14] The bureaucracy was especially strong in Java, enjoying the position which a still somewhat feudal social structure accorded them. Trading groups for their part held a higher status outside Java, where a more commercial orientation had prevailed from early times. The labor movement, concentrated in the cities, held the balance of power between them.

Against this background, three determinants of political developments in post-independence Indonesia can be isolated: (1) the continuing dominance of foreign capital; (2) the division of indigenous society into several ethnic groups; and (3) the different social positions of economic classes within different ethnic groups. Other sources of political division—and alliance—in national politics could of course be listed, among them religious, cultural, and personality conflicts. These did not, however, affect public policy to the same extent; in fact, on balance they tended to accommodate themselves to the three factors isolated here. In combination, these factors produced a logical sequence of events that led directly to the expulsion of Dutch business interests.

Three stages of development can be identified. In the first, we find an initial clash between the Dutch business community in Indonesia and the Indonesian political leadership. The Dutch attempted to minimize the economic impact of Indonesian political independence by retaining control of the central bank and by allowing Dutch enterprises to operate in an environment of maximum laissez faire. The Indonesians, for their part, thought that they could acquire some share in the economic management of their country, not yet by expropriation, but by financing the entry of new Indonesian firms into markets controlled by the Dutch. A beginning was made in the import sector.[15] Control of the nation's credit system was thought essential for the success of such a program, so the central bank was nationalized.

The nationalization of the central bank aroused little controversy within the Indonesian camp. To be sure, the sort of program it was supposed to back tended to overcrowd markets and relax financial discipline—thoroughly adverse consequences from the point of view of economic development. But it had the short-run virtue of satisfying most hostile impulses toward foreign enterprise, while at the same time leaving people free to cooperate with foreign management if they wanted to. Financial policy therefore did not as yet provide an issue to divide the political elite. Political competition continued for the time being to reflect individual ambitions for position, with no consistent divisions along social or economic lines. In fact, no such lines seemed as yet to divide society at large either, at least as long as the Korean "boom" sustained incomes for all.

But as soon as incomes dwindled with the end of the Korean War, the financial "offensive" against Dutch interests began to have serious domestic repercussions. These repercussions initiated the second stage of development. Without a reduction in government expenditures, dwindling receipts from foreign trade threatened to touch off severe inflation. The reaction was composed of three factors:

(1) Fiscal retrenchment would have required cutbacks in the support given to young enterprises. Consequently, what first seemed to be an academic debate on the merits and demerits of fiscal orthodoxy soon split the leadership sharply between those who preferred foreign domin-ance to monetary chaos and those who would jeopardize financial stability to rid the economy of Dutch control.[16]

(2) In the struggle for power between the two groups, both sides

turned to the intermediate economic classes for support. This might have seemed difficult for the financial conservatives. A program of relaxing pressure against foreign interests, while imposing austerity elsewhere, could not have held much intrinsic appeal with the Indonesian public. Financial retrenchment did, however, favor at least one of the intermediate groups, the trading interests, especially those outside Java. Combined with fixed exchange rates, domestic inflation threatened the incomes of indigenous exporters in the Outer Regions, where the bulk of exports originate. Dwindling real incomes there caused increased resentment toward populous Java, where most of the nation's imports were being absorbed.

(3) The gains to Java were unevenly distributed, however. The overvalued exchange rate benefited importers—bureaucrats who controlled exchange allocations and their friends—but did not reduce costs for trading interests outside the import sector, to whom imports were resold at high and rising prices. Price controls added further irritation. Trading groups outside Java therefore won political allies among their less powerful counterparts within Java. In combination, the trading interests provided the core of indigenous support needed to put force behind the demand for retrenchment at the top.

What backing the anti-inflationary party could muster still fell short of gaining them control of the government. Their strength merely sufficed to reduce the political base of the government parties to a precarious minimum. Progressive inflation followed, exacerbating social conflict and political instability. A showdown between exporting and importing regions was delayed as long as politicians looked to general elections for a decision in their rivalry for power. The third stage of development began with the elections of 1955. When these elections turned out merely to reflect the pattern of conflict, without deciding its issues, the representatives of the exporting regions increasingly turned to extraparliamentary means for defending their interests.[17] Some of them, in fact, in March 1958, went so far as to proclaim a rival government in Sumatra, with scattered support elsewhere.

To counteract the tendency toward political disintegration, the government parties appealed more and more "recklessly" to nationalist sentiment in the pursuit of the "unfinished" revolution against imperialism. Their chief battle-cry was against the continuing Dutch presence in West Irian, a fact used so effectively in inciting popular sentiment against

Dutch business enterprises in Indonesia that businessmen made representations in Holland favoring territorial concessions. However, while agitations within Indonesia intensified with the deepening of social strife, Indonesian efforts in the United Nations to force Holland to negotiate continued each year to end in failure. In reprisal, in December 1957 labor unions took the initiative in a forcible expulsion of Dutch economic interests from the capital. In a matter of a few days, the movement had spread across the whole country.

For a while it seemed the government had lost its power to direct events. The opposition thought to take advantage of this fact when it proclaimed its rival government in early 1958. The timing of the rebellion made its instigators seem more than ever to give aid to foreign interests. It was in some part for this reason that they lost much of the domestic support on which they had counted. The central government did not fall, but on the contrary launched a vigorous military campaign to restore its authority. Nonetheless, the rebels retained enough support to make active guerrilla warfare seem irrepressible, for a while, especially in Sumatra and Sulawesi.

IMPLICATIONS FOR THEORY

The great deterrent to expropriation of Dutch capital had always been the dislocation it would cause—at least in the short run—in the management of the Indonesian economy. When expropriation came, the price had to be paid. In 1958 the governor of the Bank Indonesia reported that "shipping space was in short supply, marketing channels to Holland had to be shifted to other countries, and there was an exodus of Dutch technicians engaged in the production sector."[18] Foreign exchange losses were particularly severe as a recession in export markets and—perhaps most important—the Sumatra and Sulawesi rebellions coincided with the Dutch exodus. Their combined impact reduced exchange receipts of the central government by 34 percent below their 1957 levels.[19] In response, imports were cut by 36 percent.[20] Even so, it was only the beginning of war reparations payments by Japan that prevented further declines in exchange reserves.[21]

For the maintenance of a reasonable degree of monetary stability, it was absolutely essential that the government deficit be cut to offset the drop in the flow of goods. Such a reduction in expenditures was unfortunately impossible—primarily because of the staggering cost of fighting the rebel guerrillas. The government's cash deficit in 1958 increased by Rp. 5,025 million over its 1957 figure, to an all-time high of Rp. 10,858 million. The whole of the increase went to finance increases in expenditures for security—which rose by Rp. 6,064 million.[22] The money supply consequently rose by Rp. 10,453 million, or by 34 percent, in 1958.[23] Combined with import cuts and an uncertain political future, inflation made orderly business management seem irrational. By early 1959, deterioration had gone so far that President Sukarno warned of an approaching "abyss of annihilation."[24]

It is tempting to use this result as evidence for "mismanagement" or "irresponsibility" on the part of the Indonesian government. Somewhat less sharply, perhaps, D. S. Paauw argues that the government had "placed too much emphasis upon essentially revolutionary goals—'sweeping away the vestiges of colonialism'—and too little upon national integration."[25] One can, on the other hand, detect a certain rationality in the behavior of the Indonesian leadership. The course of events looks very much like a simple cumulative process away from an unstable equilibrium. No stable equilibrium may have been possible within the economic structure. In countries where the control of the capital stock and the direction of public affairs are held by a single elite group, development is stimulated by the fact that the political elite identifies its interests with the expansion of capital. It is primarily this expansion which enhances elite power at home and abroad; politics will therefore be made to serve economic development. In countries where the expansion of capital will in the first instance benefit foreign managerial groups, the indigenous political elite—in spite of protestations to the contrary on grounds of general welfare—will on balance be opposed to it.[26]

Opposition to economic development will in all likelihood be accompanied by a high degree of political instability. Barred from economic careers, members of the political elite find no stable channels for the consolidation and extension of such power as they may individually aspire to, but are restricted to internecine strife in their ambitions for advancement in politics alone. Such strife will tend to crystallize around personalities rather than broad social issues at first, with alignments changing kaleidoscopically and unpredictably. Insofar as consistent lines of demarcation develop among the contestants in politics, such lines will probably divide, as in Indonesia, those who are willing to live with the economic structure that obtains from those who will insist on the need to prepare for its early destruction.[27] A showdown between the two opposing groups may be delayed. The "radicals" will have to be aware that the expulsion of foreign managerial and financial resources will cause serious economic dislocation. The "moderates," for their part, may come to realize the usefulness of political threats against established interests in winning favors and concessions from them.

The transition from stalemate to showdown may then be described as follows. As the political elite becomes increasingly divided within itself, more and more population groups will tend to lose faith in its leadership. The elite will then be faced with two alternatives: either it makes common cause with foreign interests to maintain itself against the indigenous population, or it attempts to divert the blame for economic deterioration exclusively to foreign interests, ascribing its own internal conflicts to often fictitious foreign subversion, and attempting to lead a movement of popular revolution against foreign control of the economy. The more precarious elite authority becomes, the more necessary one or the other alternative will seem, and the more irreconcilable will be the conflict between rival elite groups. The showdown will come when political strife has reached the breaking point, threatening the country with political disintegration and economic ruin.

We see, therefore, that Indonesia's present plight may not be due primarily to individual failings, but that it seems rather to have been the logical consequence of a particularly unfortunate social structure. Similar results are therefore threatened whenever an imperial power transfers political authority to a former colony without concurrently ceding economic power as well. In the process of disintegration, a new and more propitious economic order may emerge from the shambles of the old. From the point of view of economic development, a new order should unite in power those groups most dissatisfied with traditional arrangements in the agrarian sector, with those whose interests are most clearly identified with an expansion of the modern sector. In the absence of a strong indigenous managerial class, such requirements point to the industrial worker and to the "dispossessed" among the rural population. In conditions of social chaos, when old authorities are discredited, these new aspirants have every opportunity for success.

IMPLICATIONS FOR POLICY

For a variety of reasons, Western governments have shown themselves willing to assist in the economic development of their former colonies. Along with aid has gone advice. Much of the advice to underdeveloped countries concentrates on two points: (1) Domestic savings are low; they need to be supplemented from abroad; therefore one must create conditions congenial to foreign investors. (2) Capital is scarce; its marginal product is maximized in labor-intensive industries; therefore one must apply it first of all in agriculture. The danger in such advice can now be appreciated: if followed, such counsel could easily strengthen an agrarian social structure hostile to progressive capital accumulation, and leave the development of modern industry to be the concern chiefly of foreign interests. In all likelihood, the resulting "dualistic" economy will touch off a political chain reaction that may end in economic as well as political disaster.

What then is the proper role of foreign aid in the economic development of former colonies? From an Indonesian point of view, there is a double criterion by which to measure the value of foreign capital: first, foreign contributions must of course add to productive capacity; but second, they must also assist in the development of Indonesian, not foreign, vested interests. If aid cannot meet the second criterion, any contribution under the first may well become pernicious. It can be argued, therefore, that American aid funds should first of all have been used to "buy up Stanvac, Goodyear, Proctor and Gamble, National Carbon, and any other incidental American capital interests in Indonesia, turn them over to the Indonesian government to run, retaining American technicians paid by the United States government just long enough to train Indonesian replacements."[28] Unless the plausible aspect of this proposal is first recognized, workable alternatives more palatable to Western interests are not likely to be devised.

The main objection to such a scheme might be its "negative" approach. It would be preferable, rather than merely to destroy an old order, to work out new relationships between the Western business communities and the leadership of the emerging nations. Methods can be devised whereby private capital will continue to make its contribution without threatening any reversion to "colonialism." One possibility starts with the observation that a number of foreign companies operating in Indonesia had in fact long ago amortized and repatriated their investment, showing as equity a figure close to zero. One could argue that profits were being earned without the commitment of capital to justify them. Such a conviction could supply a moral justification for expropriation, but a technique is necessary to link expropriation to amortization in an orderly and institutionalized procedure to which businessmen can adapt their profit expectations and investment plans.

Suppose every firm were given the opportunity to transfer profits freely, but required each year to apply some negotiated percentage of earned profits to amortization. As soon as amortization allowances have risen to match equity, the physical plant could be considered a "natural resource" and become public domain—government property.[29] If amortization allowances are required in addition to depreciation reserves, they could perhaps take the place of the company tax. Instead of the government collecting the tax and later using it to pay compensation for expropriation, the firm would be exempt from the company tax until unpaid taxes matched the equity account.[30]

Whether such arrangements are thought feasible or not, the dilemma for which they seek a solution should not be disregarded. The scuttling of "empire" touches business empires, too. The analysis of this essay suggests that as long as Western private enterprise is unwilling to sacrifice its entrenched position in the former colonies, it invites disaster upon itself. The task is to find a way of yielding those positions, while leaving the principle of private property intact.

Notes

1. Joan Robinson, *The Accumulation of Capital*, 2nd ed. (New York: St. Martins, 1965), pp. 48 ff.
2. L. A. Mills *et al.*, *The New World of Southeast Asia* (Minneapolis: The University of Minnesota Press, 1949), p. 352.
3. W. A. Lewis, "Economic Development with Unlimited Supplies of Labor," *Manchester School*, May 1954, p. 175.
4. J. H. Boeke, *Economics and Economic Policy of Dual Societies* (New York: Institute of Pacific Relations, 1953), pp. 40 ff.
5. W. F. Wertheim, "Changes in Indonesia's Social Stratification," *Pacific Affairs*, March 1955, p. 41; and *Indonesian Society in Transition: A Study*

of Social Change (Bandung and The Hague: W. van Hoeve, 1956), pp. 135 ff.

6. D. N. Aidit, *Indonesian Society and the Indonesian Revolution* (Djakarta: Jajasan Pembaruan, 1958), p. 61.

7. On the pre-colonial Indonesian trading class, see J. C. van Leur, *Indonesian Trade and Society: Essays in Asian Social and Economic History* (Bandung and The Hague: W. van Hoeve, 1955), p. 191.

8. Even Boeke writes of the Indonesian who "finds himself hindered in reaping the rewards of his labor and in developing his paltry little business by the competition of the much more powerful and efficient Western enterprise." See *Economics and Economic Policy of Dual Societies*, p. 215.

9. "The present ruling class is hardly able to wield command over the agrarian masses." Wertheim, "Changes in Indonesia's Social Stratification," p. 52.

10. A. H. Ballendux, *Bijdrage tot de Kennis van de Credietverlening aan de "Indonesische Middenstand"* (The Hague: printed doctoral dissertation, 1951), pp. 79 ff.

11. D. S. Paauw, *Financing Economic Development: The Indonesian Case* (Glencoe: The Free Press, 1960), pp. 205 ff.

12. Lewis, "Economic Development with Unlimited Supplies of Labor," p. 157.

13. See, for example, L. H. Palmier, "Aspects of Indonesia's Social Structure," *Pacific Affairs*, June 1955; and J. H. Mysberg, "The Indonesian Elite," *Far Eastern Survey*, March 1957.

14. The importance of "intermediate groups" between the elite and the "masses" is emphasized in G. J. Pauker, "The Role of Political Organization in Indonesia," *Far Eastern Survey*, September 1958. Though examples of intermediate organizations feature economic groupings prominently, the systematic discussion totally omits economic interest as a possible source of division. The distinction between bureaucrats, tradesmen, and labor is most sharply drawn in J. M. van der Kroef, "Economic Origins of Indonesian Nationalism," in P. Talbot, ed., *South Asia in the World Today* (Chicago: University of Chicago Press, 1950).

15. For detailed expositions of these policies, see N. G. Amstutz, "The Development of Indigenous Importers in Indonesia" (Ph.D. diss., Fletcher School of Law and Diplomacy, 1958); and J. O. Sutter, *Indonesianisasi: Politics in a Changing Economy, 1940-1955* (Ithaca: Cornell University Southeast Asia Program, 1959).

16. See H. Feith, *The Wilopo Cabinet, 1952-1953: A Turning Point in Post-Revolutionary Indonesia* (Ithaca: Cornell University Modern Indonesia Project, 1958), for a variant interpretation.

17. The elections showed the Masjumi Party, which had consistently advocated

financial retrenchment, strong among trading interests and dominant outside Java, and the Nationalist Party, which had been chiefly responsible for the government's inflationary policies, strong among the bureaucracy and dominant in Java. See H. Feith, *The Indonesian Elections of 1955* (Ithaca: Cornell University Modern Indonesia Project, 1957).

18. Bank Indonesia, *Report for the Year 1957–1958* (Djakarta, July 1958), p. 128,
19. Bank Indonesia, *Report for the Year 1958–1959* (Djakarta, July 1959), p. 145. Evidence suggests that smuggling by dissidents may have accounted for two-thirds of the drop in reported exports by volume.
20. *Ibid.*, p. 151.
21. *Ibid.*, p. 133.
22. *Ibid.*, pp. 97 ff.
23. *Ibid.*, p. 86.
24. W. A. Hanna, *Bung Karno's Indonesia* (New York: American Universities Field Staff, 1960), p. 13-59-7.
25. Paauw, *Financing Economic Development*, p. xx.
26. Referring to "the Government and the national leaders" in Indonesia, Soedjatmoko writes: "It is among these circles that there is a lack of desire and determination to proceed with economic development." See Soedjatmoko, *Economic Development as a Cultural Problem* (Ithaca: Cornell University Modern Indonesia Project, 1958), p. 8.
27. Examples of a similar rift include Egypt (Nasser versus Farouk), Iraq (Kassem versus Nuri as-Said), Iran (Mossadegh versus the Shah), the Belgian Congo (Lumumba versus Tshombe), and Cuba (Castro versus Batista).
28. Hanna, *Bung Karno's Indonesia*, p. 35-59-1.
29. Compare this procedure with the arrangements used to finance the Indian railways. See D. S. Thorner, *Investment in Empire* (Philadelphia: University of Pennsylvania Press, 1950), p. 83.
30. L. A. Doyle, "Reducing Barriers to Private Foreign Investment in Underdeveloped Countries," *California Management Review*, Fall 1958, considers accounting techniques to implement this idea.

Part III

Politics, Class Conflict and Underdevelopment

Introduction

"On the Political Economy of Backwardness" is an ambitious summary of obstacles to development. In this article the late Paul Baran focuses his attention on the native capitalist middle class which, he suggests, has failed to sweep away feudal and semifeudal institutions. Having developed as a weak servant of Western capitalism, it is now fearful of popular revolution and has joined with other conservative forces in the attempt to stifle all reforms which might threaten its power. The reader should ask himself to what extent the variety of social structures in different parts of the underdeveloped world require qualification of Baran's views.

The essays by Frantz Fanon and José Nun deal with the middle classes in Africa and Latin America respectively. Like Baran, both feel that the middle classes are not a progressive force in the underdeveloped world. Fanon argues that independence has simply provided educated Africans with the opportunity to replace the formerly white administrative elite. Foreign exploitation, he argues, is merely replaced by native exploitation, while the basic structure created by colonialism remains. In his article Nun suggests that the military coup in the less-underdeveloped Latin American nations is the defensive reaction of a middle class which has allied itself with older conservative groups. The structure of Latin American society, Nun argues, inevitably leads to economic stagnation. When this stagnation produces increased popular unrest, the army is called forward in defense of established interests.

Philip Ehrensaft's study, "The Politics of Pseudo-Planning in a Primary-Producing Nation," follows the analysis formulated in Dudley Seers' article in this volume. In addition, he stresses the relationship of ethnic conflict to the lack of sectorial integration and employment opportunities characteristic of the colonial economy. A similar approach to ethnic conflict is presented by Malcolm Caldwell in "Problems of Socialism in Southeast Asia." Caldwell deftly traces the political alignments which have emerged from the colonial experience and suggests that none of the existing regimes, despite differences in composition and flexibility, will improve the economic position of the Southeast Asian peasant.

I

Paul A. Baran

On the Political Economy of Backwardness

The capitalist mode of production and the social and political order concomitant with it provided, during the latter part of the eighteenth century, and still more during the entire nineteenth century, a framework for a continuous and, in spite of cyclical disturbances and setbacks, momentous expansion of productivity and material welfare. The relevant facts are well known and call for no elaboration. Yet this material (and cultural) progress was not only spotty in time but most unevenly distributed in space. It was confined to the Western world; and did not affect even all of this territorially and demographically relatively small sector of the inhabited globe. Germany and Austria, Britain and France, some smaller countries in Western Europe, and the United States and Canada occupied places in the neighborhood of the sun. The vast expanses and the multitude of inhabitants of Eastern Europe, Spain and Portugal, Italy and the Balkans, Latin America and Asia, not to speak of Africa, remained in the deep shadow of backwardness and squalor, of stagnation and misery.

Tardy and skimpy as the benefits of capitalism may have been with respect to the lower classes even in most of the leading industrial countries, they were all but negligible in the less privileged parts of the world. There productivity remained low, and rapid increases in population pushed living standards from bad to worse. The dreams of the prophets of capitalist harmony remained on paper. Capital either did not move from countries where its marginal productivity was low to countries where it could be expected to be high, or if it did, it moved there mainly in order

This essay originally appeared in *The Manchester School of Economics and Social Studies* (January 1952), and is included in *The Longer View* (New York and London: Monthly Review Press, 1970). It is reprinted by permission of the Manchester School of Economic and Social Studies and the Estate of Paul A. Baran.

to extract profits from backward countries that frequently accounted for a lion's share of the increments in total output caused by the original investments. Where an increase in the aggregate national product of an underdeveloped country took place, the existing distribution of income prevented this increment from raising the living standards of the broad masses of the population. Like all general statements, this one is obviously open to criticism based on particular cases. There were, no doubt, colonies and dependencies where the populations profited from inflow of foreign capital. These benefits, however, were few and far between, while exploitation and stagnation were the prevailing rule.

But if Western capitalism failed to improve materially the lot of the peoples inhabiting most backward areas, it accomplished something that profoundly affected the social and political conditions in underdeveloped countries. It introduced there, with amazing rapidity, all the economic and social tensions inherent in the capitalist order. It effectively disrupted whatever was left of the "feudal" coherence of the backward societies. It substituted market contracts for such paternalistic relationships as still survived from century to century. It reoriented the partly or wholly self-sufficient economies of agricultural countries toward the production of marketable commodities. It linked their economic fate with the vagaries of the world market and connected it with the fever curve of international price movements.

A *complete* substitution of capitalist market rationality for the rigidities of feudal or semifeudal servitude would have represented, in spite of all the pains of transition, an important step in the direction of progress. Yet all that happened was that the age-old exploitation of the population of underdeveloped countries by their domestic overlords was freed of the mitigating constraints inherited from the feudal tradition. This superimposition of business *mores* over ancient oppression by landed gentries resulted in compounded exploitation, more outrageous corruption, and more glaring injustice.

Nor is this by any means the end of the story. Such export of capital and capitalism as has taken place had not only far-reaching implications of a social nature. It was accompanied by important physical and technical processes. Modern machines and products of advanced industries reached the poverty-stricken backyards of the world. To be sure most, if not all, of these machines worked for their foreign owners—or at least were believed by the population to be working for no one else—and the new refined appurtenances of the good life belonged to foreign businessmen and their domestic counterparts. The bonanza that was capitalism, the fullness of things that was modern industrial civilization, were crowding the display windows—they were protected by barbed wire from the anxious grip of the starving and desperate man in the street.

But they have drastically changed his outlook. Broadening and deepening his economic horizon, they aroused aspirations, envies, and hopes. Young intellectuals filled with zeal and patriotic devotion traveled from the underdeveloped lands to Berlin and London, to Paris and New York, and returned home with the "message of the possible."

Fascinated by the advances and accomplishments observed in the centers of modern industry, they developed and propagandized the image of what could be attained in their home countries under a more rational economic and social order. The dissatisfaction with the stagnation (or at best, barely perceptible growth) that ripened gradually under the still-calm political and social surface was given an articulate expression. This dissatisfaction was not nurtured by a comparison of reality with a vision of a socialist society. It found sufficient fuel in the confrontation of what was actually happening with what could be accomplished under capitalist institutions of the Western type.

The establishment of such institutions was, however, beyond the reach of the tiny middle classes of most backward areas. The inherited backwardness and poverty of their countries never gave them an opportunity to gather the economic strength, the insight, and the self-confidence needed for the assumption of a leading role in society. For centuries under feudal rule they themselves assimilated the political, moral, and cultural values of the dominating class.

While in advanced countries, such as France or Great Britain, the economically ascending middle classes developed at an early stage a new rational world outlook, which they proudly opposed to the medieval obscurantism of the feudal age, the poor, fledgling bourgeoisie of the underdeveloped countries sought nothing but accommodation to the prevailing order. Living in societies based on privilege, they strove for a share in the existing sinecures. They made political and economic deals with their domestic feudal overlords or with powerful foreign investors, and what industry and commerce developed in backward areas in the course of the last hundred years was rapidly molded in the straitjacket of monopoly—the plutocratic partner of the aristocratic rulers. What resulted was an economic and political amalgam combining the worst features of both worlds—feudalism and capitalism—and blocking effectively all possibilities of economic growth.

It is quite conceivable that a "conservative" exit from this impasse might have been found in the course of time. A younger generation of enterprising and enlightened businessmen and intellectuals allied with moderate leaders of workers and peasants—a "Young Turk" movement of some sort—might have succeeded in breaking the deadlock, in loosening the hidebound social and political structure of their countries and in creating the institutional arrangements indispensable for a measure of social and economic progress.

Yet in our rapid age history accorded no time for such a gradual transition. Popular pressures for an amelioration of economic and social conditions, or at least for some perceptible movement in that direction, steadily gained in intensity. To be sure, the growing restiveness of the underprivileged was not directed against the ephemeral principles of a hardly yet existing capitalist order. Its objects were parasitic feudal overlords appropriating large slices of the national product and wasting them on extravagant living; a government machinery protecting and abetting the dominant interests; wealthy businessmen reaping immense profits and not utilizing them for productive purposes; last but not least, foreign colonizers extracting or believed to be extracting vast gains from their "developmental" operations.

This popular movement had thus essentially bourgeois, democratic, antifeudal, anti-imperialist tenets. It found outlets in agrarian egalitarianism; it incorporated "muckraker" elements denouncing monopoly; it strove for national independence and freedom from foreign exploitation.

For the native capitalist middle classes to assume the leadership of these popular forces and to direct them into the channels of bourgeois democracy—as had happened in Western Europe—they had to identify themselves with the common man. They had to break away from the political, economic, and ideological leadership of the feudal crust and the monopolists allied with it; and they had to demonstrate to the nation as a whole that they had the knowledge, the courage, and the determination to undertake and to carry to victorious conclusion the struggle for economic and social improvement.

In hardly any underdeveloped country were the middle classes capable of living up to this historical challenge. Some of the reasons for this portentous failure, reasons connected with the internal make-up of the business class itself, were briefly mentioned above. Of equal importance was, however, an "outside" factor. It was the spectacular growth of the international labor movement in Europe that offered the popular forces in backward areas ideological and political leadership that was denied to them by the native bourgeoisie. It pushed the goals and targets of the popular movements far beyond their original limited objectives.

This liaison of labor radicalism and populist revolt painted on the wall the imminent danger of a social revolution. Whether this danger was real or imaginary matters very little. What was essential is that the awareness of this threat effectively determined political and social action. It destroyed whatever chances there were of the capitalist classes joining and leading the popular antifeudal, antimonopolist movement. By instilling a mortal fear of expropriation and extinction in the minds of *all* property-owning groups, the rise of socialist radicalism, and in particular the Bolshevik Revolution in Russia, tended to drive all more or less privileged, more or less well-to-do elements in the society into one "counter-revolutionary" coalition. Whatever differences and antagonisms existed between large and small landowners, between monopolistic and competitive business, between liberal bourgeois and reactionary feudal overlords, between domestic and foreign interests, were largely submerged on all important occasions by the overriding *common* interest in staving off socialism.

The possibility of solving the economic and political deadlock prevailing in the underdeveloped countries on lines of a progressive capitalism all but disappeared. Entering the alliance with all other segments of the ruling class, the capitalist middle classes yielded one strategic position after another. Afraid that a quarrel with the landed gentry might be exploited by the radical populist movement, the middle classes abandoned all progressive attitudes in agrarian matters. Afraid that a conflict with the church and the military might weaken the political authority of the government, the middle classes moved away from all liberal and pacifist currents. Afraid that hostility toward foreign interests might deprive them of foreign support in a case of a revolutionary emergency, the native capitalists deserted their previous anti-imperialist, nationalist platforms.

The peculiar mechanisms of political interaction characteristic of all underdeveloped (and perhaps not only underdeveloped) countries thus operated at full speed. The aboriginal failure of the middle classes to provide inspiration and leadership to the popular masses pushed those masses into the camp of socialist radicalism. The growth of radicalism pushed the middle classes into an alliance with the aristocratic and monopolistic reaction. This alliance, cemented by common interest and common fear, pushed the populist forces still further along the road of radicalism and revolt. The outcome was a polarization of society with very little left between the poles. By permitting this polarization to develop, by abandoning the common man and resigning the task of reorganizing society on new, progressive lines, the capitalist middle classes threw away their historical chance of assuming effective control over the destinies of their nations, and of directing the gathering popular storm against the fortresses of feudalism and reaction. Its blazing fire turned thus against the entirety of existing economic and social institutions.

The economic and political order maintained by the ruling coalition of owning classes finds itself invariably at odds with all the urgent needs of the underdeveloped countries. Neither the social fabric that it embodies nor the institutions that rest upon it are conducive to progressive economic development. The only way to provide for economic growth and to prevent a continuous deterioration of living standards (apart from mass emigration unacceptable to other countries) is to assure a steady increase of total output—at least large enough to offset the rapid growth of population.

An obvious source of such an increase is the utilization of available unutilized or underutilized resources. A large part of this reservoir of dormant productive potentialities is the vast multitude of entirely unemployed or ineffectively employed manpower. There is no way of employing it usefully in agriculture, where the marginal productivity of labor tends to zero. They could be provided with opportunities for productive work only by transfer to industrial pursuits. For this to be feasible large investments in industrial plant and facilities have to be undertaken. Under prevailing conditions such investments are not forthcoming for a number of important and interrelated reasons.

With a very uneven distribution of a very small aggregate income (and wealth), large individual incomes exceeding what could be regarded as "reasonable" requirements for current consumption accrue as a rule to a relatively small group of high-income receivers. Many of them are large landowners maintaining a feudal style of life with large outlays on housing, servants, travel, and other luxuries. Their "requirements for consumption" are so high that there is only little room for savings. Only relatively insignificant amounts are left to be spent on improvements of agricultural estates.

Other members of the "upper crust" receiving incomes markedly surpassing "reasonable" levels of consumption are wealthy businessmen. For social reasons briefly mentioned above, their consumption too is very much larger than it would have been were they brought up in the puritan tradition of a bourgeois civilization. Their drive to accumulate and to expand their enterprises is continuously counteracted by the urgent desire to imitate in their living habits the socially dominant "old families," to prove by their conspicuous outlays on the amenities of rich life that they are socially (and therefore also politically) not inferior to their aristocratic partners in the ruling coalition.

But if this tendency curtails the volume of savings that could have been amassed by the urban high-income receivers, their will to reinvest their funds in productive enterprises is effectively curbed by a strong reluctance to damage their carefully erected monopolistic market positions through creation of additional productive capacity, and by absence of suitable investment opportunities—paradoxical as this may sound with reference to underdeveloped countries.

The deficiency of investment opportunities stems to a large extent from the structure and the limitations of the existing effective demand. With very low living standards the bulk of the aggregate money income of the population is spent on food and relatively primitive items of clothing and household necessities. These are available at low prices, and investment of large funds in plant and facilities that could produce this type of commodities more cheaply rarely promises attractive returns. Nor does it appear profitable to develop major enterprises the output of which would cater to the requirements of the rich. Large as their individual purchases of various luxuries may be, their aggregate spending on each of them is not sufficient to support the development of an elaborate luxury industry—in particular since the "snob" character of prevailing tastes renders only imported luxury articles true marks of social distinction.

Finally, the limited demand for investment goods precludes the building up of a machinery or equipment industry. Such mass consumption goods as are lacking, and such quantities of luxury goods as are purchased by the well-to-do, as well as the comparatively small quantities of investment goods needed by industry, are thus imported from abroad in exchange for domestic agricultural products and raw materials.

This leaves the expansion of exportable raw materials output as a major outlet for investment activities. There the possibilities are greatly influenced, however, by the technology of the production of most raw materials as well as by the nature of the markets to be served. Many raw materials, in particular oil, metals, certain industrial crops, have to be produced on a large scale if costs are to be kept low and satisfactory returns assured. Large-scale production, however, calls for large investments, so large indeed as to exceed the potentialities of the native capitalists in backward countries. Production of raw materials for a distant market entails, moreover, much larger risks than those encountered in domestic business. The difficulty of foreseeing accurately such things as receptiveness of the world markets, prices obtainable in competition with other countries, volume of output in other parts of the world, etc., sharply reduces the interest of native capitalists in these lines of business. They become to a predominant extent the domain of foreigners who, financially stronger, have at the same time much closer contacts with foreign outlets of their products.

The shortage of investible funds and the lack of investment opportunities represent two aspects of the same problem. A great number of investment projects, unprofitable under prevailing conditions, could be most promising in a general environment of economic expansion.

In backward areas a new industrial venture must frequently, if not always, break virgin ground. It has no functioning economic system to draw upon. It has to organize with its own efforts not only the productive process *within* its own confines, it must provide in addition for all the necessary *outside* arrangements essential to its operations. It does not enjoy the benefits of "external economies."

There can be no doubt that the absence of external economies, the inadequacy of the economic milieu in underdeveloped countries, constituted everywhere an important deterrent to investment in industrial projects. There is no way of rapidly bridging the gap. Large-scale investment is predicated upon large-scale investment. Roads, electric power stations, railroads, and houses have to be built *before* businessmen find it profitable to erect factories, to invest their funds in new industrial enterprises.

Yet investing in road building, financing construction of canals and power stations, organizing large housing projects, etc., transcend by far the financial and mental horizon of capitalists in underdeveloped countries. Not only are their financial resources too small for such ambitious projects, but their background and habits militate against entering commitments of this type. Brought up in the tradition of merchandising and manufacturing consumers' goods—as is characteristic of an early phase of capitalist development—businessmen in underdeveloped countries are accustomed to rapid turnover, large but short-term risks, and correspondingly high rates of profit. Sinking funds in enterprises where profitability could manifest itself only in the course of many years is a largely unknown and unattractive departure.

The difference between social and private rationality that exists in any market and profit-determined economy is thus particularly striking in underdeveloped countries. While building of roads, harnessing of water power, or organization of housing developments may facilitate industrial growth and thus contribute to increased productivity on a national scale, the individual firms engaged in such activities may suffer losses and be unable to recover their investments. The nature of the problem involved can be easily exemplified: starting a new industrial enterprise is predicated among other things upon the availability of appropriately skilled manpower. Engaging men and training them on the job is time-consuming and expensive. They are liable to be unproductive, wasteful, and careless in the treatment of valuable tools and equipment. Accepting the losses involved may be justifiable from the standpoint of the individual firm if such a firm can count with reasonable certainty on retaining the services of those men *after* they go through training and acquire the requisite skills. However, should they leave the firm that provided the training and proceed to work for another enterprise, that new employer would reap the fruits of the first firm's outlays. In a developed industrial society this consideration is relatively unimportant. Losses and gains of individual firms generated by labor turnover may cancel out. In an underdeveloped country the chances of such cancellation are very small, if not nil. Although society as a whole would clearly benefit by the increase of skills of at least some of its members, individual businessmen cannot afford to provide the training that such an increase demands.

But could not the required increase in total output be attained by better utilization of land—another unutilized or inadequately utilized productive factor?

There is usually no land that is both fit for agricultural purposes and at the same time readily accessible. Such terrain as could be cultivated but is actually not being tilled would usually require considerable investment before becoming suitable for settlement. In underdeveloped countries such outlays for agricultural purposes are just as unattractive to private interests as they are for industrial purposes.

On the other hand, more adequate employment of land that is already used in agriculture runs into considerable difficulties. Very few improvements that would be necessary in order to increase productivity can be carried out within the narrow confines of small-peasant holdings. Not only are the peasants in underdeveloped countries utterly unable to pay for such innovations, but the size of their lots offers no justification for their introduction.

Owners of large estates are in a sense in no better position. With limited savings at their disposal they do not have the funds to finance expensive improvements in their enterprises, nor do such projects appear profitable in view of the high prices of imported equipment in relation to prices of agricultural produce and wages of agricultural labor.

Approached thus *via* agriculture, an expansion of total output would also seem to be attainable only through the development of industry. Only through increase of industrial productivity could agricultural machinery, fertilizers, electric power, etc., be brought within the reach of the agricultural producer. Only through an increased demand for labor could agricultural wages be raised and a stimulus provided for a modernization of the agricultural economy. Only through the growth of industrial production could agricultural labor displaced by the machine be absorbed in productive employment.

Monopolistic market structures, shortage of savings, lack of external economies, the divergence of social and private rationalities do not exhaust, however, the list of obstacles blocking the way of privately organized industrial expansion in underdeveloped countries. Those obstacles have to be considered against the background of the general feeling of uncertainty prevailing in all backward areas. The coalition of the owning classes formed under pressure of fear, and held together by the real or imagined danger of social upheavals, provokes continuously more or less threatening rumblings under the outwardly calm political surface. The social and political tensions to which that coalition is a political response are not liquidated by the prevailing system; they are only repressed. Normal and quiet as the daily routine frequently appears, the more enlightened and understanding members of the ruling groups in underdeveloped countries sense the inherent instability of the political and social order. Occasional outbursts of popular dissatisfaction assuming the form of peasant uprisings, violent strikes or local guerrilla warfare, serve from time to time as grim reminders of the latent crisis.

In such a climate there is no will to invest on the part of monied people; in such a climate there is no enthusiasm for long-term projects; in such a climate the motto of all participants in the privileges offered by society is *carpe diem*.

Could not, however, an appropriate policy on the part of the governments involved change the political climate and facilitate economic growth? In our time, when faith in the manipulative omnipotence of the state has all but displaced analysis of its social structure and understanding of its political and economic functions, the tendency is obviously to answer these questions in the affirmative.

Looking at the matter purely mechanically, it would appear indeed that much could be done, by a well-advised regime in an underdeveloped country, to provide for a relatively rapid increase of total output, accompanied by an improvement of the living standards of the population. There is a number of measures that the government could take in an effort to overcome backwardness. A fiscal policy could be adopted that by means of capital levies, and a highly progressive tax system would syphon off all surplus purchasing power, and in this way eliminate nonessential consumption. The savings thus enforced could be channeled by the government into productive investment. Power stations, railroads, highways, irrigation systems, and soil improvements could be organized by the state with a view to creating an economic environment conducive to the growth of productivity. Technical schools on various levels could be set up by the public authority to furnish industrial training to young people as well as to adult workers and the unemployed. A system of scholarships could be introduced rendering acquisition of skills accessible to low-income strata.

Wherever private capital refrains from undertaking certain industrial projects, or wherever monopolistic controls block the necessary expansion of plant and facilities in particular industries, the government could step in and make the requisite investments. Where developmental possibilities that are rewarding in the long-run appear unprofitable during the initial period of gestation and learning, and are therefore beyond the horizon of private businessmen, the government could undertake to shoulder the short-run losses.

In addition, an entire arsenal of "preventive" devices is at the disposal of the authorities. Inflationary pressures resulting from developmental activities (private and public) could be reduced or even eliminated, if outlays on investment projects could be offset by a corresponding and simultaneous contraction of spending elsewhere in the economic system. What this would call for is a taxation policy that would effectively remove from the income stream amounts sufficient to neutralize the investment-caused expansion of aggregate money income.

In the interim, and as a supplement, speculation in scarce goods and excessive profiteering in essential commodities could be suppressed by rigorous price controls. An equitable distribution of mass consumption goods in short supply could be assured by rationing. Diversion of resources in high demand to luxury purposes could be prevented by allocation and priority schemes. Strict supervision of transactions involving foreign exchanges could render capital flight, expenditure of limited foreign funds on luxury imports, pleasure trips abroad, and the like, impossible.

What the combination of these measures would accomplish is a radical change in the structure of effective demand in the underdeveloped country, and a reallocation of productive resources to satisfy society's need for economic development. By curtailing consumption of the higher-income groups, the amounts of savings available for investment purposes could be markedly increased. The squandering of limited supplies of foreign exchange on capital flight, or on importation of redundant foreign goods and services, could be prevented, and the foreign funds thus saved could be used for the acquisition of foreign-made machinery needed for economic development. The reluctance of private interests to engage in enterprises that are socially necessary, but may not promise rich returns in the short run, would be prevented from determining the economic life of the backward country.

The mere listing of the steps that would have to be undertaken, in order to assure an expansion of output and income in an underdeveloped country, reveals the utter implausibility of the view that they could be carried out by the governments existing in most underdeveloped countries. The reason for this inability is only to a negligible extent the nonexistence of the competent and honest civil service needed for the administration of the program. A symptom itself of the political and social marasmus prevailing in underdeveloped countries, this lack cannot be remedied without attacking the underlying causes. Nor does it touch anything near the roots of the matter to lament the lack of satisfactory tax policies in backward countries, or to deplore the absence of tax "morale" and "discipline" among the civic virtues of their populations.

The crucial fact rendering the realization of a developmental program illusory is the political and social structure of the governments in power. The alliance of property-owning classes controlling the destinies of most underdeveloped countries cannot be expected to design and to execute a set of measures running counter to each and all of their immediate vested interests. If to appease the restive public, blueprints of progressive measures such as agrarian reform, equitable tax legislation, etc., are officially announced, their enforcement is willfully sabotaged. The government, representing a political compromise between landed and business interests, cannot suppress the wasteful management of landed estates and the conspicuous consumption on the part of the aristocracy; cannot suppress monopolistic abuses, profiteering, capital flights, and extravagant living on the part of businessmen. It cannot curtail or abandon its lavish appropriations for a military and police establishment, providing attractive careers to the scions of wealthy families and a profitable outlet for armaments produced by their parents—quite apart from the fact that this establishment serves as the main protection against possible popular revolt. Set up to guard and to abet the existing property rights and privileges, it cannot become the architect of a policy calculated to destroy the privileges standing in the way of economic progress and to place the property and the incomes derived from it at the service of society as a whole.

Nor is there much to be said for the "intermediate" position which, granting the essential incompatibility of a well-conceived and vigorously executed development program with the political and social institutions prevailing in most underdeveloped countries, insists that at least *some* of the requisite measures could be carried out by the existing political authorities. This school of thought overlooks entirely the weakness, if not the complete absence, of social and political forces that could induce the necessary concessions on the part of the ruling coalition. By background and political upbringing, too myopic and self-interested to permit the slightest encroachments upon their inherited positions and cherished privileges, the upper classes in underdeveloped countries resist doggedly all pressures in that direction. Every time such pressures grow in strength they succeed in cementing anew the alliance of all conservative elements, by decrying all attempts at reform as assaults on the very foundations of society.

Even if measures like progressive taxation, capital levies, and foreign exchange controls could be enforced by the corrupt officials operating in the demoralized business communities of underdeveloped countries, such enforcement would to a large extent defeat its original purpose. Where businessmen do not invest, unless in expectation of lavish profits, a taxation system, succeeding in confiscating large parts of these profits is bound to kill private investment. Where doing business or operating landed estates are attractive mainly because they permit luxurious living, foreign exchange controls preventing the importation of luxury goods are bound to blight enterprise. Where the only stimulus to hard work on the part of intellectuals, technicians, and civil servants is the chance of partaking in the privileges of the ruling class, a policy aiming at the reduction of inequality of social status and income is bound to smother effort.

The injection of planning into a society living in the twilight between feudalism and capitalism cannot but result in additional corruption, larger and more artful evasions of the law, and more brazen abuses of authority.

There would seem to be no exit from the impasse. The ruling coalition of interests does not abdicate of its own volition, nor does it change its character in response to incantation. Although its individual members occasionally leave the sinking ship physically or financially (or in both ways), the property-owning classes as a whole are as a rule grimly determined to hold fast to their political and economic entrenchments.

If the threat of social upheaval assumes dangerous proportions, they tighten their grip on political life and move rapidly in the direction of unbridled reaction and military dictatorship. Making use of favorable international opportunities and of ideological and social affinities to ruling groups in other countries, they solicit foreign economic and sometimes military aid in their efforts to stave off the impending disaster.

Such aid is likely to be given to them by foreign governments regarding them as an evil less to be feared than the social revolution that would sweep them out of power. This attitude of their friends and protectors abroad is no less shortsighted than their own.

The adjustment of the social and political conditions in underdeveloped countries to the urgent needs of economic development can be postponed; it cannot be indefinitely avoided. In the past, it could have been delayed by decades or even centuries. In our age it is a matter of years. Bolstering the political system of power existing in backward countries by providing it with military support may temporarily block the eruption of the volcano; it cannot stop the subterranean gathering of explosive forces.

Economic help in the form of loans and grants given to the governments of backward countries to enable them to promote a measure of economic progress is no substitute for the domestic changes that are mandatory if economic development is to be attained.

Such help, in fact, may actually do more harm than good. Possibly permitting the importation of some foreign-made machinery and equipment for government or business-sponsored investment projects, but not accompanied by any of the steps that are needed to assure healthy economic growth, foreign assistance thus supplied may set off an inflationary spiral increasing and aggravating the existing social and economic tensions in underdeveloped countries.

If, as is frequently the case, these loans or grants from abroad are tied to the fulfillment of certain conditions on the part of the receiving country regarding their use, the resulting investment may be directed in such channels as to conform more to the interests of the lending than to those of the borrowing country. Where economic advice as a form of "technical assistance" is supplied to the underdeveloped country, and its acceptance is made a prerequisite to eligibility for financial aid, this advice often pushes the governments of underdeveloped countries toward policies, ideologically or otherwise attractive to the foreign experts dispensing economic counsel, but not necessarily conducive to economic development of the "benefited" countries. Nationalism and xenophobia are thus strengthened in backward areas—additional fuel for political restiveness.

For backward countries to enter the road of economic growth and social progress, the political framework of their existence has to be drastically revamped. The alliance between feudal landlords, industrial royalists, and the capitalist middle classes has to be broken. The keepers of the past cannot be the builders of the future. Such progressive and enterprising elements as exist in backward societies have to obtain the possibility of leading their countries in the direction of economic and social growth.

What France, Britain, and America have accomplished through their own revolutions has to be attained in backward countries by a combined effort of popular forces, enlightened government, and unselfish foreign help. This combined effort must sweep away the holdover institutions of a defunct age, must change the political and social climate in the under-developed countries, and must imbue their nations with a new spirit of enterprise and freedom.

Should it prove too late in the historical process for the bourgeoisie to rise to its responsibilities in backward areas, should the long experience of servitude and accommodation to the feudal past have reduced the forces of progressive capitalism to impotence, the backward countries of the world will inevitably turn to economic planning and social collecti-vism. If the capitalist world outlook of economic and social progress, propelled by enlightened self-interest, should prove unable to triumph over the conservatism of inherited positions and traditional privileges, if the capitalist promise of advance and reward to the efficient, the indus-trious, the able, should not displace the feudal assurance of security and power to the well-bred, the well-connected, and the conformist—a new social ethos will become the spirit and guide of a new age. It will be the ethos of the collective effort, the creed of the predominance of the interests of society over the interests of selected few.

The transition may be abrupt and painful. The land not given to the peasants legally may be taken by them forcibly. High incomes not confis-cated through taxation may be eliminated by outright expropriation. Corrupt officials not retired in orderly fashion may be removed by violent action.

Which way the historical wheel will turn and in which way the crisis in the backward countries will find its final solution will depend in the main on whether the capitalist middle classes in the backward areas, and the rulers of the advanced industrial nations of the world, overcome their fear and myopia. Or are they too spellbound by their narrowly conceived selfish interests, too blinded by their hatred of progress, grown so senile in these latter days of the capitalist age, as to commit suicide out of fear of death?

2

Frantz Fanon

The Pitfalls of National Consciousness—Africa

History teaches us clearly that the battle against colonialism does not run straight away along the lines of nationalism. For a very long time the native devotes his energies to ending certain definite abuses: forced labor, corporal punishment, inequality of salaries, limitation of political rights, etc. This fight for democracy against the oppression of mankind will slowly leave the confusion of neo-liberal universalism to emerge, sometimes laboriously, as a claim to nationhood. It so happens that the unpreparedness of the educated classes, the lack of practical links between them and the mass of the people, their laziness, and, let it be said, their cowardice at the decisive moment of the struggle will give rise to tragic mishaps.

National consciousness, instead of being the all-embracing crystallization of the innermost hopes of the whole people, instead of being the immediate and most obvious result of the mobilization of the people, will be in any case only an empty shell, a crude and fragile travesty of what it might have been. The faults that we find in it are quite sufficient explanation of the facility with which, when dealing with young and independent nations, the nation is passed over for the race, and the tribe is preferred to the state. These are the cracks in the edifice which show the process of retrogression that is so harmful and prejudicial to national effort and national unity. We shall see that such retrograde steps with all the weaknesses and serious dangers that they entail are the historical result of the incapacity of the national middle class to rationalize popular action, that is to say, their incapacity to see into the reasons for that action.

Reprinted from *The Wretched of the Earth* by permission of Grove Press, Inc., and MacGibbon & Kee, Ltd. Translated from the French by Constance Farrington. Copyright © 1963 by Présence Africaine.

This traditional weakness, which is almost congenital to the national consciousness of underdeveloped countries, is not solely the result of the mutilation of the colonized people by the colonial regime. It is also the result of the intellectual laziness of the national middle class, of its spiritual penury, and of the profoundly cosmopolitan mold that its mind is set in.

The national middle class which takes over power at the end of the colonial regime is an underdeveloped middle class. It has practically no economic power, and in any case it is in no way commensurate with the bourgeoisie of the mother country which it hopes to replace. In its willful narcissism, the national middle class is easily convinced that it can advantageously replace the middle class of the mother country. But that same independence which literally drives it into a corner will give rise within its ranks to catastrophic reactions, and will oblige it to send out frenzied appeals for help to the former mother country. The university and merchant classes which make up the most enlightened section of the new state are in fact characterized by the smallness of their number and their being concentrated in the capital, and the type of activities in which they are engaged: business, agriculture, and the liberal professions. Neither financiers nor industrial magnates are to be found within this national middle class. The national bourgeoisie of underdeveloped countries is not engaged in production, nor in invention, nor building, nor labor; it is completely canalized into activities of the intermediary type. Its innermost vocation seems to be to keep in the running and to be part of the racket. The psychology of the national bourgeoisie is that of the businessman, not that of a captain of industry; and it is only too true that the greed of the settlers and the system of embargoes set up by colonialism has hardly left them any other choice.

Under the colonial system, a middle class which accumulates capital is an impossible phenomenon. Now, precisely, it would seem that the historical vocation of an authentic national middle class in an underdeveloped country is to repudiate its own nature insofar as it is bourgeois, that is to say, insofar as it is the tool of capitalism, and to make itself the willing slave of that revolutionary capital which is the people.

In an underdeveloped country an authentic national middle class ought to consider as its bounden duty to betray the calling fate has marked out for it, and to put itself to school with the people: in other words, to put at the people's disposal the intellectual and technical capital that it has snatched when going through the colonial universities. But unhappily we shall see that very often the national middle class does not follow this heroic, positive, fruitful, and just path; rather, it disappears with its soul set at peace into the shocking ways—shocking because antinational—of a traditional bourgeoisie, of a bourgeoisie which is stupidly, contemptibly, cynically bourgeois.

The objective of nationalist parties from a certain given period is, we have seen, strictly national. They mobilize the people with slogans of independence, and for the rest leave it to future events. When such parties are questioned on the economic program of the state that they are clamoring for, or on the nature of the regime which they propose to install, they are incapable of replying, because, precisely, they are completely ignorant of the economy of their own country.

This economy has always developed outside the limits of their know-ledge. They have nothing more than an approximate, bookish acquaint-ance with the actual and potential resources of their country's soil and mineral deposits; and therefore they can only speak of these resources on a general and abstract plane. After independence this underdeveloped middle class, reduced in numbers and without capital, refusing to follow the path of revolution, will fall into deplorable stagnation. It is unable to give free rein to its genius, which formerly it was wont to lament, though rather too glibly, was held in check by colonial domination. The precari-ousness of its resources and the paucity of its managerial class forces it back for years into an artisanal economy. From its point of view, which is inevitably a very limited one, a national economy is an economy based on what may be called local products. Long speeches will be made about the artisan class. Since the middle classes find it impossible to set up factories that would be more profit-earning both for themselves and for the country as a whole, they will surround the artisan class with a chauvinistic tenderness in keeping with the new awareness of national dignity, one which, moreover, will bring them in quite a lot of money. This cult of local products and this incapability to seek out new systems of manage-ment will be equally manifested by the bogging down of the national middle class in the methods of agricultural production which were characteristic of the colonial period.

The national economy of the period of independence is not set on a new footing. It is still concerned with the groundnut harvest, with the cocoa crop, and the olive yield. In the same way there is no change in the marketing of basic products, and not a single industry is set up in the country. We go on sending out raw materials; we go on being Europe's small farmers, who specialize in unfinished products.

Yet the national middle class constantly demands the nationalization of the economy and of the trading sectors. This is because, from their point of view, nationalization does not mean placing the whole economy at the service of the nation and deciding to satisfy the needs of the nation. For them, nationalization does not mean governing the state with regard to the new social relations whose growth it has been decided to encourage. To them, nationalization quite simply means the transfer into native hands of those unfair advantages which are a legacy of the colonial period.

Since the middle class has neither sufficient material nor intellectual resources (by intellectual resources we mean engineers and technicians), it limits its claims to the taking over of business offices and commercial houses formerly occupied by the settlers. The national bourgeoisie steps into the shoes of the former European settlement: doctors, barristers, traders, commercial travelers, general agents, and transport agents. It considers that the dignity of the country and its own welfare require that it should occupy all these posts. From now on it will insist that all the big foreign companies should pass through its hands, whether these companies wish to keep on their connections with the country, or to open it up. The national middle class discovers its historic mission: that of intermediary.

Seen through its eyes, its mission has nothing to do with transforming the nation; it consists, prosaically, of being the transmission line between the nation and a capitalism, rampant though camouflaged, which today puts on the masque of neo-colonialism. The national bourgeoisie will be quite content with the role of the Western bourgeoisie's business agent, and it will play its part without any complexes in a most dignified manner. But this same lucrative role, this cheap-jack's function, this meanness of outlook, and this absence of all ambition symbolize the incapability of the national middle class to fulfil its historic role of bourgeoisie. Here, the dynamic, pioneer aspect, the characteristics of the inventor and of the discoverer of new worlds which are found in all national bourgeoisies, are lamentably absent. In the colonial countries, the spirit of indulgence is dominant at the core of the bourgeoisie; and this is because the national bourgeoisie identifies itself with the Western bourgeoisie, from whom it has learned its lessons. It follows the Western bourgeoisie along its path of negation and decadence without ever having emulated it in its first stages of exploration and invention, stages which are an acquisition of that Western bourgeoisie whatever the circumstances. In its beginnings, the national bourgeoisie of the colonial countries identifies itself with the decadence of the bourgeoisie of the West. We need not think that it is jumping ahead; it is in fact beginning at the end. It is already senile before it has come to know the petulance, the fearlessness, or the will to succeed of youth.

The national bourgeoisie will be greatly helped on its way toward decadence by the Western bourgeoisies, which come to it as tourists avid for the exotic, for big game hunting, and for casinos. The national bourgeoisie organizes centers of rest and relaxation and pleasure resorts to meet the wishes of the Western bourgeoisie. Such activity is given the name of tourism, and for the occasion will be built up as a national industry. If proof is needed of the eventual transformation of certain elements of the ex-native bourgeoisie into the organizers of parties for their Western opposite numbers, it is worth while having a look at what has happened in Latin America. The casinos of Havana and of Mexico, the beaches of Rio, the little Brazilian and Mexican girls, the half-breed thirteen-year-olds, the ports of Acapulco and Copacabana—all these are the stigma of this depravation of the national middle class. Because it is bereft of ideas, because it lives to itself and cuts itself off from the people, undermined by its hereditary incapacity to think in terms of all the problems of the nation as seen from the point of view of the whole of that nation, the national middle class will have nothing better to do than to take on the role of manager for Western enterprise, and it will in practice set up its country as the brothel of Europe.

Once again we must keep before us the unfortunate example of certain Latin American republics. The banking magnates, the technocrats, and the big businessmen of the United States have only to step onto a plane and they are wafted into subtropical climes, there for a space of a week or ten days to luxuriate in the delicious depravities which their "reserves" hold for them.

The behavior of the national landed proprietors is practically identical with that of the middle classes of the towns. The big farmers have, as soon as independence is proclaimed, demanded the nationalization of agricultural production. Through manifold scheming practices they manage to make a clean sweep of the farms formerly owned by settlers, thus reinforcing their hold on the district. But they do not try to introduce new agricultural methods, nor to farm more intensively, nor to integrate their farming systems into a genuinely national economy.

In fact, the landed proprietors will insist that the state should give them a hundred times more facilities and privileges than were enjoyed by the foreign settlers in former times. The exploitation of agricultural workers will be intensified and made legitimate. Using two or three slogans, these new colonists will demand an enormous amount of work from the agricultural laborers, in the name of the national effort, of course. There will be no modernization of agriculture, no planning for development, and no initiative; for initiative throws these people into a panic since it implies a minimum of risk, and completely upsets the hesitant, prudent, landed bourgeoisie, which gradually slips more and more into the lines laid down by colonialism. In the districts where this is the case, the only efforts made to better things are due to the government; it orders them, encourages them, and finances them. The landed bourgeoisie refuses to take the slightest risk, and remains opposed to any venture and to any hazard. It has no intention of building upon sand; it demands solid investments and quick returns. The enormous profits which it pockets, enormous if we take into account the national revenue, are never reinvested. The money-in-the-stocking mentality is dominant in the psychology of these landed proprietors. Sometimes, especially in the years immediately following independence, the bourgeoisie does not hesitate to invest in foreign banks the profits that it makes out of its native soil. On the other hand, large sums are spent on display: on cars, country houses, and on all those things which have been justly described by economists as characterizing an underdeveloped bourgeoisie.

We have said that the native bourgeoisie which comes to power uses its class aggressiveness to corner the positions formerly kept for foreigners. On the morrow of independence, in fact, it violently attacks colonial personalities: barristers, traders, landed proprietors, doctors, and higher civil servants. It will fight to the bitter end against these people "who insult our dignity as a nation." It waves aloft the notion of the nationalization and Africanization of the ruling classes. The fact is that such action will become more and more tinged by racism, until the bourgeoisie bluntly puts the problem to the government by saying, "We must have these posts." They will not stop their snarling until they have taken over every one.

The working class of the towns, the masses of unemployed, the small

artisans and craftsmen for their part line up behind this nationalist attitude; but in all justice let it be said, they only follow in the steps of their
bourgeoisie. If the national bourgeoisie goes into competition with the
Europeans, the artisans and craftsmen start a fight against non-national
Africans. In the Ivory Coast, the anti-Dahoman and anti-Voltaic troubles
are in fact racial riots. The Dahoman and Voltaic peoples, who control
the greater part of the petty trade, are, once independence is declared, the
object of hostile manifestations on the part of the people of the Ivory
Coast. From nationalism we have passed to ultranationalism, to chauvinism, and finally to racism. These foreigners are called on to leave; their
shops are burned, their street stalls are wrecked, and in fact the government of the Ivory Coast commands them to go, thus giving their nationals
satisfaction. In Senegal it is the anti-Soudanese demonstrations which
called forth these words from Mr. Mamadou Dia:

> The truth is that the Senegalese people have only adopted the Mali mystique
> through attachment to its leaders. Their adhesion to the Mali has no other
> significance than that of a fresh act of faith in the political policy of the latter.
> The Senegalese territory was no less real, in fact it was all the more so in that
> the presence of the Soudanese in Dakar was too obviously manifested for it
> to be forgotten. It is this fact which explains that, far from being regretted,
> the breakup of the Federation has been greeted with relief by the mass of the
> people and nowhere was a hand raised to maintain it.[1]

While certain sections of the Senegalese people jump at the chance
which is afforded them by their own leaders to get rid of the Soudanese,
who hamper them in commercial matters or in administrative posts, the
Congolese, who stood by hardly daring to believe in the mass exodus of
the Belgians, decide to bring pressure to bear on the Senegalese who
have settled in Leopoldville and Elisabethville and to get them to leave.

As we see it, the mechanism is identical in the two sets of circumstances. If the Europeans get in the way of the intellectuals and business
bourgeoisie of the young nation, for the mass of the people in the towns
competition is represented principally by Africans of another nation.
On the Ivory Coast these competitors are the Dahomans; in Ghana they
are the Nigerians; in Senegal, they are the Soudanese.

When the bourgeoisie's demands for a ruling class made up exclusively
of Negroes or Arabs do not spring from an authentic movement of
nationalization but merely correspond to an anxiety to place in the bourgeoisie's hands the power held hitherto by the foreigner, the masses on

their level present the same demands, confining, however, the notion of Negro or Arab within certain territorial limits. Between resounding assertions of the unity of the continent and this behavior of the masses which has its inspiration in their leaders, many different attitudes may be traced. We observe a permanent seesaw between African unity, which fades quicker and quicker into the mists of oblivion, and a heartbreaking return to chauvinism in its most bitter and detestable form.

> On the Senegalese side, the leaders who have been the main theoreticians of African unity, and who several times over have sacrificed their local political organizations and their personal positions to this idea, are, though in all good faith, undeniably responsible. Their mistake—our mistake—has been, under pretext of fighting "Balkanization," not to have taken into consideration the precolonial fact of territorialism. Our mistake has been not to have paid enough attention in our analyses to this phenomenon, which is the fruit of colonialism if you like, but also a sociological fact which no theory of unity, be it ever so laudable or attractive, can abolish. We have allowed ourselves to be seduced by a mirage: that of the structure which is the most pleasing to our minds; and, mistaking our ideal for reality, we have believed it enough to condemn territorialism, and its natural sequel, micronationalism, for us to get the better of them, and to assure the success of our chimerical undertaking.[2]

From the chauvinism of the Senegalese to the tribalism of the Yolofs is not a big step. For in fact, everywhere that the national bourgeoisie has failed to break through to the people as a whole, to enlighten them, and to consider all problems in the first place with regard to them—a failure due to the bourgeoisie's attitude of mistrust and to the haziness of its political tenets—everywhere where that national bourgeoisie has shown itself incapable of extending its vision of the world sufficiently, we observe a falling back toward old tribal attitudes, and, furious and sick at heart, we perceive that race feeling in its most exacerbated form is triumphing. Since the sole motto of the bourgeoisie is "Replace the foreigner," and because it hastens in every walk of life to secure justice for itself and to take over the posts that the foreigner has vacated, the "small people" of the nation—taxi drivers, cake sellers, and shoeblacks—will be equally quick to insist that the Dahomans go home to their own country, or will even go further and demand that the Foulbis and the Peuhls return to their jungle or their mountains.

It is from this viewpoint that we must interpret the fact that in young, independent countries, here and there federalism triumphs. We know that colonial domination has marked certain regions out for privilege. The colony's economy is not integrated into that of the nation as a whole. It is still organized in order to complete the economy of the different mother countries. Colonialism hardly ever exploits the whole of a country. It contents itself with bringing to light the natural resources, which it extracts and exports to meet the needs of the mother country's industries, thereby allowing certain sectors of the colony to become relatively rich. But the rest of the colony follows its path of underdevelopment and poverty, or at all events sinks into it more deeply.

Immediately after independence, the nationals who live in the more prosperous regions realize their good luck and show a primary and profound reaction in refusing to feed the other nationals. The districts which are rich in groundnuts, in cocoa, and in diamonds come to the forefront and dominate the empty panorama which the rest of the nation presents. The nationals of these rich regions look upon the others with hatred, and find in them envy and covetousness and homicidal impulses. Old rivalries which were there before colonialism, old interracial hatreds, come to the surface. The Balubas refuse to feed the Luluas; Katanga forms itself into a state; and Albert Kalondji gets himself crowned king of South Kasai.

African unity, that vague formula—yet one to which the men and women of Africa were passionately attached, and whose operative value served to bring immense pressure to bear on colonialism—African unity takes off the mask and crumbles into regionalism inside the hollow shell of nationality itself. The national bourgeoisie, since it is strung up to defend its immediate interests and sees no further than the end of its nose, reveals itself incapable of simply bringing national unity into being, or of building up the nation on a stable and productive basis. The national front which has forced colonialism to withdraw cracks up and wastes the victory it has gained.

This merciless fight engaged upon by races and tribes, and this aggressive anxiety to occupy the posts left vacant by the departure of the foreigner, will equally give rise to religious rivalries. In the country districts and the bush, minor confraternities, local religions, and maraboutic cults will show a new vitality and will once more take up their round of excommunications. In the big towns, on the level of the administrative classes, we will observe the coming to grips of the two great revealed religions, Islam and Catholicism.

Colonialism, which had been shaken to its very foundations by the birth of African unity, recovers its balance and tries now to break that will to unity by using all the movement's weaknesses. Colonialism will set the African peoples moving by revealing to them the existence of "spiritual" rivalries. In Senegal, it is the newspaper *New Africa* which week by week distills hatred of Islam and of the Arabs. The Lebanese, in whose hands is the greater part of the small trading enterprises on the western seaboard, are marked out for national obloquy. The missionaries find it opportune to remind the masses that long before the advent of European colonialism the great African empires were disrupted by the Arab invasion. There is no hesitation in saying that it was the Arab occupation which paved the way for European colonialism; Arab imperialism is commonly spoken of, and the cultural imperialism of Islam is condemned. Moslems are usually kept out of the more important posts. In other regions the reverse is the case, and it is the native Christians who are considered as conscious, objective enemies of national independence.

Colonialism pulls every string shamelessly, and is only too content to set at loggerheads those Africans who only yesterday were leagued against the settlers. The idea of a Saint Bartholomew takes shape in certain minds, and the advocates of colonialism laugh to themselves derisively when they hear magnificent declarations about African unity. Inside a single nation, religion splits up the people into different spiritual communities, all of them kept up and stiffened by colonialism and its instruments. Totally unexpected events break out here and there. In regions where Catholicism or Protestantism predominates, we see the Moslem minorities flinging themselves with unaccustomed ardor into their devotions. The Islamic feast days are revived, and the Moslem religion defends itself inch by inch against the violent absolutism of the Catholic faith. Ministers of state are heard to say for the benefit of certain individuals that if they are not content they have only to go to Cairo. Sometimes American Protestantism transplants its anti-Catholic prejudices into African soil and keeps up tribal rivalries through religion.

Taking the continent as a whole, this religious tension may be responsible for the revival of the commonest racial feeling. Africa is divided into Black and White, and the names that are submitted—Africa South of the Sahara, Africa North of the Sahara—do not manage to hide this latent racism. Here, it is affirmed that White Africa has a thousand-year-old tradition of culture; that she is Mediterranean, that she is a continuation of Europe, and that she shares in Greco-Latin civilization. Black Africa is looked on as a region that is inert, brutal, uncivilized—in a word, savage. There, all day long you may hear unpleasant remarks about veiled women, polygamy, and the supposed disdain the Arabs have for the feminine sex. All such remarks are reminiscent in their aggressiveness of those that are so often heard coming from the settler's lips. The national bourgeoisie of each of these two great religions, which has totally assimilated colonialist thought in its most corrupt form, takes over from the Europeans and establishes in the continent a racial philosophy which is extremely harmful for the future of Africa. By its laziness and will to imitation, it promotes the ingrafting and stiffening of racism which was characteristic of the colonial era. Thus it is by no means astonishing to hear in a country that calls itself African remarks which are neither more nor less than racist, and to observe the existence of paternalist behavior which gives you the bitter impression that you are in Paris, Brussels, or London.

In certain regions of Africa, drivelling paternalism with regard to the black and the loathsome idea derived from Western culture that the black man is impervious to logic and the sciences reign in all their nakedness. Sometimes it may be ascertained that the black minorities are hemmed in by a kind of semislavery which renders legitimate that species of wariness, or in other words mistrust, which the countries of Black Africa feel with regard to the countries of White Africa. It is all too common that a citizen of Black Africa hears himself called a "Negro" by the children when walking in the streets of a big town in White Africa, or finds that civil servants address him in pidgin English.

Yes, unfortunately it is not unknown that students from Black Africa who attend secondary schools north of the Sahara hear their schoolfellows asking if in their country there are houses, if they know what electricity is, or if they practice cannibalism in their families. Yes, unfortunately it is not unknown that in certain regions north of the Sahara Africans coming from countries south of the Sahara meet nationals who implore them to take them "anywhere at all on condition we meet Negroes." In parallel fashion, in certain young states of Black Africa members of parliament, or even ministers, maintain without a trace of humor that the danger is not at all of a reoccupation of their country by colonialism but of an eventual invasion by "those vandals of Arabs coming from the North."

As we see it, the bankruptcy of the bourgeoisie is not apparent in the economic field only. They have come to power in the name of a narrow nationalism and representing a race; they will prove themselves incapable of triumphantly putting into practice a program with even a minimum humanist content, in spite of fine-sounding declarations which are devoid of meaning since the speakers bandy about in irresponsible fashion phrases that come straight out of European treatises on morals and political philosophy. When the bourgeoisie is strong, when it can arrange everything and everybody to serve its power, it does not hesitate to affirm positively certain democratic ideas which claim to be universally applicable. There must be very exceptional circumstances if such a bourgeoisie, solidly based economically, is forced into denying its own humanist ideology. The Western bourgeoisie, though fundamentally racist, most often manages to mask this racism by a multiplicity of nuances which allow it to preserve intact its proclamation of mankind's outstanding dignity.

The Western bourgeoisie has prepared enough fences and railings to have no real fear of the competition of those whom it exploits and holds in contempt. Western bourgeois racial prejudice as regards the nigger and the Arab is a racism of contempt; it is a racism which minimizes what it hates. Bourgeois ideology, however, which is the proclamation of an essential equality between men, manages to appear logical in its own eyes by inviting the sub-men to become human, and to take as their prototype Western humanity as incarnated in the Western bourgeoisie.

The racial prejudice of the young national bourgeoisie is a racism of defense, based on fear. Essentially it is no different from vulgar tribalism, or the rivalries between sects or confraternities. We may understand why keen-witted international observers have hardly taken seriously the great flights of oratory about African unity, for it is true that there are so many cracks in that unity visible to the naked eye that it is only reasonable to insist that all these contradictions ought to be resolved before the day of unity can come.

The peoples of Africa have only recently come to know themselves. They have decided, in the name of the whole continent, to weigh in strongly against the colonial regime. Now the nationalist bourgeoisies, who in region after region hasten to make their own fortunes and to set up a national system of exploitation, do their utmost to put obstacles in the path of this "Utopia." The national bourgeoisies, who are quite clear as to what their objectives are, have decided to bar the way to that unity, to that coordinated effort on the part of 250 million men to triumph over stupidity, hunger, and inhumanity at one and the same time. This is why we must understand that African unity can only be achieved through the upward thrust of the people and under the leadership of the people, that is to say, in defiance of the interests of the bourgeoisie.

As regards internal affairs and in the sphere of institutions, the national bourgeoisie will give equal proof of its incapacity. In a certain number of underdeveloped countries the parliamentary game is faked from the beginning. Powerless economically, unable to bring about the existence of coherent social relations, and standing on the principle of its domination as a class, the bourgeoisie chooses the solution that seems to it the easiest, that of the single party. It does not yet have the quiet conscience and the calm that economic power and the control of the state machine alone can give. It does not create a state that reassures the ordinary citizen, but rather one that rouses his anxiety.

The state, which by its strength and discretion ought to inspire confidence and disarm and lull everybody to sleep, on the contrary seeks to impose itself in spectacular fashion. It makes a display, it jostles people and bullies them, thus intimating to the citizen that he is in continual danger. The single party is the modern form of the dictatorship of the bourgeoisie, unmasked, unpainted, unscrupulous, and cynical.

It is true that such a dictatorship does not go very far. It cannot halt the processes of its own contradictions. Since the bourgeoisie has not the economic means to insure its domination and to throw a few crumbs to the rest of the country; since, moreover, it is preoccupied with filling its pockets as rapidly as possible but also as prosaically as possible, the country sinks all the more deeply into stagnation. And in order to hide this stagnation and to mask this regression, to reassure itself and to give itself something to boast about, the bourgeoisie can find nothing better to do than to erect grandiose buildings in the capital and to lay out money on what are called prestige expenses.

The national bourgeoisie turns its back more and more on the interior and on the real facts of its undeveloped country, and tends to look toward the former mother country and the foreign capitalists who count on its obliging compliance. As it does not share its profits with the people, and in no way allows them to enjoy any of the dues that are paid to it by the big foreign companies, it will discover the need for a popular leader to whom will fall the dual role of stabilizing the regime and of perpetuating the domination of the bourgeoisie. The bourgeois dictatorship of under-developed countries draws its strength from the existence of a leader. We know that in the well-developed countries the bourgeois dictatorship is the result of the economic power of the bourgeoisie. In the under-developed countries, on the contrary, the leader stands for a moral power in whose shelter the thin and poverty-stricken bourgeoisie of the young nation decides to get rich.

The people who for years on end have seen this leader and heard him speak, who from a distance in a kind of dream have followed his contests with the colonial power, spontaneously put their trust in this patriot. Before independence, the leader generally embodies the aspirations of the people for independence, political liberty, and national dignity. But as soon as independence is declared, far from embodying in concrete form the needs of the people in what touches bread, land, and the restoration of the country to the sacred hands of the people, the leader will reveal his inner purpose: to become the general president of that company of profiteers impatient for their returns which constitutes the national bourgeoisie.

In spite of his frequently honest conduct and his sincere declarations, the leader as seen objectively is the fierce defender of these interests, today combined, of the national bourgeoisie and the ex-colonial companies. His honesty, which is his soul's true bent, crumbles away little by little. His contact with the masses is so unreal that he comes to believe that his authority is hated and that the services that he has rendered his country are being called in question. The leader judges the ingratitude of the masses harshly, and every day that passes ranges himself a little more resolutely on the side of the exploiters. He therefore knowingly becomes the aider and abettor of the young bourgeoisie that is plunging into the mire of corruption and pleasure.

The economic channels of the young state sink back inevitably into neo-colonialist lines. The national economy, formerly protected, is today literally controlled. The budget is balanced through loans and gifts, while every three or four months the chief ministers themselves, or else their governmental delegations, come to the erstwhile mother countries or elsewhere, fishing for capital.

The former colonial power increases its demands, accumulates conces-sions and guarantees, and takes fewer and fewer pains to mask the hold it has over the national government. The people stagnate deplorably in unbearable poverty; slowly they awaken to the unutterable treason of their leaders. This awakening is all the more acute in that the bourgeoisie is incapable of learning its lesson. The distribution of wealth that it effects is not spread out between a great many sectors; it is not ranged among different levels, nor does it set up a hierarchy of halftones. The new caste is an affront all the more disgusting in that the immense majority, nine-tenths of the population, continue to die of starvation. The scandalous enrichment, speedy and pitiless, of this caste is accompanied by a decisive awakening on the part of the people, and a growing awareness that promises stormy days to come. The bourgeois caste, that section of the nation which annexes for its own profit all the wealth of the country, by a kind of unexpected logic will pass disparaging judgments upon the other Negroes and the other Arabs that more often than not are reminiscent of the racist doctrines of the former representatives of the colonial power. At one and the same time the poverty of the people, the immoderate money-making of the bourgeois caste, and its widespread scorn for the rest of the nation will harden thought and action.

But such threats will lead to the reaffirmation of authority and the appearance of dictatorship. The leader, who has behind him a lifetime of political action and devoted patriotism, constitutes a screen between the people and the rapacious bourgeoisie since he stands surety for the ventures of that caste and closes his eyes to their insolence, their mediocrity, and their fundamental immorality. He acts as a braking power on the awakening consciousness of the people. He comes to the aid of the bourgeois caste and hides his maneuvers from the people, thus becoming the most eager worker in the task of mystifying and bewildering the masses. Every time he speaks to the people he calls to mind his often heroic life, the struggles he has led in the name of the people, and the victories that in their name he has achieved, thereby intimating clearly to the masses that they ought to go on putting their confidence in him. There are plenty of examples of African patriots who have introduced into the cautious political advance of their elders a decisive style characterized by its nationalist outlook. These men came from the backwoods, and they proclaimed, to the scandal of the dominating power and the shame of the nationals of the capital, that they came from the backwoods and that they spoke in the name of the Negroes. These men, who have sung the praises of their race, who have taken upon themselves the whole burden of the past, complete with cannibalism and degeneracy, find themselves today, alas, at the head of a team of administrators that turns its back on the jungle and proclaims that the vocation of its people is to obey, to go on obeying, and to be obedient till the end of time.

The leader pacifies the people. For years on end after independence has been won we see him, incapable of urging on the people to a concrete task, unable really to open the future to them or of flinging them into the path of national reconstruction, that is to say, of their own reconstruction; we see him reassessing the history of independence and recalling the sacred unity of the struggle for liberation. The leader, because he refuses to break up the national bourgeoisie, asks the people to fall back into the past and become drunk on the remembrance of the epoch which led up to independence. The leader, seen objectively, brings the people to a halt and persists in either expelling them from history or preventing them from taking root in it. During the struggle for liberation the leader awakened the people and promised them a forward march, heroic and unmitigated. Today, he uses every means to put them to sleep, and three or four times a year asks them to remember the colonial period and to look back on the long way they have come since then.

Now it must be said that the masses show themselves totally incapable of appreciating the long way they have come. The peasant who goes on scratching out a living from the soil and the unemployed man who never finds employment do not manage, in spite of public holidays and flags, new and brightly colored though they may be, to convince themselves that anything has really changed in their lives. The bourgeoisie that is in power vainly increases the number of processions; the masses have no illusions. They are hungry; and the police officers, though now they are Africans, do not serve to reassure them particularly. The masses begin to sulk; they turn away from this nation in which they have been given no place and begin to lose interest in it.

From time to time, however, the leader makes an effort: he speaks on the radio or makes a tour of the country to pacify the people, to calm them, and bemuse them. The leader is all the more necessary in that there is no party. During the period of the struggle for independence there was one right enough, a party led by the peasant leader. But since then this party has sadly disintegrated; nothing is left but the shell of a party, the name, the emblem, and the motto. The living party, which ought to make possible the free exchange of ideas which have been elaborated according to the real needs of the mass of the people, has been transformed into a trade union of individual interests. Since the proclamation of independence the party no longer helps the people to set out its demands, to become more aware of its needs and better able to establish its power. Today, the party's mission is to deliver to the people the instructions which issue from the summit. There no longer exists the fruitful give-and-take from the bottom to the top and from the top to the bottom which creates and guarantees democracy in a party. Quite on the contrary, the party has made itself into a screen between the masses and the leaders. There is no longer any party life, for the branches which were set up during the colonial period are today completely demobilized.

The militant champs on his bit. Now it is that the attitude taken up by certain militants during the struggle for liberation is seen to be justified, for the fact is that in the thick of the fight more than a few militants asked the leaders to formulate a dogma, to set out their objectives, and to draw up a program. But under the pretext of safeguarding national unity, the leaders categorically refused to attempt such a task. The only worthwhile dogma, it was repeatedly stated, is the union of the nation against colonialism. And on they went, armed with an impetuous slogan which stood for principles, while their only ideological activity took the form of a series of variants on the theme of the right of peoples to self-determination, borne on the wind of history which would inevitably sweep away colonialism. When the militants asked whether the wind of history couldn't be a little more clearly analyzed, the leaders gave them instead hope and trust, the necessity of de-colonialization and its inevitability, and more to that effect.

After independence, the party sinks into an extraordinary lethargy. The militants are only called upon when so-called popular manifestations are afoot, or international conferences, or independence celebrations. The local party leaders are given administrative posts, the party becomes an administration, and the militants disappear into the crowd and take the empty title of citizen. Now that they have fulfilled their historical mission of leading the bourgeoisie to power, they are firmly invited to retire so that the bourgeoisie may carry out *its* mission in peace and quiet. But we have seen that the national bourgeoisie of underdeveloped countries is incapable of carrying out any mission whatever. After a few years, the breakup of the party becomes obvious and any observer, even the most superficial, can notice that the party, today the skeleton of its former self, only serves to immobilize the people. The party, which during the battle had drawn to itself the whole nation, is falling to pieces. The intellectuals, who on the eve of independence rallied to the party, now make it clear by their attitude that they gave their support with no other end in view than to secure their slices of the cake of independence. The party is becoming a means of private advancement.

There exists inside the new regime, however, an inequality in the acquisition of wealth and in monopolization. Some have a double source of income and demonstrate that they are specialized in opportunism. Privileges multiply and corruption triumphs, while morality declines. Today the vultures are too numerous and too voracious in proportion to the lean spoils of the national wealth. The party, a true instrument of power in the hands of the bourgeoisie, reinforces the machine and insures that the people are hemmed in and immobilized. The party helps the government to hold the people down. It becomes more and more clearly anti-democratic, an implement of coercion. The party is objectively, sometimes subjectively, the accomplice of the merchant bourgeoisie. In the same way that the national bourgeoisie conjures away its phase of construction in order to throw itself into the enjoyment of its wealth, in parallel fashion in the institutional sphere it jumps the parliamentary phase and chooses a dictatorship of the national socialist type. We know today that this fascism at high interest which has triumphed for half a century in Latin America is the dialectic result of states which were semi-colonial during the period of independence.

In these poor, underdeveloped countries, where the rule is that the greatest wealth is surrounded by the greatest poverty, the army and the police constitute the pillars of the regime; an army and a police force (another rule which must not be forgotten) which are advised by foreign experts. The strength of the police force and the power of the army are proportionate to the stagnation in which the rest of the nation is sunk. By dint of yearly loans, concessions are snatched up by foreigners; scandals are numerous, ministers grow rich, their wives doll themselves up, the members of parliament feather their nests and there is not a soul down to the simple policeman or the customs officer who does not join in the great procession of corruption.

The opposition becomes more aggressive and the people at once catch on to its propaganda. From now on their hostility to the bourgeoisie is plainly visible. This young bourgeoisie which appears to be afflicted with precocious senility takes no heed of the advice showered upon it and reveals itself incapable of understanding that it would be in its interest to draw a veil, even if only the flimsiest kind, over its exploitation. It is the most Christian newspaper, the *African Weekly*, published in Brazzaville, which addresses the princes of the regime thus: "You who are in good positions, you and your wives, today you enjoy many comforts; perhaps a good education, a fine house, good contacts, and many missions on which you are delegated which open new horizons to you. But all your wealth forms a hard shell which prevents your seeing the poverty that surrounds you. Take care."

This warning comes from the *African Weekly* and addressed to the henchmen of Monsieur Youlou has, we may imagine, nothing revolutionary about it. What the *African Weekly* wants to point out to the starvers of the Congolese people is that God will punish their conduct. It continues: "If there is no room in your heart for consideration toward those who are beneath you, there will be no room for you in God's house."

It is clear that the national bourgeoisie hardly worries at all about such an indictment. With its wavelengths tuned in to Europe, it continues firmly and resolutely to make the most of the situation. The enormous profits which it derives from the exploitation of the people are exported to foreign countries. The young national bourgeoisie is often more suspicious of the regime that it has set up than are the foreign companies. The national bourgeoisie refuses to invest in its own country and behaves toward the state that protects and nurtures it with, it must be remarked, astonishing ingratitude. It acquires foreign securities in the European markets and goes off to spend the weekend in Paris or Hamburg. The behavior of the national bourgeoisie of certain underdeveloped countries is reminiscent of the members of a gang, who after every holdup hide their share in the swag from the other members who are their accomplices and prudently start thinking about their retirement. Such behavior shows that more or less consciously the national bourgeoisie is playing to lose if the game goes on too long. They guess that the present situation will not last indefinitely but they intend to make the most of it. Such exploitation and such contempt for the state, however, inevitably give rise to discontent among the mass of the people. It is in these conditions that the regime becomes harsher. In the absence of a parliament it is the army that becomes the arbiter: but sooner or later it will realize its power and will hold over the government's head the threat of a manifesto.

As we see it, the national bourgeoisie of certain underdeveloped countries has learned nothing from books. If they had looked closer at the Latin American countries they doubtless would have recognized the dangers which threaten them. We may thus conclude that this bourgeoisie in miniature that thrusts itself into the forefront is condemned to mark time, accomplishing nothing. In underdeveloped countries the bourgeois phase is impossibly arid. Certainly, there is a police dictatorship and a profiteering caste, but the construction of an elaborate bourgeois society seems to be condemned to failure. The ranks of decked-out profiteers whose grasping hands scrape up the banknotes from a poverty-stricken country will sooner or later be men of straw in the hands of the army, cleverly handled by foreign experts. In this way the former mother country practices indirect government, both by the bourgeoisie that it upholds and also by the national army led by its experts, an army that pins the people down, immobilizing and terrorizing them.

The observation that we have been able to make about the national bourgeoisie brings us to a conclusion which should cause no surprise. In underdeveloped countries, the bourgeoisie should not be allowed to find the conditions necessary for its existence and its growth. In other words, the combined effort of the masses led by a party and of intellectuals who are highly conscious and armed with revolutionary principles ought to bar the way to this useless and harmful middle class.

The theoretical question that for the last fifty years has been raised whenever the history of underdeveloped countries is under discussion— whether or not the bourgeois phase can be skipped—ought to be answered in the field of revolutionary action, and not by logic. The bourgeois phase in underdeveloped countries can only justify itself insofar as the national bourgeoisie has sufficient economic and technical strength to build up a bourgeois society, to create the conditions necessary for the development of a large-scale proletariat, to mechanize agriculture, and finally to make possible the existence of an authentic national culture.

A bourgeoisie similar to that which developed in Europe is able to elaborate an ideology and at the same time strengthen its own power. Such a bourgeoisie—dynamic, educated, and secular—has fully succeeded in undertaking the accumulation of capital and has given to the nation a minimum of prosperity. In underdeveloped countries, we have seen that no true bourgeoisie exists; there is only a sort of little greedy caste, avid and voracious, with the mind of a huckster, only too glad to accept the dividends that the former colonial power hands out to it. This get-rich-quick middle class shows itself incapable of great ideas or of inventiveness. It remembers what it has read in European textbooks and imperceptibly it becomes not even the replica of Europe, but its caricature.

The struggle against the bourgeoisie of underdeveloped countries is far from being a theoretical one. It is not concerned with making out its condemnation as laid down by the judgment of history. The national bourgeoisie of underdeveloped countries must not be opposed because it threatens to slow down the total, harmonious development of the nation. It must simply be stoutly opposed because, literally, it is good for nothing.

Notes

1. Mamadou Dia, *Nations africaines et solidarité mondial* (Paris: Presses Universitaires de France), p. 140.
2. *Ibid.*

3

José Nun

The Middle-Class
Military Coup

Unless a distinction is made between the structural and the circumstantial factors of military intervention in Latin American politics, important differences between countries are apt to be ignored. The number of successful coups varies independently of the degree of economic development: there were as many in Argentina as in El Salvador and fewer in Honduras than in Brazil. Evidently the intervention of the military in politics represents a different phenomenon in a country with an income per capita of $500, 70 percent of its population living in cities, and with a large middle class, than in one where less than one-third of the population lives in cities, income per capita is only $150, and scarcely 8 percent of the population can be classified as belonging to the upper and middle classes.[1]

Interpretations which tend to ignore these differences have generally been influenced either by traditional liberal anti-militarism or by the advocacy of militarism as a dynamic force for economic development.[2]

The liberal model, based on the experience of Europe in the eighteenth and nineteenth centuries, envisaged the army as the bastion of traditional and feudal values. Its officer corps was drawn from the aristocracy and was antagonistic to the liberal bourgeois state. From 1815, with the Pax Britannica contributing to a decrease of militarism and the state taking deliberate measures to insure civilian control over the armed forces, there ensued a professional revolution which reached its peak by the end of the nineteenth century. The developmentalist model conceives of the army

---

Abridged and reprinted from *The Politics of Conformity in Latin America*, Claudio Veliz, ed., published by the Oxford University Press for the Royal Institute of International Affairs. Copyright © 1967 by the Royal Institute of International Affairs.

as an intelligentsia in uniform, dedicated to progress and development and peculiarly suited to achieving them. It is based on the experience of the Afro-Asian countries, where the officer corps was mostly drawn from the popular sectors. There is a Nasserist version of this model which will be discussed later. Finally, the socialist model, which, from a rejection of militarism similar to that espoused by the liberals, has progressed to an acceptance of the integration of the military in the body politic as a means both of strengthening it and of lending additional prestige to the civilian leadership.

These three ways of approaching the problem imply that the armed forces are an independent sector, or at least that they are hardly at all integrated with the rest of society. Thus, according to one such theory, the traditional army is a step behind the modern society which is forming around it; according to another, the modern army is a step ahead of the traditional society which is disintegrating. In fact, both these theories presuppose an inverse relationship between militarism and the consolidation of the diversified social structure typical of a developed country. As one writer asserts: "Army officers in politics are typical of pre-industrial nations lacking a strong middle class."[3] How then is one to explain the military coups in countries such as Argentina or Brazil, which have strong middle-class sectors and such a high degree of industrial growth that in the former country one-third of the labor force is employed in manufacturing industry or construction, while in the second, domestic production accounts for two-thirds of the capital goods the country requires?[4]

An objective analysis shows that Latin America is lacking in two of the basic elements of the liberal model: in the first place, its armies were generally formed after the professional revolution; and, secondly, the greater part of their officers are recruited from the middle class and not from the aristocracy.

Merle Kling has proposed an interesting modification of this model. His argument may be summarized as follows: In Latin America, the oligarchy and foreign capital maintain a rigid control over the conventional bases of economic power and prevent the rise of other social groups; the government therefore appears as the only base of economic power, the ownership of which can change; and from this situation there arises the privileged position of the military in the ruthless struggle to take possession of this coveted source of potential power; instability is therefore "a function of the contradiction between the realities of a colonial economy and the political requirements of legal sovereignty among the Latin American states."[5]

Even if one ignores the economic emphasis of this theory and concedes that the personal ambition of military leaders is the basic driving force behind military interventions, it is obvious that this interpretation is only valid for very undeveloped countries, characterized by a bipolar social structure (oligarchy/masses), and a very low degree of mobility and institutional differentiation—conditions which can hardly be said to be prevalent in the more advanced countries of Latin America.

Similar objections can be raised to the "developmentalist" model—largely based on the experience of the Afro-Asian countries—which analyzes "the political implications of the army as a modern institution that has been somewhat artificially introduced into disorganized traditional societies."[6] It is applicable, in other words, to countries of very recent formation, where the civil and military bureaucracies are the only alternatives, in almost entire absence of modern institutions. It is unnecessary to emphasize the difference between such societies and those of Argentina or Brazil.

This lends added interest to an examination of instability in the more developed countries of Latin America. In the two already mentioned—Argentina and Brazil—military coups are features of the present-day situation. In the other three[7]—Uruguay, Chile, and Mexico—the last quarter-century has been marked by political stability. Is it possible, by means of an analysis of the experience of these countries, to isolate structural factors capable of explaining interventionism in situations remote from those envisaged in the traditional models? Over twenty years ago it was observed that "a government which cannot rely upon its middle classes will, almost certainly, be unable to rely upon the unbroken loyalty of its army."[8] Is this the situation? And, if so, why?

This essay attempts to analyze certain structural elements that have not generally been considered in previous interpretations of this phenomenon. For at least two reasons it makes no claim to be exhaustive; first it excludes the very important circumstantial factors, which cannot be dealt with here; and, secondly, because a model of this nature does not claim to be an exact reflection of reality, but only to place some emphasis on certain important aspects that are not immediately obvious.

THE MIDDLE-CLASS PROFESSIONAL ARMY

To understand the problem of political instability, one must look behind the military façade (just as to understand Latin American inflation, one had to look behind the monetary façade). With this end in view, both the social basis of the officer corps and some of the consequences of its recent professionalization must be considered.

Social Basis. Although statistical information on this subject is still scarce, most authorities are agreed in admitting that, since the end of the nineteenth century, the majority of Latin American officers have been recruited from the middle class.[9]

In his study of generals, brigadiers, and admirals in Argentina, José Luis de Imaz found that only 23 percent of the sample examined were descended from the traditional families. He estimated that 73 percent of the brigadiers and generals interviewed came from families belonging to the wealthy bourgeoisie, 25 percent from the lower middle class, and only 2 percent from the working class.[10] Although the category "upper middle class or wealthy bourgeoisie" is excessively large, and includes everybody from landowners to professional men, and even supposing that all the fathers concerned who were landowners, businessmen, or industrialists belonged to the upper class—which is certainly an exaggeration—this survey does indicate that two-thirds of the officer corps is of middle-class origin. Moreover, contrary to what is generally believed, the data provided by Imaz indicate that "[Argentine] generals, today just as much as formerly, come from an urban background, half of them from the capital and the Greater Buenos Aires area."[11]

John Johnson reached similar conclusions with regard to the middle-class origin of Brazilian officers,[12] even though in this case the greater part came from the small towns in the interior. For the purposes of this study this difference does not appear to be of decisive importance in view of the relative homogeneity of the system of values prevalent throughout urban Brazil. It has, for example, recently been asserted that "those who leave the small towns to take up residence in the big city find there an atmosphere that is familiar to them, and it is not so difficult for them to adapt themselves to it as might be thought."[13]

In Chile, where the officer corps represents a more typical cross-section of the urban population as a whole,[14] there has been, ever since the war of 1879, a continuous penetration of the military profession by the sons of middle-class families.[15] A similar trend has been evident in Uruguay and Mexico since the turn of the century. In the case of Mexico, it is possible that recruitment has taken place from even lower social strata: for example, an examination of the applications for admission to the Military College in 1955 reveals that 14.64 percent of the candidates were the sons of workers and 2.98 percent the sons of peasants.[16]

This description does not imply that the class situation of the officer corps entirely explains its political behavior. It does, however, restrict the field of investigation, and makes possible an assessment of the importance and relative autonomy of outside factors inhibiting or determining the behavior of this group.[17] It is, after all, not entirely fortuitous that the liberal model which prevailed in the nineteenth century should have paid particular attention to the basis of recruitment of those destined for military command: "after all, their origins constitute the source of the 'non-Armed Force' opinions of the armed force organizations."[18]

In the countries under discussion, there are other factors which presumably tend to strengthen this class affiliation, owing to continual contact between the civil and military spheres. Among these are the lack of a tradition of active warfare, which diminishes the separation between the daily life of the officers and that of the rest of the population. Another factor that has still not been investigated is the mediating role fulfilled by retired officers: the available data do, in fact, indicate a tendency toward "rejuvenation" among the higher ranks of the armed forces,[19] which means that the retirement—voluntary or enforced—of the officer occurs when he is still fully active and capable of embarking on a civilian career, while at the same time keeping in touch with his old comrades in arms. Moreover, whereas in technologically backward societies the increasing technical specialization of the army tends to link the officer more closely to foreign sources, in societies of a higher cultural development, such as those we are analyzing, the same phenomenon leads to increased contacts between the officer and his civilian colleagues.

Finally, it is worth pointing out an obvious fact which is too often forgotten, namely the "civilianization" of the officers that is a direct consequence of their continual political activity. Although one should not exaggerate the importance of such contacts, which in any case are limited to certain social sectors, this is nevertheless an argument against the traditional conception of the army as an institution completely isolated from its social context, and the consequent exaggeration of the uniqueness of the armed forces' attitudes and behavior. It would, of course, be absurd to deny the existence of characteristics peculiar to the army as such but so far no attempt has been made to determine how important these are in determining an officer's behavior.[20] Several studies devoted to this question apply to the military establishment the concept of the "total institution" formulated by Goffman.[21] However, such studies pay less attention to the distinctions drawn by the same writer with regard to methods of recruitment and the permeability of the institution to the influences surrounding it,[22] and ignore his assertion that "total institutions do not really look for cultural victory,"[23] which explains the relative ease with which its members are able to become reintegrated into the society outside the institution.[24]

Organization. While it is true, on the one hand, that the greater part of the officer corps comes from the middle class, the military establishment can, on the other hand, count on a degree of cohesion and institutional solidity which is entirely lacking in the Latin American middle class.

The tendency to consider social phenomena in isolation and in the abstract has led some writers to suppose that professionalization per se induces officers to withdraw from politics, by placing a barrier between them and the rest of society. Oddly enough, Mosca argued with equal conviction, and for well-founded reasons, that the contrary was true and, more recently, Finer has supported his arguments.[25] With regard to the Latin American armed forces, one observer asserts: "On the contrary, in those countries in which they have been most highly professionalized, they seem to have become even more closely linked with the rest of society than formerly."[26]

What happens in reality is that every system of domination attempts to internalize violence by the means most suited to its values and interests. Thus professionalism became generally accepted in European armies only at the end of the nineteenth century and as a result of deliberate government policy. The bourgeois state had experimented with various formulae for the control of the armed forces—examples of which are the unsuccessful French and American attempts to have the highest posts of command submitted to popular election—until the logic of capitalist society eventually dictated the solution. In the framework of a general tendency toward fragmentation and division of labor, the exercise of violence was also converted into a specialized field calling for high professional qualifications, and became part of a series of particular sub-systems enjoying a relative degree of autonomy. In this way "military institutions have taken on more and more the characteristics common to civilian large-scale organizations."[27] Professionalization is therefore the means by which the armed forces are incorporated into a determined place in the structuralization of society as a whole, and it is this, and not professionalism as such, that explains the apparent political neutrality of the army in the Western democracies.

This process of professionalization was bound to produce different results in Latin America, since it not only took place in armies at different stages of development but did so in the context of pre-industrial societies with structures based on the hegemony of the oligarchy and not that of the bourgeoisie.

In Europe "military organization had established its form centuries before professionalization definitely began."[28] This explains in part the successful establishment of organizational controls designed to counteract the possible centrifugal tendencies which might result from increased professionalization. In Latin America organization and professionalization take place almost simultaneously, increasing the probability of discrepancies leading to open conflict.[29]

This early professionalization had two important social consequences: first, as has been indicated above, the middle class was admitted to the career of arms through the creation of military academies; and, secondly, in contrast to its own organizational weakness,[30] this class was now allied to a sector with a remarkable degree of institutional cohesion and articulateness. In other words, the armed forces became one of the few important institutions controlled by the middle class.[31]

This relationship partly explains political instability due to military intervention, but it is open to two important criticisms: first, from those who consider that the profession of arms conditions its followers so thoroughly that one may ignore any other variable in seeking for explanations of their behavior; and, secondly, from those who maintain that the middle class, by its very nature, is dedicated to the support of political stability and democratic institutions.

I have already given some of the reasons why I consider the first objection to be valid only in a relative sense. With regard to the second, it will be necessary to touch briefly on some of the factors that lead the middle class to associate with military intervention in politics.

MIDDLE CLASS AND BOURGEOISIE

Hitherto I have deliberately used the expression "middle class" rather than "bourgeoisie." G. D. H. Cole has drawn the distinction:

> Bourgeois, to any historically-minded person, calls up at once the image of a body of citizens asserting their collective, as well as their individual, independence of a social system dominated by feudal power based on landholding and on the services attached to it; whereas the words "middle class" call up the quite different image of a body of persons who are placed between two other bodies—or perhaps more than two—in some sort of stratified social order.[32]

The same writer goes on to say that the bourgeoisie as such is not in the middle of anything, at least not consciously so.

At this point it is necessary to consider the degree of relative independence of the rural and urban sectors of the same national society; it is on this supposed independence that the hypothesis of structural dualism, so frequently met with in studies concerned with Latin America, is based. The concept of a middle class implies, by definition, a system of unified vertical stratification. But the application of the hypothesis of dualism to the Latin American situation admits of two different interpretations; in the first, the traditional and modern "poles" are analysed as if they were relatively independent entities, with the result that some writers speak of "two countries within the same territory." Hence the tendency to transfer mechanically to the Latin American situation a technologically determinist hypothesis like Ogburn's "cultural lag." The observer "isolates" São Paulo from the Northeast, for example, and assumes that for the latter to attain the level of development of the former, all that is required is to transform the Northeast without considering whether such a transformation would involve equally profound changes in São Paulo. On the other hand, the dialectic interpretation finds the key to the situation in the internal unity of a historically determined system of domination. This is the unity explaining the frustration of a middle class which is prevented from fulfilling the role of a bourgeoisie. In order to analyze such an interpretation, it is necessary to distinguish between two principal stages in the evolution of the system: that of the unity of the oligarchy and that of its crisis.

THE HEGEMONY OF THE OLIGARCHY

G. D. H. Cole's observation was based on a study of the urbanization of Central Europe which, according to the well-known theory of Henri Pirenne, was the consequence of the rise of the mercantile sectors, potentially antagonistic towards the feudal order and the power system on which it was based. A different situation obtained in Southern Europe—a typical example being the Italian cities—corresponding more closely to Werner Sombart's interpretation: here it was the nobility that played a leading role in the formation of the new urban centers, which were thus integrated into the prevailing power structure.[33]

The characteristics associated with the process of colonization, in the case of the urbanization of Latin America, made it from the very beginning resemble more closely the second of the processes described above, in that there was never any real dissension between the urban centers and the nascent landowning aristocracy. "Colonization was in large part an urban venture, carried out by urban-minded people,"[34] and the city represented both the point of departure and the residence of the owners of land. The difference, of course, lay in the fact that, whereas in Italy "the power of the city becomes so strong that it becomes independent of any central government,"[35] in Latin America it was precisely the urban centers which served as the instrument of colonial rule. Nevertheless, *mutatis mutandis*, a basically similar tendency was apparent: "More typical than the struggle between burgher and feudal groups was the conflict between local rural-urban oligarchies and agents of the royal bureaucracy."[36]

This initial "unitary" characteristic becomes even more pronounced in the second half of the nineteenth century, with the rapid integration of the Latin American national economies into the world market. As Celso Furtado has observed, "the entrepreneurial attitude that made the rapid development of lines of export possible had its origin within the merchant groups which operated from the urban centers."[37] Instead of a divergence developing between the interests of the dominant groups in the cities and those in the rural areas, the urban mercantile sector consolidated its position as a landowning and capitalist oligarchy.[38]

It was thus that the great Latin American capitals became the places of residence of the privileged sectors during the era of "outward" economic growth.[39] Beside them there developed the middle class, of the primary-products export model, composed of the exporters and importers, small industrialists, professional men, and civil servants, all integrated into the hegemonic system of the oligarchy.

This did not mean that the state was simply the expression of the subjective will of one social class, as if the underlying unity of the hegemonic structure were given by the ideology of the dominant group. On the contrary, this unity must be sought in the total structure of society, in which this ideology was only one element among many. The function fulfilled by the state—providing a framework for the oligarchy—must not be obscured by being forced into the nineteenth-century liberal model imported from Europe. In Latin America there was no question of the status quo being challenged; laissez-faire was in practice the political instrument which consolidated the economic system, and its application constituted "a deliberate measure consciously designed to achieve specific ends and not the spontaneous and automatic expression of an economic situation."[40] Structure and superstructure thus became fused into an extremely solid historical block, and found their expression in an advanced juridical and institutional system. Marx asserts that a particular class can only maintain its supremacy by exercising it in the name of the general rights of society. On the basis of a particular economic system, this "conquérante" oligarchy was able to evolve a systematic justification of its dominant position by means of a normative structure which defined those general rights in terms which applied to the existing internal relationships among social groups. The fundamental reason for its success was undoubtedly the high degree of efficacy of the system itself: the bonanza arising from the export of raw materials convinced all its beneficiaries—direct and indirect—that Argentine meat, Brazilian coffee, Uruguayan wool, and Chilean minerals guaranteed permanent economic expansion. To be optimistic, it was enough to conceive of the future as an extension of the present, and the middle class enthusiastically adopted that conservative outlook which takes no account of the future or the vicissitudes it may bring. It was members of the oligarchy, not of the middle class, who were responsible for the first industrial expansion of any importance, and it was they who organized the new industrial and commercial enterprises, in which the middle class participated only as a second-rate but acquiescent partner. This is why it raised no protest when the Chilean government handed over to foreign companies the exploitation of the nitrate deposits which it had cost the country five years of war to acquire, nor when the Brazilian authorities frustrated the energetic attempts at industrialization made by Viscount de Maúa; for this reason, it neither protested nor gave support to a contrary policy when lack of protection led to the breakdown of the incipient process of industrialization encouraged by the First World War. Since the basic principles of the system were never called into question, commercial or industrial collapse was regarded as a problem affecting only the individual concerned, or, at most, held to be the result of corruption of a system that, in its uncorrupt state, was considered unsurpassable.

The expanding middle class made no attempt to change the system as a whole: it merely demanded recognition of its legitimate right to play a part in it. Its aspirations were limited to a desire for participation in political affairs and for defense of its moral status.[41] The most interesting features of this process were the speed with which these aspirations were satisfied and the instrumental role of the military.

THE MIDDLE CLASS AND DEMOCRACY

It is a commonplace to compare the rapid expansion of the Latin American political arena with the very gradual evolution of the British electoral system.[42] Without underestimating the undoubted interest of this kind of analysis, it is fair to say that "it conveys the impression that England became a democracy primarily as a result of statutory changes in the electoral system, whereas in fact the historical process involved was a good deal more complex."[43]

One of the decisive elements in that process was precisely the efficacy of the Victorian bourgeoisie in articulating the popular consensus. For this purpose, it skillfully utilized the deferential attitudes still persisting in the working class; it ceaselessly diffused the values associated with its capitalist, liberal, and Christian ethical system; it gave enthusiastic encouragement to a complex of institutions "devoted to self-improvement and self-help,"[44] and, above all, it proved able, from the middle of the last century, to effect a considerable improvement in the economic position of a labor aristocracy which responded eagerly to such encouragement.[45] Without this intermediate process, which made possible the ending of the original identification of the "laboring classes" with the "dangerous classes," the electoral reform of 1867 would be incomprehensible: the workers only began to be accepted as citizens when their conformism had extinguished the old Chartist fervor.[46] It was for that reason that the suffrage lost its disruptive character and was able to fulfill in the political sphere the legitimizing function that the contract fulfilled in the economic sphere. In other words, the validity of the classical Marxist proposition according to which representative democracy is the form of government which most closely corresponds to the interests of the bourgeoisie depends on the previous consolidation by the latter of its hegemonic supremacy, its development of a metaphysical justification of its leading role, and its demonstration of its efficacy as a ruling class.

In the course of the above analysis, we have tried to point out some of the reasons for the failure of the Latin American middle class to achieve this position. The central nucleus of its problem is that, when it has still not succeeded in working out a stable political compromise with the oligarchy, it is already having to face the problem which Disraeli formulated a century ago: "The Working Class Question is the real question, and that is the thing that demands to be settled."[47]

Electoral data provide only an approximate indication of the magnitude of the problem. At the outbreak of the First World War, in a somewhat similar stage of industrial development, only 10 to 15 percent of the population of Europe took part in elections;[48] in the countries we are considering, however, the proportion is often three or four times as great, e.g., Argentina, 43.9 percent (1963); Uruguay, 36.4 percent (1958); Chile, 30.5 percent (1964). These figures are close to the most recent ones for the United States, e.g., 38 percent in 1964.

Unable to consolidate themselves as a bourgeoisie, the most that the progressive sectors of the Latin American middle classes have been able to do has been to offer the popular sectors programs based on fundamentally quantitative goals, mobilizing them to seek the satisfaction of their demands within the existing structural framework. This is the essential ingredient in the populism of Perón, Vargas, and Ibáñez; and it provides one of the clues to its unique character: whereas elsewhere— e.g., the United States and Canada—populist movements have had an agrarian basis, and arose in periods of depression, in Latin America these movements were fundamentally urban and were associated with periods of prosperity.

For this reason economic stagnation fixes the limits of such movements, as is shown by the change of orientation of Perón's regime around 1950, and the swing of Ibáñez to conservatism which coincided with the falling-off of the Korean War boom.[49]

It has often been alleged that the Latin American middle class was progressive as long as it needed popular support to achieve power and, once established there, became reactionary.[50] Although this observation is more or less valid as a mere description of actual events, the formula is dangerous on account of the class-subjectivism to which it may lead: it can tempt the observer too easily to make a metaphorical association with a psychological "vertigo" supposedly felt by that class when it reaches the heights of power.

If this analysis is correct, it is its internal composition and the manner in which it has achieved power within the framework of the hegemony of the oligarchy which is beginning to disintegrate that explains the behavior of this middle class. Moreover, if we employ for a moment the hypothetical representation of history recommended by Weber, it is probable that if the process of import-substitution had been accompanied by opportunities of exploiting an external colonial market, these countries would have achieved self-sustained growth without radical internal changes and with a Fabian-style working-class participation in political affairs.

What actually happens is quite different, and tends to aggravate the instability of the middle class. In the first place, it lacks the internal cohesion of the upper class, which not only still dominates strategic sectors of the economy but has firm control over the symbols of prestige. Secondly, it can no longer fulfill the only promises it is able to formulate to the masses whose organization is now increasing dangerously, in contrast to the middle class's own institutional weakness.

It is necessary at this point to introduce a word of warning—even though this is not the place to go more fully into the matter—in view of the tendency of many interpreters to refer to the "massification" of the Latin American societies which we are considering;[51] one must be careful to distinguish between the points of view of the observer and the person observed, even though they may use similar terminology. It is in this case that the observation of Raymond Williams is particularly oppropriate: "There are in fact no masses; there are only ways of seeing people as masses."[52] To the oligarchies at the turn of the century, the "masses" were the rising middle classes, just as for the latter the "masses" are now the rural and urban workers: "If you disapprove of the changes you can, it seems, avoid open opposition to democracy as such by inventing a new category, mass-democracy, which is not such a good thing at all."[53]

In these conditions, and in spite of the objective indicators of "massification" that the observer may detect, the concept of the masses does not express a general tendency toward levelling but merely identifies the proletariat, conceived as such by the propertied classes regardless of the degree of internal solidarity that those masses have been able to achieve.

If we concentrate our attention on the low level of class-consciousness of the new working class, we are apt to forget that an essential ingredient in a social class, as T. H. Marshall has emphasized, is the way in which a man is treated by his neighbor. I do not mean by this that the Latin American political struggle will assume the form of the nineteenth-century conflicts: both the context and the protagonists have changed greatly. Nevertheless, as the populist atmosphere wears off, the central contradiction takes visible shape in somewhat similar terms. For this reason, even though Furtado may be right in emphasizing the differences in revolutionary potential between the urban and the rural workers,[54] it is worth remembering that the continued existence of such differences is a function of the ideological vigor of the dualistic structure as a confusing form assumed by Latin American capitalist development. On the economic plane, the underlying unity of the process is increasingly revealed by the chronic tendency to stagnation; on the political plane, it is the alliance of the middle class with the oligarchy that fully reveals that unity.

THE MIDDLE-CLASS MILITARY COUP

Schumpeter maintained that "without protection by some non-bourgeois group, the bourgeoisie is politically helpless and unable not only to lead its nation but even to take care of its particular class interest. Which amounts to saying that it needs a master."[55] He was obviously referring to Great Britain, in view of the "protective" flexibility with which the aristocracy managed to adapt itself to the rise of the bourgeoisie.[56] Moreover, in the case of France, the disintegration at the time of the Revolution of the traditional "protecting strata" was responsible for the high degree of instability that characterized the nineteenth century. However, in order to understand the peculiar synthesis achieved by the Third Republic—which "was throughout, in spirit and operation, middle class rather than either aristocratic or peasant or proletarian"[57]—it must be borne in mind that in France too there existed a "protecting stratum," namely, the civil service, the pre-revolutionary organization of which was maintained almost intact, and which established an element of continuity which has lasted through five republics and two empires.[58]

If Schumpeter's proposition is valid for a "bourgeoisie conquérante," it must be even more so in the case of a class fragmented by the particularism of its outlook and formed in a context of bargaining and compromises. For this reason, translated into the terms of this theory, my thesis is that in the Latin American countries we are considering, owing to the absence of an English-style adaptation facilitated by a remarkable economic development, and also of a French-style bureaucracy capable of absorbing the shocks originating from political conflict, it is the armed forces which assume the responsibility of protecting the middle class. It was with their support that the middle class achieved, as the beginning of the century, political recognition from the oligarchy; it was with their protection that it later consolidated itself in power; and now it is with their intervention that it seeks to ward off the threat posed by the popular sectors that it is incapable of leading.

This explains the continuous civilian pressure in favor of military intervention, which a mere chronicle of the events rarely reveals.[59] Although he does not draw all the possible conclusions from his assertion, Imaz observes:

> Thus, the appeal to the armed forces as a source of legitimation—quite apart from all the other explanations given—has become a tacit rule of the Argentine political game. It is a rule that no one explicitly invokes, but from which all political groups have benefited at least once. Publicly they would all deny the existence of such a rule, but in reality it can never be ignored by Argentine politicians, who, at one time or another during this quarter of a century, have all gone to knock on the door of the barracks.[60]

The oligarchy, of course, has recourse to this expedient, and attempts to influence the military in its favor. However, the history of the coups that have taken place in the twentieth century shows that the military have only exceptionally shown a tendency to act as the representatives of the oligarchy. In other words, if the connection between the upper class and military interventionism serves to explain an exceptional case such as the overthrow of Yrigoyen advocated also by the middle class, nevertheless, it is the connection between the army and the interests and values of the middle class which explains most of the remaining interventions.

Thus, failure to emphasize and distinguish between the structural factors that cause the chronic instability of this class and its penchant for interventionism can be doubly misleading; first, because it prevents a full understanding of the peculiar characteristics of Latin American political development, and thus fails to relate to their historical context the very concepts of parliamentary democracy and of the middle class;[61] and, secondly, because it leads the observer to treat the armed forces as external factors, who interfere with the supposed normal evolution of a political process, either through personal ambition or because they have been beguiled by the upper class into serving its interests. The problem is inevitably reduced to psychological terms, and the political development of Latin America comes to be interpreted as depending less on social transformation than on a change of mentality on the part of the army officers.

PROVISIONAL STABILITY

We must now make brief reference to the cases of Uruguay, Chile, and Mexico. Although, as I pointed out above, the army in these countries supported the rise to power of the middle class, their apparent political neutrality since that event seems to constitute an objection to my main argument, which up to now has been principally illustrated by reference to the cases of Argentina and Brazil. I believe, however, that it can be seen to corroborate my argument, if we identify certain peculiar characteristics on which this apolitical behavior is based.

In Uruguay, the civil war at the beginning of the century resulted in the triumph of the middle class through a tacit pact with the oligarchy, the interests of the stock-breeders being so scrupulously respected that—although it was a country based on agriculture and stock-raising—there was no direct taxation based on landholding which might have affected that sector.[62] Besides this compromise with a comparatively weak traditional sector, the government of Batlle embarked on an intensive process of centralization and modernization of the state, transforming it from then on into the "common denominator" of Uruguayan life,[63] to a degree then unknown in other Latin American countries. As in the case of France, a civil bureaucracy was consolidated and became the backbone of the system. In 1961 it was calculated that 21.1 percent of the active population was employed in the public sector,[64] which has undoubtedly created a strong complex of interests in favor of stability, and has diffused throughout the country that middle-class outlook that has become associated with Uruguay. Another contributory factor was the satisfactory rate of growth achieved by Batlle's *étatiste* program initially, and later by the benefits deriving from a process of import-substitution accompanied by thriving foreign trade. In this context, most middle-class aspirations have been connected with the obtaining of better government employment, and the patronage system of the political parties and state paternalism have been appropriate instruments for the satisfaction of these demands.

These and other factors which have helped to make the case of Uruguay exceptional have become less operative in recent years. First, the reduced size of the internal market resulted in a rapid exhaustion of the process of import-substitution; and, secondly, as in the case of Argentina, the persistence of an agrarian structure based on big estates has caused a fall in productivity in the rural sector, to such an extent that since 1943 there has been no increase in the volume of the essential exports of meat and wool. The result is complete economic stagnation, and the gross product per capita has remained practically stationary for the last twenty years. This has coincided with a period of intense rural migration, accompanied by the familiar "revolution of rising expectations." Once again the public sector has tried to canalize these pressures: the number of people employed by it grew between 1955 and 1961 at a rate of 2.6 percent per year, and the private sector by only 0.9 percent. As Solari observes, "it is now a question of how long the state can continue to fulfill this function."[65] One of the first symptoms of the disintegration of Uruguay's *aurea mediocritas* was the victory in 1958 of the Blanco Party, which replaced the Colorados, who had enjoyed ninety-three consecutive years of power.[66] In this decade, industrial conflicts have become more frequent, and some civilian sectors have significantly begun to urge a military intervention to thwart the "Communist menace."[67]

In the case of Chile, the expansion of the foreign-owned nitrate and copper concerns resulted in a rapid increase in the public sector, since owing to the system of taxation "it was the government and not the native owners of the exporting sector which was the agent administering, spending, and distributing a considerable proportion of the revenue generated by foreign trade."[68] To these elements—which lend the

Chilean case some of the characteristics previously mentioned of the French and British cases—there were added two circumstances that are especially relevant to this discussion: first, the reduced size of the Chilean political arena—until 1946, the number of voters never exceeded 8–9 percent of the population;[69] secondly, and for this very reason, the fact that the system made it possible to pass on the benefits derived from mining and the first stage of industrialization to those popular sectors which participated in political life, thus facilitating their acceptance of the rules of the game. It is worth noting, for instance, that "Chile is probably the only country in the world that instituted a legal minimum salary long before a minimum wage."[70] In other words, the military interventions of the 1920's consolidated the power of the middle class vis-à-vis a particularly flexible oligarchy; this regime integrated a limited proportion of the population into the national political system ("probably about a fifth to a quarter of all Chileans live in what we think of as a modern society")[71] and, at the same time, gave it access to its benefits.

It is not necessary to emphasize that I have pointed out only a few of the factors that explain Chile's stability: despite everything, it may be noted that every broadening of the political framework has been accompanied by the thread of its complete breakdown: between 1946 and 1952 the number of voters increased by 75 percent, and in the latter year, in a context of open rejection of the parties of the Establishment, Carlos Ibáñez was elected; between 1958 and 1964 the electorate increased by a further 78 percent, the entire political spectrum was displaced leftward, and the Christian Democrats were elected on a platform which can certainly be described as populist. Moreover, the Chilean economy has been virtually stagnant since 1954. In these circumstances, it seems safe to assume that, in the short term, stability will be maintained as long as the government succeeds in preserving a compromise with the higher levels of the urban wage-earning sector. However,

> the political significance of these groups as spokesmen for the working class as a whole has . . . been small and has probably been decreasing, especially since the stagnation of the Chilean economy during the last decade began to reduce the opportunities of employment and to endanger the standards of living which these groups had gained for themselves.[72]

It is, therefore, probable that the pressures exercised by the lower strata of the urban and rural proletariat will become stronger in the future and—if the government fails to satisfy their demands—may cause break-down of the stability which a limited degree of democracy has made possible in Chile. Thus conditions would again favor a middle-class military coup, the possibility of which was widely rumored when an electoral triumph of the Frente de Acción Popular was feared.

Finally, with regard to Mexico, as we have already observed: "Apart from the important peasant group of Zapata's followers which remained politically marginal until the assassination of Carranza, the Mexican Revolution from the outset had middle-class leanings."[73] The historical importance of the movement—and what made it exceptional in the Latin American context until the Bolivian and Cuban revolutions occurred—lies in its elimination of the landowning oligarchy. It thus opened the way to the formation of an authentic bourgeoisie, with an original normative structure and a collective sense of direction capable of mobilizing the politically active part of the population. As a further illustration of the difference between the form and the content of social institutions, in this case it was not a liberal state but an interventionist one that organized the hegemony of the bourgeoisie, while at the same time the atmosphere of the revolution lent a "universality" to its particularist aspirations. This explains the misgivings expressed by a decided supporter of the movement:

> This bourgeoisie has seized its potential, has become strong and becomes stronger with every day that passes, not only in the national sphere but in the international as well . . . and, like every bourgeoisie, it tends not only to become independent of the force that created it, the government, but to convert the latter into a mere instrument of its interests; the government thus ceases to be a mediator, capable of balancing the interests of the bourgeoisie against those of the rest of the nation.[74]

In this process, the armed forces played a decisive role, and their present neutrality is in fact a function of the consolidation of the hegemony of the bourgeoisie:[75] "The military element is the permanent reserve of order; it is a force which acts 'in a public way' when 'legality' is threatened."[76] The greatest problem facing this "legality" is the fact that at least 50 percent of the population has been denied the benefits of development:[77] "The self-same people who made the agrarian revolution, or their descendants, have little but poverty for their reward now that the revolution has passed into the industrial stage because it has been channeled through the capitalist system."[78] The stability of Mexico, therefore, depends much less on the good humor of its generals than on the ability of its bourgeoisie to incorporate these internal colonies into the life of the nation.

THE EXTERNAL FACTOR

Up to this point I have avoided referring to external pressures in favor of military intervention because it is these internal factors that determine the efficacy of any external pressure that may be brought to bear.

I mean by this that the density of social relationships in the countries under discussion is such as to make highly improbable a military coup pure and simple, in the sense that a group of officers supported by the United States Embassy seizes control of the government at midnight. The size and complexity of the military establishment, combined with the frequent divergences of opinion among the officers themselves, tend to make relatively impracticable a putsch that does not enjoy a relatively high degree of consensus.

With this consideration in mind,[79] two points must now be emphasized. The first directly concerns the armed forces: namely, the extent to which their outlook is influenced by the strategic revolution closely linked to the development of the Cold War and the rise of national-liberation-front movements. It is in this sense that Horowitz is right when he affirms that "United States policies of military globalism tend to make obsolete earlier efforts at a standard typology of Latin American military styles and forms based exclusively on internal political affairs."[80] Here we are not only considering the greatly expanded program of military aid, but the fact that, since 1961, the United States has reappraised the basic policy underlying such aid, replacing the principle of hemispheric defense—for which it assumes sole responsibility—by that of internal security.[81]

What is most important to remember is that, by definition, the counter-insurgency operational projects blur the distinction between the military and the political spheres of action. In the context of the *guerre dans la oule*—a permanent war, which needs not be declared—there is no longer any sense in the classical distinction according to which the civil power was responsible for the direction of the war and the military power for the conduct of military operations. In such a war, since the enemy is not immediately recognizable, his identification depends on the military operations themselves; this limits considerably the sphere of civilian decision.

In other words, political intervention has now become, for the Latin American officer, a matter of professional interest. In this connection, it would be interesting to study the probable increase of the potential conflict of loyalties already mentioned: to the organization and to their profession. The tactics of imperialism may affect one more than the other, insofar as it may concentrate on the sending of missions to the country concerned, or on inviting selected officers for training in its own establishments. One may hazard a conjecture that the second alternative will be preferred in the case of the more advanced countries of the continent, where direct manipulation of the military establishment as such would not be so easy. This accounts for the increased importance attributed by the United States military academies to the political indoctrination of their Latin American guests.[82]

I said above that I would draw the reader's attention to two points. The second of these is, in fact, essential to an understanding of the first. I refer to the particular vulnerability of the Latin American middle class in the face of the strategies used during the Cold War. This corresponds exactly to the worsening of its relations with the popular sectors, and thus systematic anticommunism appears as the kind of rationalization most appropriate to its interests. Moreover, as a correlative of the absence of any vocation for hegemony among its various component fractions, the middle class only achieves a precarious unity on the basis of negative principles. It is opposed to corruption and to communism, without realizing that the former is a function of the irrationality of the system that the middle class helps to perpetuate, while the latter is merely the name that its own fears give to the aspirations of the popular sectors. This sufficiently explains why, in the five countries under discussion, it is in those where the middle class is least stable and feels most threatened that this type of outlook most flourishes. It was a Brazilian officer, General Golberi do Couto e Silva, who formulated the "ideological frontiers" doctrine, and an Argentine officer, General Onganía, who demonstrated enthusiastic adherence to it.

SOME CONCLUSIONS

Precisely because the military establishment is inseparable from the society surrounding it, it is legitimate to infer in these cases a different pattern of civil-military relations from those described at the beginning of this essay. Military interventionism does not threaten the middle class (as in the liberal model), nor is it a substitute for its absence (as in the developmentalist model); it tends to represent that class and compensate for its inability to establish itself as a well-integrated hegemonic group.

Several consequences follow from this interpretation.

1. The ideologists of the middle class—whose interests, according to one partisan observer, coincide not only with those of Latin America but also with those of humanity in general[83]—would be wrong to interpret my analysis as a justification of interventionism; I have, on the contrary, tried to demonstrate why the middle class is not in a position to contribute to the development of these countries. Moreover, in its present form military interventionism tends to prevent rather than favor the possibility of certain sectors of that class ever transcending their profoundly traditional outlook.

In this connection, the observation of Gramsci is perfectly valid when he distinguishes between "progressive" and "regressive" varieties of Caesarism.[84] Despite its compromising and its limitations, the first variety does assist the consolidation of new social groups, whereas the second tries to preserve the elements of a social order that has exhausted its possibilities of development. This is the fundamental difference between a Vargas and a Castelo Branco.

Just at the moment when the loss of the dynamic impulse of the import-substitution model is creating the objective conditions for ending the agrarian-industrial pact, free elections are becoming an essential instrument of political bargaining, which makes possible the gradual union of the progressive groups. This possibility is, however, eliminated by the fears of the upper and middle classes; it is for this reason that both Brazilian and the Argentine military governments have lost no time in suspending the electoral process, and are tending to search for forms of functional representation which avoid the risk inherent in normal elections.[85]

We are not concerned here with advocating territorial representation in the abstract, nor must corporativism in general be identified with one of its manifestations, i.e., fascism. However, given the present degree of development of the societies I am considering, the danger inherent in projects of this kind is that they constitute an institutional "freezing" of a system of relationships which must be changed. For this reason, the price that is paid for reducing the electoral influence of the popular sectors is the maintenance of the self-same structure that has led to the crisis. Therefore, not only is this a transitory solution, since it does not deal with the fundamental causes of the problem, but it already reveals what it leads to in the long term; as the tendency to stagnation increases, so will popular discontent, and the corporativist system will develop an increasingly rightward bias. This will happen even though, in the short term, fortuitous movements of economic expansion—due, for instance, to a temporary fluctuation in the foreign market—may favor compromises with trade-union organizations of a reformist outlook.

2. The other point worth mentioning is the possibility of a "Nasserist" variant; this is a frequent theme in present-day Latin American writing.

There are, of course, two possible meanings of the term Nasserism. One of them, on an extremely vague and theoretical level, applies the term to any military group whose objectives are "a mixture of radical independence, the reconquest of national identity and emphasis on social progress."[86] According to this interpretation, Kemal Ataturk and Perón were Nasserists "*avant la lettre*." Obviously, this greatly reduces the scientific usefulness of the concept, because what it gains in general applicability it loses in precision.

The other meaning, however, is specific, and refers to one prototype of national development—the Egyptian—and is the only one that appears relevant to a concrete analysis. From this point of view, I believe that the Nasserist variant as such is inapplicable in the context of these countries. I will give briefly some of the reasons on which I base this assertion, leaving out of account obvious ethnic and religious differences between the two contexts.

In the first place—as in the Afro-Asian model in general—the degree of integration of the Egyptian army into the society around it was considerably less than in the case of Latin America. It should be remembered that, after the defeat of the precursory movement led by Ahman al-'Urabi in 1882, Egypt underwent for seventy-four years, in one form or another, British military occupation. This not only limited the opportunities for natives in the military profession, but deprived this career of patriotic appeal. As recently as 1936 the Anglo-Egyptian Treaty reopened the Military Academy to the sons of the petty bourgeoisie—especially the rural petty bourgeoisie—and it was then that Nasser and most of the future Free Officers entered the army.[87] In addition to this lack of integration of the Egyptian officer into the context of the influential sectors in the country, there was also the impact of the immediate colonial situation and, later, the "experience of the concrete Fatherland"[88] as a result of the disastrous Palestine campaign.

In addition to these peculiar characteristics, it is necessary to take into account the circumstances of the country. In 1952 Egypt was an essentially agricultural country, with nearly 70 percent of the population consisting of "fellahs,"[89] a per capita income of under $120, nearly 80 percent illiteracy, and an industry contributing only 10 percent of the Gross National Product.[90] At the same time, as a consequence of underdevelopment and foreign control over important sectors of the economy, there was an absence of national bureaucratic and entrepreneurial cadres.

Finally, the degree of popular participation in the system was extremely low. Thus, one writer observes:

> It is incorrect to argue that the old regimes in Egypt and Syria were overthrown because the people ceased to accept their legitimacy. Legitimacy was not yet an issue in nations in which few classes and groups of the population had entered politics at all. In spite of the constitutional formula for male suffrage in both countries, the predominantly poor and illiterate masses did not achieve a high voting rate, and to expect from them active and discerning participation in political affairs would be absurd.[91]

It will be observed that we have here the characteristics peculiar to the developmentalist model, with the addition of the colonial factor, which tended to increase the nationalism of this first generation of Egyptian officers drawn from the popular sectors. Given this context, it is understandable that, after the 1952 movement, the army should become, in theory and in practice, "the real backbone of the state,"[92] and that the degree of mobilization of the urban and rural workers should be very limited. At the same time it explains the extreme economic liberalism which characterized the first phase of the revolution (1952–1956) when desperate efforts were made to attract foreign capital and thus encourage the incipient industrialization process.

The nationalization of the Suez Canal Company represented the watershed of the regime, and its change of orientation was further emphasized by the legislation of 1961 and 1963, which transferred 80 percent of industry to state ownership.[93] But it is precisely now, when Egypt has succeeded in doubling its industrial production, that the future success of Nasserism depends on its ability to supersede the factors that have characterized it hitherto. In other words, the previous absence of popular participation, to which I referred above, and an especially favorable international situation—due, above all, to Soviet support—made it possible to liquidate the aristocracy and the foreign interests " 'from above' bureaucratically, without the bourgeois revolution being obliged to resolve the problem of democracy and that of the rural sector."[94] It is this specific development of Nasserism that establishes the limits of the movement. Therefore, Abdel Malek is correct in thus summarizing the alternatives now facing the regime:

> The choice is between, on the one hand, a coalition of the two currents of the national movement—Nasserism and Egyptian Marxism—which would allow Egypt to realize to the full its potential internally, in the Arab world, and in the global struggle against Imperialism, and to take the first steps toward socialism; and, on the other hand, the elimination of these possibilities by the combined action of the pro-imperialist forces in the Arab world and the reactionary forces inside the Egyptian establishment.[95]

It is obvious, even from this brief outline, that there is a great difference between the Egyptian case and that of the Latin American countries under discussion, as regards the integration of the military into civilian society, a much higher degree of popular participation, and the absence of an immediate colonial experience. The most important factor, however, is the greatly superior level of development as compared with Egypt in 1952; in the Latin American countries under discussion, therefore, the chief problem is not that of introducing technical innovations but of organizing rationally and establishing social control over those that already exist.

Whereas the slogan *"enrichissez-vous,"* coined in the Europe of the nineteenth century, simultaneously fulfilled a social function, creating new techniques of production and imposing on society as a whole a growing need for rationalization, first formal and later substantive, in the conditions of Latin American economic growth the principle of private profit has resulted in a considerable increase in the irrationality and imbalance of the system. A good illustration of this is the "over-equipment" of the modern sector of industry by imported labor-saving machinery, that is to say, machines which economize on what is precisely the most abundant factor. This made it necessary to give protection to the small quasi-craft industries, which even if they operate with very low productivity, give employment to a considerable proportion of the labor force otherwise threatened with technological unemployment. This resulted in a division of the market in the only practicable way, that of regulating the system of prices in accordance with the high costs of the least efficient concerns. These have therefore managed to survive, while modern businesses make profit margins high enough to compensate them for maintaining in idleness a part of their installed capacity; which is clearly prejudicial to the interests of society as a whole. That is why these economies have suffered all the disadvantages of a paramonopolistic market structure,[96] without enjoying the benefits of increased productivity that have resulted from such a structure in the developed capitalist countries. Moreover, this increases the dependence of industry on the traditional exports: since it is prevented by its high costs from competing in the international market, the primary sector still has to be relied on to supply the foreign exchange the country needs.

At the risk of oversimplifying the problem, it can, therefore, be asserted that these countries have already passed the Nasserist stage as far as their industrial expansion is concerned—and also as regards the degree of popular mobilization—though not as regards the confrontation with the oligarchy and the foreign interests. The immediate task facing the continent is the appropriation for social ends of the potential economic excedent, through a radical transformation of its existing structures.[97] However, both the level of development and of institutional complexity, and the vulnerability of various sectors of the army to pressures exercised by the beneficiaries of the status quo would appear to condemn to failure a revolution "from above" directed by the armed forces. It must be remembered that, in order to succeed, such a movement would have to acquire a populist character; and the stagnation of the economy, the fears of the propertied classes, and the increased maturity of the urban and rural proletariat all militate against such a development.

Even if there are in Latin America groups of officers of a Nasserist outlook—which seems doubtful—and supposing that the present character of the groups in the higher command remains unchanged, their position would necessarily be very weak; and to imagine that, in the countries we have considered, such officers could come into power by means of a coup, would be to transfer into the military sphere the Utopianism that underlies advocacy of the "Cuban way" in the civilian sphere.

It is precisely the potential existence of such a fraction among the army officers—I am now referring to the more general meaning attached to the term Nasserism—that can encourage confidence in an alternative to violent revolution, which both the international situation and internal factors (among them, the very strength of the armed forces), render, for the moment, impracticable. In Latin America, however, the efficacy of such a progressive group cannot make itself felt *before*—as in the Egyptian case—but only *after* an intensive mobilization of the popular sectors. It is on this, and not in any *appel au soldat*—which, thus, introduces an element of confusion—that the success of a coalition based on a program of revolutionary reforms will depend.[98] And it is the struggle to achieve such a program that can lead to the organization, from below, of a new hegemonic consciousness capable of putting an end to the crisis.

De Tocqueville once said that "it is not in the army that one can find the remedy for the ills of the army, but in the country."[99] In this study I have tried to give a contemporary twist to this proposition in the context under discussion; the concluding reflection would be that "neither is it in the army that one can find the remedy for the ills of the country."

Notes

1. Intentionally, the data given in this example correspond approximately to those of Argentina and Guatemala. In a recent study of Latin American militarism, the case of the latter country was considered as a paradigm of events in the rest of the continent. See Fedro Guillén, "Militarismo y golpes de estado en América Latina," *Cuadernos americanos*, 140/3 (1965), pp. 12–16. Lieuwen makes equally far-sweeping generalizations in his examination of the coups that occurred between 1962 and 1964. See Edwin Lieuwen, *Generals vs. Presidents—Neo-Militarism in Latin America* (New York: Praeger, 1964).

2. For a critical commentary on the literature dealing with this subject, see Lyle N. McAlister, "Changing Concepts of the Role of the Military in Latin America," *The Annals*, 360 (July 1965), pp. 85–98; and my study "A Latin American Phenomenon: The Middle-Class Military Coup," in *Trends in Social Science Research in Latin American Studies* (Berkeley, March 1965), pp. 55–59. For a typical expression of the liberal theory, see Edwin Lieuwen,

Arms and Politics in Latin America (New York: Praeger, 1961); the best exposition of the developmentalist theory is John J. Johnson, *The Military and Society in Latin America* (Stanford: Stanford University Press, 1964).

3. James H. Meisel, *The Fall of the Republic—Military Revolt in France* (Ann Arbor: University of Michigan Press, 1962), p. vi.

4. Cf. ECLA, *Problemas y perspectivas del desarrollo industrial latinoamericano* (Buenos Aires, 1964), p. 21.

5. Merle Kling, "Toward a Theory of Power and Political Instability in Latin America," in John H. Kautsky, ed., *Political Change in Underdeveloped Countries* (New York: Wiley, 1962), p. 201.

6. Lucian W. Pye, *Aspects of Political Development* (Boston: Atlantic, Little Brown, 1966), p. 173.

7. I have omitted Cuba from this analysis both because of the incongruence of its indicators of development and because of the exceptional situation resulting from the Revolution. Together with Mexico—as we shall see later—and Bolivia, it provides the only case in Latin America illustrating the socialist model of civilian-cum-military rebellions. Thus, Article 6 of the law establishing the new Bolivian army lays it down that "military academies must be constituted fundamentally of elements of the middle class, working class, and peasantry, which in addition to the technical training relating to the military art, will be educated to respect and protect the national sovereignty and the aspirations of the people, and to defend the riches of the country against the ambitions of the oligarchy." See McAlister, "The Military," in J. J. Johnson, ed., *The Military and Society in Latin America* (Stanford: Stanford University Press, 1964), p. 146.

8. Katharine Chorley, *Armies and the Art of Revolution* (London, 1943), p. 78.

9. Cf. McAlister, in Johnson, *The Military & Society*, p. 145; and Johnson, *ibid.*, pp. 102 ff. For a discussion of the same tendency in Europe, see Morris Janowitz, "Armed Forces in Western Europe: Uniformity and Diversity," *European J. of Sociology*, 6 (1965), p. 232.

10. José Luis de Imaz, *Los que mandan* (Buenos Aires, 1964), p. 58.

11. *Ibid.*, p. 56.

12. Johnson, *The Military & Society*, pp. 235–238. Also Charles Wagley, *An Introduction to Brazil* (New York: Columbia University Press, 1963), pp. 253–254.

13. Maria Isaura Pereira de Queiroz, "Les classes sociales dans le Brésil actuel," *Cahiers internationaux de sociologie*, 39 (1965), p. 162.

14. Johnson, *The Military & Society*, p. 108.

15. Cf. Liisa North, *Civil-Military Relations in Argentina, Chile and Peru*, (Berkeley, Calif.: University of California Press, 1966), pp. 17–20.

16. Javier Romero, *Aspectos psicobiométricos y sociales de una muestra de la*

juventud mexicana (Mexico City, 1956), quoted by McAlister in Johnson, *The Military & Society*, p. 147.

17. Cf. Louis Althusser, *Pour Marx* (Paris, 1966), pp. 85–128.
18. Marion J. Levy Jr., *Modernization and the Structure of Societies—A Setting for International Affairs* (Princeton: Princeton University Press, 1966), Vol. II, p. 595. Contrast: "Social origins and early backgrounds are less important to the character of the professional military man than to any other high social type." C. Wright Mills, *The Power Elite* (New York: Oxford University Press, 1956), p. 192. However, Mills himself adds that "the point should not, of course, be pushed too far" (*ibid.*); and, moreover, he does not offer any empirical evidence to support his thesis. Incidentally, although the latter is expressed in such categorical terms, it is weakened by its relative nature, insofar as little is known of the importance of the social origin of the other "high social types."
19. Imaz, *Los que mandan*, p. 68.
20. As far as Latin America is concerned, the only study I know that compares attitudes of cadets before and after their military training is: Mario Monteforte Toledo, *Guatemala—monografía sociológica* (Mexico City, 1959), pp. 367 ff.
21. Erving Goffman, *Asylums—Essays on the Social Situation of Mental Patients and Other Inmates* (New York: Aldine, 1961), *passim*.
22. *Ibid.*, pp. 118–119.
23. *Ibid.*, p. 13.
24. *Ibid.*, p. 73.
25. See Gaetano Mosca, *The Ruling Class*, A. Livingstone, ed. (New York, 1939), Chap. 9; and S. E. Finer, *The Man on Horseback: The Role of the Military in Politics* (New York: Praeger, 1962), pp. 26–30. See also Stanislav Andreski, "Conservatism and Radicalism of the Military," *European J. of Sociology*, 2 (1961), pp. 55–58, and Philip Abrams, "The Late Profession of Arms: Ambiguous Goals and Deteriorating Means in Britain," *ibid.* 6 (1965), pp. 241–242.
26. Arthur Whitaker, "Nationalism and Social Change in Latin America," p. 99, in J. Maier and R. W. Weatherhead, eds., *Politics of Change in Latin America* (New York: Praeger, 1964), pp. 85–100.
27. Janowitz, "Armed Forces in Western Europe," p. 226.
28. Jacques Van Doorn, "The Officer Corps: a Fusion of Profession and Organization," *European J. of Sociology*, 6 (1965), p. 270.
29. One example of this tension was provided in 1965 by the resignation of General Juan Carlos Onganía from the post of commander-in-chief of the Argentine army because of the government's failure to take account of professional perquisites in the appointment of the secretary for war.

30. See below, pp. 333 ff.

31. I believe it would be fruitful to reinterpret from this point of view the hypotheses of Merle Kling mentioned above, even though I would insist that I consider them to be only applicable to the less-developed countries of Latin America, which I am not dealing with in this study.

32. G. D. H. Cole, *Studies in Class Structure* (London, 1955), pp. 90–91.

33. Cf. Alessandro Pizzorno, "Sviluppo economico e urbanizzazione," *Quaderni di sociologia*, 11 (1962), p. 35.

34. Richard Morse, "Urbanization in Latin America," *Latin American Research R.*, vol. 1, no. 1 (1965), p. 38.

35. Pizzorno, "Sviluppo economico e urbanizzazione," p. 35.

36. Morse, "Urbanization in Latin America," p. 38.

37. Celso Furtado, *Development and Stagnation in Latin America: A Structuralist Approach*, mimeographed (New Haven: Yale University, 1966), p. 13.

38. I am, of course, giving a general outline of a long-term process. In the short term, however, there are conflicts which derive precisely from the activities of the urban mercantile sectors in their attempts to displace the pre-capitalist landowning sector.

39. It is unnecessary to emphasize that I am greatly simplifying the discussion. Among the five countries to which I am referring, the one that most deviates from the pattern is Brazil; this country, together with Ecuador and Colombia, constitutes an exception to the Latin American rule of the unique "primate" city. In any case, during the period we are discussing, the situation in Brazil becomes increasingly similar to that which I have described, owing to the centralization imposed from the beginning of this century onwards by the coffee-growing economy of São Paulo. Thus here too "the leading strata of urban society were composed for the most part of members of the great landowning families." Furtado, "Political Obstacles to the Economic Development of Brazil," in Claudio Veliz, ed., *Obstacles to Change in Latin America* (New York and London: Oxford University Press, 1965), p. 152.

40. Antonio Gramsci, *Notas sobre Maquiavelo, sobre política y sobre el estado moderno* (Buenos Aires, 1962), p. 54.

41. On the moral outlook of the middle class—possibly a constant in Latin American political life—see, in general, Svend Ranulf, *Moral Indignation and Middle Class Psychology* (New York: Schocken, 1964), and, more specifically, IBESP, "O moralismo e a alienação das classes medias," *Cadernos do nosso tempo*, 2 (1954), pp. 150–159.

42. See, for example, Gino Germani, *Política y sociedad en una época de transición* (Buenos Aires, 1962), pp. 153 f.

43. Trygve R. Tholfson, "The Transition to Democracy in Victorian England," *International R. of Social History*, vol. 6, no. 2 (1961), p. 226.

44. *Ibid.*, p. 232.

45. For an excellent analysis of this subject, see E. J. Hobsbawm, *Laboring Men—Studies in the History of Labor* (New York: Basic Books, 1965), pp. 272–315.

46. Cf. Royden Harrison, "The 10th April of Spencer Walpole: The Problem of Revolution in Relation to Reform, 1865–1867," *International R. of Social History*, vol. 7, no. 3 (1962), pp. 351–397.

47. R. A. J. Walling, ed., *The Diaries of John Bright* (New York, 1931), p. 297.

48. Cf. Stein Rokkan, "Mass Suffrage, Secret Voting, and Political Participation," *European J. of Sociology*, vol. 2, no. 2 (1961), pp. 132–152. Even in Great Britain it has been estimated that around 1913 no more than 17 percent of the population had the right to vote.

49. In the case of Brazil, observers have recently noted the tendency toward the adoption of an ideology on the part of the politician operating the patronage system, as his possibilities of immediately satisfying the demands of the electorate become increasingly restricted. It is obvious that this transition from being "Savior of the Poor" to being "Savior of the Fatherland" implies, eventually, the negation of the patronage system and as such represents a risk that the dominant groups do not seem prepared to take. See Carlos Alberto de Medina, *A favela e o demagogo* (São Paulo, 1964), pp. 95–96.

50. See, for example, ECLA, *The Social Development of Latin America in the Post-War Period* (Santiago, 1963).

51. Thus, Torcuato S. Di Tella *et al.*, eds., *Argentina, sociedad de masas* (Buenos Aires, 1965).

52. Raymond Williams, *Culture and Society* (New York: Harper and Row, 1958), p. 300.

53. *Ibid.*, p. 299.

54. Cf. Celso Furtado, "Reflections on the Brazilian Pre-Revolution," in Claudio Veliz, ed., *The Politics of Conformity in Latin America* (New York: Oxford University Press, 1967), pp. 62–73.

55. Joseph A. Schumpeter, *Capitalism, Socialism, and Democracy* (London, 1947), p. 138.

56. So decisive was this factor that it has recently been argued that the British bourgeoisie never succeeded in becoming a hegemonic group. See Perry Anderson, "Origins of the Present Crisis," *New Left R.*, vol. 23, pp. 26–53. For a discussion of the existence of a protecting Establishment in the United States as well, see the interesting study by Andrew Hacker, "Liberal Democracy and Social Control," *American Political Science R.*, vol. 5, no. 1 (1957), pp. 1009–1026.

57. David Thomson, *Democracy in France* (London, 1958), p. 58.

58. Compare Charles Frankel, "Bureaucracy and Democracy in the New Europe," in Stephen R. Graubard, ed., *A New Europe?* (Cambridge, Mass.: Harvard University Press, 1964), p. 541. See also Stanley Hoffman, "Paradoxes of the French Political Community," in Hoffman *et al.*, *In Search of France* (Cambridge, Mass.: Harvard University Press, 1963), pp. 1–117.

59. The reader has only to glance at the Argentine or Brazilian press in the months before the recent military coups. An analysis of the contents of such publications as *Confirmado*, *Primera Plana*, or *Estado de São Paulo* would be extremely revealing.

60. Imaz, *Los que mandan*, p. 84.

61. This is the fundamental mistake made by studies which attempt to describe in the abstract the developmentalist strategy of a middle-class elite. Compare Clark Kerr *et al.*, *Industrialism and Industrial Man* (Cambridge, Mass.: Harvard University Press, 1960), Chap. III. One thus loses sight of the essentially relational nature of the notion of social class. Compare Stanislaw Ossowski, *Class Structure in the Social Consciousness* (London, 1963), p. 133.

62. Johnson, *Political Change in Latin America* (Stanford: Stanford University Press, 1958), p. 61.

63. Aldo E. Solari, *Estudios sobre la sociedad uruguaya* (Montevideo, 1964), p. 167.

64. *Ibid.*, p. 136.

65. *Ibid.*, p. 156.

66. See Carlos M. Rama, "La crisis política uruguaya," *Ciencias políticas y sociales*, vol. 5, no. 16 (1959), pp. 233–242.

67. For a significant appeal to the army from the left, see Carlos María Gutiérrez, "Reflexión para los militares uruguayos," *Marcha*, Oct. 16, 1965, p. 11: "In contrast to the generals, voicing official policy and given to political bickering, subservient to United States strategy and fearful of the economic and social transformation for which the people are clamoring, one observes the different attitude of the junior officers, who realize the stupidity of the way the country is being governed."

68. Aníbal Pinto, *Chile, una economía difícil* (Mexico City, 1964), p. 160.

69. See Federico C. Gil, *The Political System of Chile* (Boston: Houghton Mifflin, 1966), p. 213.

70. Albert O. Hirschman, *Journeys Towards Progress* (New York, 1965), p. 264. The law establishing minimum salaries for employees was passed in 1937, whereas this measure was extended to the workers only in 1955.

71. Silvert, "Some Propositions on Chile," in Robert D. Tomasek, ed., *Latin American Politics* (New York: Doubleday Anchor, 1966), p. 387.

72. Osvaldo Sunkel, "Change and Frustration in Chile," in Claudio Veliz, ed.,

Obstacles to Change in Latin America (New York: Oxford University Press, 1965), p. 129.

73. Moisés González Navarro, "Mexico: The Lop-Sided Revolution," in Veliz, *Obstacles to Change in Latin America*, p. 226.

74. Leopoldo Zea, "La Revolución, el gobierno y la democracia," *Ciencias políticas y sociales*, vol. 5, no. 18 (1959), p. 543.

75. It is interesting to note that the structure established by Cárdenas for the Partido de la Revolución Mexicana increased the similarity of this case to the socialist model of civil-military relations. The PRM, in practice, comprised four sectors: agrarian, workers, popular, and military. In other words, the armed forces, whose officers in any case held at that time over half the posts in the government, were considered to be an active part of the political system. However, this sector was dissolved in 1940 after three years of existence, and the officers holding elective posts were absorbed into the popular sector. "This does not mean that the army divorced itself from politics. On the contrary, having returned to its old position behind the throne, the military's role in Mexican politics has remained strong and partisan." Robert E. Scott, *Mexican Government in Transition* (Urbana: University of Illinois Press, 1964), p. 134.

76. Gramsci, *Notas sobre Maquiavelo*, p. 81.

77. Cf. Pablo González Casanova, *La democracia en México* (Mexico City, 1965), p. 81.

78. González Navarro, in Veliz, *Obstacles to Change in Latin America*, p. 228.

79. It is important to relate this consideration to the new forms assumed by imperialist activities, especially the growing tendency to replace direct investment by various types of association with local concerns. This is even more valid in the case of the relatively advanced countries such as those we have been describing, and it is symptomatic of the internalization of the external influence to which I have referred in the text. See Hamza Alavi, "Imperialism, Old and New," in John Saville and Ralph Miliband, eds., *The Socialist Register* (New York: Monthly Review Press, 1964), pp. 116 ff.

80. Irving L. Horowitz, "The Military of Latin America," in Seymour Lipset and Aldo Solari, eds., *Elites in Latin America* (New York: Oxford University Press, 1967). Horowitz analyses in detail the incidence of the external factor, and I therefore refer the reader to his work.

81. Cf. Lieuwen, *Generals vs. Presidents*, pp. 114 ff.

82. "*Dr. McAlister:* I would like to ask a simple-minded question about it. As conceived, is this primarily done for military or for political purposes? The college, that is. [He is referring to the Inter-American Defense College, Fort McNair, Washington, where about thirty-five Latin American officers receive training every five months.]—*Col. Hicks:* I imagine I can respond

to that. Anything that we do in the military I believe has a political overtone to it.—*Dr. McAlister:* Right.—*Col. Hicks:* And we are . . .—*Dr. Milburn* (interposing): That is one of the more sophisticated statements I have heard made at the conference. (Laughter).—*Col. Hicks:* So definitely there is a political connotation to the school.—*Dr. McAlister:* But is it just a connotation?—*Col. Hicks:* Yes." U.S. Naval Ordnance Test Station, *A Symposium on Military Elites in Latin America*, Louis D. Higgs, ed. (China Lake, Calif., March 1965), pp. 137–138. Referring to the training received by the officers at this College, Lieuwen observes: "They are taught much about Communism here but little about democracy." *Generals vs. Presidents*, p. 148 n.

83. Víctor Alba, "La nouvelle classe moyenne latinoaméricaine," *La Revue Socialiste*, 133 (1960), p. 468.

84. Gramsci, *Notas sobre Maquiavelo*, pp. 84 ff.

85. Referring to the corporativist tendencies in Latin America, a writer observes: "The major social purpose of the syndicalist approach is to find a way of subsuming the new class complications of modernism to hierarchy, preserving a kind of Latin *Führerprinzip*, leaving inviolate the privileges and powers of the traditional, and thus escaping the secularization and, to their eyes, immorality of the nation-State." Silvert, "National Values, Development, and Leaders and Followers," *International Social Science Journal*, vol. 15, no. 4 (1963), p. 563.

86. Anuar Abdel Malek, "Nasserismo y socialismo," in R. García Lupo, *Nasserismo y marxismo* (Buenos Aires, 1965), p. 186.

87. Cf. Bernard Vernier, "L'évolution du régime militaire en Egypte," *Revue française de science politique*, vol. 13, no. 3 (1963), p. 604.

88. Jean Ziegler, *Sociologie de la nouvelle Afrique* (Paris, 1964), p. 294.

89. Abdel Malek, *Egypte—société militaire* (Paris, 1962), p. 26.

90. Charles Issawi, *Egypt in Revolution* (London, 1963), pp. 46–47.

91. See P. J. Vatikiotis, *The Egyptian Army in Politics* (Bloomington, Ind.: University of Indiana Press, 1961), pp. 99–100.

92. Ziegler, *Sociologie de la nouvelle Afrique*, p. 347.

93. Abdel Malek, in *ibid.*, p. 170.

94. Hassan Riad, "Las tres edades de la sociedad egipcia," in *ibid.*, pp. 38–107.

95. Abdel Malek, in *ibid.*, p. 188.

96. ECLA, *Problemas y perspectivas* . . . , pp. 22–24. For a perceptive analysis of the distortions of Latin American industrialization, see Aníbal Pinto, "Concentración del progreso técnico y de sus frutos en el desarrollo latinoamericano," *El Trimestre económico*, vol. 32, no. 1 (1965), pp. 3–69.

97. For an analysis of the concept of "potential economic excedent," see Paul A. Baran, *The Political Economy of Growth* (New York: Monthly

Review Press, 1957). In this connection, it is necessary to submit to objective examination the supposed need for foreign capital in these countries. This is generally the "technical" pretext for operations that provide good profits for foreign investors and at the same time help to preserve the status quo. For a demonstration of the fallacy of the argument see among others, the excellent study of the Chilean case included in Nicholas Kaldor, *Essays on Economic Policy* (New York: W. W. Norton, 1965), pp. ii, 233–287.

98. The idea of "revolutionary reformism" is discussed by, among others, André Gorz, *Stratégie ouvriére et néo-capitalisme* (Paris, 1965), and Lucio Magri, "Le modéle de développement capitaliste et le probléme de 'l'alternative' prolétarienne," *Les Temps modernes*, nos. 196–197 (1962), pp. 583–626.

99. Alexis de Tocqueville, *De la démocratie en Amérique* (Paris, 1963), Bk. II, chap. 26, p. 349.

4

Philip Ehrensaft

The Politics of Pseudo-Planning in
a Primary-Producing Nation

The failure of primary-producing nations like the country of Trinidad
and Tobago to attain rapid economic growth is first of all a political
failure. Political action failed to change structures which prevent the
nation from effectively utilizing the surplus generated by its economy to
spur national development. Using the small island-nation of Trinidad
and Tobago as a case study, the nature of these structures and the reasons
why politics failed to transform them will be outlined. Trinidad has been
chosen as the object for a case study because: (1) It exhibits in polar form
crucial characteristics common to the political economies of primary-
producing nations; (2) its small scale makes it easier to simultaneously
comprehend the intertwining of economic, political, and social power
than would be the case if one began with a larger nation; (3) the range and
quality of statistics are better than for many other primary-producing
nations.

As national societies go, the country of Trinidad and Tobago is relatively young. Nearly all of the original Amerindian population was deci-
mated by the Spanish. Of the nation's 827,957 inhabitants as of 1960,
43.5 percent were classified as Negro, 16.3 percent as Mixed (mainly
Negro-White mixtures, commonly referred to as Coloreds), 47.8 percent
as East Indian, and 1.9 percent as White. The island of Trinidad lies
seven miles from the northern coast of Venezuela and is 65 miles long
and 48 miles wide. It contains nearly all of the nation's large East Indian
minority. The smaller island of Tobago is more typical of the British

---

Originally published in a slightly different form as "Authentic Planning or Afro-
Asian Appalachia?" in *American Behavioral Scientist*, vol. 12, no. 2 (November–
December 1968). Copyright © 1968 by Sage Publications, Inc.

West Indies: the population of 33,333 is overwhelmingly of African descent; the economy is predominantly agricultural and tourist. Trinidad's economy, on the other hand, is based upon the mining and refining of oil and asphalt. Because the overwhelming majority of the nation's population, production, and decision-making powers are located in the larger of the sister islands, this essay focuses upon Trinidad.

THE COLONIAL DIVISION OF LABOR

The linchpin of the structures which prevent Third World nations like Trinidad and Tobago from effectively utilizing their economic surplus is a division of labor exhibiting three characteristics:

1. Low interdependence. The society is divided into primary-producing localized segments having a low rate of exchange with one another.[1]

2. Openness. The rate of interchange between segments within the same nation is low relative to the rate of interchange between these segments and other nations.[2]

3. Appendage functions. Extra-national interchange is almost exclusively with the industrialized countries of the North Atlantic, the metropoles of colonial empires; localized segments serve less as complements of a national society than as appendages supplying primary products and profits to metropolitan economies. The colonial division of labor does not constitute an optimal distribution of benefits generated by each nation's specializing in what is relatively cheapest for it to produce, as a static theory of international trade would teach us. It is not the result of a "natural evolution" of economic relations, but a pattern imposed under the aegis of political domination.[3]

Europe's industrial development witnessed the welding of isolated segments within a given territory into an interdependent national network. Links within segments were replaced by links between segments. This interdependent network is termed the "metropolitan division of labor." Economic development in the Third World entails replacing the external links of isolated social segments to metropolitan economies with links between segments within the nation. The metropolitan and colonial divisions of labor are schematically contrasted in Charts I and II.

The colonial division of labor extends to social and political relations. This organization of production operates so as to place different ethnic groups in different sectors of the economy. Hence, the colonial division of

Chart I
The Metropolitan Division of Labor

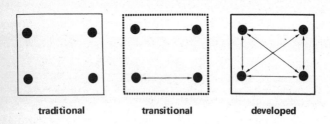

traditional   transitional   developed

Chart II
The Colonial Division of Labor

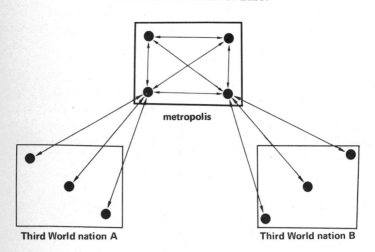

metropolis

Third World nation A   Third World nation B

labor is simultaneously an *ethnic* division of labor. In turn, the ethnic division of labor contributes to and is enhanced by political rivalry between ethnic groups. This political rivalry weakens the ability of the nation to transform structures so as to more effectively utilize its economic surplus.

THE ETHNIC DIVISION OF LABOR

As in many other primary-producing nations, Trinidad's principal ethnic groups are, on the whole, regionally, economically, culturally, and politically differentiated from one another. After the emancipation of slaves, the Negroes spurned plantation agriculture. Sugar-planting interests replaced them with indentured laborers from India. Most Indians remained in Trinidad after the five-year period of indenture terminated and settled on small plots of land. Negroes, on the other hand, tended to seek work in urban areas, the service sector, the factories of sugar plantations, and other nonagricultural pursuits. Moreover, the slavery system had been much more destructive of African culture than was the indenture system. After five years' service, Indians left the plantation barracks for an Indian village and restored many traditional social patterns.

Most Indian villages were established in mid-southern Trinidad around the sugar plantations. Thus, economic, regional, and cultural differentiation between Negroes and Indians were intertwined. Even where the two groups lived side by side, they tended to coexist rather than mingle. Although the transition from a sugar-based to a petroleum-based economy carried large numbers of Indians to all parts of Trinidad, the regional concentration of Indians in the original areas of settlement continues. Of Trinidad's 300,813 Indians, 229,978 are located in such areas.[4] For the nation as a whole, there is still a disproportionate concentration of Indians in agriculture.

Economic differentiation between Negroes and Indians is evidenced by an ethnic breakdown for major industrial groups in the male working population.[5] The method of analysis is to compare the proportion of a particular race in a specified industrial group with the proportion of that race in a given administrative ward.[6] An index of ethnic differentiation in economic pursuits can be formed by taking the ratio of the ethnic composition of industrial groups to what would be the case if each ethnic group contributed exactly the same percentage to the industrial group as its percentage of the total work force in a given area. Space prevents presentation of the data in detail. What emerges is a demonstration of relative concentration of Negroes in mining, manufacturing, and construction. Indians are relatively concentrated in agriculture, commerce, and transportation.

Ecological data is subject to compositional errors. It is preferable to have surveys where calculations can be made from the individual level. Ecological data, however, was all that was publicly available. Other studies also imply a continuing ethnic division of labor. For example, data from a sample survey of voting behavior is reworked in Table I. It shows clear differences between Indian and Negro respondents in income and education, which are in turn good indicators of different positions in the system of production. The ethnic division of labor is also associated with cultural differentiation in areas such as religion, mating and fertility, and psychological orientations. Space limitations prevent the presentation of supporting data and necessitate a direct shift to the political implications of the ethnic division of labor.

Table I

	INCOME					
	Lower[a]		*Upper*		*Total*	
	%	n	%	n	%	n
Negro	31.8	47	68.2	101	100	148
Indian	54.9	100	45.1	82	100	182

	EDUCATION							
	None		*Primary*		*Secondary*		*Total*	
	%	n	%	n	%	n	%	n
Negro	1.9	3	87.1	135	11.0	17	100	155
Indian	26.0	56	70.7	152	3.3	7	100	215

[a] Lower income defined as less than $100.00 W.I. per month. $1.00 U.S.= $1.70 W.I.
Source: Calculated from data in K. Bahadoorsing, "Trinidad Electoral Politics: The Persistence of the Race Factor" (Ph.D. diss., University of Indiana, 1966), pp. 65, 71.

The ethnic division of labor makes Trinidadian society more prone to conflict than would be the case if membership in the various social categories were to crosscut rather than reinforce one another. Crosscutting memberships mediate conflict at two levels:

1. By creating personal ambivalence, which in turn dampens the individual's propensity to engage in conflict. For example, a person's occupation impels him to take one side in the conflict while his ethnic status pressures him toward the other side.

2. By hindering the unification of all the members of a particular social category, since a significant proportion of the members belong to other groups with differing interests from that of the first group.

To the degree that memberships are crosscutting, a society may rely to a greater extent upon the diffuse, informal network of interpersonal and intergroup relations, in preference to formal state controls, to mediate conflict, than is the case if memberships are reinforcing. Because the colonial division of labor leads to reinforcing rather than crosscutting memberships, there is a corresponding reliance upon state agencies to regulate conflict. When a majority ethnic group or majority coalition of ethnic groups controls the state, it controls the very agencies which frequently regulate conflicts between the majority and the minority. Ethnic competition for control of state adds a fierce earnestness to politics, for there is little trust between the rival ethnic-economic-regional-cultural groups.

In a developed national economy, memberships are more likely to crosscut. At intermediate stages of development, only the first trends

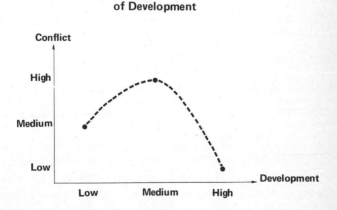

Chart III
Ethnic Conflict and Degree
of Development

toward crosscutting appear, and they are likely to *increase* rather than decrease conflict. For example, ethnic group A is likely to resent the appearance of group B in an area of employment traditionally the preserve of A. Most of all, rivalry for control of the state increases consciousness of ethnic differentiation and hostility between groups. The trends of ethnic conflict through time are schematically represented in Chart III.

As formal de-colonization approached and the Trinidadian masses became increasingly mobilized into the political arena, relations between Negroes and Indians deteriorated. When Britain ruled, there could be peaceful if unfriendly coexistence. When it became possible for an indigenous group to control the state, the other group became increasingly anxious about the treatment it would receive. Ethnic conflict reached a height in the 1961 elections, because the party which won would probably lead Trinidad to independence under a new constitution.

Two major parties contested the election. The People's National Movement's social base was Negro and Colored. It first assumed joint power

Chart IV

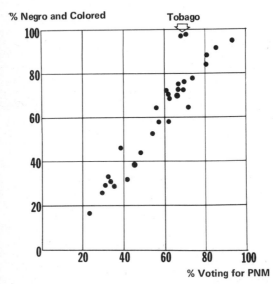

Source: Data from S. Ryan, "The Transition to Nationhood in Trinidad and Tobago, 1797–1962" (Ph.D. diss., Cornell University, 1966), pp. 494–502.

with the Crown in 1956, and since that time had almost fully West Indianized the civil service. The bulk of these appointees, however, were either Negro or Colored.[9] In addition, most of the government's development expenditure was concentrated in predominantly Negro urban areas. Hence, ethnic conflict involved not only control of agencies which had ultimate control over social conflict, but also of ethnic differentiation in the distribution of scarce jobs and funds.

Opposing the PNM was the Democratic Labor Party, whose social base was predominantly Indian. Choice between the two parties was nearly entirely determined by race. Chart IV cross-tabulates the proportion of Negroes and Coloreds in each of thirty constituencies against the proportion of votes going to the PNM. A similar pattern of racial polarization is revealed when proportions of Indians and DLP votes are compared. Sample survey data supports this ecological evidence of racial polarity (see Table II). Although the PNM's majority ethnic base won it twenty of the thirty legislative seats, the corresponding alienation of the large Indian minority weakened the PNM's ability to transform the colonial division of labor. The reasons for this will be clear after describing the structures supporting the colonial division of labor and the evolution of the PNM from a normatively oriented movement to a remuneratively oriented machine.

Table II
Race and Reported Vote in Three Sampled Constituencies

	Indians (n=215)	Negroes (n=167)	Total (n=382)
Voted for:			
DLP	95.8	7.8	57.3
PNM	4.2	92.2	42.7
Total	100.0	100.0	100.0

Source: Bahadoorsingh, "Trinidad Electoral Politics," p. 60.

THE CRISIS ECONOMY

The economy of Trinidad, based upon mining and refining of oil and asphalt, makes the nation one of the wealthiest primary-producing territories on a per capita basis.[8] Its slow rate of growth is explained not in terms of the lack of a sufficient surplus to spur development, but in terms of structural arrangements which prevent this surplus from being effectively utilized. The main feature of an economy organized around the colonial division of labor ". . . is that the long period rate of growth is very largely determined by one exogenous variable (export) and one structural relation (the income elasticity of demand for imports)."[9]

This exogenous variable interacts with the structural relation to produce recurrent *short-run* crises due to continual pressure on the nation's foreign exchange position. The income elasticity of demand for imports is greater than one, while the net total of foreign exchange rises less than expansion of exports. The resulting pressure on the nation's foreign exchange position is eased by measures such as private capital inflows, foreign aid, and commercial credit. All these measures require metropolitan cooperation.

The economy is also under *long-run* pressures because production organized around the colonial division of labor fails to satisfy the aspirations of rapidly growing population. Institutions controlled by and profiting the metropoles are key components of the colonial division of labor. Hence, transforming the colonial division of labor not only damages short-run aggregate metropolitan interests by ending the appendage functions of the primary-producing economy, but also damages specific, politically powerful metropolitan corporations.

In response to primary-producers' attempts at basic structural changes, metropolitan participation in measures alleviating foreign exchange pressures can be withdrawn. Withdrawal of metropolitan participation leads to a severe economic crisis intended to bring down the primary-producer's government or change its policies. The dilemma is this: in order to alleviate *long-run* pressures which cannot be handled within the framework of the colonial division of labor, the nation must move against institutions controlled by metropolitan corporations. Due to the foreign exchange pressure generated by the colonial division of labor, the nation is vulnerable to *short-run* sanctions which can cripple its economy and thus thwart attempts toward rapid structural transformation. The ability of the nation to withstand these sanctions depends upon: (1) Internal political mobilization creating the collective will to endure hardships; (2) mobilizing support from other nations to counter metropolitan sanctions.

The *short-run* crises due to pressure on Trinidad's foreign exchange position frequently result from these factors: (1) Because export sectors are controlled by metropolitan corporations, a significant percentage of expanded export earnings flows to metropolitan countries as profits; (2) since import-substitution is often directly financed by private metropolitan capital, foreign profits reduce the foreign-exchange savings. Furthermore, import-substituting operations frequently involve assembly of finished components into final goods, e.g., assembly of television sets or radios. Such assembly operations are often financed by metropolitan firms in order to hold primary-producers' markets. Metropolitan control of import-substitution can also snuff out existing or potential indigenous efforts in the same industry. When the above factors are added to the tax and tariff holidays granted to newly established firms, the result is that there is little net savings in foreign exchange for the national economy from import-substitution.

Thirdly, price manipulations by foreign firms can also add to the foreign exchange squeeze. The petroleum firms in Trinidad are branches of integrated international corporations. "Integration" means that the same corporation controls the firm extracting a raw product and the firm purchasing this product. Integrated firms set buying and selling prices so as to maximize financial benefits through comparison of tax arrangements in different nations. For example, if taxes in the country of extraction get too high, the integrated corporation sells the raw product at a very low price to its metropolitan branch. Since the corporation is selling its product to itself, it takes a large markup at home where there is a better tax arrangement. Only the corporation knows the actual costs of extraction and refining. A large part of Trinidad's public revenue is raised from taxes based on a profit-sharing formula with the petroleum corporations. Hence, price manipulations by the oil firms exert a direct and deleterious effect on Trinidad's development financing and its foreign exchange earnings from petroleum exports.

Fourthly, demand for imports is high both in average and marginal terms. Tariffs are relatively low and there are a few quantitative restrictions on imports. Demands for imports is raised by such commonly noted characteristics as the demonstration effect created by the life styles of expatriates and the upper ranks of bureaucrats and politicians; the shift of population to urban areas, which involves life styles characterized by a higher propensity for imported goods; and the effects of mass media. The net result is that, as the economy grows, spending of foreign exchange is likely to outstrip earnings of foreign exchange, unless steps are taken by the government.

The response of the government to this foreign exchange pressure has been to run down reserves somewhat, increase the rate of taxation on mineral corporations, and institute mild increases in tariffs. Reliance has also been placed upon private capital inflows from the metropoles, aid from metropolitan governments, and commercial credit.[10] The National Planning Commission recognizes that these measures do not alleviate *long-run* pressures on the economy. Among these long-run pressures are: (1) A population expansion and density matched by few other nations.[11] (2) The rapid expansion of population, which leads to an increasingly broad-based age pyramid—i.e., an increasing percentage of the population is under 15. Because most of these young people have not yet entered the work force, an increasing percentage of the economic surplus must be used to support nonproductive persons. Furthermore, expansion of the school system to accommodate these young people requires increasing recurrent capital expenditures, some of which could be used to finance current industrialization. Finally, age and unemployment vary inversely. Associated with this is a drift of young people to the cities, where a concentration of young, unemployed, and restive persons accumulates. (3) There is the secular, downward trend in prices paid for primary products. (4) Trinidad's oil resources will only last about another five years or so, unless new offshore deposits are discovered. The National Planning Commission states that revenue from oil is a short-run windfall which must be used wisely to speed industrialization based on light manufactures for export. Little progress has been made in this direction: the export of manufactures amounted to only $4.4 million W.I. in 1964. The explanation is to be found in a government policy which avoids a confrontation with metropolitan interests controlling the peaks of the economy; hence, the distribution of its surplus.

Trinidad's present policies may be labeled "weak planning" or "the open, orthodox model." This model restricts governmental functions to providing infrastructure, financial incentives, and other services to private firms, many of which are expected to be directly financed by metropolitan capital. Weak planning is planning largely on paper. The objectives of the plan are voluntary goals honored largely in the breach by private enterprise. Heavy reliance is placed upon metropolitan investment and aid, especially to meet short-run foreign exchange crises. The failure of weak planning to effectuate rapid growth has been patent in all the primary-producing nations.

Authentic planning, in contrast, entails direct mobilization of the nation's resources, material and human, by a relatively draconian state. The purpose of authentic planning is to rapidly create links within the economy in place of subservient links to metropoles. The objective is not autarchy, but a new pattern of trade in which the primary-producing nation is a partner rather than an appendage. Metropolitan opposition to even the initial moves toward authentic planning by a primary-producing nation is not due to a mere distaste for draconian government:

> The possibility of conflict with foreign interests is inherent in planning. The realization of this, perhaps largely subconscious, helps explain why in some instances the governments of the great powers, and their associated financial organizations, try to prevent the adoption of exchange control and an expansionist policy; these involve, particularly in the long run, raising issues of the treatment of foreign companies, which the latter would prefer not to be on the agenda of public discussion.[12]

If Trinidad were to abandon the patent failure of the open, orthodox model of development and move toward authentic planning, commodity agreements and the measures easing its short-run foreign exchange pressures could be terminated by the metropoles. Ensuing hardships would require strong internal political mobilization to support the government. External aid would be required to shelter the small island-nation from economic strangulation or military intervention by the metropoles. Neither of these supports is likely to be forthcoming under present conditions. Internal support is eroded by ethnic polarity in politics. Secondly, reliance of PNM rule upon distribution of patronage and the failure of any viable alternative to appear makes it an unlikely vehicle to rally the populace to endure the hardships of authentic planning. The likelihood of external support will be treated at the end of the next section.

MONEY-MAKING AND POLITICS

The peaks and a good part of the middle echelons of the Trinidadian economy are controlled by metropolitan interests: oil, asphalt, sugar, banking, and larger commercial enterprises. Metropolitan control has meant exclusion of nonwhites from decision-making positions in the economy. Consequently, politics and administration, in addition to medicine, law, and smaller-scale commerce, emerged as the chief routes to upward social mobility for the indigenous population. Politics became a primarily remunerative affair:

> To the professional, politics provided the fastest way out of obscurity. In a claustrophobic society which offered non-whites so few opportunities for social and economic advancement, politics became the principal instrument for the achievement of status and wealth.[13]

There arose a politics of patronage which was reminiscent of ethnic politics in turn-of-the-century American cities. The professional politician delivered services which the average ill-educated and low-paid Trinidadian was unable to obtain for himself from a state which was aloof and complicated. Like the ward heelers of old Chicago and New York, the professional politician needed funds to pay professional canvassers, opinion leaders of ethnic communities who could deliver a bloc of votes for a price, and enumerators to pad voting lists and/or ferret out dead voters who might become posthumous enthusiasts for the opposition. Politics was an entrepreneurial activity which led to upward social mobility.

The limitations of entrepreneurial politics was the scarcity of services which could be provided. Only some politicians could win, and only a limited number of voters could then receive favors. The system was not successful in satisfying mass desires for a rapid expansion in employment opportunities, better wages, improved housing, and so on. Political competition became vicious, because to lose an election was to lose a higher standard of living made possible by payoffs for services rendered. Politics was popularly labeled dirty and corrupt.

The People's National Movement first appeared in 1956, with the intention of replacing entrepreneurial politics by a disciplined, normatively oriented party which would lead Trinidad to political independence and rapid economic growth. After the PNM won a plurality of legislative seats in the 1956 elections, Britain helped consolidate the party's power because it espoused the open, orthodox model of planning. By 1956, Britain had learned from her Asian experiences that formal de-colonization did not mean the destruction of her business interests if the reins of power were handed to "responsible" nationalists.

Responsible meant "not radical." The PNM had never enunciated policies which entailed an assault upon the metropolitan-controlled institutions dominating Trinidad's economy. It would be riskier to face a chaotic situation later, in which there was strong agitation for independence spearheaded by more radical leadership, than to gradually relinquish power to a "reasonable" PNM. There was little danger in letting orthodox blacks and browns replace whites in the political and administrative agencies keeping order within the framework of the colonial division of labor.

Once in power, the PNM announced an orthodox, open model of development which still provides the framework for the regime's development activities. Both the metropolitan corporations and the Crown were content. But the Trinidadian masses expected a new order once black and brown faces appeared in government offices. These high expectations provided the incentives which changed Trinidadian politics from a remunerative to a normative activity during the early years of PNM rule. These expectations reached a peak during a dispute in 1959 over the location of American military bases in Trinidad.

Though none of the PNM's demands were radical, the rhetoric and style of its public stance gave the impression of radicalism. Years of pent-up mass resentments against the white-dominated social and economic order were focused on the dispute. Making the Americans evacuate their base at Chaguaramas became the great symbol of the impending new order. (Substantively, the demand was that the United States pick another site *within* Trinidad, not make a final exit.)

When the PNM accepted a settlement which allowed the Americans to remain at Chaguaramas in return for increased foreign aid and other benefits, the popular shock was profound. It became clear that the PNM was not leading Trinidad down the path toward a new order. This realization undercut the system of incentives which contributed to the rise of the PNM. If the PNM's past statements and actions had been kept in mind, the shock would not have been so profound. Perhaps the PNM had adopted its radical style in the dispute in order to strengthen its bargaining position with the United States. Yet the fact remains that hopes were aroused and then dashed, hopes which had provided the incentives for a transition from entrepreneurial to normative politics.

When independence was attained in 1962, the PNM found itself governing within the same socioeconomic structure as had the Crown. Like the Crown, it became occupied with the same tasks of preserving "law and order" within the framework of the colonial division of labor.

There had arisen a core of politicians and administrators whose new positions of wealth and power gave them a stake in the smooth functioning of the existing system. It was not long before the government moved against its earlier supporters such as trade unionists or intellectuals who now threatened to disrupt the system.

Because the upper reaches of the economy remained essentially a white preserve, politics and the newly won control over the civil service still provided the chief means for social mobility. Opportunities for mobility through politics and administration were more abundant than under the colonial regime, but the basic facts remained the same. Only the political rhetoric had changed. When it became clear in the popular consciousness that no new order was in store, the people copied the actions of Economic Man. Rationally ignoring the rhetoric, they acted to maximize their interests within the opportunity structure provided by the colonial division of labor. Entrepreneurial politics returned, but under the aegis of a strong, permanently organized party instead of the shifting alliances of individuals and short-lived parties that characterized the forties and early fifties. This was not without advantage for the Trinidadian people, because the PNM's organization could—and did—strike better bargains with metropolitan interests than could shifting alliances. But the net gain constituted marginal returns within the confines of the colonial division of labor.

The evolution of the PNM from normative to entrepreneurial politics did not take place without bitter incriminations from former supporters. It was possible for the PNM to ignore these incriminations because there was not any readily available alternative. The PNM, despite its sincere efforts, had never been able to attract many Indians. Most Indians remained anti-PNM, but did not have enough votes to elect a new government. It was unlikely that they could form a coalition with a sufficient number of Negroes and Coloreds to form an electoral majority.

Most Negroes and Coloreds viewed the PNM as *their* party, despite disillusion with the PNM's evolution. They could look at the color of the large majority of faces in government bureaus and the uses to which development funds were put and conclude that the party had diverted a segment of the economic surplus from whites to people of African descent. They expected that an Indian-led party would do the same for its own. In an underdeveloped and slowly growing economy benefits were scarce and likely to remain so. At least what was available had been directed toward blacks.

Given the lack of any present viable alternative for the Negro and Colored majority, the PNM can maintain its power in the short run. Because Indians are reproducing at a faster rate than Negroes and Coloreds, they will eventually be able to outvote blacks at the polls. More importantly, the open, orthodox model of development is failing to generate sufficiently rapid growth and structural changes to alleviate *long-run* economic pressures. Despite initial sincere beliefs that weak planning would spur development, Trinidad's politicians and administrators are painfully conscious of its failure.

Moves toward authentic planning would bring metropolitan sanctions. Because Trinidad is so small, its location not very strategic, and its oil not a very important part of world supplies, nations of the Eastern block would have no strong incentive to come to its aid. Nor is it likely that other primary-producing nations would be willing or able to provide help. The first condition necessary for a successful transition to authentic planning is a changed world context in which other nations exhibit greater capacities and determination to resist metropolitan actions against primary-producers.

Secondly, the PNM's advocacy of weak planning and the failure of the open, orthodox model would have demonstrated to the Trinidadian people that no new order was in store, even if the issue of the military bases had never arisen. The Chaguaramas dispute merely hastened this consciousness. Metropolitan aid and capital inflow alleviates *short-run* pressures on the nation's foreign exchange position, but does not alleviate *long-run* pressures. These long-run pressures will lead to increasing tendencies toward social disorder and discontent. From this disorder and discontent there must arise an intense political mobilization which creates the collective will to endure the hardships of authentic planning and draconian action by the state. It is unlikely that the entrepreneurial PNM could serve as the vehicle for this mobilization. A new team of political organizers which can bridge the gap between Indians and Negroes must arise. The alternative to authentic planning will be economic stagnation and a repressive state propped up by the metropoles. Only through *political mobilization*, both of its own populace and of external aid to encounter metropolitan sanctions, can Trinidad gain control over her economic surplus and avoid becoming a permanent and impoverished appendage to corporate capitalism.

Notes

1. When the ratio of total intermediate output is computed from a thirteen-sector input-output matrix on a basis which excludes imports so as to gain a measure of interdependence within Trinidad's territorial economy, the level of interindustry relations is seen to be very low. The computed ratio of .233 compares, for example, with figures of .431 for Japan and .409 for the United States. See A. Francis, "A Note on Inter-Industry Relations in the Economy of Trinidad and Tobago, 1962" (Trinidad, Central Statistics Office, Research Paper No. 2, 1965), p. 70.

2. Openness may be measured by the ratio of foreign trade to national production. The *World Handbook of Political and Social Indicators* ranks countries in terms of a ratio of exports plus imports to Gross National Product. The highest ratio assigned to any nation included in the table is 103. Using GNP as a base, which would lower the ratio, Trinidad exhibits a ratio of 123.8, based on figures from W. Demas, *The Economics of Development in Small Countries* (Montreal: McGill University Press, 1965), p. 104.

3. For example, agricultural resources are still skewed toward plantations exporting sugar. Consequently, in a nation where agriculture is still the largest single employer of manpower, $76 million W.I. worth of food was imported out of a total food consumption of $235 million W.I. See Trinidad and Tobago Chamber of Commerce, *Trinidad and Tobago Yearbook*, 1965, pp. 208–210. Nearly all their food imports came from metropolitan nations. Neither technological nor cost restraints appear to prevent Trinidad from producing a good deal more of its own food supply. Rather, it is the institutional legacy of the plantation system.

4. Government of Trinidad and Tobago, *Census, 1960*, II A, Table 5.

5. *Ibid.*, III G, Table 8.

6. For example, in the ward of Tacarigua, 70 percent of the males employed in agriculture are Indians, while only 45.9 percent of the male working population in that ward is Indian. Similarly, while 35.2 percent of the male working population in Tacarigua is Negro, only 13.6 percent of those employed in agriculture are Negro.

7. S. Ryan, "The Transition to Nationhood in Trinidad and Tobago, 1797–1962" (Ph.D. diss., Cornell University, 1966), p. 487.

8. In a list of 122 nations, Trinidad ranked 33 in GNP per capita, with only six other Third World nations ahead. See B. Russet *et al.*, *World Handbook*

of Political and Social Indicators (New Haven: Yale University Press, 1964), pp. 154–155.

9. D. Seers, "The Stages of Economic Development of a Primary Producer in the Middle of the Twentieth Century," *Economic Bulletin* (Ghana), 1963, p. 58. See pp. 163–180 above.

10. The foreign exchange squeeze is evidenced by a significant gap between Gross *Domestic* Product and Gross *National* Product. For example, net factor payments to the rest of the world in 1962 amounted to $113.6 million W.I. out of a GDP of $1,005.7 million W.I. (Government of Trinidad and Tobago, 1964). The foreign exchange implications of the colonial division of labor are revealed in starker form by comparing total merchandise exports in 1964—$694 million W.I.—with the $288 million W.I., short of unrequited receipts, accruing to the national economy. Unrequited receipts amounted to $63 million W.I.: $17 million from foreign capital inflow, $13 million from public foreign loans, and $33 million from bank financing.

11. Trinidad and Tobago ranks sixteenth out of 131 nations in terms of population per square mile, and fifteenth out of 155 in terms of population per 1,000 hectares of agricultural land. It is rated seventeenth in annual rate of natural increase in population.

12. Seers, "The Stages of Economic Development," p. 64.

13. Ryan, "The Transition to Nationhood in Trinidad and Tobago," p. 246.

Malcolm Caldwell

Problems of Socialism in Southeast Asia

Southeast Asia is a vast fragmented tropical area occupying the southern
fringe of the Asian continent between India and China. It extends more
than 3,000 miles east to west, and 2,000 north to south. The population
of over 225 million is growing with explosive force, and is expected to
more than double before the end of the century. Seventy-five to 80 percent
of the people are still engaged in agriculture, and primitive methods,
inadequate education, the absence of incentives, landlordism, and lack of
capital spell very low living standards. All the countries of the region,
with the exception of Thailand (which was never colonized), have attained
political independence since the Second World War.

One must be careful of generalization. Southeast Asia is not homogeneous: there are national, ethnic, linguistic, cultural, and religious
divisions, to a greater extent, in fact, than is true of Europe. There are
wandering hill tribes living by hunting and·"slash and burn" cultivation,
as well as modern commercial-industrial cities. The historical experiences
of the countries that go to make up Southeast Asia have differed sharply,
before, during, and since the colonial period.

Still, there are common problems which should not be overlooked.
The rural masses are everywhere oppressed by the same, or similar,
congeries of circumstances—growing population, fragmentation of
holdings, chronic indebtedness, usury, concentration of landownership,
low productivity. Politically, the outstanding problem is the evolution of
appropriate institutions, with viable indigenous roots, which will afford
the peasants and other classes an opportunity to voice and right their

Originally published in *The Socialist Register 1966* (New York: Monthly Review
Press, 1966). Copyright © 1966 by The Merlin Press, Ltd.

grievances—in societies whose entire previous experience has consisted of either despotism, whether local or colonial, or grafted representative democracy, the social impact of which has only been skin-deep, since it has in fact disguised "top-down" rule.

The countries of Southeast Asia are, on the mainland, Burma, Thailand, Laos, Cambodia, and Vietnam, and, in the Malay world of isthmus and archipelago, Malaysia and Singapore, Indonesia and the Philippines.[1] Present boundaries correspond, at best, only roughly with precolonial cultural-historical realities; map-making was left to the colonial powers, and was still in process in the post-1945 period.

Western contact dates from the sixteenth century, and the objective was the purchase or seizure of commodities prized in the markets of Europe. In the early stages, European merchants fitted themselves in to the existing pattern, as traders, plunderers, and rulers of the ports they were able to capture and hold. Penetration into the hinterland was sporadic and temporary, contingent upon the needs of security or acquisition of local produce. The indigenous social structure remained unaffected: at the base the homeostatic, amoeboid, and broadly self-sufficient[2] village community, growing rice and, depending upon geographical location, fishing, holding land in common, but with hereditary familial tenure of plots, and to a large extent in normal times self-governing; superimposed upon this, the local ruler and his retinue of advisers, soldiers, concubines, etc., with whom should be included the craft specialists such as silversmiths and ordnancers, dependent upon engrossing the agricultural surplus by means of exactions on the villages and, often, upon piracy; and, finally, the traders—inland peddlers and coastal and ocean-going merchants—both indigenous and foreign. (Compared with neighboring India and China, Southeast Asia as a whole was, for geographical and related administrative-logistical reasons, lightly populated and also, and partly as a result, comparatively prosperous, and so always exerted a strong demographic pull.)

Expansion inland by the European powers and extension of their political authority and economic mastery (and therefore of their intrusion into and influence upon indigenous class structure) was patchy and piecemeal until the second half of the nineteenth century, when a more uniform pattern of "forward movement" emerged. The two most affected regions prior to the nineteenth century were Java, first ranking island of Indonesia in terms of population though not in size, and the Philippines.

In Java, the Dutch East India Company introduced, in addition to mere collection of produce, a system of forced production and delivery of commercial crops, some of them, such as coffee, specially introduced for the purpose; basically, however, as regards impingement upon local social organization, this was still tribute, and the company's major impact was felt in the elimination of the Javanese merchant classes in the interests of Dutch monopoly. In the Philippines, most of the islands, with the excep-ion of those in the south, which were largely Muslim, were brought under direct Spanish administration and their inhabitants converted to Catholicism; huge landholdings were amassed by the Church, Spanish corporations and individuals, and wealthy Filipinos and mestizos (those of mixed blood), as a result of colonial land policy, while former peasant owner-occupiers were progressively impoverished by debt and forced to surrender their land and become tenants, sharecroppers, and laborers.

The tempo of Western interest in the region changed and quickened in the nineteenth century in tune with economic developments in Europe and North America and concomitant world price changes.[3] The accent shifted from consumption crops—tea, sugar, coffee, tobacco—though production of these continued and indeed greatly increased—to the growing and extracting of industrial raw materials; tin, copra, cinchona, petroleum, and rubber. The tribute system was inappropriate to the satis-faction of the new demands and a great surge of direct Western investment characterized the last half of the century and the years before the First World War. From 1853 to 1873 world primary product prices were rising, and around the latter year a whole series of developments carried the process of economic development of Southeast Asia forward—the opening of the Suez Canal (1869), the extension of the telegraph cable to Singapore, the improvement of steamships, the onset of falling prices in the industrial countries, the industrialization of further Western countries, the growth of the canning industry, the popularity of bicycles with their solid rubber tires, and so on. From 1896 onward, with rising primary product prices again and the introduction of the automobile, the surge of investment became a tidal wave, which swept over and transformed the Southeast Asian society.

Western direct investment necessitated Western direct political control, both to safeguard investments and to ensure to the European, as opposed to the indigenous and alien Asian, investor every possible advantage. Everywhere that control was consolidated, with the sole exception of

Thailand, which nevertheless was forced, by the Bowring (1855) and subsequent treaties, to accept certain restrictions on her sovereignty which operated in favor of Western commerce and industry. In 1874, following the Pangkor Engagement with the Sultan of Perak, Britain expanded from her commercial footholds in Penang, Malacca, and Singapore, into the tin, and later rubber, estates of Pahang, Negri Sembilan, Perak, and Selangor in Malaya. In 1873, Holland launched the Atjeh war, to complete the pacification of Sumatra, focus of the new wave of investments in Indonesia. French occupation of Cochinchina (completed 1867) in southern Vietnam foreshadowed engulfment of the rest of Vietnam, Cambodia, and Laos. British conquest of Burma, begun in 1826, was completed by 1886. The Dutch and British defined their sphere of influence in Borneo in 1871. Spain opened tentative doors in the Philippines, long cocooned in feudal and theocratic stagnation, to international trade and investment.

Indigenous social structures could not survive this assault. By the introduction of money economy, by the destruction of local enterprises, by the incorporation of the traditional ruling classes into their administrative systems, and by the recruitment of local and attraction of alien wage labor, the European colonialists shook self-sufficient subsistence village economy to its foundations, uprooting, transplanting, and beheading the living organism with ruthless effectiveness.

The village now needed money, for paying taxes, for buying imported European goods, and for other transactions hitherto avoided or conducted by barter. How was it to be got? Men were reluctant to leave their homes to work in European-owned factories and plantations, and in any case wages were pitifully low, and competition from the imported Indian and Chinese coolies fierce. Villagers could, and did, turn from rice production to the growing of commercial crops, but in marketing and shipping these they were subject to the cheating and discrimination of the middlemen, often aliens, and the discouragement of the colonial authority, and in addition prices fluctuated in bewildering and apparently capricious ways. In these circumstances, the demand for money in the village invariably exceeded the supply.

This being the case, moneylending could hardly fail to be a lucrative business. Chinese and Indian usurers moved in to meet the steady demand for cash, charging rates of interest as high as the market could bear, and of course the more desperate the borrower the weaker his bargaining position. Traditional village usages had limited the harm a man could do to himself and his family by prodigality or lack of foresight. Now all limitations were swept aside. Apart from those places where the responsible political authority took positive steps to prevent land alienation—as with the Dutch in Indonesia, and the Thai government—more and more villagers found themselves surrendering the plots they had unwisely pledged as security for loans. Few understood the implications of either compound interest or European land law. They became rack-rented tenants or sharecroppers on the soil which had once been their own, or else were forced to move on to work as landless laborers or plantation coolies elsewhere. Naturally, it became no easier to escape from debt; in fact, the average peasant could anticipate a lifetime of almost unalleviated indebtedness. Even on Java, where the 1870 Dutch Agrarian Law sought to safeguard "native" rights in the soil, the sheer increase in numbers and consequent fragmentation of holdings, plus the distending pressures of the new money flows, helped to break up the village.

It was not only Chinese and Indian, and sometimes local, moneylenders who capitalized on the plight of the peasant catapulted into the money economy. Local landlords found the lending of money to their tenants and neighbors an extremely rewarding way of stepping up the extraction of profit from the soil. A tenant owing money to his landlord was in no position to haggle about his share in the harvest, and an indebted neighbor could be pressed to the point of surrendering his plot. But although a section of indigenous society was thus accumulating capital, it was not being used by the landlords in a productive way, but rather to step up traditional modes of expenditure and saving (purchase of buffaloes and precious stones and metal, ostentatious consumption).

Where enterprise and capital were required, and the Europeans did not care to, or were in no position to, provide it, it was forthcoming mostly from the Chinese, Indian, and other foreign communities. Often, as on Java, this was in large measure the outcome of preceding colonial policy which had actively encouraged the alien and discouraged local enterprise. But the result exacerbated the resentment and sense of injustice among the exploited rural masses, who, having been depressed into conditions of misery and hopelessness from Burma to the Philippines, neverthelesss saw aliens waxing fat in their midst.

In these circumstances, an amorphous protopolitical consciousness developed among the peasantry. As long as rural society had survived in its traditional form more or less intact, the notion that any action on their part could materially change their way of life had not arisen among the villagers. At infrequent intervals and in isolated incidents the peasants might rise in blind anger and despair to murder and pillage in protest against cruel oppression or intolerable exactions. Such action could be construed as nothing but a gesture of hopelessness. Western penetration forged important changes. Dissatisfaction was no longer local, but widespread throughout the rural areas. In Burma, where by the First World War the best part of Lower Burma was in the hands of absentee alien landlords, lawlessness and violence were endemic. Significantly, indications of more coordinated protest first appeared in Java[4] and the Philippines,[5] the areas which had endured the most disturbing Western presence. The dissatisfaction was not at first directed exclusively against the colonial powers. The peasants' concern was land, and their anger was vented against the immediate agents of their disinheritance—the Indian and Chinese moneylenders and middlemen, and the indigenous landlords (the Saya San rebellion in Burma in 1930 affords an example). But here is to be sought the germ of nationalism. Awareness of their social dislocation gave the peoples of Southeast Asia a consciousness of common destiny.[6]

As regards the nonagricultural sector, it was no part of the Western purpose to encourage local industry; it was markets that were sought, not competition. Traditional handicraft industries were hard hit by the competition of cheap mass-produced Western imports, and many disappeared or shrank. Modern manufacturing industry did not appear to replace them on the spot, except to the extent convenient to the European sector. The main sources of nonagricultural employment open to local people apart from mining and the public services were in the processing of commercial crops, the repairing and servicing of machinery and vehicles, and in the handful of factories producing such commodities as it was uneconomic to ship from Europe (cement, beer, soft drinks, biscuits, etc.). There was, therefore, a negligible proletariat, although many Marxist movements in Southeast Asia concentrated, in the first instance, the greater part of their energies on what workers there were. It was not until 1953, for example, that Aidit, secretary-general of the Indonesian Communist Party (PKI), in an important article reoriented the party with the statement that "The agrarian revolution is the essence of the people's democratic revolution in Indonesia."[7]

The stirrings of nationalism in the countryside were at first, therefore, headless. But parallel developments were in process of making good the deficiency. The colonial powers were increasingly in need of all kinds of clerical, technical, and semiprofessional services. A small section of the local people were therefore granted the privilege of Western education. However narrow this education in practice, it did facilitate the acquisition and dissemination of Western ideas. Once employed, the educated Southeast Asian was most commonly in a humiliating position of inferiority with respect to Europeans of equivalent education; this, coming on top of the subjugation of his country, naturally attracted him to the revolutionary stream of Western thought, to the Leninist explanation of imperialism, the liberal ideal of national self-determination, the socialist blueprint for economic development. These enabled him to rationalize, articulate, and systematize his, and his country's experience. Moreover, socialist ideas matched his own ambivalence: they were both of the West and critical of the West. The spread of literacy also brought knowledge of the achievements of existing nationalist movements, such as those in China and India, and awareness of external events as shattering in their implications as the victory of Japan over Russia in 1905, and the European civil war of 1914–1918.

This predominantly urban and often Western-orientated petite bourgeoisie was not ideally adapted to the task of harnessing the energies of the profoundly discontented rural people, and in fact religious revival in many cases preceded them out into the countryside; Islam and Buddhism were more immediately available rallying points than imported ideas of nationhood and anti-imperialism. For various reasons, however, religious teachers failed to consolidate their hold, and the organizations they had helped bring into existence—the Young Men's Buddhist Association in Burma and the Jam Yat Khain and Sarekat Dagang Islamiyah in Indonesia, for example—fell most often into the hands of leaders who, though nominally of the appropriate religion, were far more secular-political in their outlook and aims.[8]

In the aftermath of the First World War, nationalism and anti-colonialism developed rapidly. The example of the Philippine revolution of 1896–1902 struck no immediate echoes, but there were uprisings led by the Communist Party (PKI) in Indonesia (1926–1927) and by the Viet Nam Quoc Dan Dang (Vietnamese Nationalist Party) in Vietnam (1930). The first Southeast Asian trade union, the Union of Rail and Tramway

Personnel (VSTP) in Indonesia, founded in 1908, was the precursor of many, and militant unionism had spread even to Malaya by the 1930's.

Two things strengthened the association of nationalist and socialist thinking: the Russian Revolution and the impact of the interwar depression. The obvious direct attraction of the first was quickly followed up by the forging of links between the nationalist movements and Russian leaders. The depression had catastrophic consequences for Southeast Asia, since the bottom completely fell out of the market for most of the commodities produced in the region.[9] "Few countries," wrote an economist, "suffered a more violent contraction of economic activity in the thirties than the Netherlands Indies."[10] Some paid-off Indian and Chinese labor drifted home, but there had been in the prosperous twenties a marked tendency for immigrant labor to bring over wives and families and make the countries of Southeast Asia "home." Political events in India and China were reflected in movements among the Indian and Chinese communities in Southeast Asia—notably in the growth of communism among the latter. Paid-off local labor could return to the village, but this simply meant that the village, which could ill afford it, had to provide the "welfare services" that the colonial authorities failed to provide. Smallholders, who had taken to the commercial production of export crops during the boom years, were now driven back to subsistence farming. Moreover, under the various commodity control schemes adopted to shore up prices, the local smallholder was blatantly discriminated against in the interests of the generally high-cost European estates.[11] As a microcosm of capitalism in action, the interwar years could hardly fail to leave a clear imprint upon nationalist thinking; poverty, injustice, and inefficiency were seen to accompany the wild and irrational economic fluctuations, in the grip of which the capitalist Western powers appeared to be powerless.

The development of representative institutions during these years was extremely uneven from country to country. The Volksraad in Indonesia remained unrepresentative and virtually powerless, while the French made little attempt to satisfy even the mildest of nationalist demands in Indochina, crushing all opposition with indiscriminate ruthlessness (and thus helping to sow the seeds of Vietnam's subsequent agony). On the other hand, British Burma by 1937 had moved by stages to the point where there was virtual internal self-government, and the Commonwealth of the Philippines was inaugurated in 1935. Thailand, by the revolution of 1932, moved from control by the royal family to a constitutional monarchy, with at least the relevant apparatus of parliamentary institutions.

Development in this direction was abruptly halted by the Japanese invasion. Southeast Asian nationalists had long had their eyes on Japan, and some of the leaders had visited and studied there. Before Pearl Harbor, the Japanese had already begun to train Southeast Asian nationalists in guerrilla warfare, looking to their assistance in defeating the European colonial powers.[12] Between Pearl Harbor and the middle of 1942, the Japanese in effect took over the whole of Southeast Asia; the Vichy French handed over Indochina, Thailand agreed to come into the war on the Axis side, and the other countries were invaded.

The Japanese period was important for a variety of reasons. First of all, the speed and decisiveness with which the Japanese forces defeated and humiliated the European armies made an indelible impression on the peoples of the region. The myth of white supremacy had been dealt a death blow, and it would never again be possible for a handful of white troops and administrators to hold down millions of Asian subjects. The Japanese rammed home the point by publicly exposing European prisoners to the most menial of tasks. Second, the Japanese presence gave the nationalists training and experience in the use of arms. This was partly by intention, as with the Indonesian-manned and officered auxiliary armies of Java, Sumatra, and Bali, and the Burmese Independence Army. But it was also a result of the resistance movements that grew up throughout Southeast Asia as the initial goodwill or at least neutrality toward the Japanese gave way to disillusion and hatred. Naturally, it was allied policy to help these resistance movements to the maximum extent possible, and this was an extremely useful source of arms for the guerrillas—the Malayan People's Anti-Japanese Army, the People's Anti-Japanese Resistance Army in the Philippines (usually known as the Hukbalahap), the constituents of the Anti-Fascist People's Freedom League in Burma, the Viet Nam Doc Lap Dong Minh Hoi (Viet Minh), in Indochina. A third important result of Japanese occupation was the precipitous promotion of layers of Southeast Asian administrators, who had, under the colonialists, been restricted to the lower echelons of the service. This was important training for the tasks that lay ahead, because all the European powers had to some extent or another been guilty of culpable neglect of education and of discrimination in employment.[13] A fourth factor was the encouragement, direct and indirect again, given to the development of local nationalism. Of course it was the Japanese intention to pass themselves off as "liberators," but their concessions were extremely limited until defeat began to loom. In Burma and the Philippines, where ready collaborators were found among the politicians, "independence" was declared by the Japanese in 1943. In Indonesia, where the nationalist leadership divided between those who took to the hills and those who tried to wrest every advantage from cooperation with the invaders, the Japanese allowed the collaborators, who included Sukarno and Hatta, to propagate the national language (Bahasa Indonesia), and to travel widely throughout the country stirring up anti-colonialist feeling and organizing. Later, an Independence Preparatory Committee was sanctioned, headed by Sukarno, and it was the deliberations of this body which laid the foundations for post-independence policy and organization. Sukarno proclaimed independence two days after the Japanese surrender. Finally, the Japanese afforded the Southeast Asian Communists an opportunity which they grasped to some effect. In the Philippines, Vietnam, and Malaya, Communists gained control of the resistance movement, and in Burma and Indonesia they played a substantial, though not controlling, part; only in the Free Thai underground was their role negligible.

The Japanese surrender found militant and uncompromising nationalist movements in being in all the former colonies, and their attitude and state of preparedness undoubtedly took the returning Western powers by surprise. I do not propose here to deal, except in passing, with Vietnam, for which an already voluminous and rapidly expanding literature exists,[14] but the postwar fate of the others I intend to review briefly before turning to analysis of the present position and the prospects for socialism.

The countries may be distinguished in terms of a number of variables. The Philippines, Burma, Malaya, and Singapore, all formerly American or British possessions, attained independence peacefully, at least in respect of relations between the colonial authority and the authority recognized by the colonial power as its successor. The two countries which had, prewar, advanced furthest along the road, the Philippines and Burma, were the first to secure independence, the former in 1946 and the latter in 1948. Indonesia, on the other hand, had to wage a long armed struggle against the Dutch before freedom was conceded in 1949, and the French fought until beaten at Dien Bien Phu in 1954, by which time, unfortunately for the Vietnamese, the Americans had taken over their role.

However, among the countries attaining independence peacefully, a distinction has to be made between Burma on the one hand, and the Philippines and Malaya on the other. Burma cut itself off completely on attaining independence, leaving the Commonwealth and embracing policies of nonalignment and internal self-reliance. Britain and America, however, maintained important economic and strategic links with Malaya and the Philippines. There were various significant reasons for this. Malaya and the Philippines both housed important military bases commanding areas considered strategically vital for the West, while Burma did not. Moreover, Burma got its independence before Dulles became the dominant figure in the American administration in 1953 and launched his aggressive brand of anti-communism in Southeast Asia. It is doubtful if he would have approved of the political complexion of the leaders to whom Britain entrusted power in 1948, for the Burmese nationalist movement, for all its divisions, was pretty much left-wing in character throughout its spectrum and Dulles would have interpreted the British grant of independence as a "surrender to Communism." In economic terms, Burma was of less importance to Western investors and manufacturers than either Malaya or the Philippines, and she had emerged from the war utterly devastated, half the national capital (excluding land) having been destroyed. These considerations, together with the adamant desire for freedom in all sections of Burmese society, undoubtedly carried weight with the British leaders.

Burma had had a singularly unfortunate colonial experience in terms of the demoralization and disintegration of traditional social structure and way of life, and it was natural that all sections of society should be anti-Western, to the extent of eventually virtually closing the Burmese borders to visitors from the West. There were, in contrast, important sections in Malayan and Philippine society that had benefited from colonial rule, and were therefore prepared to work with the West even after independence. Western policy was, in turn, predicated on their assumption of responsibility. The early introduction of "Filipinization" by the Americans meant that lucrative careers were open to talented Filipinos; moreover, it was indigenous businessmen who, along with Americans, benefited from the economic development of the islands—

in marked contrast to the situation in Burma where it was mainly immigrant Indians who benefited from Western rule. In Malaya, the Malays feared Chinese domination, and it had been British policy, by and large, to counterbalance Chinese wealth by placing political power in the hands of those who were regarded as the original inhabitants of the country; also, Malaya had enjoyed in the past, and was to enjoy again, unexampled prosperity under British rule, and there were therefore not lacking businessmen in the Chinese community who thought of British rule, and the continuation of British protection after independence, as safeguards for the profitable and untroubled continuation of private enterprise.

We have already noted, however, that there were left-wing, nationalist movements in Malaya and the Philippines, both dominated by the Communists, and having their origin in the anti-Japanese resistance. At the end of the war, both had ambitions to take over: the Huks (short for Hukbalahap cadres) declared a "people's democratic government," and the Malayan People's Anti-Japanese Army (MPAJA) had like pretensions. Both were short-lived, but that was not the end of the matter. The Huks continued fighting, and the Malayan Communist Party (MCP—former MPAJA) rose in rebellion in 1948. The subsequent campaigns against these two Communist-led insurrections were of great importance for the political future of the countries concerned. In both cases, the metropolitan powers played a significant, and in the case of Malaya at least, a decisive part; American military aid and advice at a vital point in the campaign against the Huks enabled Magsaysay (more or less) to break the back of their resistance, while it was British troops and police that bore the brunt of the long war against the Communists in Malaya.[15] Certain factors favored the security forces. In Malaya, the MCP was almost entirely Chinese in composition, and it was forced to operate in the predominantly Malay rural areas; during and immediately after the war, moreover, communal tensions had been heightened by Chinese reprisals on Malays who had collaborated with the Japanese (whose main repressive measures were, of course, aimed against the Chinese). In the Philippines, although the Filipino people had, to a much greater extent than the inhabitants of any other Southeast Asian country, resisted the Japanese with great tenacity and ferocity, and, therefore, had much sympathy with the old resistance now operating in their midst in the shape of a movement of social protest, the elites remained solidly committed to the American cause (as they had during the war gone over solidly to collaboration), and the flow of U.S. money and support in the end was the telling factor. Both emergencies had unfortunate repercussions for the trade union and labor movements, which were purged and suppressed for suspected sympathies with the guerrillas.

In Malaya and the Philippines, therefore, the elites who inherited power were confirmed in their anti-communism and in their pro-Western policies by the nature of the postwar internal events that faced them and by the way these were tackled. Although Burma's Communists also staged an insurrection, the governing groups there did not think it necessary to call in Western help to suppress it, and the matter remained a domestic one which did not mold foreign policy. It should be noted that the divergent experiences of the men who came to make up the armed forces of the Southeast Asian independent countries had great influence in determining their political outlooks: in Indonesia the army had been blooded in a long and bitterly contested anti-colonial war, and subsequently in fighting rebels who were aided by the imperialist powers, and therefore remained indelibly anti-imperialist in outlook (to the extent that the recent army take-over in Indonesia is unlikely to foreshadow radical changes in Indonesian foreign policy); in Malaya and the Philippines, however, the armed forces had gained their experience against left insurrectionary movements, with civilian allies, and therefore remained basically conservative in outlook.

Much that has been said about Malaya and the Philippines is true too for Thailand. As a result of the 1932 revolution, the greater part of the middle classes obtained satisfaction in terms of participation in power, prestige, and monetary reward, and the revolutionary left was therefore to a degree starved of articulate educated leadership. The army was, and is, an established, conservative, security-minded social group. The decision to side openly with the Americans after the war had critics at the time, but active opposition to it has, until recently, been slight. American aid has certainly benefited the urban areas, and the comparatively comfortable standard of living in the countryside has up to now afforded advocates of radical social change little in the way of purchase. It is convenient in much of what follows to regard Thailand as being in the same category as Malaya (after 1963, Malaysia) and the Philippines, while Burma has, in some important respects, more parallels to offer with Indonesia.

In Burma, as in Indonesia, the army developed directly out of the anti-Japanese resistance. In the years immediately following the end of the war, the armed forces of the Burmese Anti-Fascist People's Freedom League were an important factor in defeating British attempts to foist something less than full independence upon Burma, while in Indonesia the armed nationalists went straight from fighting the Japanese to fighting the returning Dutch. In neither country could the colonial power find any worthwhile body of local support against the translated resistance movements, and in general it may be said that the independent governments of the two countries arose out of the war and immediately postwar national liberation movements, whereas those of Malaya and the Philippines arose out of opposition to the equivalent movements in their own countries.

The distinction between what have come to be known as the "neocolonial" and the "nonaligned" powers in Southeast Asia is a significant one, and must be seen in connection with class relationships in the respective societies, in particular the relationship between the traditional ruling classes and landlords on the one hand, and the Western-educated middle classes on the other. In prewar Burma, big landlordism itself was largely a product of colonial rule, and aliens were the main beneficiaries. In addition, the educated Burmese was subject to restrictions on the kind of employment he might have expected, since Indians filled large sections of such employments as the public services and the professions. Nor was it easy for the local capitalists to take advantage of what business opportunities were available, since Indian capital had a stranglehold on petty trading and small business. A like situation prevailed in Indonesia, where internal trading was almost a monopoly of the Chinese, and the traditionally business-orientated indigenous groups, such as the Minangkabau, were hard pressed to keep a corner open for their own entrepreneurial activities. Here, too, the landlord was alienated from the Western-educated middle classes. The Dutch had absorbed the traditional ruling classes and big landowners into their local administration, and accorded them high material rewards and prestige, to the point almost of social equality in certain respects. For the Indonesian who had scrambled his way up the narrow and steep path of education, in contrast, all was different. Once employed, it would be at an inferior salary as compared with Europeans performing the same work and with equivalent or even inferior qualifications, and there were humiliating social discriminations to endure. At least in Burma the representative legislative institutions offered some opportunity for power, but in Indonesia the Volksraad was virtually powerless, and in any event, Indonesians were not in the majority.

All was different in Malaya and the Philippines. In the former, the nationalist movement right up to the Second World War was formless—there were extremely left-wing and anti-imperialist Chinese unions by the thirties, and, especially on the east coast, foci of discontent centered on Islam among the Malays. For the rest, the situation bore no strict comparison with that of its neighbors. For the educated Malays, there were privileged positions in the British administration, for the Chinese unlimited business opportunities, and in the professions employment for Indians and the educated of all communities. The poorer classes were fractured by racial differences—Indians on the estates and public services, Chinese in the mines and as city wage labor, Malays in the subsistence agricultural sector. The position was, then, that the educated of all communities could find chances to deploy their talents and earn satisfactory rewards, and at that stage there was insufficient resentment against the entrenched position of the Malay feudal classes in the civil service, police, etc., to generate much heat. Moreover, whatever their poverty, the Malay rural masses felt more loyalty to their own traditional ruling classes than they felt common cause with the poor of other communities. British policy kept possible sources of friction to a minimum by emphasizing separate development of the communities and sectors rather than integration. (The consequences are being felt today, since the chance to start promoting a national language and building up a common educational system was let slip, and newly independent Malaya had to start more or less from scratch in these touchy areas.)

The nationalist movement of the Philippines was, of course, by contrast, the oldest in Southeast Asia. But after its frustration at the hands of American power in the period 1899–1902, American policy successfully diverted its energies in the direction of cooperation in the attainment of independence by constitutional means. Especially after American entry into the First World War, "Filipinization" of the civil service, other public services, the judiciary, etc., was so rapid that for the large numbers of educated Filipinos there were plenty of opportunities to attain satisfactory positions of power, prestige, and high income. American respect for property rights had prevented them from touching the power and wealth of the landowning classes. Further, the Filipino businessman had greater scope than his counterpart in either Burma or Indonesia; there were Chinese in the Philippines, but their grip on commerce was weaker than in Indonesia, since Spanish policy had discouraged them whereas the Dutch had encouraged them. American policy, therefore, succeeded in creating a Filipino oligarchy of landowners, businessmen, and educated middle classes in the bureaucracy and the professions.

It can be appreciated, then, that the educated middle classes in Burma and Indonesia naturally wanted not just a political revolution leading to independence, but also a *social* revolution to blow the resented groups—alien traders, privileged landowners—out of their entrenched positions which were identified with colonial power. In Malaya and the Philippines, on the other hand, the landlords, businessmen, and educated middle classes could work together for political independence without seeking to disrupt the existing social system—indeed, their aim was to take over the system as it was, and simply fill the vacuum left by the departing colonialists; this identification of interests was immensely strengthened by the events of the postwar period, when the revolutionary uprisings exposed clearly the common danger which the privileged groups ran.

Not surprisingly, all the nationalist movements in Burma and Indonesia were "socialist," at least in vocabulary.[16] Colonialism was identified with the Western capitalist countries; to be anti-colonialist was to be anti-capitalist. For Indonesians the adjective "capitalistic" had the indelible connotation of ". . . selfish, predatory, forsaking of human and social interests in the search for profits, and thus inconsistent with the spirit of democracy,"[17] and the same could be said of the Burmese. Even those nationalist leaders with rather moderate views in practice had learned to apply Marxist vocabulary, as the most apt and appropriate available, to the situation in which they found themselves as colonial subjects. Moreover, unlike their counterparts in Malaya and the Philippines, the educated middle classes in Burma and Indonesia could, in a dichotomous class situation, see themselves as on the side of the workers and the peasants as against not only the colonialists and their alien Asian agents but also as against those indigenous elements of society (big landowners, top feudal administrators), committed to, and supported by, the colonialists. They could, therefore, formulate decidedly revolutionary aims. Moreover, all the nationalist groups paid at least lip service to the need for planning of some kind after the attainment of independence in order to promote development; "planning" was held up against the social chaos created by unregulated capitalism-colonialism. Socialism, then, was a broadly accepted, if rather undefined, aim of most of the nationalist groups.

The situation was different in Malaya and the Philippines. Although objectively it could be seen that whomever capitalism had benefited it had signally and flagrantly failed to benefit the mass of the people, here as in Burma and Indonesia, yet here those who might otherwise have given articulation to the misery of the masses were themselves integrated into, and interested in the survival of, the capitalist system. Anti-colonialism was not anti-capitalism; it was simply a search for a bigger role in the partnership with the colonial power, and a jockeying for advantage in the commercial and business fields. It was, in fact, part of the independence agreements with the metropolitan powers that they should retain military bases, important investments, and economic privileges, and that the new independent governments should favor private enterprise and foreign investment. Nor was there any incentive to tackle landlordism and feudalism in the countryside, since the big landed interests were fused in a coalition, which, whatever its internal strains, held together in a situation where there was the threat of organizations like the Huks and the MCP. The neo-colonial arrangement was one in which both parties benefited in the short run.

But the regimes which emerged in Burma and Indonesia were also coalitions, representing a great variety of interests, such as the bureaucracy, the local business community, intellectuals (writers, academics, teachers, etc.), religious groups, trade unions, peasant organizations, those landowners who had not been fatally identified with the colonial power, the armed forces, and so on. It is obvious that these were not, and could not be, cohesive or progressive coalitions: united, more or less, in the pursuit of independence, they were susceptible to divisive strains very quickly thereafter. For many of the social groups concerned, there was no desire for further social change now that the goal of independence had been attained, and with it greatly enhanced power, prestige, and wealth. The bureaucrats, for example, heirs to the top posts and privileges of the evicted colonial administrators, saw no reason for further social upheaval. Nor, by and large, did the army. For others, something remained to be accomplished, but that something fell far short of being revolutionary in scope or implications: for example, the local businessmen or would-be businessmen sought to take over some of the economic interests of the colonial power and to dislodge the "second layer of imperialism" in the shape of foreign Asian entrepreneurs. For yet others, the winning of political independence was but the first step in a long process of reshaping society on a socialist pattern. It was clear that these groups, whose intended social revolution went far beyond the displacement of the colonialists and alien Asians from the plum positions in society, were bound to clash with the new establishments, for their aims of land reform, progressive taxation, state enterprises, and egalitarianism clashed at almost every point with the interests of the new, national, bourgeoisie. The point has been well put by the Dutch historian Jan Pluvier, talking about Indonesia:

> In all governments between 1949 and 1957 the parties who predominated represented what might be called the middle classes—the economic bourgeoisie, the Western-educated intellectuals, the civil servants. It is true that only a very small minority belonging to these groups can be classed as bourgeois-capitalist and, as a result, the majority were able to adhere to some Socialist ideas without embarrassing consequences for themselves. But their socialism was directed more negatively against foreign (Dutch and Chinese) capitalism than positively towards any real program of socialization. Moreover, whatever disharmony might exist among these parties and on whatever issues they were fighting each other openly or intriguing against each other in secrecy, they were in complete agreement that the proletariat, whether rural or urban, should be kept in its place.[18]

Of the forces to the left, neither Social Democrats nor Communists fared very well. The Communists in both Burma and Indonesia staged armed revolts in 1948; the first goes on in the remoter parts of Burma to this day without seriously threatening to take over power, while the PKI was fairly easily crushed, and its recovery was slow and painful. As for the acknowledged Social Democrats, that is, those who believed that it would be possible to introduce land reform, redistributory legislation, and nationalization by constitutional means, they suffered from certain grievous weaknesses. Although exceptionally strong in the sense of counting in their ranks some of the ablest and finest men in Southeast Asia, they were woefully weak in terms of popular support and in organization. Also, they were, despite their intelligence, rather formalistic in their approach, transferring mechanically procedures and approaches appropriate in the West to the quite different circumstances of Southeast Asia.

However desirable it might be to have free elections, cabinet government, and stable parliamentary majorities as the bases for sound and rational (and incorrupt) economic planning, these things were quite simply Utopian and unattainable. The most elementary prerequisites and conditions for the establishment and working of the necessary institutions were absent.[19]

One partial exception must be noted, and that is the case of the island state of Singapore. But this is a very special case. Singapore is a modern city, whose per capita standards are the highest in Asia, outside Japan. The present ruling party, the People's Action Party (PAP) inherited excellent municipal services and has built and improved upon them. Their record in the provision of housing and in public health has justifiably attracted international notice. The PAP is predominantly Chinese, reflecting in this the racial composition of the city. Its leaders are extremely shrewd politicians, theoretically well-versed and adept veterans of the most practical aspects of political maneuvering. They have to cope with a very strong, persistent, and clamorous body of left-wing criticism and action, and so far they have succeeded in containing it. Their formula is a consciously moderate and empirical one, preferring "gas and water socialism" plus economic planning to full-scale nationalization plus radically redistributive policies. In this, they are simply adjusting to the facts of life in Singapore, which is a commercial and industrial center where the powerful Chinese business interests have the power to make or break governments. The PAP has to accommodate profit-making to its scheme of things, and this it has done by-trying to encourage and steer investment in desired directions. In doing so, the party has of course exposed itself to the charge of "selling out." In handling this criticism, the leadership has argued that the preservation of parliamentary democracy, free trade unions, and high living standards are good in themselves, and that these things would be jeopardized and probably lost under a more dogmatic socialist regime, which might well not only chase away Singaporean capital across the Straits of Johore into Malaya, but also kill the city as an international entrepôt.[20]

However, Singapore is in rather a special position. There is, for example, no peasantry engaged in subsistence farming, since the city's hinterland is devoted to the cultivation of commercial crops and market gardening. Even so, there is always the possibility of a government much further to the left taking over. Despite the efforts of the PAP there is much serious poverty,[21] and gross inequalities of wealth are all too obtrusive. Moreover, there are social and educational grievances among a section of the educated—the Chinese-speaking—which provide a constant pool of actual and potential left leadership. There are also, in practice, limitations on the operation of democracy and the labor movement. So that even in Singapore, the chances of this kind of pragmatic, manipulative, democratic, and compromising "welfarism" enduring are problematical. It may well be questioned, further, how far this welfarism is entitled to the epithet of "democratic socialism," since the operations of the PAP, however much they benefit the people in the way of modern municipal housing, TB clinics, etc., obviously create excellent conditions for capitalism in the way of a healthy labor force, and a division of the left into those supporting and those attacking the PAP.

That Singapore's experience is not exportable was demonstrated very clearly by the short marriage with Malaya in the Federation of Malaysia (1963–1965). The PAP sought to extend its organization into Malaya, and to seek a role in Federal politics. In this it was absolutely frustrated by the conservative Malayan feudal-business ruling groups in the Federal capital of Kuala Lumpur. They showed unequivocally that even the mild reformism of the PAP was totally unacceptable to them, and, indeed, that they had no intention of allowing democracy to operate to the extent that it might conceivably pose a threat, however remote, to their own hold on power.[22]

Outside Singapore, then, those politicians describing themselves as Social Democrats fared badly. In Malaya, Thailand, and the Philippines there was, as there still is, no real role or future for them in the conventional political arena, which is dominated by the feudal and business and/or military groups. In Indonesia, their impatience with administrative and legislative inefficiency drove some of them into unwise involvement in the anti-Sukarno Sumatran revolt of 1958, from which the whole Socialist Party of Indonesia (PSI) ultimately suffered, since it was banned in 1960. In Burma, the inability of the parties prepared to work within a democratic framework to produce durable governments with the capacity to govern led to the imposition of military rule, and the Social Democrat politicians went down with the rest.

One of the problems which genuine Social Democrats had to face, apart from the totally inauspicious objective circumstances of the contexts within which they had to work, was that the word "socialist" continued to be appropriated by other parties, as an incantation possessed of great popular power. This is a matter to which I return shortly.

For the present three-quarters or four-fifths of Southeast Asia, the fruits of independence proved meager and sour. Nothing much changed in strict economic terms. Population continued to rise, and the size of holdings to fall; landlords still collected disproportionate rents, money-lenders still charged usurious rates of interest, middlemen still bought cheaply and sold dearly. Rural living standards showed no tendency to rise, and indeed in parts of the region were demonstrably falling.[23] It was small consolation to see and hear that it was some of one's own people who were now enjoying the rewards of top government posts, or of having taken over the businesses of Europeans, Chinese, or Indians.

The peasants found themselves, as a political force, virtually headless again. But things had decisively changed in one respect. Having once demonstrated that they could exercise crucial political leverage, they could no longer be safely ignored. There were many calls on their attention, not least from the governments they had helped to create.

The ruling groups were aware of the problem of the countryside, and knew that it had to be tackled as a political necessity. But they had to work, because of the social interests they represented and depended upon, within constraints that were shackling. For the sake of appearances, piece-meal installments of legislation, aimed at specific abuses, were introduced, and showcase projects for rural development mounted. But the truth was that they could not afford, politically, to make these reforms effective. To produce any significant change in the rural areas beneficial to the peasantry would necessarily have entailed hurting powerful groups in the ruling coalitions. The fate of these shop-window reforms was in practice to be quietly stifled or universally evaded.[24]

Another important weapon resorted to by governments was nationalism. Nationalism had flowered in the rural masses, and its symbols and trappings could be used to appeal to their emotions. In Burma, the military Revolutionary Council gave rein to the anti-Indian sentiments of the people, and encouraged a heightened chauvinism which took the form of expelling thousands of Indians, and, as we have seen, virtually closing the borders to Westerners. Indonesian leader Sukarno created his own ideology to give his people pride in their past, their achievements, and their potential. His "Marhaenism," a blend of elements from

Marxism, Islam, and Indonesian ideals, was specifically aimed at the villages, glorifying them as examples of indigenous democracy and socialism in practice. In terms of infusing Sukarno's speeches, and the speeches of his colleagues, with peculiarly Indonesian slogans, phrases, and words, Marhaenism worked very well. But in terms of genuinely influencing actual administration, its impact was, not altogether surprisingly, slight. Cambodian leader Norodom Sihanouk sought to focus nationalist feelings on the traditional princely line.

In all three cases, the leaders claimed a right to the use of the word "socialist" to describe their aims and actions. Yet it is doubtful how far they were justified in doing so. What it often amounted to in practice was a combination of anti-Western sentiments and moves, plus the desire to modernize and industrialize. It is true that much could be done which had every appearance of socialism in action. For example, Burmese and Indonesian leaders could expropriate Western businesses. But the beneficiaries of these operations were not so much the common people as the bureaucrats or military men or local businessmen who took over their running. It is true that the Burmese Revolutionary Council appears to be pushing ahead with serious land reform, but the facts are hard to establish when Western visitors, including journalists, are excluded. Cambodian "Royal Socialism" is insufficiently radical for some of the younger intellectuals.[25]

It is important to note, too, how particularly the government of Indonesia used international issues as a means of curbing and harnessing the revolutionary left. Now that the nationalists were in power, it was dangerous to have the continuing social unrest channeled into anti-government feeling by the Communists. But there were a large number of issues upon which the rulers could enlist the backing of the Communists—the returning of West Irian, for example. The anti-Western militancy of the governments of Indonesia and Burma and Cambodia has often been thought of as "Communist" in the Western press. This is a misunderstanding. It is in fact a measure of the embarrassment of the ruling groups who had in the fight for independence allied themselves with groups further to the left and now found themselves the targets of the unrest they themselves had been partly responsible for arousing during the struggle for freedom.

The manipulation of the symbols of nationalism and socialism in some of the countries, and of the symbols of nationalism alone in others, is in fact to do with the retention of political power. But the nationalism of the peasantry is to do with land. As long as their demand for land on fair terms is unsatisfied, the revolution is incomplete and the ruling groups are simply fighting a delaying action. Their regimes cannot be toppled without the use of force. There is, for reasons suggested above, only a negligible proletariat in Southeast Asia.[26] The dynamic for radical social change can only come from the peasantry.

But the calls on the emotions of the rural people come not only from the direction of revolutionary socialism. Religious leaders, communalists, and regionalists are all trying to harness the feelings of resentment and frustration. On the rural east coast of Malaya, the theocratic and anti-Chinese Pan Malayan Islamic Party flourishes among the Malay peasants. The peoples of the South Moluccas in Indonesia seek independence from Djakarta.[27] The hill tribes of Burma rise against the central government.

Revolutionary socialist forces must seek to focus the discontent and wrath of the rural masses on the gross disparities of wealth between themselves and the urban elites,[28] and to guide them to the correct conclusions. This is not an easy task. This emerges from the history of the Indonesian Communist Party (PKI), Asia's oldest and the third largest in the world. Despite economic stagnation and hardship, despite years of propagandizing by devoted cadres, and despite a membership of three million, plus perhaps another seven million sympathizers in front organizations, the PKI in 1965 could not openly challenge the Indonesian army.[29] The PKI leaders have been cautious because they have appreciated all along how far they have to go before they can make a reasonable bid for power. Yet the PKI is far and away the largest and best organized body of its kind in Southeast Asia. The Malayan Communist Party consists of a few hundred guerrillas encamped in southern Thailand, plus an unknown number of agents and sympathizers in Malaysia and Singapore. The Hukbalahap guerrillas in the Philippines, although still active in parts of Central Luzon, are well below their peak postwar strength. In Thailand, a left challenge to the ruling elites is an unfulfilled promise rather than a reality. In Burma, the Communist Parties are in rather impotent revolt—but here the interesting question is how far and how fast the left military administration itself will go in the direction of bringing socialism to the countryside.

That the peasantry will eventually act to assert their human dignity and their human rights is certain. In most parts of Southeast Asia, they have deeply entrenched anti-capitalist ideas, which is a sound starting point. There are also features of traditional Southeast Asian life which make the soil rather hopeful for the seed of socialism. In the first place, there is a very strong tradition of mutual self-help in the village.[30] In Indonesia this is called *gotong royong*, and has played a large part in Sukarno's ideological thinking. Selosoemardjan has shown[31] that whereas large, officially fostered cooperatives often fail, small spontaneous ones limited to the traditional horizons of the village have worked. There is certainly a strong cooperative tradition upon which to build.

Second, as compared with South Asia and the Far East, Southeast Asia has fewer paralyzing social traditions and institutions through which to break in order to start modernizing. It is interesting to speculate on the reasons for this, but it is safe to say that part of the explanation lies in the extremely broken nature of Southeast Asia geographically, for this has always militated against the establishment of extensive and enduring empires, such as were possible on the larger land masses of India and China. Therefore, nothing so elaborate as the Hindu caste system or the Chinese mandarinate system had a chance to evolve and fossilize in the region.[32] It is very noticeable, to take one point, how emancipated the Southeast Asian female is as compared with her pre-1949 Chinese counterpart, or her counterpart in Indian rural society today.[33]

Little has been said here about the development of Southeast Asian trade unionism, which is politically divided, and almost everywhere subject to strict limitations on freedom of action.[34] But something should be said about the objective external conditions favorable to the development of socialism in Southeast Asia. As Martinet has pointed out,[35] small socialist countries cannot adopt a Chinese-style economic self-sufficiency vis-à-vis the Western capitalist powers. They would have to rely, in present circumstances, on Western trade and markets. This dependence puts strong neo-colonial weapons in the hands of the Western powers, and they are undoubtedly ready to take advantage of this leverage to influence internal events in the Southeast Asian countries. The fight for greater international control over trade and aid policies is, therefore, also part of the fight for the liberation and advancement of the peoples of the developing countries.

This is an exciting and crucial period in the evolution of socialist thought as the European movement lifts its eyes outward from the limited and, to some extent, unrepresentative problems of the West to the problems of the world as a whole. Familiar controversies, about violence, power, redistribution, are seen in fresh perspective and given a new lease of life. No position founded on a complacent view of the European achievement in raising working-class living standards can call itself socialist. The poor and underprivileged that ought to concern us include the poor and underprivileged of Asia, and our socialist theory must account for their plight and draw the correct conclusions or else fail in its purpose. It should be clear from what has gone before that the related tasks of socialism in Southeast Asia are the smashing of neo-colonialism, which protects and supports the most reactionary ruling groups, and the raising of the living standards of the rural masses, who have so far gained little from the political upheavals of the postwar period.

Notes

1. The standard geographical work is C. A. Fisher, *Southeast Asia* (London, 1964). Short specialist historical-political accounts, country by country, are contained in G. McT. Kahin, ed., *Government and Politics of Southeast Asia* (Ithaca: Cornell University Press, 1964), which is also useful for the descriptive bibliographies following each section.

2. But see J. C. Leur, *Indonesian Trade and Society* (The Hague, 1955) for a discussion of early Southeast Asian patterns of internal and international trade.

3. See my articles in C. D. Cowan, ed., *The Economic Development of Southeast Asia* (New York: Humanities Press, 1964), and in *Journal of the Historical Society of the University of Malaya* (October 1964).

4. See G. McT. Kahin, *Nationalism and Revolution in Indonesia* (Ithaca: Cornell University Press, 1952).

5. See, for instance, T. A. Agoncillo, *Revolt of the Masses* (Quezon City, 1956).

6. See E. H. Jacoby, *Agrarian Unrest in Southeast Asia* (London, 1961), pp. 38–39, and *passim*.

7. D. N. Aidit, "Haridepan Gerakan Tani Indonesia" [The Future of the Indonesian Peasant Movement], *Bintang Merah* [Red Star] (July 1953).

8. See F. R. von der Mehden, *Religion and Nationalism in Southeast Asia* (Madison: University of Wisconsin Press, 1963).

9. Sugar collapsed from over 25s. per cwt. in the early 1920's to 5s. per cwt. in the mid-1930's. Tin, which had hovered around the £300 per ton mark in 1926–1927, averaged £142 a ton for 1930 as a whole. Rubber, which had

been as high as 4s. 8d. per pound in 1925, reached a low of just 1½d. a pound in 1932.

10. B. and J. Higgins, *Indonesia* (New York: Van Nostrand-Reinhold, 1963), p. 64.

11. See, for instance, P. T. Bauer, *The Rubber Industry* (Cambridge, Mass.: Harvard University Press, 1948).

12. See W. H. Elsbree, *Japan's Role in Southeast Asian Nationalist Movements* (Cambridge, Mass.: Harvard University Press, 1953).

13. In 1940 only 240 Indonesians, out of a population of 60 to 65 million, graduated from high school.

14. An excellent recent account is J. McDermott, *Vietnam Profile* (London, 1965), which can be obtained from CND, 14 Gray's Inn Road, London, W.C. 1.

15. For an orthodox interpretation of the emergency in Malaya (1948–1960), see G. Z. Hanrahan, *The Communist Struggle in Malaya* (New York, 1954). For a left-wing view, see *Berita Pemuda*, vol. 3, no. 3 (March 1965). For the Hukbalahap movement, see W. J. Pomeroy, *The Forest* (New York: International Publishers, 1963).

16. See Jeanne S. Mintz, *Mohammed, Marx, and Marhaen* (New York: Praeger, 1965): ". . . every significant organ of political expression in Indonesia . . . has been or has claimed to be socialist" (p. 6).

17. Selosoemardjan, *Social Changes in Jogjakarta* (Ithaca: Cornell University Press, 1962), p. 291.

18. J. Pluvier, *Confrontations* (New York: Oxford University Press, 1965), p. 36. This is an excellent class analysis of the Indonesian revolution.

19. For a fuller discussion of this, see my *Problems of Independence in Asia*.

20. For some typical articles by PAP leaders, see Dr. Wong Lin Ken, "Social Democracy, the Intellectual Left, and the Nation"; Lee Kuan Yew, "The Future of Democratic Socialism in Afro-Asia"; Dr. Goh Swee, "The Economic Problems of Democratic Socialism in Malaysia"; all in the PAP's Tenth Anniversary Souvenir entitled *Our First Ten Years* (Singapore, 1964).

21. An account of the slums of Singapore, which is startlingly reminiscent of early nineteenth-century British reports on the housing of the laboring classes, is to be found in Barrington Kaye, *Upper Nanking Street, Singapore* (Kuala Lumpur, 1961).

22. For an account of the political background to Singapore's breakaway, see M. Leifer, "Singapore in Malaysia: The Politics of Federation," *Journal of Southeast Asian History*, vol. 6, no. 2 (September 1965).

23. This was the impression even in prosperous Malaya. See, for instance, Professor Ungku Aziz, "Poverty and Rural Development in Malaysia,"

Kajian Ekonomi Malaysia, vol. 1, no. 1 (June 1964). The peasant economy of Malaya is ". . . an economy of poverty and chronic debt, relieved only in years of exceptional prosperity . . . and normally at levels not much above the appalling poverty of most of Asia." T. H. Silcock, *The Economy of Malaya* (Singapore, 1957), p. 1.

24. For a Philippine example, see D. Wurfel, "The Philippines" in G. McT. Kahin, *Government and Politics of Southeast Asia*, pp. 750–751.

25. For the program of the Burmese Revolutionary Council's Burma Socialist Program Party, see *The Burmese Way to Socialism* (Rangoon, 1962); for a review of agrarian problems in Burma, see *Narodni Azii i Afriki*, no. 5 (1965); for a discussion of the socialist content of Sukarno's ideas, see Jeanne S. Mintz, *Mohammed, Marx, and Marhaen*, and J. M. Pluvier, *Confrontations;* for an introduction to the Cambodian background (and a bibliography), see R. M. Smith in G. McT. Kahin, *Government and Politics in Southeast Asia*.

26. Even in Malaya, nearly 60 percent of the population is still engaged in agriculture. See E. L. Wheelwright, *Industrialization in Malaysia* (Melbourne, 1965), p. 2.

27. See G. Decker, *Republik Maluku Selatan* (Gottingen, 1957), and J. C. Bouman *et al.*, *The South Moluccas* (Leyden, 1960).

28. It is very striking how wealth is concentrated around one or two major cities. This is particularly so with Bangkok in Thailand, but can also be seen in Penang, Ipoh, and Kuala Lumpur in Malaysia. This point is made by the Thai and Malaysian contributors (Dr. Puey Ungphakorn and Lim Chong Yah) in Cranley Onslow, ed., *Asian Economic Development* (New York: Praeger, 1965), but later ignored in the editor's discussion at the end of the book.

29. See my analysis in *New Society*, September 7, 1965. I am not suggesting here that the Communist parties are the only possible vehicles for revolutionary socialism in Southeast Asia; only that they are at present the best organized and most experienced, and yet are *still* far from power anywhere (outside of Vietnam). Alternative revolutionary socialist movements are by comparison hardly visible.

30. See, for example, references to mutual cooperation in M. G. Swift, *Malay Peasant Society in Jelebu* (New York: Humanities Press, 1965); J. E. de Young, *Village Life in Modern Thailand* (Berkeley and Los Angeles: University of California Press, 1955); G. C. Hickey, *Village in Vietnam* (New Haven: Yale University Press, 1964).

31. See Selosoemardjan, *Social Changes in Jogjakarta*, pp. 285 *et seq.*

32. I am aware of the exceptions that could be made to this statement.

33. See R. Burling, *Hill Farms and Paddy Fields* (New Jersey, 1965), p. 2 and *passim*.

34. See W. Galenson, *Labor in Developing Economies* (Berkeley and Los Angeles: University of California Press, 1962); T. H. Silcock, *Commonwealth Economy in Southeast Asia* (Duke University Commonwealth Studies Center Series, No. 10, 1959); for a bibliography on labor organization, see Iskandar Tedjasukmana, *The Political Character of the Indonesian Trade-Union Movement* (Ithaca: Cornell University Press, 1958); Charles Gamba, *The National Union of Plantation Workers* (Singapore, 1962); Alex Josey, *Trade Unionism in Malaya* (Singapore, 1957).

35. See G. Martinet, *Marxism of Our Time* (New York: Monthly Review Press, 1964), pp. 92 *et seq.* Also Kwame Nkrumah, *Neo-colonialism* (New York: International Publishers, 1969), *passim.*

Selected Bibliography

This bibliography excludes many items that can be found on any standard list. Thus, for example, the Marxist classics and standard historical works have not been included. Also, in those areas where a great many excellent books are now available, such as Cuba, I have included only the most recent discussions. The reader will be able to trace his way backward from these works.

Generally speaking, two kinds of items have been given precedence. First, I have tried to include strong summary articles written in recent years; and second, I have given special emphasis to discussions of rural social structures. Despite the recent interest in peasant politics and revolution, few students of development have any real familiarity with these areas. Hopefully, this bibliography will help to remedy this deficiency.

There are presently several groups of radical scholars doing research on development problems. I have not listed their publications. Instead, their addresses are given at the end of the bibliography.

I would like to thank Andre Gunder Frank, Terence K. Hopkins, Allen M. Howard, James O'Connor, Peter Roman, Al Szymanski, and Richard Wolff for the use of their unpublished bibliographies and for their helpful suggestions.

CAPITALIST DEVELOPMENT AND UNDERDEVELOPMENT

Agarwala, A. N., and Singh, S. P., eds. *The Economics of Underdevelopment.* London: Oxford University Press, 1958.

Avineri, Shlomo, ed. *Karl Marx on Colonialism and Modernization.* New York: Doubleday, 1968.

Balogh, Thomas. *The Economics of Poverty.* London: Weidenfeld & Nicholson, 1966.

Baran, Paul A. *The Longer View: Essays Toward a Critique of Political Economy.* New York: Monthly Review Press, 1970.

———. *The Political Economy of Growth.* New York: Monthly Review Press, 1957.

———, and Hobsbawm, E. J. "The Stages of Economic Growth." *Kyklos*, vol. 14 (1961), pp. 234–242.

Bottomley, Anthony. "Monopolistic Rent Determinations." *Kyklos*, vol. 29 (1966), pp. 106–117.

Caspary, William. *American Economic Imperialism: A Survey of the Literature.* Radical Education Project, Box 56-A, Detroit. Mimeographed.

Cipolla, Carlo M. *Guns and Sails in the Early Phase of European Expansion, 1400–1700.* London: Collins, 1965.

Clairmonte, Fédéric. *Economic Liberalism and Underdevelopment: Studies in the Disintegration of an Idea.* London: Asia Publishing House, 1960.

De Vries, Margaret G. "Trade and Exchange Policy and Economic Development: Two Decades of Evolving Views." *Oxford Economic Papers*, NS, vol. 18, no. 1, pp. 19–44.

Dobb, Maurice. *Studies in the Development of Capitalism.* New York: International Publishers, 1963.

Dolci, Danilo. *Waste.* New York: Monthly Review Press, 1964.

Dumont, René. *Lands Alive.* New York: Monthly Review Press, 1966.

Engler, Robert. *The Politics of Oil: A Study of Private Power and Democratic Directions.* Chicago: University of Chicago Press, 1961.

Feis, Herbert. *Europe, the World's Banker, 1870–1914.* New Haven: Yale University Press, 1930.

Frank, Andre Gunder. *Latin America: Underdevelopment or Revolution.* New York and London: Monthly Review Press, 1970.

Frankel, S. H. *The Economic Impact on Underdeveloped Societies.* Oxford: Basil Blackwell, 1953.

Furtado, Celso. *Development and Underdevelopment.* Berkeley: University of California Press, 1964.

Gallagher, J., and Robinson, R. "The Imperialism of Free Trade." *Economic History Review*, 2nd ser., vol. 6 (1953), pp. 1–15.

Gardner, Lloyd C. *Economic Aspects of New Deal Diplomacy.* Madison: University of Wisconsin Press, 1964.

Genovese, Eugene. *Political Economy of Slavery.* New York: Pantheon Books, 1965.

———, and Foner, Laura, eds. *Slavery in the New World.* Englewood-Cliffs, N.J.: Prentice-Hall, 1969.

Gustafsson, Bo G. "Rostow, Marx and the Theory of Economic Growth." *Science & Society*, vol. 25, no. 3, pp. 229–244.

Hazelwood, Arthur. "The Economics of Colonial Monetary Arrangements." *Social and Economic Studies*, vol. 3, pp. 291–315.

Horowitz, David, ed. *Containment and Revolution.* Boston: Beacon Press, 1967.

Jalée, Pierre. *The Pillage of the Third World.* New York: Monthly Review Press, 1968.

––––––. *The Third World in World Economy*. New York: Monthly Review Press, 1969.

Jenks, L. H. *The Migration of British Capital to 1875*. New York: A. A. Knopf, 1927.

Kemp, Tom. *Theories of Imperialism*. London: Dobson, 1967.

la Feber, Walter. *New Empire: An Interpretation of American Expansionism, 1860–1898*. Ithaca: Cornell University Press, 1970.

Magdoff, Harry. *The Age of Imperialism*. New York: Monthly Review Press, 1969.

Mandel, Ernest. *Marxist Economic Theory*. 2 vols. New York: Monthly Review Press, 1969.

Miliband, Ralph and Saville, John. *The Socialist Register 1964–1969*. Annual. New York: Monthly Review Press. (Includes many excellent articles on development questions.)

Moore, Barrington Jr. *Social Origins of Dictatorship and Democracy: Lord and Peasant in the Making of the Modern World*. Boston: Beacon Press, 1966.

Nadel, George, and Curtis, Perry, eds. *Imperialism and Colonialism*. New York: Macmillan, 1964.

Nirumand, Bahman. *Iran: The New Imperialism in Action*. New York: Monthly Review Press, 1969.

Ober, John David, and Corradi, Juan Eugenio. "Pax Americana and Pax Sociologica: Remarks on the Politics of Sociology." *Catalyst* (Summer 1966), pp. 41–54.

O'Connor, Harvey. *World Crisis in Oil*. New York: Monthly Review Press, 1962.

O'Connor, James. "International Corporations and Economic Underdevelopment." *Science & Society*, vol. 34 (1970), pp. 42–60.

Pomeroy, William J., ed. *Guerrilla Warfare and Marxism*. New York: International Publishers, 1968.

Rhodes, Robert I. "The Disguised Conservatism in Evolutionary Development Theory." *Science & Society*, vol. 32 (1968), pp. 383–412.

Rosenberg, Nathan. "Capital Goods Technology, and Economic Growth." *Oxford Economic Papers*, NS, vol. 15, no. 3 (1963), pp. 217–227.

Samuelsson, Kurt. *Religion and Economic Action*. Stockholm: Bonniers, 1961.

Science & Society. *The Transition from Feudalism to Capitalism: A Symposium*. 2d printing. New York: 1963.

Seers, Dudley. "Big Companies and Small Countries." *Kyklos*, vol. 16 (1963), pp. 599–607.

––––––. "The Mechanism of an Open Petroleum Economy." *Social and Economic Studies*, vol. 13 (1964), pp. 233–242.

Stinchcombe, Arthur L. "Agricultural Enterprise and Rural Class Relations." *American Journal of Sociology*, vol. 67 (1961–1962), pp. 165–176.

Strachey, John. *The End of Empire*. New York: Random House, 1960.

Sweezy, Paul M. *The Theory of Capitalist Development*. New York: Monthly Review Press, 1956.

——, and Magdoff, Harry, "Notes on the Multinational Corporation." *Monthly Review*, Part I, vol. 21, no. 5 (1969), pp. 1–13, and Part II, vol. 21, no. 6 (1969), pp. 1–13.

Tanzer, Michael. *Political Economy of International Oil and the Underdeveloped Countries*. Boston: Beacon Press, 1969.

Van Alstyne, Richard W. *The Rising American Empire*. New York: Oxford University Press, 1960.

Williams, Eric. *Capitalism and Slavery*. New York: G. P. Putnam, 1966.

Williams, William Appleman. *The Roots of the Modern American Empire*. New York: Random House, 1969.

Wolf, Eric R. *Peasant Wars of the Twentieth Century*. New York: Harper & Row, 1969.

Worsley, Peter. *The Third World*. 2nd ed. London, 1967.

Wright, Harrison M., ed. *The "New Imperialism": Analysis of Late Nineteenth-Century Expansion*. Boston: D. C. Heath, 1961.

AFRICA

American Committee on Africa. "A Special Report on American Investment to the South African Economy." *Africa Today*, vol. 13, no. 1 (1966).

Anderson, Perry. "Portugal and the End of Ultra-Colonialism." *New Left Review*, May-June 1962, pp. 83–102, and July-August 1962, pp. 88–123.

Arrighi, Giovanni, and Saul, J. S. "Socialism and Economic Development in Tropical Africa." *The Journal of Modern African Studies*, vol. 4, no. 2 (1968), pp. 141–169.

Austen, Ralph Albert. *Native Policy and African Politics: Indirect Rule in Northwest Tanzania, 1889–1939*. Cambridge, Mass.: Harvard University Press, 1965.

Baldwin, R. E. "Wage Policy in a Dual Economy: The Case of Northern Rhodesia." *Race*, vol. 4, no. 1 (1962), pp. 73–87.

Barnett, Donald, and Njama, Karari. *Mau Mau from Within*. New York: Monthly Review Press, 1966.

Berg, Elliot J. "Backward-Sloping Labor Supply Functions in Dual Economies—The African Case." *Quarterly Journal of Economics*, August 1961.

——. "The Economics of the Migrant Labor System." In Hilda Kuper, ed., *Urbanization and Migration in West Africa*. Berkeley: University of California Press, 1965.

Chaliand, Gérard. *Armed Struggle in Africa: With the Guerrillas in "Portuguese" Guinea*. New York: Monthly Review Press, 1969.

Clower, Robert W. *Growth Without Development: An Economic Survey of Liberia.* Evanston: Northwestern University Press, 1966.

Crocker, W. R. *On Governing Colonies: Being an Outline of the Real Issues and a Comparison of the British, French and Belgian Approach to Them.* London: Allen and Unwin, 1947.

Cruise O'Brien, Conor. *To Katanga and Back: A UN Case History.* New York: Simon and Schuster, 1963.

Davidson, Basil. *Black Mother: The Years of the African Slave Trade.* Boston: Little, Brown and Co., 1961.

Diamond, Stanley. *Nigeria: Model of a Colonial Failure.* New York: American Committee on Africa, 1967.

———. "Who Killed Biafra." *The New York Review of Books*, vol. 14, no. 4 (1970), pp. 17–27.

Du Bois, W. E. B. *The World and Africa.* Rev. ed. New York: International Publishers, 1965.

Dumont, René. *False Start in Africa.* 2d ed. New York: Praeger, 1966.

Fallers, Lloyd A. *The King's Men: Leadership and Status in Buganda on the Eve of Independence.* Chicago: University of Chicago Press, 1965.

———. "The Politics of Land Holding Busoga." *Economic Development and Cultural Change*, vol. 3, no. 3 (1955), pp. 260–270.

———. "Social Stratification and Economic Processes." In M. J. Herskovits and M. Harwitz, eds., *Economic Transition in Africa.* Evanston: Northwestern University Press, 1964.

Fanon, Frantz. *The Wretched of the Earth.* New York: Grove Press, 1965.

Fitch, Bob, and Oppenheimer, Mary. *Ghana: End of an Illusion.* New York: Monthly Review Press, 1966.

Gann, L. H., and Duignan, Peter. *The History and Politics of Colonialism, 1870–1914. Colonialism in Africa, 1872–1960*, vol. 1. Cambridge: Cambridge University Press, 1969.

Garbett, C. K. "The Rhodesian Chief's Dilemma: Government Officer or Tribal Leader?" *Race*, vol. 9, no. 2 (1966), pp. 113–128.

Gifford, P., and Louis, W. R. *Britain and Germany in Africa: Imperial Rivalry and Colonial Rule.* New Haven: Yale University Press, 1967.

Goldthorpe, J. E. *An African Elite: Makerere College Students, 1922–1960.* Nairobi: Oxford University Press, 1966.

Gordon, David C. *The Passing of French Algeria.* New York: Oxford University Press, 1966.

Green, Reginald H., and Seidman, Ann. *Unity or Poverty? The Economics of Pan-Africanism.* Baltimore: Penguin, 1968.

Grundy, Kenneth W. "The Class Struggle in Africa: An Examination of Conflicting Theories." *Journal of Modern African Studies*, vol. 2, no. 3 (1964), pp. 379–393.

Gutkind, Peter C. W., and Webster, John B. *A Select Bibliography on Traditional and Modern Africa.* Program of Eastern African Studies, Syracuse University, Syracuse, 1968. Mimeographed.

Hodgkin, Thomas L. *Nationalism in Colonial Africa.* London: Muller, 1956.

Institute of Race Relations. *Angola: A Symposium. Views of Revolt.* London: Oxford University Press for the Institute of Race Relations, 1962.

Jones, W. O. "Economic Man in Africa." *Food Research Studies*, vol. 1, no. 2 (1960), pp. 107–134.

Kuper, Leo, and Smith, M. G., eds. *Pluralism in Africa.* Berkeley: University of California Press, 1969.

McLoughlin, P. F. M. "The Class Struggles in African Economic Development." *Civilizations*, vol. 15, no. 4 (1965), pp. 471–476.

———. "Economic Development and the Heritage of Slavery in the Sudan Republic." *Africa*, vol. 32, no. 4 (1962), pp. 355–391.

Middleton, John. *Land Tenure in Zanzibar.* London: H.M.S.O., Colonial Research Studies, 1961.

Morel, E. D. *The Black Man's Burden: The White Man in Africa from the Fifteenth Century to World War I.* Orig. pub. 1920. New York: Monthly Review Press, 1969.

Murray, Roger, and Wengraf, Tom. "The Algerian Revolution." *New Left Review*, vol. 22 (1963), pp. 14–65.

Neumark, F. Daniel. *Foreign Trade and Economic Development in Africa.* Stanford: Stanford University Food Research Institute, 1964.

Nkrumah, Kwame. *Neo-colonialism: The Last Stage of Imperialism.* New York: International Publishers, 1965.

Oliver, Roland A., and Fage, J. D. *A Short History of Africa.* Baltimore: Penguin, 1962.

Ottaway, David, and Ottaway, Marina. *Algeria: The Politics of a Socialist Revolution.* Berkeley: University of California Press, 1970.

Sacks, Benjamin. *South Africa: An Imperial Dilemma.* Albuquerque: The University of New Mexico Press, 1967.

Van den Berghe, Pierre L. *The Dynamics of Race Relations: An Ideal Type Study of South Africa.* Cambridge, Mass.: Harvard University Press, 1959.

———. *Caneville: The Social Structure of a South African Town.* Middletown, Conn.: Wesleyan University Press, 1964.

Wallerstein, Immanuel. *Africa, The Politics of Independence: An Interpretation of Modern African History.* New York: Vintage Books, 1961.

———. *Africa, The Politics of Unity: An Analysis of a Contemporary Social Movement.* New York: Random House, 1967.

Wilson, Monica. "Land and the Kikuyu: A Study of the Relationship Between Land and Kikuyu Political Movements." *The Journal of Negro History*, vol. 40, no. 2 (1955), pp. 103–153.

Woddis, Jack. *Africa : The Lion Awakes*. London: Lawrence & Wishart, 1961.
————. *Africa : Roots of Revolt*. London: Lawrence & Wishart, 1960.
————. *Introduction to Neocolonialism*. New York: International Publishers, 1967.
Woolf, Leonard. *Empire and Commerce in Africa : A Study in Economic Imperialism*. New York: Macmillan, 1919.
Yudelman, Montegue. *Africans on the Land : Economic Problems of African Agricultural Development* . . . . Cambridge, Mass.: Harvard University Press, 1964.

ASIA

Bailey, F. G. *Caste and the Economic Frontier*. Manchester: Manchester University Press, 1957.
Bauer, P. T. *Report on a Visit to the Rubber-Growing Smallholders of Malaya, July-September 1946*. Colonial Research Publication, Colonial Office, London, 1948.
Bettelheim, Charles. *India Independent*. New York: Monthly Review Press, 1969.
Boeke, J. H. *The Structure of the Netherlands Indian Economy*. New York: Institute of Pacific Relations, 1942.
————. *Economics and Economic Policy of Dual Societies*. New York: Institute of Pacific Relations, 1953.
Chandra, Bipan. *The Rise and Growth of Economic Nationalism in India, 1880–1905*. New Delhi: People's Publishing House, 1966.
Crippen, H. R. "American Imperialism and Philippine Independence." *Science & Society*, vol. 11, no. 2 (1947), pp. 97–126.
Crook, Isabel, and Crook, David. *Revolution in a Chinese Village : Ten Mile Inn*. London: Routledge and Kegan Paul, 1959.
————. *The First Years of Yangyi Commune*. London: Routledge and Kegan Paul, 1966.
Curtis, Robert. "Malaysia and Indonesia." *New Left Review*, no. 28, pp. 5–32.
Desai, Akshayakumar R. *Social Background of Indian Nationalism*. Rev. ed. Bombay: Popular Book Depot, 1954.
Fan, K. H. *The Chinese Cultural Revolution : Selected Documents*. New York: Monthly Review Press, 1968.
Fei, Hsiao-Tung. *Peasant Life in China : A Field Study of Country Life in the Yangtze Valley*. London: Kegan Paul, Trench, Trubner and Co., 1939.
————, and Chih-I, Chang. *Earthbound China : A Study of Rural Economy in Yunan*. Chicago: University of Chicago Press, 1945.
Feuerwerker, Albert. *The Chinese Economy, 1912–1949*. Michigan Papers in

Chinese Studies, No. 1. Center for Chinese Studies, University of Michigan, Ann Arbor, 1968.

Fox, Richard G. *From Zamindar to Ballot Box: Community Change in a North Indian Market Town*. Ithaca: Cornell University Press, 1969.

Furnivall, John Sydenham. *Colonial Policy and Practice: A Comparative Study of Burma and Netherlands India*. Cambridge: Cambridge University Press, 1948.

———. *Progress and Welfare in Southeast Asia: A Comparison of Colonial Policy and Practice*. New York: Institute of Pacific Relations, 1941.

Geertz, Clifford. *Agricultural Involution: The Process of Ecological Change in Indonesia*. Berkeley: University of California Press, 1963.

———. *Peddlers and Princes: Social Change and Economic Modernization in Two Indonesian Towns*. Chicago: University of Chicago Press, 1963.

Gough, Kathleen. "Peasant Resistance and Revolt in South India." *Pacific Affairs*, vol. 41 (Winter 1968-69), pp. 526–544.

———. "Communist Rural Councillors in Kerala." *Journal of Asian and African Studies*, vol. 3, nos. 3–4 (1968), pp. 181–202.

Hinton, William. *Iron Oxen: A Documentary of Revolution in Chinese Farming*. New York: Monthly Review Press, 1970.

Jacoby, Erich H. *Agrarian Unrest in Southeast Asia*, 2d ed. rev. London: Asia Publishing House, 1961.

Kahin, George McT., and Lewis, John W. *The United States in Vietnam*. New York: Dial Press, 1967.

Kidron, Michael. *Foreign Investments in India*. London: Oxford University Press, 1965.

Kurian, K. Mathew. *Impact of Foreign Capital on Indian Economy*. New Delhi: People's Publishing House, 1966.

Lacouture, Jean. *Ho Chi Minh: A Political Biography*. New York: Random House, 1968.

Legarda, Benuto Jr., and Garcia, Roberto y. "Economic Collaboration: The Trading Relationship." In Frank H. Golay, ed., *The United States and the Philippines*. Englewood Cliffs, N.J.: Prentice-Hall, 1966.

Lockwood, W. W. "Foundations of Japanese Industrialism." In B. Supple, ed., *The Experience of Economic Growth*. New York: Random House, 1963.

Maniruzzaman, Talukder. "Group Interests in Pakistan Politics, 1947–1958." *Pacific Affairs*, vol. 39, nos. 1–2 (1966), pp. 83–98.

Marriott, McKim, ed. *Village India: Studies in the Little Community*. Chicago: University of Chicago Press, 1955.

McAlister, John T. Jr., and Mus, Paul. *The Vietnamese and Their Revolution*. New York: Harper & Row, 1970.

McCormick, Thomas J. *China Market: The Quest for Informal Empire, 1893–1901*. Chicago: Quadrangle Books, 1967.

Mukherjee, Ramrishna. *The Rise and Fall of the East India Company: A Sociological Appraisal.* 2d ed. rev. Berlin: 1958.

Nee, Victor, with Layman, Don. *The Cultural Revolution at Peking University.* New York: Monthly Review Press, 1969.

Needham, I. "The Past in China's Present." *Centennial Review,* vol. 4, no. 2 (1960), pp. 145–178 and vol. 4, no. 3 (1960), pp. 281–308.

Schurmann, Franz. *Ideology and Organization in Communist China.* Berkeley: University of California Press, 1966.

Segal, Ronald. *The Crisis of India.* Baltimore: Penguin, 1965.

Shand, R. T. *Agricultural Development in Asia.* Berkeley: University of California Press, 1970.

Smith, Thomas Carlyle. *The Agrarian Origins of Modern Japan.* Stanford: Stanford University Press, 1959.

Snow, Edgar. *Red Star over China,* 2d ed. rev. New York: Grove Press, 1968.

Taira, K. "Ryukyu Islands Today: Political Economy of a U.S. Colony." *Science & Society,* vol. 22, no. 2 (1958), pp. 113–128.

Tawney, R. H. *Land and Labor in China.* London: Allen, 1937.

Tsuru, Shigeto. *Essays on Japanese Economy.* Tokyo: Kinokuniya Bookstore, 1958.

Wertheim, W. F. *East-West Parallels: Sociological Approaches to Modern Asia.* The Hague: Van Hoeve, 1964.

Yang, C. K. *Chinese Communist Society: The Family and the Village.* Cambridge, Mass.: M.I.T. Press, 1959.

LATIN AMERICA

Astiz, Carlos A. *Pressure Groups and Power Elites in Peruvian Politics.* Ithaca: Cornell University Press, 1970.

Béjar, Héctor. *Peru 1965: Notes on a Guerrilla Experience.* New York: Monthly Review Press, 1970.

Bello, José Maria. *A History of Modern Brazil, 1889–1964.* With a concluding chapter by Rollie E. Poppino. Stanford: Stanford University Press, 1966.

Boorstein, Edward. *The Economic Transformation of Cuba: A First-Hand Account.* New York: Monthly Review Press, 1968.

Bottomley, Anthony. "Planning in an Underutilization Economy: The Case of Ecuador." *Social and Economic Studies,* vol. 15, no. 4 (1966), pp. 305–311.

Cumberland, Charles C. *Mexico: The Struggle for Modernity.* New York: Oxford University Press, 1968.

de Vries, Egbert, and Medina Echavarría, José. *Social Aspects of Economic Development in Latin America.* Paris: UNESCO, 1963.

Debray, Régis. *Revolution in the Revolution?* New York: Monthly Review Press, 1967.

————. *Strategy for Revolution: Essays on Latin America.* New York: Monthly Review Press, 1970.

Erasmus, Charles J. "Upper Limits of Peasantry and Agrarian Reform: Bolivia, Venezuela, and Mexico Compared." *Ethnology*, vol. 6, no. 4 (1967), pp. 349–380.

Fals Borda, Orlando. *Subversion and Social Change in Colombia.* New York: Columbia University Press, 1969.

Frank, Andre Gunder. *Capitalism and Underdevelopment in Latin America.* New York: Monthly Review Press, 1969.

Furtado, Celso. *Diagnosis of the Brazilian Crisis.* Berkeley: University of California Press, 1965.

————. *The Economic Growth of Brazil: A Survey from Colonial to Modern Times.* Berkeley: University of California Press, 1963.

Galeano, Eduardo. "De-nationalization and Brazilian Industry." *Monthly Review*, vol. 21, no. 7 (1969), pp. 11–30.

————. *Guatemala: Occupied Country.* New York: Monthly Review Press, 1969.

Gerassi, J. *The Great Fear in Latin America*, 2d ed. rev. New York: Collier Books, 1965.

Griffin, Keith B. "Reflections on Latin American Development." *Oxford Economic Papers*, NS, 18, 1, 1966, 1–18.

Guevara, Ernesto Che. *Reminiscences of the Cuban Revolutionary War.* New York: Monthly Review Press, 1968.

————. *Guerrilla Warfare.* New York: Monthly Review Press, 1961.

Hanson, Simon G. "The Alliance for Progress: The Sixth Year." *Inter-American Economic Affairs*, vol. 22, no. 3 (1968).

————. "The Experience with the International Coffee Agreement." *Inter-American Economic Affairs*, vol. 19, no. 3 (1965), pp. 27–65.

Horowitz, Irving Louis, ed. *Masses in Latin America.* New York: Oxford University Press, 1970.

————; de Castro, Josué; and Gerassi, John. *Latin American Radicalism.* New York: Vintage Books, 1969.

Huberman, Leo, and Sweezy, Paul M., eds. *Régis Debray and the Latin American Revolution.* New York: Monthly Review Press, 1969.

————. *Socialism in Cuba.* New York: Monthly Review Press, 1969.

Jagan, Cheddi. *The West on Trial: My Fight for Guyana's Freedom.* New York: International Publishers, 1967.

Landsberger, Henry A., ed. *Latin American Peasant Movements.* Ithaca: Cornell University Press, 1969.

Lewis, Gordon K. *The Growth of the Modern West Indies.* New York: Monthly Review Press, 1968.

————. *Puerto Rico: Freedom and Power in the Caribbean.* New York: Monthly Review Press, 1963.

Marini, Rui Mauro. "Brazilian Interdependence and Imperialist Integration." *Monthly Review*, vol. 17, no. 7 (1965), pp. 10–29.

Mintz, Sidney. *Worker in the Cane*. New Haven: Yale University Press, 1960.

———. *Puerto Rico : An Essay in the Definition of a National Culture*. San Juan: University of Puerto Rico, 1968.

Munro, D. G. *Intervention and Dollar Diplomacy in the Caribbean, 1900–1921*. Princeton: Princeton University Press, 1964.

Nearing, Scott, and Freeman, Joseph. *Dollar Diplomacy*. Orig. pub. 1925. New York: Monthly Review Press, 1969.

O'Connor, James. *Origins of Socialism in Cuba*. Ithaca: Cornell University Press, 1970.

Petras, James. *Politics and Social Forces in Chilean Development*. Berkeley: University of California Press, 1969.

———. *Politics and Social Structure in Latin America*. New York: Monthly Review Press, 1970.

———. "U.S.-Latin American Studies: A Critical Assessment." *Science & Society*, vol. 32, no. 2 (1968), pp. 148–168.

———, and Zeitlin, Maurice, eds. *Latin America : Reform or Revolution?* Greenwich, Conn.: Fawcett Publications, 1968.

Reno, Philip. *The Ordeal of British Guiana*. New York: Monthly Review Press, 1964.

Rhodes, Robert I. "Mexico—A Model for Capitalist Development in Latin America?" *Science & Society*, vol. 34, no. 1 (1970), pp. 61–77.

Scobie, James. *Argentina : A City and a Nation*. New York: Oxford University Press, 1964.

Stein, Stanley J., and Stein, Barbara H. *The Colonial Heritage in Latin America : Essay on Economic Dependence in Perspective*. New York: Oxford University Press, 1970.

Studies in Comparative International Development, vol. I–IV (1965–1970). (The best single source on Latin American development. Includes translations of major articles published in Spanish.)

Veliz, Claudio, ed. *Obstacles to Change in Latin America*. New York: Oxford University Press, 1965.

———. *Politics of Conformity in Latin America*. London: Oxford University Press, 1967.

Williams, William Appleman. *The United States, Cuba and Castro : An Essay on the Dynamics of Revolution and the Dissolution of Empire*. New York: Monthly Review Press, 1962.

Womack, John Jr. *Zapata and the Mexican Revolution*. New York: Knopf, 1969.

Wood, Dennis B. "The Long Revolution: Cuba." *Science & Society*, vol. 34, no. 1 (1970), pp. 1–41.

Zeitlin, Maurice. *Revolutionary Politics and the Cuban Working Class.* Princeton: Princeton University Press, 1967.

SCHOLARLY ORGANIZATIONS PUBLISHING RESEARCH ON IMPERIALISM AND UNDERDEVELOPMENT

Africa Research Group, P.O. Box 213, Cambridge, Mass. 02138.

North American Congress on Latin America, P.O. Box 57, Cathedral Park Station, New York, N.Y. 10025.

Union For Radical Political Economics, P.O. Box 287, Cambridge, Mass. 02138.

Pacific Studies Center, 1963 University Ave., East Palo Alto, Calif. 94303.